TAIFA

NEW AFRICAN HISTORIES SERIES

Series editors: Jean Allman and Allen Isaacman

*Books in this series are published with support from
the Ohio University National Resource Center for African Studies.*

TAIFA

Making Nation and Race in Urban Tanzania

⮍

James R. Brennan

OHIO UNIVERSITY PRESS ⮍ ATHENS

Ohio University Press, Athens, Ohio 45701
ohioswallow.com
© 2012 by Ohio University Press
All rights reserved

Printed in the United States of America
Ohio University Press books are printed on acid-free paper ∞ ™

21 20 19 18 17 16 15 14 13 12   5 4 3 2 1

Library of Congress Cataloging-in-Publication Data

Brennan, James R.
  Taifa : making nation and race in urban Tanzania / James R. Brennan.
    p. cm. -- (New African histories)
  Includes bibliographical references and index.
  ISBN 978-0-8214-2001-0 (pb : alk. paper) -- ISBN 978-0-8214-4417-7 (electronic)
  1. Ethnicity--Tanzania--Dar es Salaam--History. 2. Nationalism--Tanzania--Dar es
Salaam--History. 3. Urbanization--Tanzania--Dar es Salaam--History. 4. Dar es Salaam
(Tanzania)--Race relations--History. 5. Dar es Salaam (Tanzania)--Social conditions.
I. Title. II. Series: New African histories series.
  DT449.D3B74   2012
  967.8232—dc23

                                                             2012004955

Contents

Illustrations

Abbreviations

ACS	Assistant Chief Secretary
ANC	African National Congress (Tanganyika)
AO	Administrative Officer
CCM	Chama cha Mapinduzi (Revolutionary Party, successor to TANU in 1977)
CO	Colonial Office, U.K. National Archives (London)
CS	Chief Secretary
DAR	District Annual Report
DC	District Commissioner
DO	District Officer
DOS	Department of State (US)
DPO	District Political Officer
DSM	Dar es Salaam
EACFIN	East African Command Fortnightly IntelligenceNews Letter
ECB	Economic Control Board
EO	Executive Officer
KAR	King's African Rifles
LC	Labor Commissioner
LO	Land Officer
PAR	Provincial Annual Report
PC	Provincial Commissioner
RH	Rhodes House (Oxford)
Rs.	Rupees (Tanganyika's currency from *ca.* 1916 to 1921)
Shs.	Shillings (Tanganyika's currency from 1921 to the present)
TA	Township Authority
TAA	Tanganyika African Union
TACSA	Tanganyika Asian Civil Service Association
TAGSA	Tanganyika African Government Servants Association

TANU	Tanganyika African National Union
TAWCA	Tanganyika African Welfare and Commercial Association
TNA	Tanzania National Archives (Dar es Salaam)
TTACSA	Tanganyika Territory African Civil Services Association
UDSM	University of Dar es Salaam
UTP	United Tanganyika Party

Acknowledgments

This book began long ago as an idea that I had at the end of my first quarter at Northwestern University, when a small seminar of first-year African History graduate students—Greg Mann, Sarah Lozowski, Jeff Strabone, and I—met in Jonathon Glassman's apartment in Rogers Park to discuss Moyez G. Vassanji's *The Gunny Sack*. I must first thank all of the people in that seminar, whose influence on my way of thinking about African History was formative. My debt to Jonathon Glassman will become apparent to readers familiar with his work. He convinced me that a history of nationalism and race in Dar es Salaam would be an important project, and helped to sharpen my arguments through his powerful if sometimes unnerving criticisms. In ways that are obvious and not obvious, this book could not have been produced without his influence and support. I must also thank Sara Berry for helping move this project into a fundable state during her brief but quite influential time at Northwestern. Other faculty—James Campbell, John Rowe, Ivor Wilks, John Hunwick, Jane Guyer, the late Harold Perkin, Thomas Heyck, David Schoenbrun, Jock McLane, and Richard Lepine—were all intellectually generous to me at key moments during my years at Northwestern. David Easterbrook at the Melville Herskovits Library was and remains particularly helpful.

I was fortunate to share the company of a tremendous group of graduate students during those years, whom I would like to thank for their ideas and friendship: Brett Shadle, Greg Mann, Jeremy Prestholdt, Sarah Lozowski, Giulia Barrera, Jeff Strabone, Pius Nyambara, Chris Hayden, Lorelle Semley, Amy Settergren, Rebecca Shereikis, Chris Beneke, Mike Guenther, Elizabeth Prevost, Neil Kodesh, Mike Bailey, Guy Ortolano, Pat Griffin, Rhiannon Stephens, Jeremy Berndt, Karen O'Brien, and Mike Tetelman.

In Tanzania I encountered a delightful group of people whose advice, kindness, and support I deeply appreciate: Isaria Kimambo, Nestor Luanda, Yusuf Lawi, Fred Kaijage, the late Hasnain Panjwani, Anja Panjwani, Ralf Orlik, Bruce Heilman, Paul Kaiser, Abdul Sheriff, Fatma Aloo, Hamisi Msumi, Mohamed Kibanda, Luna Mkayula, Jonathan Walz, Stephen Hill, Blandina Giblin, Hasnain Virjee, Ned Bertz, Cymone Fourshey, Rhonda Gonzales,

Rashida Sharif, Franck Raimbault, Tadasu Tsuruta, Joseph Kironde, Sospeter Mkapa, Issa Shivji, Walter Bgoya, Geoffrey Owens, Peter Bofin, Elector Kilusungu, Gary Burgess, Paul Bjerk, Stephanie Wynne-Jones, and Robyn Pariser. A special word of thanks must go to Mohamed Said, who has generously hosted me in Tanga and introduced me to several important interlocutors around Dar es Salaam. I must also thank Ned Alpers, who generously wrote long and thoughtful answers to a long set of questions that I e-mailed to him when I was just beginning graduate school.

I spent five very rewarding years at SOAS, where I enjoyed the advice and support of Wayne Dooling, John Parker, Cedric Barnes, Richard Reid, James McDougall, William Gervase Clarence-Smith, Rachel Dwyer, Barbara Spina, Elke Stockreiter, Lutz Marten, Farouk Topan, Tom Cadogan, Mike Jennings, Pedro Machado, Ed Simpson, Felicitas Becker, Cyp Stephenson, Carol Miles, David Martin, and Adam Waite. I would also like to thank other people who assisted me in one way or another while I was in the UK: the late Randal Sadleir, Ruth Watson, Martin Walsh, Jason Mosley, Dan Branch, Emma Hunter, Gez McCann, Ethan Sanders, Justin Willis, Shane Doyle, Karin Barber, Terence Ranger, Philip Murphy, Gareth Austin, Sloan Mahone, Sana Aiyar, Kate Luongo, David Killingray, and Steven Pierce. Derek Peterson and John Lonsdale warmly hosted me during visits to Cambridge University, as did David Anderson and Jan-Georg Deutsch during visits to Oxford University. I was also fortunate to visit Berlin a few times, where I received much valuable support and advice from Katrin Bromber, Andreas Eckert, Kai Kresse, Achim von Oppen, and Katharina Zoeller. At the University of Illinois I have had wonderful colleagues who have each helped in some way with this project: Diane Koenker, Antoinette Burton, Terri Barnes, Carol Symes, Don Crummey, Craig Koslofsky, Mark Leff, Nils Jacobsen, Ken Cuno, Julie Laut, Brian Dill, Claire Crowston, Leslie Reagan, Fred Hoxie, Al Kagan, and Mary Stuart.

The following institutions have provided support and assistance for this project: The History Department, Program of African Studies, Melville Herskovits Library, and Graduate College at Northwestern University; Fulbright-IIE; NSEP; COSTECH (Tanzania); the History Department and East Africana Library at the University of Dar es Salaam; the Tanzanian National Archives; the United Kingdom National Archives; Rhodes House Library, Oxford University; the National Archives and Records Administration, College Park, Maryland; the History Department and Faculty of Arts and Humanities at the School of Oriental and African Studies; and the History Department and Center for African Studies at the University of Illinois at Urbana-Champaign.

I would also like to thank those who read parts of what became this manuscript closely and with great care at one point or another: Andrew Burton, Emily Callaci, Jim Giblin, Leander Schneider, and Andy Ivaska. John Iliffe provided his customarily professional and thorough comments when this was a just-finished dissertation, and he has also generously lent me his notes on files that are no longer accessible at the Tanzanian National Archives. The debt that I and other historians of colonial Tanganyika owe to him is enormous. Ron Aminzade gave me extremely useful comments in the late stages of this project, as did Erika Stevens and Deborah Wiseman. Claudia Walters ably provided this book's maps. I would like to thank Gill Berchowitz, Jean Allman, and Allen Isaacman for their support and patience with this project, and I also thank the two anonymous reviewers for their helpful criticisms.

The above list of acknowledgments is long and incomplete. I would like to conclude by thanking Theresa Kircher for her patience, love, and kindness over these years. Her support made this book possible.

Introduction

The title of this book asks the reader to learn one Swahili word from the outset. *Taifa* (pronounced tă-ēfə) is today translated as "nation," but seventy years ago, "race" would have been an equally accurate translation. I have titled this book *TAIFA* not only because this is a historical study of nation and race in a city and country where Swahili is the first language, but also because this is a study of the language of identity. Terms of identity like *taifa* often resist simple translation to contemporary English equivalents; moreover, the meanings of the terms themselves change over time. I employ categories such as "nation" and "race" as modes of thought rather than as elements of social structure; they are best understood by paying attention to the changing meaning of words and the deeper linguistic and cultural grammars in which the words are embedded.

This is also a study of colonial rule, which is what made English the country's second language. The imposition of European colonial rule on what is today mainland Tanzania—first by Germans (1890–1916) and then by the British (1916–1961)—shaped in formative ways the social, economic, and intellectual lives of those who inhabited its capital city of Dar es Salaam. Colonial rulers oversaw urban segregation; they reserved for themselves the best housing and services; they instituted inferior and racially segregated systems of education and government employment for Indians and Africans; and they did much more that will be examined in the pages to come. Yet the impact of colonial rule did not fully reinvent the language with which people identified one another. Rather, this book demonstrates that categories of belonging like nation, race, and ethnicity (or "tribe") were shaped as much by the limitations and contradictions of colonial rule and by local cultural understandings of hierarchy and difference as they were by the imposition of new colonial categories. In this work we will embark on a tour of identity categories as they were created by the colonial and postcolonial state, as well as by those states' subjects and citizens, over the period of British rule and the early years of postcolonial rule in what became the independent nation-state of Tanganyika (1961–1964) and shortly after, Tanzania (1964–present).[1]

The identity of "African" is not one that can be taken for granted. *TAIFA* tells the story of how one particular African racial identity formed and came to provide the guiding assumptions of nationalism in Tanzania. Such stories cannot be told only from the towering perspectives of colonial rulers, who imposed racial modes of thought and hierarchical social structures, or those of Pan-Africanist elites, who offered a racial ideology of liberation that deliberately ignored cultural diversity. Local thinkers in Dar es Salaam made sense of both colonial categories and Pan-Africanist arguments, but did so through the lens of local Swahili categories of thought. Swahili has since been appropriated as a main language of postcolonial Pan-Africanism, most notably in a North American context, by providing the vocabulary for African American names and festivals such as Kwanzaa. It is an ironic appropriation—Swahili had become a national language across Tanganyika through the nineteenth-century slave and ivory trading, and then through its application as the chosen language of German colonial administration. But this appropriation has also been vindicated; Swahili shapes Tanzania's polity, and few other African countries can boast a more durable and successful national identity or a postcolonial history that has been comparatively untroubled by ethnic strife. This is not a survey of the many and varied reasons often given for Tanzania's relative political tranquillity, except only to explore what is in plain sight— that Tanzania marks perhaps the continent's most successful example of an African racial political identity.

Every group has its constitutive "Other." For most Africans in colonial and early postcolonial Dar es Salaam, that "Other" was neither the town's tiny European community, which figured so prominently in Africa's settler colonies, nor its similarly small Arab population, which figured so prominently in neighboring Zanzibar. Rather, it was the town's Indian community, who outnumbered Europeans and Arabs combined by nearly four to one, and who constituted roughly one quarter of colonial Dar es Salaam's population. The existence of East African Indians became globally known in the late 1960s and early 1970s when they emigrated out of the region's increasingly inhospitable countries, most notoriously Idi Amin's Uganda, to countries in the West, particularly Great Britain, where this instance of the empire "striking back" provoked a wave of anti-immigrant populism that opened a new chapter in British history. Most of these Indians had originated earlier—in some cases far earlier—from northwest India in the area bounded roughly by Bombay and Karachi, but had developed deep roots in East Africa, with some families dating back well over a century. Although the Indian presence in East

Africa had predated European colonialism, many more immigrated during the years of colonial rule, primarily drawn to communities with prospering commercial networks, but some came also to take up artisanal and clerical positions. Examined closely, East African "Indians" splinter into a dizzying array of regional, religious, and caste-based communities. If considered as a microcosm, East African Indians appear to be a privileged community that, by and large, had profited from their participation in systems of colonial rule. Wealthy and endogamous, Indians appeared to many Africans as a privileged insular merchant minority who generally refused to participate in a new post-colonial nation. Thus, figures like Idi Amin and many others could speak reliable applause lines by railing against the exploitative presence of Indian foreigners, whose wealth was widely perceived as coming at the expense of African farmers and consumers.

This is a study of racial and national thought, but also one that does not seek to divine the "origins" of such thought in East Africa; rather, it examines the specific processes by which historical actors come to identify and politicize humanity's alleged divisions. Race cannot be assumed to be a universal mode of thought, but its ubiquity, as Jonathon Glassman argues, is perhaps born of "a universal propensity to categorize."[2] Understanding the contingent and historically unique ways in which this "propensity to categorize" is realized is one of the central tasks of this book, which proposes to chart the growth and intensification of racial and national thought in the context of colonial and postcolonial urbanization. Prevailing terms of identity such as "African," "Indian," "Zaramo," et cetera, thus bear the burden of being interrogated and historicized while also having to perform important descriptive work. I have tried to historicize these terms throughout, even in my employment of them as objective categories, and emphasize the subjective and processual nature of identity formation where appropriate. But the amount of descriptive work is simply far too great to avoid regular usage of "African" and "Indian" in this study of identity. Thus we begin and end with frequent descriptions of historical actors as Indians and Africans, but in the minds of these actors, both terms varied considerably in their meaning, utility, and intensity across the intervening decades.

HOUSING A NATION

Let us begin at the end of this book's story. On April 22, 1971, residents of Dar es Salaam heard over the radio that Tanzania's National Assembly had passed a law nationalizing all buildings worth more than 100,000 shillings (£5,000) and not solely occupied by their owners. Handled with utmost secrecy before its parliamentary introduction, the law was the boldest move yet in Tanzania's socialist makeover of its cities. Dar es Salaam's Indian community, who owned nearly all of the buildings in question, waited nervously to hear which specific properties were affected. The next day brought a massive political parade. Such parades had become routine events since independence in 1961, but this one was different. Several thousand Africans joined in a celebratory march, which grew loud and unruly as it traversed the predominantly Indian neighborhood that was most heavily affected by the new law. President Julius Nyerere triumphantly proclaimed to celebrants that the goal of the law was "to prevent the emergence of a class of people who live and thrive by exploiting others."[3] The following Saturday at midnight, Indians leaving the city's late cinema shows scrambled to buy fresh copies of the *Sunday News*, which carried the first listings of nationalized buildings. Hundreds learned that night that the government had taken over their properties, and so began planning their departures from Tanzania.[4] Fiction captures the moment's emotions. Hassan Uncle, an Indian character in Moyez G. Vassanji's novel *The Gunny Sack*, reports the devastating news to his sister:

> "Did you hear? Washed out, I said. We are washed out—"
> "Washed out what, brother?"
> "Aré, in which world do you all live? Haven't you heard? Our buildings, our property, our houses, all gone. Saaf! Clean! Nationalised. Mali ya uma. Property of the masses. He's betrayed us, this stick-wielder [Julius Nyerere]."[5]

More than any other African leader of his time, this "stick-wielder" had elevated the principle of nondiscrimination to a philosophy of governance. Seven years earlier, an abortive army mutiny had unleashed riots that destroyed several Indian shops in Dar es Salaam. President Nyerere had toured the wreckage shortly after, apologized to shop owners, and promised them security. After Tanzania's banks were nationalized in 1967, he allegedly promised Habib Punja, Dar es Salaam's wealthiest property investor, that his buildings would be secure. As late as February 1971, Nyerere had joined the Aga Khan, leader of the region's largest and wealthiest Indian community, for the ceremonial opening of the Investment Promotion Services (IPS) skyscraper. All such buildings became "property of the masses" two months later.[6]

Was this betrayal or fulfillment? *Ujamaa*, postcolonial Tanzania's policy of "African socialism," had promised to remove exploitation, and Nyerere had identified "landlordism" as a principal source of exploitation and class conflict—a practice carried out with alacrity by all groups, but most visibly in the dense clusters of multistory buildings owned by Indians. For many *ujamaa* supporters, however, removing exploitation meant removing the enemies of African socialism, enemies whose qualities blurred economic and racial characteristics. In the months following passage of the Building Acquisition Act of 1971, more than 96 percent of the properties nationalized were revealed to be owned by Indians, who had invested heavily in housing in part to prove their commitment to living in independent Tanzania.[7] These investments were now taken away by a government hostile toward both capitalist development and the widely perceived failure of Indians to integrate with Africans. For many, nationalization removed the heavy inheritance of racial inequality symbolized by Uhindini (Swahili for "Indian area"), Dar es Salaam's prosperous Indian neighborhood that consisted of expensive, multistoried buildings situated apart from the nearest African neighborhood. H. M. Makaranga, a member of Tanzania's Parliament, reflected on how his walks through Uhindini would now be different:

> I think this bill will make legislators known today when they walk in this city of Dar es Salaam, and citizens will see that we truly rule ourselves, because every day when I left Parliament I passed these buildings, it seemed to me as if I was not actually leaving this Parliament. Because when those people saw me they were sitting up high in their buildings and asking, "Where are they coming from? Legislators, no way! They run the country? How!" From today they know that we have the real power to tear out the horns of the elephant and rhinoceros.[8]

Africans would no longer have to endure such postcolonial humiliation. By 1973, upward to half of Tanzania's Indian population had left the country. Of those who remained, the wealthy hedged their African futures by obtaining multiple passports; the poor simply adjusted to new conditions.[9] The rapidity of the Indian exodus only confirmed to most Africans what was then widely felt to be self-evident: that Indians never "belonged" to the new Tanzanian nation. Their houses had not been their homes.

This is a historical study of the connection between "houses," the urban site of economic investment and social life, and "homes," the intellectual site of racial thought and debates over national belonging. In exploring this connection, this book brings together two modes of analysis that rarely speak to one another. The first is that of colonial urban social history. Driven principally by materialist concerns, this approach typically focuses on the policies of the colonial state and African responses to them, as well as on the history of class development and social movements that occur within colonial cities.[10] The second mode of analysis is that of intellectual and cultural history, which for non-Western, ex-colonial sites like East Africa has been loosely termed "postcolonial studies." Driven principally by concerns about discourse and representation, this approach typically focuses on colonial, anticolonial, and nationalist political discourses, primarily by integrating the study of elite philosophy with that of more popular discourse, and interpreting subsequent communication and miscommunication between elites and masses. The most intellectually fruitful example of this approach has been the work of the "Subaltern Studies" school, whose examinations of nonelite agency and discourse in colonial India pioneered efforts to disrupt master narratives of anticolonial nationalism in the postcolonial world.[11] But before this study is situated within these two wider literatures—urban history and the study of nationalist and racial discourse—it will first be situated within the geographical and diasporic context of this book's primary "Other," East African Indians and the wider Indian Ocean world that they represent.

A CITY ON THE INDIAN OCEAN

Except for a brief examination of African soldiers in wartime South Asia, our spatial focus is the city and surrounding area of Dar es Salaam, which lies both on the African continent and along the Indian Ocean littoral. As a bustling site of peoples, goods, and ideas, Dar es Salaam housed multiple political discourses that were regional, extraterritorial, and supraterritorial in their ambition. One prominent discourse concerned "Greater India," an idea elaborated by Indian patriots in East Africa and other diasporic locales during the half century before India's independence in 1947. Extending across a far-flung South Asian diaspora, the primary aim of Greater India was to secure a set of national rights within an imperial context. The idea flourished where anti-British grievances ran sharpest; it was particularly pronounced along the Indian Ocean littoral. Neither a derivative discourse of European nationalism nor a modular replication of a proto-nation-state's "imagined community," Greater India was instead an argument formed out of diasporic grievances in dialogue with a constant stream of news from home, carried over imperial and commercial networks that tied London, Bombay, Delhi, and the diaspora together. Such networks formed, Sana Aiyar argues in her study of Kenya, a "united political realm" into which Indian diaspora figures inserted themselves and political intermediaries between local East African concerns, the global imperial project of Britain, and anticolonial nationalism then ascendant in India. Subsequent anticolonial discourse enabled East African Indians to create paths for inclusion in both colonial governance and African national movements.[12] Yet "Greater India" enthusiasts were not only apostles of anticolonialism but also importers and imposers of a tutelary nationalism to East Africa, in which the much-vaunted cosmopolitanism of the Indian Ocean world revealed its hierarchical underpinnings.

The Indian Ocean of the British Empire was a capacious arena of political debate, pregnant with multiple and contradictory forms of diasporic politics.

Such "polyphony" had potential to cohere around anti-imperial targets. In *A Hundred Horizons*, Sugata Bose stresses the virtues of cosmopolitan and universalist anticolonialism forged by "expatriate patriots" of the Indian Ocean unconcerned with "false binaries" of the secular and the religious. The anticolonialism of South Asians in the Indian Ocean, Bose argues, was "nourished by many regional patriotisms, competing versions of Indian nationalism, and extraterritorial affinities of religiously informed universalisms." Across this sprawling littoral, Indians sought "creative accommodation of differences" rather than pursuit of any singular type of anticolonialism.[13] It takes determined listening, however, to discern only the anticolonial tendencies from this oceanic political cacophony. Bose's portrait celebrates the patriotic vigor of South Asia's Indian Ocean diasporas while silently passing over their subimperial roles and aspirations. Much of Britain's Indian Ocean littoral, as Thomas R. Metcalf has demonstrated, owed its colonial administrative machinery, labor, and capital to British India.[14]

Another theme plainly audible across Britain's Indian Ocean after 1920 was the rivalry between "Indian" and "Muslim" political parties. The spirit of India's Pan-Islamic *khilafat* campaign and salt tax protests manifested themselves in East Africa, where they were similarly both secular and religious. But it would be an equally false binary to disentangle the religious from the secular as embodied in the imperial loyalism and bitter communal struggles that also flourished among East African Indians, who breathlessly exercised colonial privilege and anticolonial activism in tandem. In the eyes of many Africans in Dar es Salaam, the institutions of what Jon Soske terms "diasporic endogamy," which include marriage, religion, domestic space, dress, and even music and food, become "signifiers of social hierarchy and racial exclusion."[15] Blithe celebrations of Indian Ocean cosmopolitanism tend to obscure these deeper currents of racial resentment upon which African nationalist thought and practice would be built.

The task here is not to trace Indian diasporic networks in their movements across great distances, but rather in their social, economic, and political investments within one revealing corner, to show how what was once termed "plural society" forms, hardens, and dissipates. The descriptive sociology pioneered by J. S. Furnivall posited plural societies as one "with different sections of the community living side by side, but separately, within the same political unit."[16] Lacking the organic unity of common values, such a society, Furnivall argued, could be held together only through exercise of political force by its dominant section; by extension, only nationalism could reconstruct the connectedness lost with colonial rule and global economic integration. While offering little in way of either analysis or prescription, Furnivall's vision of pluralist social fracture reflects a sensibility that actors in Dar es Salaam's colonial public would readily acknowledge. Within this public, "different sections" had different and well-defined roles.

Indians famously became colonial East Africa's most important "middlemen" minority. Like European Jewry and the Chinese of Southeast Asia, they were the penetrating "strangers" of Simmelian sociological literature, middlemen who enjoyed freedom from expected reciprocal obligation, thus well-positioned to create money-based market relations but also reviled for their unassimilability, and therefore vulnerable to scapegoating. Neither alien nor citizen, the archetypal stranger was an economically aggressive actor who served to mediate between society and state.[17] For Africans, Indians were the shopkeepers on the other side of the counter who bought low and sold high, extracting African wealth between the margins. While such typologies have comparative utility, they cannot account for how Indians formed a *politically* aggressive diaspora, whose ultimate frailty was a product of both local and imperial histories. Such typologies also risk conflating popular imaginaries with sociological categories, as when Van den Berghe characterizes East African Indians as a middlemen minority that "shared little more in common than a broad geographical origin and membership in a despised, powerless, vulnerable, defenseless group of pariah capitalists."[18] Most important, comparative typologies lose sight of how immigrant communities historically shape the very categories of identity that they inhabit, and how these communities act as a mirror via which "host" populations define themselves.

Indians in Dar es Salaam, similar to their cousins in Durban, were both "insiders and outsiders," accorded privileges denied to Africans but also disenfranchised in relation to Europeans. Yet in contrast to South Africa, Indians in East Africa wielded significantly more political influence and economic power—power that originated from access to capital and its husbanding within profitable mercantile circuits. Moreover, Indians in Tanganyika had access to land, particularly urban land, which offered not only secure returns on investment but also collateral for credit, upon which all mercantile circuits relied. Enthusiastic Indian investment in urban property would form the basis not only for regional merchant networks but also for local political influence over the shape and direction of Dar es Salaam's urbanization.

CREATING URBAN SPACE

Histories of colonial African cities are most frequently cast in broad terms of material conflict between colonial states and their unruly African subjects. While isolated urban enclaves have a long history across Africa, one particularly significant dimension of the twentieth-century colonial town, as Bill Freund argues, was the way in which it began "to dissolve older relations of production in the countryside."[19] The most rigorous analytical framework cast in such terms is the subtle Marxist argument offered by Frederick Cooper in his studies of colonial Mombasa. Political conflict over space and mobility are revealed to be part of a deeper economic struggle over the control of labor. Cooper highlights the wide-ranging significance of African *straddling* of different modes of production—working part of the time as wage laborers and part of the time as peasant or subsistence farmers—which largely obstructed the full-scale proletarianization desired by colonial officials and capital investors alike. Late-colonial efforts to overcome straddling and finally achieve a permanent African urban workforce through labor stabilization policies created new forms of urban and national politics that would prove inordinately influential in Africa's decolonization. The analytical key was to investigate the actual relations of production, or what Marx termed the "hidden abode of production."[20] In this framework, colonial urbanization is one semiproletarianized end of a larger spatial conflict over class formation.

This book is not primarily a study of class formation and labor extraction, but it does examine these themes from the two main perspectives that it takes on colonial urbanization—the analysis of local cash-generating strategies that include but are not limited to labor, and the analysis of the changing regulatory commitments of the colonial state. Besides wages and the profits of petty commerce, there were two other major cash-generating strategies that urban residents relied upon—for creditors, rents; for debtors, consumer credit. Struggles over property indeed form a central motor of urban history, but my point of departure is Ricardian rather than Marxist. The most diffuse and accessible strategy of capital accumulation in cities was the accumulation of rents. Dar es Salaam's high rents for rooms and houses were not only indicators of urban immiseration for those on the economic margins, though they were certainly that, but also powerful evidence of successful strategies of capital accumulation by landlords of varying means and all colors. Urban newcomers suffered to pay because overall they derived comparative advantages from living in cities. Expensive rents emerge not only as a function of scarcity, but also from the consequent spillover or "externality" of human capital that in turn binds cities and their willing renters together.[21] The work of landlords who set out to capture these expensive rents did considerably more to determine the physical shape of colonial and particularly postcolonial urban growth than did colonial urban planners.

A subtheme of this study is the gradual rise and partial dismemberment of an urban *rentier* class of landlords in Dar es Salaam.[22] As the term is used here, *rentier* refers not only to those who passively derive their main incomes from returns on property, but also to those who actively *seek and collect economic rent*. Conventionally defined, economic rent is not simply payment for use (i.e., rent), but rather the *surplus of income over opportunity cost*.[23]

The *rentier's* capture is the excess value beyond what is minimally needed to elicit the sale of a given object. Inelastic by nature, land cannot respond to price changes that accompany population growth in the way that elastic factors of labor and capital can. Land works instead, in David Ricardo's words, for whatever is given to it by competition. A surplus above perfectly competitive market conditions is a regular and obvious phenomenon enjoyed by landowners throughout history—a history that may largely turn on the story of changing *rentier* fortunes.[24] In cities, growing scarcity of urban land generates rising incomes and power for *rentiers*. Commodification of urban space occurred in Dar es Salaam through shifting and competing institutions of petty and diffuse landlords, developers, farmers, and squatters. While the colonial state treated rising rents as a problem best handled by rent controls and other forms of regulation, the postcolonial state shook off lingering ambivalence and confronted landlordism directly, initially with a gradual euthanasia of land *rentiers* through rising taxes and changing land laws, and finally through a dramatic expropriation of private property that overwhelmingly targeted Indian "exploiters" in April 1971.

Although *rentiers* were key urban economic actors, urban identities were formed not primarily from landlord-renter relationships but rather through participation in wider urban economic circuits. The most concentrated site of such circuits was the *duka* (store), where food, clothing, and credit changed hands across shop counters, typically dividing African producers and consumers from Indian traders. Urban Africans on marginal wages survived on credit—primarily the consumer credit of pawnshops and store advances. Sharply diverging approaches to the meaning and use of wealth characterized this commercial nexus on the East African coast. Explicating the relationship between desire and wealth, Jeremy Prestholdt has demonstrated that for nineteenth-century Mombasans, the "proper social use of wealth was to consume it, not to store it up for future use." A Mombasan aphorism philosophized that "the property of the miser is eaten by worms."[25] Powerful regional caricatures portray Indians as tightfisted and self-denying, forgoing present satisfaction for future-oriented accumulation. Africans, by contrast, understood wealth as a means to the social end of mobilizing supporters and clients—or, as they were caricatured by Indians, living lives only in the here and now without reckoning for future investments. Such caricatures, while carrying grains of truth, also serve to obscure the history of successful African urban businessmen, as well as the extravagant use of wealth within Indian households and communities. This sort of social caricature is a major theme of this study; it plays an important constituent role in forming urban identities. But caricature is a process, not a timeless given. Racial caricature grew in tandem not only with the economic interactions for which it was a shorthand but also with a more fundamental rethinking of territorial origins, descent, and belonging, the core elements of identity in this Indian Ocean city. Credit, more than any other element of daily life, entwined strategies of urban survival with processes of racial caricature.

The other major perspective on urbanization that this study takes up has to do with the colonial state itself. There was a peculiar ambivalence at the heart of British interwar policy. In a materialist sense, this ambivalence was owing to what John Lonsdale and Bruce Berman termed the "contradictions of accumulation and control"[26] (i.e., the contradiction between the need to extract labor and the need to be seen to act on behalf of the social order as a whole). The latter primarily took the form of the paternalist protection of Africans, which was enshrined in the League of Nations mandate that granted Tanganyika to Britain. The British arrived after Dar es Salaam had already experienced thirty-odd years of racial segregation, and they proceeded to retain most of the urban policies of their German predecessor. For two decades, officials drifted between two poles of thought—that Tanganyika's "non-native" Indian and European population be encouraged to invest and gentrify urban space, and that Tanganyika's "native" African population be protected from the encroachment of "non-natives," with the former pole generally winning out in practice. The very language of this debate provided the major categories of identity—"native" and "non-native"—that the British colonial state formally imposed upon its Tanganyikan subjects.

The threat of war in 1939 ended this ambivalence and placed colonial urban policy on an entirely new footing. Unlike rural areas, which were heavily targeted for accumulation, urban areas posed an immediate threat to political security, and as such became primary sites to impose control, even at the expense of accumulation. The wartime urban colonial state was a regulatory state that extended basic minimum guarantees of food and clothing in return for visible full employment. Urban space grew within this regulatory texture of price and mobility controls, with several far-reaching effects, including providing the foundations for what development economists term "urban bias"—the unfair pricing of goods and services that flow between rural and urban areas.[27] What becomes clear in these processes is that African cities like Dar es Salaam increasingly became primary sites of consumption. Local politics thus became increasingly concerned with how scarce commodities were regulated by the state, as well as how the state should best manage hitherto opaque commercial distribution networks. The colonial state's particular answer to this crisis in Dar es Salaam was similar to what it had chosen to do elsewhere in East Africa—to distribute resources according to community "needs," which had the effect of putting distribution and consumption on a thoroughly racial basis.

In colonial historiographies the state occupies center stage as principal manu-
facturer of identity categories, although the limitations of this approach have
been increasingly appreciated. Recent literature has begun to stress that the state
itself was both less ambitious and more confused about entrenching categories
of identity. The goal of what Ann Laura Stoler terms "taxonomic states" was to
create not detailed sociological knowledge but rather "sorting codes" that were
easy to think through and useful to master, and whose fullness of implementation fell well short of Foucauldian expectations. Subsequent racial taxono-
mies were "not the unilateral inventions of colonial and metropolitan states,"
but rather mutually constituted through conflict and intimacy.[28] Colonial-era
identities in East Africa were partly products of legal-administrative strategies
and expediencies of colonial states, although their classificatory powers were
mainly suggestive outlines. Early literature on the subject has stressed the ri-
gidification of identity that accompanied colonial rule and colonial thinking.
Justin Willis shows how identity in Mombasa was once "intensely negotiable"
and defined "by attachments, the nature of obligations and claims," but that,
in the subsequent imposition of colonial ideas, ethnicity had lost "much of its
negotiability."[29] In the work of Willis, as well as Laura Fair's study of colonial
Zanzibar, colonial subject participation in identity building usually consists of
the straightforward and rational pursuit of legal improvement and social status
that imparted new meanings to old categories. The startling numerical rise in
self-identifying "Arabs" and "Shirazi" in colonial Zanzibar between 1924 and
1931 reveals a growing stigma attached to the category of Swahili. Distancing
oneself from the category of Swahili was an assertion of "independence and
transcendence" and, crucially, rising landownership on Zanzibar's neighboring
island of Pemba.[30] This process became even more straightforward during the
Second World War, when one could secure access to scarce cloth and rice, as
well as avoid forced labor, by successfully claiming Arab or Shirazi identity.
Pursuit of superior ration cards led the population of Zanzibar's "superior" races
to grow suspiciously large.[31] However, whatever the ultimate cause for this sharp
rise in claims to Shirazi identity happened to be, as Jonathon Glassman has
argued, "in the minds of its participants it involved more than rationing cards."[32]
This study takes up Glassman's insight by examining the trajectories of racial
thought, as well as examining the ambivalences of the colonial state.

Colonial identity categorization was not a unilateral process of realizing
state hegemony; it was always relational. Indeed, as we shall see, for Tanganyika the categories of "native" and "non-native" were not only poor guides
to urban development, they were also categories that were neither sharply
defined nor sharply applied by colonial officials. Nor were these categories
eagerly appropriated by colonial subjects. Instead, the process of identity

formation had multiple if unequal participants, who expressed a variety of material, intellectual, and psychological motivations—the pursuit of legal improvement, social status, intellectual rearticulation of community, and visceral resentment were all at work, if not in concert. The pursuit of identities necessarily required the manufacture or appropriation of useful vocabularies. The English-language category of "African" is a product of that continent's enslaved diaspora in the Americas.[33] Coexisting with its synonymous referents "negro" and "black," "African," however, was appropriated by Africa-descended authors and activists in the late eighteenth century. According to James Sidbury, it was these actors who transformed "African" from a term "so laden with connotations of primitivism and savagery into a source of pride,"[34] before its fading from nationalist discourse by the 1820s. "African," in Swahili *mwafrika*, had existed as a term of identity throughout the twentieth century but became the touchstone claim of origin, descent, and belonging in Tanganyika only during the 1940s. The term's political success owed much to the local, regional, and postwar international context, but it also reflected a new language for an old need. Robin Fox has speculated that the human need to reckon descent and claim ancestries may originate from the psychological security "derived from a sureness about one's ancestry," for such knowledge "rids us of anonymity."[35] This book traces specific efforts to "rid anonymity" within a relatively short period, from the 1920s to 1970s in Tanzania, by focusing on processes that formed categories of race, nation, and ethnicity. All of these categories can be understood theoretically as metaphors of descent; and all could be expressed in colonial East Africa with the Swahili word *taifa*.

National categorical thought need not be "modular" (i.e., portable and universally adaptable from country to country), let alone a modular import. In Benedict Anderson's *Imagined Communities*, nationalism begins with Europe's post-Enlightenment disenchantment, in which print capitalism replaces church authority to produce an exportable and modular nationalism that forms nation-states out of shared horizontal imaginations seeking territorial states.[36] In their wide-ranging critique of Anderson's model, John D. Kelly and Martha Kaplan explain that there is "both less and more to the nation-state and its genealogy" than Anderson suggests. "Communities" were not simply imagined, but fundamental political institutions that were legally and bureaucratically routinized within colonial states.[37] In British colonial Africa, "community" transformations were institutional phenomena. Put roughly, unrepresented "natives" in colonial Africa before the Second World War became poorly represented "Africans" who resented other better-represented races during the 1940s; better-represented "Africans" of the 1950s became citizens of sovereign nation-states in the 1960s. What *was* modular, symmetrical, and homogeneous about nationalism in Africa was not its specific contents but instead the symmetrical and singular world system of postwar UN sovereignty that welcomed the accession of colonial territories to nominally equal independent nation-states.[38] Out of shared disgust with the violent wartime elisions of nationalism and race, postwar metropolitan elites created a new international order that separated nation from race. But throughout the late colonized world, in sharp contrast, aspiring citizens expected their nations to value the shared descent that formed communities of visceral nationalist attachment.

Nationalisms precede nations, and require articulation by nationalist intellectuals who presume the world to be constructed of natural units of nations. Strictly speaking, few such intellectuals imagine themselves to be "creating" nations; they rather see themselves doing the simpler work of identifying what is already immanent in a "natural" grouping of peoples. Guiding assumptions about national fealty in Tanganyika involved race, which is an inherently exclusive rubric. There was a widespread conviction among academics as well as some political actors, including Julius Nyerere, during the first decades of Africa's independence, that nationalism was inclusive and based on shared civic values that could be realized in the future, within a secular and sovereign nation-state. This vision was partially secured in Tanzania's legal code, most notably its nonracial citizenship laws, yet its appeal was thin, and wilted in the face of "popular" nationalists who were less troubled by conflations of nation and race.

Although much of this book studies the subjective side of identity formation, it also must account for objective social structures that become racialized in practice. The analytical value of the term "identity," as Frederick Cooper and Rogers Brubaker have observed, is often compromised by its tendencies to conflate categories of analysis and categories of practice.[39] Therefore, it is important to distinguish terms of analysis from terms of practice at the outset. This book analyzes nation, race, and ethnicity alike as modes of thought in which "groups" are subjectively presumed to be authentic cultural wholes that define themselves by metaphors of shared descent.[40] By showing how both political language and political will of Tanzanian actors changed over time, this book demonstrates the connection between intellectual engagement with identity and the urban socioeconomic context, through which these actors defined national belonging and exclusion. Although this book is not primarily a study of women and gender, women figure prominently in the male African political imagination as the vulnerable barriers through which other "nations" and "races" undermine the African *taifa*. Indeed, what emerges as the most enduringly hegemonic aspect of racial and national thought in Tanzania is the reckoning of descent along patrilineal lines. Yet the messy material realities of urban life, in which women increasingly exercise autonomy within the colonial and postcolonial economies through informal and unregulated activities such as beer-brewing, trading, and prostitution, make poignant the enormous gaps between that world that African nationalist intellectuals would like to have had and the world that they had.

A NOTE ON SOURCES AND METHODOLOGY

The language of identity in Dar es Salaam survives mostly in the voluminous documentary sources that this book examines. Covering the period from roughly 1916 to 1976, these sources reflect the biased perspective of their authors, who were overwhelmingly educated men—be they European, Indian, or African—who produced documents to be read either by or within formal institutions of government, voluntary associations, and newspapers. I also conducted a large number of formal interviews and less-formal conversations, which included conversations with Indians, Africans, and one particularly helpful former colonial official, the late Randal Sadleir. These oral interlocutors provided me with valuable social and economic perspectives on urban history, but discussions with them about the language of identity were both nonabstract and "postcolonial," by which I mean that my interlocutors showed little interest in discussing categories of identity themselves (race, nation, etc.), and that their use of identity categories usually matched the postcolonial sensibilities that are mapped out in this book's final chapter rather than recalling colonial-era usages that survive in print.

There were, however, important exceptions; in particular, the oral discourse of firstcomers and outsiders discussed at length in this book's second chapter. Through my research assistants, Hamisi Msumi and Mohamed Kibanda, I conducted a series of interviews with elderly African men and a few women—as few of the latter agreed to be interviewed—in the neighborhoods of Kariakoo, Gerezani, and Buguruni, framed around questions of race relations between Indians and Africans and more-general economic issues. This is where I first learned that many Shomvi and Zaramo, Dar es Salaam's "original" African inhabitants, remain deeply embittered about their displacement from positions of wealth and authority in the city and continue to use the discourse of firstcomers and outsiders to convey their complaints. They and others alerted me to the significance of this vital language of identity that structured large parts of urban African social life during the colonial period, which I would have otherwise missed—its presence in written sources is often oblique and lacking in consistent terminology. This is also where I first learned of the deep resentment and occasional misogyny that some men displayed in reference to successful and independent women in Dar es Salaam, which correlates with what survives in documents, in particular letters published in newspapers.

This is primarily a work of documentary history, in which institutions and educated men loom large. The most important of these institutions was the colonial and postcolonial state, which plays a central role by shaping and administering policies—and in adjudicating disputes—relevant to identity. The historian must not only reconstruct legal and administrative histories but also trace conceptual genealogies of identity in order to discern points at which the state is creating, shaping, or simply receiving ideas about who its subjects are. This book attempts to meet this challenge through a systematic reading of colonial-era documents that pays careful attention to shifts in language employed by both the state and its subjects. The state's unrivaled capacity to generate and preserve documents, at least during the colonial period, exaggerates its importance to local life. This also makes for an ironic challenge, as one of my arguments is that previous historians have attributed too much significance to the state—colonial and postcolonial alike—in generating categories of identity. Yet at certain junctures the interventions of the state *were* critical, and this is reflected in the chapter structure, which acknowledges that the Second World War and independence were both watershed moments in Tanzania's social and intellectual history.

This book also traces the contours and trajectories of print debates as they appeared in newspapers, educational primers, poetry, and literature in order to recover a history of African political thought. Dar es Salaam's press richly chronicles and debates urban developments for a preponderantly urban readership. The most important newspapers were owned either by the government (*Mambo Leo*), European-owned corporations (*Tanganyika Standard*), private individuals (*Tanganyika Opinion, Kwetu, Ngurumo*), or the ruling party (*Uhuru, Nationalist*).[41] Both short- and long-term intellectual debates emerge through an exhaustive reading of these sources, which rarely challenged political authority but gave surprisingly generous latitude to social criticism. In the last two chapters, I delineate a forum of political debate that lies somewhere between the structural determinism of discourse and the detached elite agency of African intellectual history, a midway realm termed a "public." Karin Barber has defined *public* as "an audience whose members are not known to the speaker/composer of the text, and not necessarily present, but still addressed simultaneously, and imagined as a collectivity." This shift to print, among other media technologies, marks a fundamental change in the relationship between author/speaker and recipient. This requires a new form of address to meet the challenge of anonymity, while also striving to form what Barber terms "a real, single, co-present collectivity."[42] Ridding oneself of this anonymity was a central if unstated task for authors of the country's print public. One answer to this challenge was the employment of wider descent-based categories of identity like *taifa*, as well as the use of racial caricatures and class-based personifications like *kabwela* and *naizi* (chapter 5).

Tanganyika's print public had numerous limitations. The African population literate in Roman-script Swahili or English, the language of the major print media examined in this study, was limited and mostly male in colonial Dar es Salaam—in 1956, 42 percent of men and 12 percent of women were literate in Roman-script Swahili—although overall literacy rates had surpassed 60 percent by the 1960s.[43] Yet this print public always had a significant oral component. Tanganyikan writers wrote to be heard. Reading was often a social event, in which the reach of the press extended to the nonliterate through the practice of reading aloud. Much of what was published in Swahili independent newspapers, and the poetry that was published in all Swahili newspapers, followed spoken rather than standardized written conventions.[44] Tanganyikan writers also wrote to be seen. The sense of honor that was attached to the acquisition and public demonstration of literacy noticeably shaped how male African writers—in particular those associated with the military—represented themselves, colonial society, and elements of that society that they felt were dishonoring them—namely women and non-African men. Although honor is not taken up as a central category of analysis, it nonetheless features in key moments when racial and nationalist convictions harden. John Iliffe argues that honor, minimally defined as the right to respect, was a powerful ideological motivation in Africa's twentieth-century history.[45] The language of Tanganyika's print public supports this claim, as it is saturated with references to honor (*heshima*) and shame (*aibu*). As an "ideological motivation," honor does not lend itself to systematic thought like that of race and nation, but its thick presence does reveal the versatility of Tanzanian documentary sources to convey the rich combinations of thought, posture, and sentiment at work in the minds of its authors.

ORGANIZATION OF THE BOOK

We begin with an analysis of urbanization under colonial law and administration in the 1920s and 1930s. This was not the beginning of imperial rule in Dar es Salaam, which was founded in the 1860s as an imperial outpost of Zanzibar, and later served as the capital of German East Africa from 1890 until its evacuation in 1916. Chapter 1 instead begins by examining how British officials adopted much of the German administration's segregationist spatial urban planning, yet departed from German practices by raising the legal status of Indians from "native" to "non-native." The distinction between "native" and "non-native," premised on the postwar paternalist principle to protect "native" Africans from "non-native" predations, became the critical fulcrum through which urban policies were pursued, to self-contradicting ends. The enormous wealth generated and invested by the town's Indian community over this period dramatically improved conditions in the "Asian" or "Commercial Quarters," but also drove poorer Indians to seek cheaper housing in the (theoretically) segregated "Native Quarters" ostensibly reserved for Dar es Salaam's African population. Resulting ripples of gentrification challenged the very purpose and logic of policies ostensibly designed to protect "native" interests, and gave unintended meanings to the categories of native and non-native.

Chapter 2 examines the social and political lives of Africans and Indians in Dar es Salaam during the interwar period. Despite abiding divisions along "communal" lines based on religion and caste, Indian nationalists based in Dar es Salaam during the 1920s often united in criticism of British policy to direct effective protests against the colonial state. Yet the growing salience of Hindu-Muslim division in India disrupted East African anticolonial unity in the 1930s. This also coincided with the increasing communalization of commercial networks to better adapt to global depression that had reduced territorial trade and tightened commercial regulations. Indian political activism also stimulated new forms of African political activism. Racial self-identification as "African" was growing but enjoyed no political monopoly. It instead competed with an older dynamic in which Dar es Salaam's "indigenous" inhabitants would claim firstcomer status and ancestral rights to all aspects of urban life vis-à-vis more recent, and frequently more successful, African immigrants. Associational life in Dar es Salaam straddled not only this moiety-like dynamic that pitted self-proclaimed "owners of the town," or *wenye mji*, against more recent immigrants, or *watu wa kuja*, but also the aspirations of new actors and groups that identified along racial rather than firstcomer lines. "Race relations" between Indians and Africans were largely commercial relations, and the urban economy became the prism through which both groups would understand, misunderstand, and caricature each other.

Chapter 3 analyzes the radical demographic, economic, and administrative changes that the Second World War brought to Dar es Salaam. Facing massive growth in urban population and inflation, the colonial state exercised unprecedented control over Dar es Salaam's urban economy. Their intrusions, which guaranteed a low but reliable level of subsistence to town residents, in effect created "urban entitlement" in a time of territorial scarcity. To put urban entitlement on a sustainable basis, the colonial government restricted urban space to those it deemed productive and fully employed, while targeting the unemployed through heavy-handed rural repatriation campaigns. The major issues of urban politics were the distribution and consumption of food, clothing, and housing. To contain inflation, the colonial state took over distribution of these goods for which it used a racialized rubric, which effectively organized urban life along racial lines as never before. Black markets thrived, and Africans identified and vilified Indians as unscrupulous profiteers. Labor disputes were increasingly organized around racial resentments, and labor leaders insisted on the duty of non-Africans to pay Africans a living wage. From these tensions developed a race-based popular politics among Africans in Dar es Salaam. The creation of urban entitlement—macroeconomically speaking, the rural subsidization of urban life—had the political effect of entrenching racial divisions.

The term *taifa* comes under examination in chapter 4, which is an intellectual history of racial and nationalist writers, mostly based in Dar es Salaam, who made sense of these wide-ranging urban and territorial changes by articulating the idea of nation and race during the 1940s and 1950s. "Civilization" provided the principal theme upon which ideas of racial difference were cast. African writers embraced the "uplift" provided by plainly paternalistic notions of civilization, but also discerned that civilization bestowed racial self-identification and a duty to maintain racial integrity. Racial advancement depended on racial purity, whose greatest transgressors were the numerous "mixed-race" offspring of "immoral" African women and non-African men. The Second World War had a decisive effect on those African men who served in South Asia and Burma; these men returned with memories scarred not only by racial inequalities but with newly gained knowledge of comparative Indian poverty. The African racial identity paradigm flourished under political leadership of the African Association, which by 1954 had become the Tanganyika African National Union (TANU). TANU embraced and pursued ideas of racial purity and virtue contained within the concept of civilization and its more secular successor, development, although its leader, Julius Nyerere, tempered racial logic by his pragmatic participation in "multiracial" politics, as well as by his personal conviction to pursue nonracial politics when possible. TANU also mobilized mass support by adopting local idioms of exploitation to explain the demoralizing persistence of non-African economic successes and African economic failures. So complete was TANU's monopoly over racial discourse, and its monopoly of racial thought over most Tanganyikans, that formal and informal political opposition to TANU failed to effectively contest Nyerere's ideal of a nonracial, patrilineal-based national citizenship for Tanganyika.

Chapter 5 examines the development of an urban socialist ideology that combined local ideas of exploitation and its eradication with international socialist concepts and colonial ideas of development. The discursive categories of *ujamaa* targeted non-Africans, Indians in particular, as unwilling participants in the project of nation-building. Long-standing mistrust, combined with long-standing discursive conflation of nation and race, helped nationalists to identify the "Indian" as the most fitting example of the new nation's purge category, "exploiter." This culminated in the expropriation of mostly Indian-owned buildings in 1971, which inspired a massive Indian exodus that fulfilled the doomsayers' prophecy that Indians never intended to join the new African nation. Despite these racial transformations of urban policy, much of the colonial inheritance endured, in particular systematic removals of under- and unemployed Africans.

Racialized purge categories offered little to aspiring urban residents who lived in constant fear of being removed from Dar es Salaam to labor in *ujamaa* villages. Instead, a new language was born that transcended the official rhetoric of party and state, crafted by urban residents who sought to carve out discursive space to critique the totalizing conceits of the postcolonial state.

A final note on term usage: the language of identity categories is the principal focus of this book, and thus much thought has been given to descriptive group terms that require frequent and consistent usage. I use the term "Indian" throughout to refer to people of South Asian descent for two reasons. First, "Indian" was the main term of reference and self-reference throughout most of the period covered in this study. Second, the alternative terms, "South Asian" and "Asian," are far too artificial and inexact, respectively, to bear constant repetition. "South Asian" is the preferred postpartition term of academics, but it is a term that is simply not used, either then or now, in East Africa. "South Asian" can be relied upon not to offend, but it lacks any and all emotive or intellectual force that is sometimes contextually conveyed—with both joy and discomfort—by the term "Indian" and its Swahili equivalent, *Mhindi*. The term "Asian" and its archaic variant "Asiatic" were frequently used to describe people from South Asia, but these were also shifting legal and political terms that sometimes, but not always, joined Arabs and Indians together, and sometimes Chinese as well. Although "Asian" became considerably more popular as a term of reference and self-reference after 1950, which is reflected in its usage in this book, any systematic usage of this term throughout would require frequent and tedious qualification. That said, "South Asian" and "Asian" are used in those instances when they are the better terms and require little or no elaboration. More problematic are the terms "native" and "non-native," which were not only the principal legal categories used until the 1940s, but also terms frequently used for popular identification and self-identification. When I employ the terms "native" and "non-native" in the chapters below, I attempt to ameliorate the condescending connotations they inevitably carry by sometimes using scare quotes ("native" and "non-native") to indicate their historically specific and, on occasion, ironic usage. I do not do this consistently, however, as systematic usage of scare quotes becomes burdensome and tedious for the reader and writer alike. Understand that the absence of scare quotes in no way condones the degrading connotations associated with the term "native," any more than my un-scare-quoted usage of the acrid epithet *mshenzi* (savage) condones the degradation of mainland Africans by "civilized" coastal chauvinists.

1 ⤳ Native and Non-Native

Colonial Urbanization and the Legal
Foundations of Identity

IN BRITISH COLONIAL AFRICA between the 1890s and 1940s, a person's first legal identity was either native or non-native. While there was no one definition, in general "natives" were indigenous Africans, and "non-natives" were European and Asian immigrants. The legal ordering of colonial identities was thus first the mediation of relations between indigenes and immigrants. This chapter examines how legal identities and colonial administrative processes entrenched racial categories in interwar Dar es Salaam. The most important of these processes involved regulating interaction between "native" Africans and "non-native" Indians. Nominally intended to protect African "native" interests, the implementation of Tanganyika's colonial laws revealed two competing visions for urban Africa. One championed urban growth driven by non-African commerce and capital improvements; the other pursued the paternalistic protection of Africans from non-African market forces. Urban life, however, ran well ahead of either vision, and a distinctly reactive and ad hoc character of governance emerged during these years. Although the main actors of this chapter are British officials, their work and debates provided contradicting visions of urbanization that Africans and Indians would appropriate and reshape to make claims on urban life.

This chapter investigates how colonial categorization shaped urban development. Legal and administrative categories of colonial rule have left lasting imprints on Africa's subject population. The most influential author to stress this point has been Mahmood Mamdani, who argues that the legal-administrative complex of colonial states "framed and set in motion particular political identities," which produced subsequent racial and ethnic identities.[1] Like Tutsis in Rwanda, Indians in East Africa were a middle-ground "subject race"; immigrants who enjoyed the partial fruits of "non-native" status without the full political power exercised by "non-native" Europeans. But the most important development was the colonial state's initial inscription of "native" and "non-native" upon subject populations. *"The greater crime of colonialism,"* Mamdani stresses, *"was to politicize indigeneity in the first place."*[2] Legal privileges only underlined the essential foreignness of "non-natives." Popularly stigmatized, these middle-ground communities found themselves vulnerable to the inevitable Fanonist violence that accompanied decolonization.

This chapter argues that the colonial legal-administrative system *was* vital to the production of identities in urban Tanganyika, but—contra Mamdani's uniform model—it was a system with multiple constituencies that forged competing sets of priorities. The path between colonial policy and internalized colonial identity was mediated by several factors, in particular the constant improvisation of colonial officials and the selective political appropriation of their colonial subjects. The resulting paths were rarely straightforward. In Dar es Salaam, the clearest physical inscription of colonial identity production lay in urban spatial planning. Following German precedent, the British colonial government divided the city into three zones, ostensibly based on economic activity but effectively legalizing racial patterns of residence. As we shall see, Dar es Salaam's European, Asian (i.e., Indian), and African zones were formed by legal codes and administrative initiatives that sought to secure de facto if not quite de jure racial segregation. Yet, in practice, the power of the colonial state to specifically inscribe segregation and, more generally, ontological identity categories was limited by three principal factors. First, the state had limited resources to realize its visions; second, these visions were multiple and contradictory. Finally, colonial identity categories were selectively appropriated by colonial subjects themselves, who pursued political projects that exploited colonial contradictions in order to secure certain protections and to reject certain forms of authority. Legal-administrative categories were unavoidable tools of colonial bureaucracy. The goal of this chapter is to place the legal-administrative intent of urban policies in the context of the limited capacity of British colonizers to effect change. Though fundamental to the colonial project, "native" and "non-native" were not fully realized categories of colonial power, but instead a language of policy and administration used to justify and rationalize improvised action.

NATIVE/NON-NATIVE: THE POLITICS OF AN INCOMPLETE LEGAL PROJECT

The legal categories of native and non-native in British Tanganyika (1919–1961) represent standard imperial tools reforged in the language of international paternalism of the immediate postwar years. Originally an anodyne reference to one's birthplace, the term "native" had transformed into a British imperial category used to describe non-European subjects during the nineteenth century. Coinciding with administrative challenges posed by Bengal and other post-American, non-Western possessions, "native" came to conflate birthplace, residence, and culture, and implicitly contrasted the cosmopolitan mobility of European non-natives with the relative immobility of non-European subjects.[3] The term became a popular antonym to "non-native," the legal category that represented "civilized" settlers, officials, and—on occasion—non-European immigrants. Native/non-native became the legal diptych through which the rules of interaction between territorial subjects and imperial immigrants were prescribed.

Tanganyika's legal code was heavily freighted with paternalistic legislation ostensibly designed to protect indigenous people from foreign encroachment. The League of Nations Class B Mandate granted to Britain over ex-German East Africa in 1922 directed the new ruler to "respect the rights and safeguard the interests of the native population,"[4] and this principle was enshrined in the major legislative acts of the early administration. Most important was the Colonial Office's decision to ensure that Tanganyika, like West Africa, be "primarily a Black man's country,"[5] relieving itself of the volatile pressures that accompanied white settler political influence elsewhere in East and Central Africa. Subsequent laws were designed to prevent land commercialization, not only to avoid settler domination but also to avoid land speculation from Indians who enjoyed protection from legal discrimination under the mandate.[6] Land and conveyance laws prohibited transfer of land between natives and non-natives without written government permission. The governor held all land in trusteeship for its inhabitants except those freehold areas (i.e., private land owned in perpetuity) previously alienated under German rule. All other land could be allocated to individuals only on the basis of time-fixed leases, the maximum being ninety-nine years. Credit restrictions prohibited non-natives from recovering native debt collateral to prevent Africans from selling or encumbering their land, their one principal asset.[7] Horace Byatt, Tanganyika's first British governor, promised to "discountenance the giving of credit to natives by refusing to the creditor any redress in the courts."[8] Taken together, these land and credit policies ideally bifurcated Tanganyika's population between native producers living on communal lands and non-natives confined to either urban areas or commercial estates.

As the legal category of "native" gained in significance, the legal category of "non-native" widened in membership. Previous German East African laws had classified Indians, Arabs, and Africans alike as "natives." This classification had stimulated the formation of the colony's first Indian political organization in 1914, which petitioned for the privileged "non-native" status enjoyed by Europeans.[9] This desire for higher legal status only sharpened during and after the war. Under Article 7 of the mandate, all nationals of League of Nations member states were to receive equal treatment in Tanganyika, thus placing nationals of India, an original League member, at theoretical par with those from European states. Moreover, Indians were generally much wealthier than Africans, and thus expected to afford non-native house taxes instead of far cheaper native hut taxes for the revenue-hungry administration.[10] Finally, between 1916 and 1920, the Colonial Office had been faced with demands from Indians in East Africa, Britain, and India to make German East Africa a colony of India as a reward for service in the First World War. Although Britain did not accede to this demand, it could not support legislation that made Indians legally distinct from Europeans in the conquered colony, as occurred in Kenya with significant political turmoil. With these various pressures in mind, officials in Dar es Salaam and London in effect "promoted" Indians from native to non-native status during the drafting of Tanganyika's foundational laws.

Creating obstacles to protect "native interests" against non-native predations became a priority among a discernible faction of officials. Internal debates did not address how protectionist laws obstructed African commercial aspirations in Dar es Salaam; Africans themselves would be the first to raise this point. Rather, debate centered on which priority should guide urban development: improving public health, maximizing state revenue, or protecting the security of African tenure in and around Dar es Salaam. The notorious frugality of British rule was especially evident in Tanganyika, and often those policies that cost the colonial power the least and extracted the most from the colonized won out. Yet Dar es Salaam was also home to hundreds of British officials, and therefore costly public health projects often received favor, helped by strident support from the town's small but vocal white business community.[11] Other officials embraced the mandate's injunction to protect "native" interests against "non-natives." In 1929, Indians accounted for 78 percent of non-native population of Dar es Salaam; non-natives overall accounted for 9,024 or 28.5 percent of the town's 31,656 residents, with "native" Africans totaling 22,632 or the majority 71.5 percent.[12]

Although "native" and "non-native" constituted the principal terms of administrative debates, Tanganyika's state project of identity categorization was incomplete in both intent and effect. Officials across East Africa were well aware that "native" was a shorthand for race that risked becoming absurd upon closer scrutiny and application, such as with manifestly ambiguous cases like Swahili, Somali, and Arab. Neighboring colonies had offered cautionary examples. In coastal Kenya during the 1910s, a politically reckless closer application of "native" and "non-native" categories was used to distinguish "Swahili" from "Arab" populations, politicizing those coastal identities for decades.[13] In 1925 the Zanzibar government abolished the category "native" and replaced it with the category "African" in all but a few of its laws, which marked an early regional entrenchment of continent-based identity categories.[14] Leading officials in Tanganyika, by contrast, resisted demands from lobbyists within the territory and across the empire who sought clarity and consistency. Rather than declaring constitutional definitions of who was or was not a "native," they opted to decide ambiguous matters on a case-by-case rather than categorical basis. Two criteria were generally followed: in the handful of legal decisions, cases usually turned on one's *descent*; in the far more numerous administrative decisions, cases usually turned on one's *mode of living* or class. Arabs presented the most consistently vexing cases. Arabs numbered 581 in Dar es Salaam's 1929 census, and were defined as "native" in some laws but "non-native" in others. Many strategically straddled these inconsistencies—claiming to be "native" Arabs to avoid paying higher "non-native" taxes, while claiming to be "non-native" Arabs to avoid being called out to labor on public works by local Native Authorities. Their numbers were deemed sufficiently small to avoid having to apply consistent categorization.[15] In cases where decisions had to be made, class was the determining factor.

As law was open to international scrutiny and Tanganyika was an internationally mandated territory, its government was comparatively sensitive about giving appearances of legal discrimination. During the 1920s "native" had been a lax category of administrative convenience, but demands for closer definition stimulated by an obscure court case in Nyasaland in 1929 had moved the Colonial Office to clarify the designation throughout East and Central Africa. The legal status of mixed-race people reveals uniquely explicit discussions about this taken-for-granted category.[16] Most officials in Tanganyika were keenly aware that, aside from its implicit but obvious universal exclusion of white Europeans, "native" was not a term of any racial precision. Rather, the language was, like so much else about colonial rule, improvised to accommodate the kaleidoscopic diversity of East Africa, particularly its coastal area. When considering a form of native administration for Dar es Salaam in 1929, the provincial commissioner stated that "native" was

> hardly suitable when we are speaking of the towns people, since they include not only Africans but many of other races, Arabs of several kinds, certain of the poorer Indians, and the greater number of persons of mixed African and Oriental descent; and also Somalis. . . . I would, therefore, wish to be understood as including in the convenient term "native" all those who live according to native standards in what we call the native quarters of the towns.[17]

As the Nyasaland case worked its way through the imperial bureaucracy, a practical consensus formed that legal status of "native half-castes" should depend "primarily upon the standard and mode of their life," and that no legal obstacles should be placed to prevent this.[18] Philip Mitchell, then Tanganyika's Secretary of Native Affairs, was tasked to address once and for all the question of "native" status territorially. Mitchell answered by refusing to establish constitutional identities. Categories of "native" and "non-native," he reasoned, should not be "mutually exclusive terms in the administrative sphere indefinitely," for within a few decades, one can reasonably expect urban "natives" to be fully participating as citizens in colonial towns.[19] As typical in other British African territories, his legal research found numerous differing and conflicting definitions. In Tanganyika's statutes, "native" was most frequently defined as "any member of an African race and includes a Swahili and a Somali"; next most frequent was "any native of Africa not being of European or Asiatic race or origin." Such messiness, however, was preferable to the potential political trouble that legal clarity might bring.

To Mitchell's paternalistic mind, the purpose of colonial law was not to fix the identities and rights of separate racial groups, but to achieve stable political development through the exercise of judicial discretion. "No amount of theorising," Mitchell argued, "can alter the fact that certain classes of all communities require specific protection in the laws." A descriptive definition of "native" that allowed for individual exceptions, he felt, should remain the principle of territorial legislation for protective purposes:

> The whole question is full of difficulties and demonstrates the complications you cannot escape once you let racial discrimination into the law, unless you are prepared to go the whole way and make the broad distinction of white and coloured, which is not practical politics. As far as Tanganyika is concerned, it is a sleeping dog that I would let lie.[20]

The Secretariat finally responded to Colonial Office definitional inquiries by drafting a bill that allowed mixed-race people to claim "non-native" status if they met three criteria—that the person be partly of "non-native" descent; the person not occupy land on "native" terms; and the person not live among "members of any African tribe or community *in accordance with their customary mode of life*."[21] Thus descent, class, and culture all served as definitional markers to minimize constitutional identity categories and to maximize individual discretion for British colonial officers charged with ruling on such distinctions. "Native" remained colonial Tanganyika's principal if ill-defined legal identity category, while "African" remained a secondary term for use in tautological definitions of "native." They were improvised categories designed for improvised projects.

Colonial urban planners have both taken and been given too much credit for their ability to transform the urban space of African cities. Ambitious blueprints were rarely if ever implemented. Far from regularizing and rationalizing urban space, the colonial state and its policies were, as William C. Bissell has noted for neighboring Zanzibar, "marked by contradiction, confusion, even chaos."[22] Thrift and expediency perpetually trumped planning and design. Indeed, "planning" is a rather misleading term to characterize the tactical improvisations of separate government departments that ultimately shaped the spaces and created the infrastructures of colonial urban Africa. The term "planning" furthermore implies a unity of policy and implementation that did not exist, just as common usage of the term "the colonial state" often implies a unitary actor. As this chapter shows, "the colonial state" in Dar es Salaam was a group of separate departments with distinct and sometimes conflicting priorities. The main institutional actors during the interwar years were the Medical Department, the District Office, and the Public Works Department. Each had separate functions and remits, none of which were firstly "urban." The Dar es Salaam Township Authority (est. 1920) was staffed mostly by representatives from these departments, and the only fully "urban" administrator in Dar es Salaam was the Municipal Secretary, a post created only in 1930. Government efforts to shape the urban space of interwar Dar es Salaam amounted to the implementation of building codes and land laws for segregationist ends, and a handful of modest public health and public works projects. Post-1945 interventions remained ad hoc and project-specific. Dar es Salaam's three "master plans" (1949, 1968, 1979) are significant as snapshots of "blueprint" aspiration, but as guides to subsequent urban development, they are for the most part irrelevant fantasies.[23] Urban planning was ultimately the collective sum of interventions carried out by separate bureaucracies, driven by different and often competing visions.

The new colonial government's first goal was the restoration of a workable political stability. Deprivations of war and years of unregulated growth confronted officials after British military forces occupied Dar es Salaam on September 4, 1916, following a protracted siege. The former German-colonial capital initially swelled after it became the principal military cantonment for allied forces in East Africa.[24] Urban security was charged to military contingents, and later to a new police force based on a core of twenty white South Africans who arrived in Dar es Salaam in late 1917.[25] Yet the stresses of feeding and housing military forces and interned enemy subjects, a massive drought in 1917–1918, and the collapse of both local German currency and hinterland trade networks brought economic breakdown and severe food shortages to the town and surrounding areas that did not abate until 1920.[26] Interned German families at least enjoyed guaranteed sustenance provided by humanitarian conventions; food shortages forced many Africans to decamp. Another 4,000 Africans in Dar es Salaam, mostly demobilized military soldiers and porters, were forced from town in 1919, "either to their own districts or to the country to cultivate."[27] Combined with the eventual expulsion of interned Europeans, the net result was a massive decrease in the town's population, from perhaps as high as 34,000 in 1914 to 16,886 by 1921.[28]

Amid these dramatic population movements, medical officers emerged as the new regime's first urban administrators. They were comparatively powerful and well-funded, in no small part because their public work ensured the private health of several hundred European residents. These officers had arrived shortly after Britain's occupation of Dar es Salaam in 1916, and had generally worked in the town longer and knew it better than officials from other departments. The Dar es Salaam that German officials had abandoned lacked any public water supply or sewage system, depended on poorly constructed wells, and suffered an alarmingly high rate of malarial infection.[29] Household rubbish, cut vegetation, and sweepings piled up far more quickly than could be disposed of by town ox-cart removals.[30] R. R. Scott, the first Medical Department head, characterized their immediate postwar work as cleaning an "Augean stable," blaming the unsanitary conditions on Indian and African indifference to sanitation. Water drainage was a chronic problem, particularly in the open depression of Chafukoga (from *Mchafu-Kaoge*, which translates roughly as "who is dirty go and bathe"), where, after heavy rains, water stood for weeks in a pond of green algae until the depression was gradually filled with burned rubbish and drained by culverts.[31] The town would later be described as a "sponge lying on a large plate"—the sponge being the town's centrally placed, malarial reservoir, which derived its parasite supply from the periphery.[32] Surface wells provided nearly all of the town's water supply, which was described as precarious and unsafe.[33] Like Bombay, Dar es Salaam was a drainage nightmare, with inadequate sewage perpetually endangering public health. Thick with humidity and irritants, town air was difficult to breathe. Strong ocean breezes stirred up such large amounts of sand and dirt that the township regularly watered streets to reduce blowing dust.[34] Costly public health works in Dar es Salaam consumed more than one-third of Tanganyika's entire sanitation and public health budget in the early 1920s. Costs were heavily subsidized by central government, as the town's tax base alone could not support such projects.[35] During the 1920s, medical officers were the only effective zoning authorities who alone curtailed unapproved building.[36] In recognition of their prominent role, the executive office of Dar es Salaam Township Authority was held by the head of the Medical Department from 1920 to 1930.[37]

Segregationist public health logic that had guided German urban planning was appropriated in Britain's reconstruction. The German Building Code, promulgated just weeks before the First World War in 1914, had divided Dar es Salaam into three zones according to racial categories: Zone I for European residences in detached buildings, Zone II for "Asiatic" businesses and residences in contiguous buildings, and Zone III for a planned "native" quarter. This division would facilitate separate development based on different building and sanitation standards, as well as establish sanitary corridors separating each zone to isolate "racially endemic" diseases.[38] Out of expediency and lack of alternative vision, Dar es Salaam's Town Planning and Building committee largely adopted this German legacy. Seeking a separate European residential area, yet also finding legal racial segregation politically "impracticable" as well as in conflict with the mandate, the committee dropped explicitly racial references and posited "a standard to which all new buildings must conform" that "will secure the 'same advantages'" as de jure segregation.[39] Byatt vainly hoped that Europeans and Indians could be separated through enforcement of building codes, but close proximity between European and Asian zones, divided by a single street along which expensive buildings already stood, imposed formidable costs and obviated plans to create a second sanitary corridor.[40] "Segregation for Europeans and Asiatics in Dar-es-Salaam, and probably also in Tanga, appears to be impracticable," the land officer concluded in 1920. "There does not appear to be anything, however, to prevent segregation of other races from natives."[41]

The government settled for urban segregation between "native" Africans and "non-native" Europeans and Indians. State segregation was most intrusive in respect to African mobility. Township rules prohibited "natives" from loitering in Zones I, II, or the open space after 6 p.m., and fully excluded "natives" after 11 p.m. without a dated and signed certificate from an (non-native) employer. To calm fears about nocturnal crime, "natives" were also required to carry lights between 9 p.m. and sunrise anywhere in Dar es Salaam.[42] Indians who could afford expensive houses were reluctantly allowed to build in the European zone. British colonial officials, who represented roughly half of Dar es Salaam's European population, were not allowed to own property until 1947, and were thus less invested in maintaining neighborhood "purity."[43] Ramshackle African premises located in the areas zoned to Europeans would in due course be demolished, as had been the practice under German rule. Only houses of European standards would be built. "If that rule is maintained, then in all probability there will arise no necessity for any law compelling 'community segregation,'" the chief sanitation officer suggested, resigned to the irritants of Indian wealth but confident in African poverty. "The problem solves itself."[44]

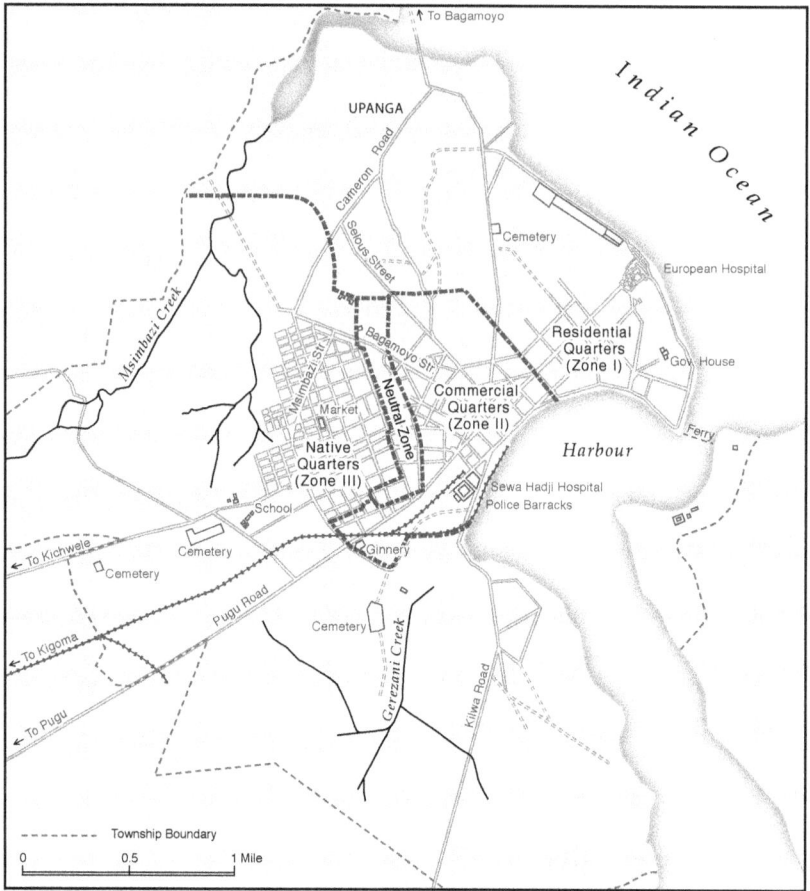

Map 1. Based on 1925 map of Land, Survey & Mines Department, TNA 12589/I.

Building and sanitation codes provided the first major tool used to reorder and segregate Dar es Salaam.[45] The chairman of the Town Planning and Building Committee explained the new policy:

> The policy of segregation by sanitary standards was adopted instead
> of that of racial segregation; it is a policy to which no thinking person
> can take exception. Put bluntly, it consists in dividing the town's in-
> habitants into two classes: those who use a water closet, whether of
> Eastern or Western pattern, and those who can only afford primitive
> means of the privy pit and untrapped soakage pits, both of these being
> responsible for much fly and mosquito breeding.[46]

Africans displaced from the harbor area by Germans long ago could theoretically return under British policy, but almost none would have "the wherewithal to build the type of house required in Zone I or Zone II."[47] Structural improvements to standing "native" houses in "non-native" zones were forbidden in 1920. To further encourage African decampment, in 1923 more than five hundred new plots in the "native" quarter were offered, on condition that residents quit plots located in European and Indian quarters. Those slow to shift faced demolition orders by 1928.[48] Many refused—there were still 380 "native" houses in Zones I and II by February 1931. Most Africans residing in the sparsely settled Zone I lived in *makuti* (thatched) huts on Upanga coconut plantations; many were evicted in 1931 by health officials on the grounds that they negated costly antimalarial measures through their carelessness toward standing water.[49] Those who were allowed to remain were tolerated for "doing good work in keeping down the bush" by working as plantation caretakers and watchmen to prevent coconut theft.[50] Zone I merged into a peri-urban area in which ethnic Shomvi, who claimed to be the indigenous people of Dar es Salaam, successfully protested against their removal by convincing officials that they enjoyed freehold tenure over plots they occupied.[51] Africans living in the Kisutu area of Zone II were not so lucky—334 were evicted for building code violations.[52] Unlike the Shomvi in Upanga, Africans in Kisutu failed to convince officials that they owned freehold tenure plots through *adverse possession*—possession through continuous occupation in absence of the original owners. By 1936, the remaining African residents received cash, new plots, and permits to cut building materials at no cost in return for quitting Indian-zoned Kisutu, which removed the last major African settlement from the "non-native" zones of Dar es Salaam.[53]

To achieve physical separation between "natives" and "non-natives," the cornerstone of segregationist urban planning was the reclearance of the old German sanitary corridor, or "neutral zone," known today as Mnazi Mmoja. The "native" area was meant to be separated from European and Asian zones by clearing a sanitary neutral zone of 300 yards between Zone II and Zone III, to protect "non-natives" from the theoretical malarial tendencies and endemic diseases of Dar es Salaam's African population. In 1915, German administrators had cleared out many of the homes in the proposed neutral zone, but the scheme lapsed upon British occupation, during which time Africans, Arabs, and Indians alike rebuilt in this well-placed location.[54] A major fire in 1921—locally remembered as no accident—conveniently destroyed dozens of area homes, and facilitated the reclearing of the neutral zone, renamed the "open space."[55] Yet even after this, owing to a lack of both resources and urgency, no firm planning commitment was even made until 1924, when the administration settled on a more modest 100-yard open space. Remaining structures were cleared through snail-like enforcement of building codes and land policy, which took nearly a decade. Most evicted Africans were relocated to Ilala, a new "native" residential quarter created in 1930 and named after the district where Livingstone died; "non-native" evictees were left to their own devices.[56]

Urban land policy provided the second major tool for restructuring and segregating interwar Dar es Salaam. In the early years of British rule, plots with stone structures were given renewable government leases usually lasting thirty years, while plots of *makuti* huts were given annual tenancies.[57] All structures required payment of an annual non-native house or native hut tax, payment of which granted recognition of tenancy. Earlier in 1905, the German state had instituted a *kiwanja* (Swahili, "plot") tax for urban residents requiring residents to pay a 50 percent fee in addition to the original house or hut tax. *Kiwanja* was unevenly enforced, and in 1914 the governor exempted "natives proper of German East Africa" from payment.[58] The new British administration, however, fully implemented *kiwanja* and enforced "native" payment because it simultaneously raised revenue and expressed urban land tenure in the absence of land records.[59] Theoretically, there could be no African customary tenure within township boundaries, unlike rural areas, where the convenient notion of "communal" ownership freed the colonial government from having to register landowners or collect land taxes. African urban plot ownership, however, was necessarily a contract between an individual and the state. In the 1920s, *kiwanja* tenure thus provided urban residents with an indefinite tenure on government land subject to termination upon six months' notice.[60]

This makeshift *kiwanja* system of urban land tenure facilitated forced removals, but its unrestrictive terms—one had to pay only a fixed annual fee, and it imposed no building improvements on the holder—prevented the collection of market-value land rents and hindered urban "improvement" or gentrification. As Dar es Salaam grew more prosperous over the 1920s, the government sought to raise revenues and improve building standards. In 1926 it proposed to replace *kiwanja* tenure with rights of occupancy tenancies, which required that structures on leased plots conform to the Township Authority's grid layout and be worth an agreed-upon value.[61] Although a handful of wealthy Africans in Zone III did take out new tenancies, the law was primarily designed to shape the development of the town's Indian community. This new urban tenure offered officials greater control over building standards and offered Indian investors the rights to mortgageable properties. Urban plots offered Indian traders not only income but, above all, collateral to borrow against necessary advances on goods or harvest purchases.[62] In Zone II or Uhindini (Swahili for "Indian area"), these tenancies usually called for two-storied, permanent stone structures with waterborne waste disposal.[63] More than five hundred non-natives, overwhelmingly Indians, were instructed in 1926 to replace *kiwanja* tenure with rights of occupancy with rents determined at public auction, or to quit their plots by the following year. Poorer Indians were reluctant to accept the new system. They understood *kiwanja* tenure to be, if not freehold tenure, certainly more than a yearly tenancy agreement, and balked at being compelled to pay higher rents and make expensive capital improvements.[64] When the government issued a more forceful notice in 1931, the Indian Association—the main representative body for Dar es Salaam's Indians—responded by forming a *kiwanja* tenure committee, which after protracted negotiations agreed to a complete conversion to rights of occupancy by 1935.[65] As the depression deepened, the Indian Association demanded relief for distressed owners unable to meet building code improvements, asking to ease building covenants and create government-subsidized loans in order to free people from the clutches of moneylenders.[66]

This imposition of more-coercive tenancies guided the gentrification of Dar es Salaam's Indian neighborhood. New multistory buildings quickly replaced ramshackle premises and single-storied veranda shops across Uhindini. Investor acceptance of these terms had spurred building construction, while speculators rushed in to acquire cheap plots with dilapidated buildings on them, anticipating their rising value.[67] The rapid success of Indian property investors bred unease among Tanganyika's British settler community—one leading figure exaggeratedly lamented that "95% of the property in Dar-es-Salaam is owned either by Indians or aliens."[68] Valuable sites were obtained at competitive auctions, and carried covenants to build properties with high minimum values within two years of purchase. Average plot rents increased threefold in conversion from *kiwanja* to rights of occupancy.[69] New constructions housed an increasingly wealthy and professional Asian population. By 1931, one female resident recalled that "things had completely changed in Dar"; accompanying the rapid construction of stone buildings in the Indian quarter was the arrival of women, doctors, masons, carpenters, engineers, and architects—the latter importing the multistory architectural designs of urban Gujarat.[70] Visiting in 1931, Evelyn Waugh described the town as hideously hot and uninteresting—"some relics of Arab and German occupation, a rash of bungalows, a corrugated-iron bazaar full of Indians."[71] A town planner warned that streets would soon be lined with "lodging houses and chawls" to benefit the Indian speculator who had "so little regard to the welfare of his tenants."[72]

The rapid gentrification of Uhindini undermined the segregation of Zone III or the "native quarter," which in the 1920s consisted of four principal neighborhoods—Kariakoo, Gerezani, Mission Quarter, and Kisutu.[73] Kariakoo, Dar es Salaam's main African neighborhood, was a dense, cosmopolitan, and largely Muslim neighborhood. A small "Mission Quarter" of forty residential houses was established in southwest Kariakoo by special plot allocations in 1923–1926 at the behest of the Anglican Bishop of Zanzibar, on grounds that

Muslim landlords were reluctant to rent rooms to Christian tenants.[74] Rising rents and growing population density pushed both Indian renters and aspiring landlords to consider alternatives beyond their allotted area of Zone II. Despite the ongoing building boom, rents in 1929 remained "at a fictitiously high figure," while housing conditions for most Indians could "only be classed as scandalous and worse than the slum areas of European cities."[75] E. C. Baker, the most observant of Dar es Salaam's interwar officials, noted that Indians could "obtain greater privacy and more attractive surroundings at a lower debt" in the African quarter.[76] Between 1931 and 1939, the number of native-owned houses in Zone III rented by Indians rose from 32 to somewhere between 200 and 300.[77] Legal rights and administrative encouragement had secured the conditions in which Dar es Salaam's Indian community flourished over the 1920s and 1930s. "Non-native" Zone II and "native" Zone III were separated by only 100 yards but two opposite visions of urban development. Indian settlement in the African quarter raised knotty questions of managing interactions between "natives" and "non-natives," which revealed the impotence of protectionist policies, as well as fundamental legal and administrative confusion.

URBAN COMMERCE AND THE PARADOXES OF PROTECTION

Indians in colonial East Africa are often characterized by historians as a mediating "buffer" of colonial rule between Europeans and Africans. Through their ubiquitous shops where they sold imported goods and purchased African produce, Indians constructed commercial infrastructures upon which colonial rule depended, freeing Europeans to pursue more-leisurely tasks of estate management and colonial administration. Indians, not Europeans, interacted with Africans on a daily basis and bore the brunt of African frustrations with the cruel vicissitudes of market economies. The European was *bwana shauri*, the distant official who took political decisions and resolved disputes; the Indian was *dukawallah*, the familiar shop owner who set prices. One historian of Dar es Salaam has even described its Indian quarter as a "buffer zone" between its European and African quarters.[78] This racially stratified, extractive view of colonial state and economy is accurate in many respects, but it overlooks a long history of contradictions generated by coeval paternalist policies and practices.[79] As Bruce Berman and John Lonsdale observe, colonial officials in East Africa had to balance revenue-raising prerogatives with their role as the "even-handed arbiter, or defender of the weaker, African, interest," upon whose guardianship state legitimacy rested.[80] Balancing extractive and protective priorities was at its thorniest where regulating the interactions between "native" and "non-native," which in Dar es Salaam primarily took the form of interaction between Africans and Indians. The theoretical reasoning behind land and credit restrictions confronted daily realities of this interaction. What exact rights did Indian "non-natives" have to acquire urban plots owned by African "natives"? What exact rights did African "natives" have to borrow money from Indian "non-natives"?

Pursuit of both extractive and protective principles lay behind efforts to regulate urban commerce. All produce had to be sold at public auction at township markets, on grounds that auctions ensured higher prices to producers than would be obtained by bargaining.[81] Economic exchanges occurring beyond surveilled markets raised fears that traders would exploit African producers and consumers alike. "Asiatics and Waswahili are very apt to persuade strangers to part with their goods for less than their market value," one official observed. "Indians, especially, are fond of making payment in kind, and the 'Shenzi' [up-country] native seldom receives full value."[82] Seen as particularly abusive was the "hawker system," where agents working for Indians, typically on a 10 percent commission, would tempt producers with goods to buy or take on credit, indebting future crops and demonetarizing exchange.[83] Considerable produce nonetheless failed to reach Dar es Salaam's official market and entered instead through the black market, which appears to have thrived from the very outset of British rule. "The Indian merchant sends his native agents who buy the food at the shambas [farms]," the town's senior officer lamented, "but the native producer also takes his surplus stocks to the Indian." Although much food passed through the market, "a lot of food coming into the town goes direct to their [Indians'] shops."[84]

During the interwar period, market regulation was an important site of contest between three separate and distinct strains of urban policy: ensuring political security through protectionism, maximizing revenues, and raising public health standards. Internal government debates produced no single victor, only a tendency to secure local European convenience. Township boundaries themselves were the product of this interbureaucratic contest. In 1931, public health officers proposed incorporating farmlands around Msimbazi Creek (in today's Hanna Nassif) into the township to better control mosquito breeding. They were rebuffed by the District Office, whose first task was to administer the town's "native" population, and which sought to avoid the displacement of sixty African farmers who had settled there.[85] In the District Office's view, the Indian shopkeeper, or *dukawallah*, was the primary obstacle to affordable living for African consumers. Most consumers lacked sufficient capital or trust to pool capital and buy food in bulk, leaving them vulnerable to "Indian and middlemen of the market," who purchased country produce bulk and retailed "at 50 to 100% profit, and the consumer's monthly pay is expended within a few hours of receipt in settlement of his past month's account at the Indian shop."[86] Yet the alternative of an ambulatory urban commerce directed by undercapitalized and "unsanitary" African hawkers was objectionable on public health and segregationist grounds. District Office efforts to relax antihawking regulations in order to loosen market congestion and address Hindu protests concerning proximity of meat and fish to vegetables were vetoed by Secretariat officials who feared that inadequate supervision would expose foods to sun and dirt, spread disease, and raise chances of theft and "annoyance to European ladies" in the European quarter by itinerant vendors.[87]

No single law discouraged African commercial development more than the Credit to Natives Ordinance, which required written government permission for transactions between "natives" and "non-natives" in order for the latter to recover debt, and banned outright recovery of collateral. Yet credit, as we shall see, was the very lifeblood of urban commerce, without which no trader and very few consumers could survive. In practice, "non-natives" frequently breached the law and sacrificed legal recourse, sued for debt recovery in subordinate courts through dummying Africans, or simply refused to extend credit to African traders.[88] Legal prohibitions against utilizing accumulated collateral for credit legally reinforced steep economic barriers that limited African merchants to the petty side of retail trade. Urban Africans' chief assets were their houses, valued by Indians particularly for their location, but were legally considered collateral and therefore a prohibited source to collateralize credit. Rarely do official records document property transfers between natives and non-natives that resulted from debt seizures, though probably a larger number of Indian acquisitions of African houses in Kariakoo (see below) were exactly that. A handful of Africans had opened small shops during the 1923 Indian commercial strike upon official encouragement, yet the number of African shopkeepers had decreased to two by 1931.[89] Indulging in racial speculation, the Township Authority concluded that coastal Africans "have not the trading instinct sufficiently developed to run the business of a shop in competition with non-natives already established."[90] For their part, public health officials closed many marginal opportunities by canceling African trading licenses upon finding their premises unsatisfactory.[91] By 1939 there were only twenty African shops in Dar es Salaam, all of which carried stock worth no more than shs. 600/-.[92] Whatever else "native" protections may have brought, they surely helped to secure Indian commercial dominance.

Despite prohibiting commercial credit, the government permitted consumer credit to Africans by legalizing pawnshops, which were exempted from credit legislation and became the principal financial institution for Africans living in Dar es Salaam. Movable property, particularly jewelry and clothing, served as the basis for African collateral rather than land or housing. By 1928 the town had eight licensed pawnbrokers, all Ismaili Khoja Indians who charged customers 6 percent monthly interest on pawned items redeemable up to three months. Some officials considered pawning exploitative and the institution illegal because it permitted seizures of "native" collateral; others considered it a necessary evil that sustained Africans' threadbare urban existence.[93] Interwar officials gave only slightly more consideration to African urban workers than they had to aspiring African traders. Tanganyika's Labor Office operated on the conviction that wage migrants had targeted goals and would not work more efficiently for higher wages, obviating reasons to offer Africans an urban living-wage and relegating them to the ideological as well as economic margins. Orde-Brown, Tanganyika's Labor Commissioner, refused suggestions to increase wages on grounds that it would only attract "the flow of deluded victims towards the maw of the town harpy," resulting in increased prices and no one better off "except the vampires among the landlords and middlemen."[94] District Office personnel proved willing to intervene in the urban economy to regulate African living costs if the perceived difficulty lay in non-native commercial abuse, particularly those of Indian traders. They would not yet be willing, however, to commit sufficient government machinery to make such interventions effective, nor would they begin to address employer responsibilities until the Second World War.

SEGREGATION VERSUS GENTRIFICATION

Segregationist works such as clearing the "neutral zone" and Kisutu were exceptional for their unambiguous consequences. Africans were forced out and moved to Zone III; Indians were forced out and moved (mostly) to Zone II. More typical of Dar es Salaam's legal-administrative regime, however, were the contradictory results that laws with segregationist intent produced when they intruded upon inevitable interactions between Africans and Indians—interactions that challenged the intent and viability of housing, trade, and land laws. Officials wrestled with ever-widening contradictions that emerged from implementing the legal-administrative principle that inherently communal "natives" needed protection from inherently individualist "non-natives." But colonial law also protected "non-native" rights to property, livelihood, and freedom of movement. What happened to individual and communal rights when the two conflicted?

The absurdity of creating a "commercial" Zone II for Indians and a "native" Zone III for Africans not only ignored inevitable questions of racial mobility and interaction, but also assumed that commercial space would not expand. It quickly did. In 1923, Dar es Salaam's official market was relocated from Zone II to Kariakoo in Zone III, stimulating development of the town's most vital neighborhood. The new market became the center of African social life, attracting traders, consumers, preachers, "religious maniacs," salesmen, and thieves.[95] Yet, in stunning contradiction to the logic of racial-cum-occupational zones that had guided urban planning, officials had not only relocated the central market from the "commercial" to the "native" quarter, but also established a "non-native" trading area surrounding the new market. The market relocated to the eponymous Carrier Corps Building (Swahili, "Kariakoo"), built originally in 1914 as a market but converted into a depot for German—later British—military porters.[96] British officials surveyed more than 600 plots along the surviving German-era grid plan with the new market as its focal point, dramatically raising neighborhood property values.[97] Hundreds of Indians relocated to Kariakoo to seize trading opportunities as the new market opened. Kariakoo's commercial life was swiftly dominated by Indian traders, who by 1927 occupied 396 of Zone III's 420 trading sites.[98] Many "non-natives" also made Kariakoo their residence, owning 142 of 2,035 houses in the "native" quarter by 1931. "It is hard to foresee the future of Zone III," Baker observed, "the population of which is becoming very mixed."[99]

Kariakoo grew amid the conflicting expectations of Indians and Township Authority officials on the one hand, who hoped the neighborhood would become a commercial area with a strong "non-native" presence, and African traders, renters and District Office officials on the other, who hoped it would remain a predominantly African residential neighborhood. There was no singular "colonial state" shaping interwar Kariakoo, but rather conflicting departments and lobbies pursuing opposite visions of urban development. Their battle line was the boundary of commerce. In 1925, the Township Authority shifted the commercial boundary from the neutral zone to Msimbazi Street, declaring east of Msimbazi a commercial zone and west a residential area, thereby circumventing protectionist land laws that had forbade "non-natives" from acquiring "native" property in eastern Kariakoo.[100] Opponents of Indian settlement in Kariakoo discovered that segregationist urban planning laws offered little positive protection of African interests. Building codes, the legal basis of Dar es Salaam's "non-native" European and Asian zones, stated only that "native" Zone III should be reserved as "an area for native quarters only." The Township Authority removed even this nominal prohibition in 1932, on grounds that non-native businesses had been long-established and provided "convenient shopping facilities for the Native residents." The District Office countered that Zone III should be confined to "native quarters."[101] A Township Authority official admitted that rising land values were pushing poorer African inhabitants from Kariakoo, but explained that "nothing we can do will enable people with Whitechapel incomes to live in Mayfair. . . . It may be unfortunate, but it is inevitable." Imposing maximum building standards, he felt, would be a mistake of the first order, as better buildings benefit everyone, including Africans.[102] The chief secretary sided with the Township Authority, and the building ordinance was amended in 1933 to retroactively legalize "non-native" building types in the area. The following year, "non-natives" were permitted to purchase native houses. Improved building standards, increased land rents, and high license fees generated by this Indian-led gentrification of Kariakoo proved irresistible to higher officials.[103] The political costs of African discontent would not match the economic benefits of gentrification until the 1940s.

District Office officials, allocated the task of protecting urban "native" interests and general political security, retreated west to Ilala to establish an exclusively "native" residential and commercial area. "You are doubtless perceiving the fact," the district officer appealed to the Land Office, that "native owned land in the township of Dar-es-Salaam is rapidly passing into the possession of non-natives who are mostly of Asian nationality."[104] Even the Township Authority recognized the political value of protectionist gesture by reserving plots around the Ilala market exclusively for Africans in 1932.[105] This knotted legacy of competing segregationist and gentrifying policies and interdepartmental compromise, however, was shattered when Philip Mitchell, now chief secretary, overruled a Land Office refusal to permit a "non-native" purchase of a "native" property in Ilala. He reasoned that it was never government policy "to establish a racial standard in this or in any similar area, nor to prevent a native from selling his plot to a non-native, when he could advantageously do so."[106] Protectionism was now decreed inexcusable racial discrimination against individuals. A court later bolstered Mitchell's view by finding township notices that established separate residential and trading areas within Zone III *ultra vires* (outside the law) in 1937. The whole of Zone III was now declared a trading area, formally ending the theoretical division between Indian commercial and African residential space. Africans could legally trade in their own houses with proper license, but such was the reigning confusion that officials continued to deny Africans permission to do so.[107] The protectionist defeat was formally complete, yet district officers nonetheless continued to reject non-native house purchases, lettings, and sublettings in Zone III on a discretionary ad hoc basis. Kariakoo's housing boom had posed perhaps the greatest paradox for urban protectionists. It formed the greatest source of wealth for the African individual, and the greatest source of spatial dislocation for the renting African community.

REGULATING RENTIERS: AFRICAN LANDLORDS AND INDIAN TENANTS

"There is no home life in Dar es Salaam Town," a 1939 report observed. "Every house is a boarding house."[108] This exaggerates the transience of the town's population but correctly stresses the central role that landlords and *rentier* economic strategies played in Dar es Salaam's history. *Rentier* is used here to refer to forward-minded, rent-seeking behavior in which capital accumulation from rising economic rents is the primary goal (see introduction). Towns were locations where wealth easily dissipated. The point of becoming a landlord was to trap wealth, best captured in the Swahili word for investment, *kitegauchumi*, literally "profit trap." *Rentier* behavior is certainly not uniquely African, but it is particularly pronounced among the broad and successful urban landlord classes of East Africa. During the German period, Indians in Dar es Salaam let rooms to African tenants, though this appears to have been more common among humbler Indian traders living on the margins.[109] Wealthier Indians were landowners rather than landlords, collecting land rents from African tenants while limiting construction to Indian-occupied shops and houses. Even in largely African neighborhoods like Kariakoo, Indian landlords let rooms mostly to Indians.[110] It was the figure of the African landlord, like that of the Indian shopkeeper, who happily did business with all races.

Becoming a landlord was the most durable and profitable business strategy available to urban Africans. In Dar es Salaam there were roughly three thousand African house owners in 1939, roughly 20 percent of the town's African population.[111] The housing market in Tanganyika's capital was, as Frederick Cooper suggests for Mombasa, "the paradise of the petty capitalist."[112] Women and men alike could accumulate wealth while providing necessary shelter that colonial governments had neither the will nor the means to produce. Urban property provided a means to join, as Luise White argues for Nairobi, "the ranks of the urban petty bourgeoisie, to construct classes."[113] Urban property also promised security. "The great aim of the urbanized African," Baker suggested, "is to buy or build a house in the Township as a safeguard against indigence in his old age."[114] Most houses constructed in Kariakoo during the 1920s were five- or six-room "Swahili" houses made of mud, wattle, and *makuti* roofs situated within relatively spacious compounds. Land rent and construction costs were expectantly borne in part by rent-paying tenants.[115] Capital accumulated through wages, trading, prostitution, and alcohol (see chapter 3) was also rechanneled into housing construction and urban plot speculation. Unable to hide his confusion, a district officer confessed that "when it is realized that the average native house is valued at shs.1200/- to shs. 1500/- when newly completed, one wonders where all the money comes from to build the 600 houses that have been built. . . . It represents a capital outlay by natives of shs. 720,000/-."[116] Such figures bear scant obvious relation to prevailing African wages, then roughly between fifteen and twenty shillings per month, and hint at the size of the informal economy. "It is often a mystery," a puzzled E. C. Baker admitted in his 1931 survey of Dar es Salaam, "how natives manage to build their houses," particularly those seemingly indigent older women "with no ostensible means at their disposal but what they can make from the sale of rice cakes and fried fish."[117] Construction took several months if not years, rewarding those who could mobilize communal labor, patiently acquire necessary materials, and attract solvent renters.

African landlords in Kariakoo were positioned to prosper from its gentrification but vulnerable to renter nonpayment. They had profited during the boom years of 1926 to 1930, but economic depression put lodgers out of work—one-third of adult African males in Dar es Salaam were unemployed in 1931.[118] A wealthy Nubian landlady complained that she did not rent to "Waswahili" because they could not pay even half of what Indians could, they did not stay in one place for long, and they were often repatriated from town by the government for not paying their poll taxes.[119] Baker similarly noted that "native rents are often one or two months in arrears and the lodger not infrequently decamps at night in order to avoid paying his debts."[120] Yet fortunes could be made. African landlords in Kariakoo happily charged "non-natives," mostly Indians, as much as shs. 120/- per month for a house, while average African room rent was shs. 5/-.[121] Among District Office officials, the rhetoric and policy of "native protection" increasingly meant protection of the African tenant. But their administrative tools were blunt, limited to discretionary approvals for the transfer or subletting of plots from "native" to "non-native." Municipal Secretary E. H. Helps described the conundrum officials faced:

> Properties leased by natives to non-natives are almost invariably purchased by the lessees at a later date. Non-natives are interested in all properties in Zone III which are valuable for trading purposes but no others. I am personally in favor of natives being given every encouragement to trade among themselves in Zone III, possibly to the exclusion of non-natives whose true locale for trading purpose is Zone II. My reason for this is that natives are gradually surrendering all the best plots in Zone III to non-natives. They cannot resist the temptation of a good offer for their premises, but not infrequently the riches thus acquired become dissipated within a short time.[122]

This was Dar es Salaam's gentrification of its "native" quarter—Indian "immigration," rising wealth for African and Indian landlords, and rising rents for African and Indian tenants. Such was their rising wealth that by the late 1930s, African landlords who rented to non-natives were required to take out "non-native" rights of occupancy at market rents rather than profiting from low *kiwanja* rents.[123] Indian tenants in Kariakoo demanded that maximum rents be fixed for those living in rooms of African-owned houses.[124] Facing impossibly high rents, African tenants often left Kariakoo to settle in areas lying just beyond township limits, where a far grander "non-native" appropriation of "native" lands was passing almost unnoticed.

LAW, LAND, AND IDENTITY IN THE URBAN PERIPHERY

Today, most of Dar es Salaam's four million residents live in a ten-mile radius beyond the original township boundaries that ended at the harbor, Ilala and

Oyster Bay. Yet, during the interwar period, this peri-urban area was sparsely populated, comprising plantations, farmlands, and villages on land of coral rock and poor soils, intersected by five creeks that yielded rich black soil where most area crops were sown. Drier and more-elevated land was covered almost entirely by coconut trees. Owners of freehold land received rents and labor from tenants to guard coconut trees and clear bush; in return, "squatters"—as formal tenancy agreements were rare—received cultivation and residency rights. Coconut plantations, generally situated on higher and drier lands, yielded low rents while rice-producing valley land generated high ones. Owners of land near town could charge full payment in advance; lands farther out commanded only partial advance payment. Many people came forward as "landlords." Africans squatting on government-owned land were found to sublet portions of land to other squatters at a fee or hire laborers for cultivation.[125] Over the interwar period, "non-native" investors came to recognize that the primary value of peri-urban land lay not in coconut production but rather in urban food production and for suburban residences. Yet the majority of peri-urban land in the surrounding farms and villages outside Dar es Salaam were neither freehold nor governmental but rather "communal" lands and represented, far less ambiguously than the individually-owned urban plots of Kariakoo, a clear mandate imperative to prevent "non-native" alienation. Over the interwar period, commercial investment regularly overpowered abstract principles opposing land alienation in these valuable peri-urban areas. The overall effect was to privatize the most valuable tracts of Dar es Salaam's future land.

Overall, Tanganyika's foundational restrictions on credit, land, and conveyance had succeeded in preventing land commercialization during the 1920s, which spared the territory from the political unrest in the 1930s that resulted from default and foreclosure on mortgaged land elsewhere in the British Empire.[126] However, around the commercial center of Dar es Salaam itself, a variety of factors conspired to create and commercialize freehold land: the odd legacy of German land policy, British unwillingness to abandon legal precedent, the low costs of confiscated lands sold at enemy property auctions, and the lack of administrative supervision beyond the township. Lack of supervision was particularly important, as Tanganyika land laws relied heavily on administrative discretion rather than a coherent system of adjudicatory land rights.[127] In other words, land claims were far more frequently settled through administrative decision than through judicial process. In small cases, the governor customarily approved decisions made by officials on the spot, who were woefully uninformed and poorly trained to handle the historical and legal complexities upon which individual land claims turned. By the Second World War, expansion of "non-native" freehold land around Dar es Salaam had engendered frenzied land speculation that drove up prices to astronomical levels, greatly increasing future urban planning costs. Though often absentee as landlords, "non-natives" grew as firmly ensconced in peri-urban areas as they had in "native" Zone III.

The dead hand of legal precedent guided British administrative responses to peri-urban development. The Colonial Office recognized three forms of land tenure in ex-German East Africa—an "ancient tribal system" of communal ownership, a "purely private and individualistic Arab system" that putatively emerged in the nineteenth-century colonization of the coast by Zanzibar, and a European system based on "responsible" development concessions.[128] Each form represented not only a race but an epoch, in which fortunes of the "Arab" system declined with coastal slavery, but left a legal legacy that both Germany and Britain felt politically compelled to acknowledge. Recognition of freehold tenure (i.e., unlimited individual ownership) along a ten-mile-wide "coastal strip" of East Africa, German officials reasoned, had already begun with Zanzibari-Omani alienation of plantations in the nineteenth century, including the original Arab settlement of Dar es Salaam. German officials recognized preceding Arab claims and further alienated large tracts surrounding Dar es Salaam as plantations for German and Indian settlers. The German administration also established the legal principle of acquisition of title by prescription, through which long or "immemorial" right to land use gives right to continued use, by Arabs and "natives" occupying the former coastal belt of the Zanzibar Sultanate. In other words, if one could prove long-standing continued use of land along the coast, one could acquire individual title to that land. Recognition of title by prescription enabled Africans and Arabs to create and sell land as freehold property.[129]

And sell it they did. The German government was so alarmed by the rate of land alienation around Dar es Salaam that it ordered a field survey (Flurbuch) in 1913 to determine which lands were occupied or ownerless and therefore government land, although the war prevented the survey's completion.[130] Despite mandate and legal obligations to protect native landownership, the British administration—seeking the quickest means to auction German enemy properties in order to recoup war costs—privileged an interpretation of German precedent that accepted Flurbuch entries as proof of freehold.[131] Furthermore, the principle of recognizing title by prescription continued in attenuated form under British rule by approval of claims based on *adverse possession* (i.e., possession through continuous occupation in absence of original owner that dates at least thirty years before passage of the 1923 Land Ordinance).[132] Recognition of German Flurbuch entries and/or claims to adverse possession thus could "create" freehold property where none existed before, offering legal loopholes that were exploited to great profit by land-hungry investors and savvy coastal leaders. Twenty years later, these loopholes would be recognized as giving "title which is against the whole spirit and intention of the land law and Government policy."[133] When asked by Lord Frederick Lugard at the Permanent Mandates Commission about the dangers of "native" land dispossession by such freehold recognitions, Governor Donald Cameron replied that he had received very few such requests, and in any event "these had nearly all come from sophisticated Swahilis and Arabs, quite capable of looking after their own interests for themselves."[134] Coastal land was seen by many officials as still vaguely "Arab" land and therefore fair game for commercial investment.

The fundamental confusion surrounding the legal status of Dar es Salaam's peri-urban lands reflected wider uncertainties about who its "natives" were. European administrators across colonial-era Africa assumed that "natives" enjoyed cultivation rights through membership in a collective body, usually the "tribe," while rights to individual creative improvements such as crops were recognized, separate from communal land, as individual property.[135] British officials defined customary tenure around Dar es Salaam in similar terms, concluding that it was based on usufructuary occupation with individual ownership applicable to trees and crops alone—and would adjudicate ownership of trees and crops only in land disputes between "natives" beyond the township, refusing to recognize the many claims of individual ownership on tribal land.[136] As Elizabeth Colson argues, the larger assumption at work was that an African political community occupied a region and used its resources, and therefore "there was no need to distinguish rights of ownership from rights of sovereignty."[137] African land security thus depended on the integrity of an assumed "native" collectivity. In peri-urban Dar es Salaam, no such collective unit or sovereign existed. British officials blithely attributed community anomie to the corrupting wealth of "non-natives":

> The Speculative and Settling Non-Native has shewn the native that land has a value. The native therefore tries to make money out of this unexpected source and goes to great trouble to provide himself with a marketable title. This is, one may venture to say, a bad thing, because by tribal custom the land should belong to the community in which it is situated and not to any individual.[138]

Officials also ascribed blame to German rule, which was alleged to have dissolved "local custom" and loosened communal bonds. British authorities' answer was to reconstitute community through indirect rule. The relevant "native" governing body was the Uzaramo Native Authority, ostensibly modeled on "native custom" of indigenous Zaramo who populated the surrounding area, and tasked with maintaining the political and economic integrity of the "native." It proved generally unpopular, particularly among the many non-Zaramo of peri-urban Dar es Salaam who preferred to pay fixed rents to non-native landowners rather than rely on the Native Authority to secure cultivation rights.[139] Yet, in order to avoid endless administrative work, ownership had to be communal where it could be. Officials formulaically dismissed thorny issues concerning land and ethnic differences by asserting that "alien natives" (i.e., non-Zaramo) who purchased land from local natives were regarded "as having become absorbed in the indigenous population," and were therefore subject to prevailing custom.[140]

Peri-urban land alienation thus turned on administrative processes of identity creation and recognition. Officials lumped together high-status Swahili clans with up-country migrants into the singular communal category of "native." Hugh McCleery, a specially appointed land investigator, proposed that all claims of adverse possession on communal land be dismissed in order to preserve native custom and community:

> The land is wanted by a non-native and the native wishes to sell. Who else is to be considered? Not the native community since Government had disallowed the community's interest in the land. The seller's children? He might argue that with money realised by the sale he could go and settle elsewhere, as indeed he could. And so, as a rule, consent is given and yet another bit of this Mandated Territory, held in trust for the native, is permanently alienated.[141]

An anonymous official answered McCleery's suggestion by stating, "There does not appear to be any real native custom about Dar es Salaam and there has not been for years."[142] Both "native custom" and "communal land" had been British legal fictions without a constituency all along. Africans had contested "native" land sales to "non-natives" by employing the same terms of individual or lineage-based freehold ownership that were busily extinguishing "communal" tenure in the first place.[143] "Native custom," invoked primarily by officials in order to protect communal interests, proved powerless to prevent acquisition of Dar es Salaam's choicest plantations and future residential neighborhoods by "non-native" investors.

As with urban land, the defeat of "native" protectionism in peri-urban Dar es Salaam had secured the economic foothold of Indians while politicizing indigeneity among Africans. Yet this politicization was not the straightforward process that Mamdani suggests, but one that instead revealed the colonial category of "native" for what it was—an impotent bureaucratic tool that promised protection in principle but mocked the existence of an African community in practice. It would be for Africans themselves to create and define terms of identity that would explain what indigenous communities were, and what their relationships with outsiders should be.

CONCLUSIONS

The laws and institutions of the new British administration entrenched racial categorization in Dar es Salaam, but in contradictory ways that produced un-intended consequences. Tanganyika's legal-administrative structure assigned to non-natives positive individual protections for the accumulation of capital and for the ownership of freehold land, and assigned to natives only nega-tive communal protections *from* non-native predation. Within the township, native and non-native became the legal language to implement a strategy of racial segregation. Yet colonial legal-administrative categories did not simply inscribe political consciousness of "indigeneity" upon "native" Africans, any more than they inscribed a dangerously privileged "subject race" conscious-ness upon Indians. Nor did such categories realize their theoretical tasks of neatly separating urban populations—implementation was necessarily pragmatic, limited, and uneven. Although legal-administrative processes of urbanization sharpened colonial racial categories, it overstates the matter to characterize colonial Dar es Salaam as a site of rigid and firmly entrenched racial segregation.[144] "Natives" continued to live in "non-native" Zone I, al-beit with scant legal security, while "non-natives" from Zone II immigrated to "native" Zone III with alacrity. Racial interaction was both inevitable and complex, and the desultory and contradictory attempts to regulate interaction through the legal diptych of native/non-native revealed to Africans the admin-istration's racial double standards and its unaccountable discretionary powers. Institutions of colonial governance did not create racial or national sentience alone, but did guide spatial and commercial urban development, and offered a new layer of argumentation as urban life brought Africans and Indians into increasing interdependence. Identity and racial consciousness formed more substantially within social groups and their interactions with one another, to which we now turn.

2 ꙅ Identity and Social Structure in Interwar Dar es Salaam

THIS CHAPTER EXAMINES the formation of group identities in interwar Dar es Salaam to show the dialectical interaction between external categorization and internal self-understanding.[1] These identities formed, this chapter argues, primarily through the exercise of claims to exclude others from access to political and material resources. Two modes of identification among groups can be usefully distinguished—a *relational* mode, dependent on direct connections between local individuals; and a *categorical* mode, defined beyond local individuals and external to direct interaction.[2] A relational mode based on firstcomer claims loomed large among Dar es Salaam's African residents, while a categorical mode based on race became simultaneously entrenched during the interwar decades, and would eventually displace relational modes in the 1940s. The language of group identity in all of these cases was suffused with idioms of kinship and descent. This poses a challenge to the analytical utility of certain group identity terms—namely "nation," "race," and "ethnicity"—which contemporary sociological literature often treats as discrete and separable categories of belonging.

To generalize, this literature holds that a nation necessarily carries with it the project to realize a state where race and ethnicity do not; while a race is necessarily hierarchical, and more likely biological or somatic, ethnicity and nation are not.[3] Both propositions hold true, to an extent, for colonial East Africa: European, Asian, and African "races" formed a ranked hierarchy; while "national" politics were loosely those that challenged imperial sovereignty. Yet two objections also arise. First, race, nation, and ethnicity were not understood as discrete categories by historical actors themselves, but rather as overlapping and commonsensical ways to group people. Second, privileging state-building, hierarchy, or somatic traits to separate race, nation, and ethnicity obscures the powerful presence of shared descent expressed in all three as categories of analysis, let alone as categories of practice. Like ethnicity and nation, race implies, as Max Weber argues, a normative community bounded by many factors, but above all by subjective belief in common descent.[4] Interwar reckonings of descent in Tanganyika—be it by British officials, community leaders, or local intellectuals—did not hinge on genetic traits or other biological inheritances that obsessed armchair racial theorists in Europe, nor did they necessarily invoke challenges to imperial sovereignty. Rather, descent was the simplest device available to describe group difference, upon which colonial hierarchies and anticolonial movements subsequently constituted themselves.

Dar es Salaam's major group identities were united by idioms of descent, but distinguished by factors of scale. Race was a category used in the first instance by outsiders. With plainly greater differences in territorial origins, marital patterns, somatic features, economic resources, language, and religion, few interwar Africans would describe Indians as just another local tribe. As we have seen in the previous chapter, legal-administrative distinctions between "native" and "non-native" fostered racial consciousness among Indians and Africans, albeit in a crooked manner. But three additional processes were also at work during the interwar decades. First, anticolonial nationalisms from abroad and shared economic interests at home moved Tanganyika's Indian community to make ambitious political claims in the 1920s followed by a retreat into communalism and imperial loyalism over the 1930s, entrenching categorical modes of racial, national, and religious identity. Second, African identity incorporated the language of a long-standing relational mode of identification based on rivalry between self-styled indigenes and more recently arrived townspeople in Dar es Salaam, expressed in the autochthonous Swahili-language terms of native (*mwenyeji*) and foreigner (*mgeni*). The native had self-evident rights over land and political offices that foreigners—frequently in reference to up-country Africans—did not. Finally, "race relations" between Africans and Indians, based primarily on commercial and labor interactions, moved Africans to rethink the scope and content of urban identities in light of their subordinate position to Asians and Europeans. Europeans played a significant role as state agents, but overall they were few in number compared to Asians and Africans. Between 1921 and 1943, Europeans totaled roughly 3 percent, Asians 23 percent, and Africans 74 percent of the town's population.[5] Racial consciousness sharpened at the boundaries—spatial, economic, and political—formed by interactions between Africans and Indians, as well as from each group's relations with the state. Organizational politics, like the colonial state, played an important but not defining role in these processes. Rather, it was at the level of popular negotiation with urban structures of economic and social exclusion—employment, property, credit, and the right to respect—where the core political work that went into transforming "Indian" and "African" from the lazy shorthand of outsiders into categories of self-understanding and aspiration was first carried out. This chapter investigates that work and the context in which it was undertaken.

INDIAN IDENTITIES: "GREATER INDIA," COMMERCE, AND COMMUNAL POLITICS

The history of Indians in East Africa is one of consistent economic strategies and changing political ambitions. Resident for centuries along the Swahili coast, Indian immigrants over the course of the nineteenth century increasingly chose to settle in Zanzibar, where commercial links between Gujarat, Oman, and the African interior intersected.[6] Most originated from the regions of Saurashtra in western Gujarat and Kachchh—regions under control of various princely states from the 1860s, and from which came most of East Africa's future Indian traders.[7] Characteristic of the South Asian diaspora across the Indian Ocean, capital and labor formed separate streams of movement to East Africa. Gujarati and Kachchhi merchants immigrated to trading centers; Punjabi workers immigrated to construction sites.[8] Indian immigration shifted largely northward to Kenya following the construction of the Uganda railway in the 1890s. Punjabis made up the bulk of indentured railway workers, and many continued to German East Africa via Zanzibar from the 1890s until the First World War. Construction of German East Africa's central railway began in 1905, attracting Indian immigrants who numbered 6,723 by 1910, with more than one quarter living in Dar es Salaam.[9]

Seen from a distance as a singular merchant minority group, up close Dar es Salaam's Indian community was stratified along complex lines of religion, caste, language, and class. Defined as "non-natives" or "Asians" by the colonial government, the daily lives of Indians revolved around communal rather than racial institutions. "Community" was firstly religious. In 1931, Tanganyika's Indian population was 57 percent Muslim, 31 percent Hindu, 7 percent Goan, and 3 percent Sikh.[10] Within religious communities, further social striations occurred. Muslims were divided among three large Shia factions—Khoja Ismailis, Khoja Ithnasheris, and Bohoras—most of whom came from Gujarat, Kachchh, and Sind. A smaller and more diverse Sunni population originated from Gujarat, Kachchh, and Punjab. Tanganyika's Hindus organized largely around endogamous units known as *jati*, which are more popularly if less accurately termed "castes"; the two most significant being Kachchhi Lohana and Gujarati Patidar (Patel). Other relatively prosperous *jati* include Brahman and Bhatia; among the poorer groups were Bhoi, Rana, and Divecha. The Shia groups were overwhelmingly merchants; Hindus and Sunni Muslims

Map 2. Western Indian Ocean and Gujarat.

were often artisans as well as shopkeepers.[11] Most Sikhs were low-ranking Ramgarhias dominated by craftsmen. Most Goans worked as clerks or artisans; nearly all were Roman Catholic, and most had come from Bombay rather than directly from Goa.[12] Communal associations proved the most durable of Tanganyika's Indian institutions for collecting and redistributing financial resources, as well as for political lobbying. The two most significant were the Hindu Mandal and Ismailia Council.[13] Communal identities of religion and caste coexisted with competing affinities of regional origin, language, and class. Gujarati and Kachchhi were most Indians' mother tongue, followed distantly by Punjabi, Marathi, and Tamil.[14] Of Tanganyika's employed Indian men, 58 percent worked in commerce, mainly as importers, shopkeepers, and produce purchasers; 14 percent were government employees; 3 percent agricultural or professional; and the remaining 25 percent "other," most likely nongovernmental clerks and artisans.[15]

Despite the social significance of these "subracial" complexities, Indian public discourse within Tanganyika favored the employment of colonial-ascribed racial categories in order to pursue subimperial and nationalist ambitions. During and after the First World War, prominent political figures demanded that German East Africa become a colony of India in return for India's wartime support. Among them was Sultan Muhammad Shah, Aga Khan III (1877–1957), or simply "the Aga Khan," leader and living Imam of East Africa's largest Shia community, the Ismaili Khojas, and also a trusted imperial loyalist. The British India government in Delhi lobbied London in support.[16] Subcolonization had support among East African Indians, who in Kenya and Zanzibar rallied to support the proposal; in German East Africa a territorial rally was planned.[17] The project's loudest European voice was Theodore Morison, former Principal of Aligarh College, who had commanded Indian forces during the war and had become a political officer in British-occupied German East Africa. He petitioned Whitehall to accept German East Africa's subcolonization in order to redirect India's surplus population of farmers and the educated to develop the "under-manned" former colony, in order for India to establish "her claim to rank with the white man."[18] In his 1918 memorandum *A Colony for India*, Morison argued that Indian agriculture would make a more appropriate model for "native" farmers, and that an Indian subcolony would pacify anti-British ire as "compensation for her exclusion from the Dominions." India could now prove its right to "higher status in the Empire" by accepting this invitation "to share the white man's burden."[19] Nairobi's Indian Association led the regional campaign by petitioning that German East Africa be reserved "for Indian colonization" and placed under "direct control of the Government of Indian" in return for India's military service.[20] Dar es Salaam's Indian Association lobbied Gandhi for support.[21] After plans for a subcolonization rally in Tanga became known, African elders quickly organized a counterprotest and petitioned Horace Byatt, civil administrator and soon-to-be governor, that Britain "may have mercy upon us, and may not place us under Indian rule," and that they would rather "be subjects under your direct rule just like the Indians."[22] Most of Whitehall agreed, considering the proposal a reckless fantasy. Gandhi himself vehemently opposed subcolonization in principle, and directed his deputy Charles Andrews to discourage East Africa Indians.[23] Byatt opposed the plan, and used a visit by an India government official to establish that settlement of Indian peasants would be "unsound and unwise."[24] The plan effectively died in 1921.

During the war, most Indians in German East Africa had aligned their fortunes with a British victory, a wager that paid off handsomely. The new administration protected delinquent Indian firms from German creditors, allowed unfettered access to acquire former German properties, and expanded Indians' share of import-export trade with Europe.[25] Indians purchased one-third of all ex-enemy properties sold—considerably less than the share bought by British nationals, but larger than all other nationals combined over the period 1917–1933.[26] Leftover sale proceeds formed a liquidation fund that many Indians made successful claims upon to recoup wartime damages inflicted by Germany. British Indian nationals owned 20.8 percent of "non-native" agricultural landholdings by 1930, falling to 16.4 percent by 1938 as Indian investors sold property back to returning German planters.[27] Tanganyikan Indians enjoyed the advantage of experience. Indian creditors in German East Africa had controlled key trade circuits along the coast, through which they collaborated with German firms.[28] With German merchant houses now displaced, a small group of South African and British importers and wholesalers—most undercapitalized, callow opportunists concerned mainly with removing German and Indian competitors—offered a weak replacement. In 1919 they formed the Dar es Salaam Chamber of Commerce, which alienated officials with shrill demands to create settler-friendly civil courts, land tenure policies, and enemy property allocations. Byatt considered them "young, enthusiastic, and inexperienced commercialists" who lacked any "weight, status, and influence."[29] Indians became significant importers in their own right; Tanganyika's European merchants never exercised the monopoly over the territory's import-export trade that their German predecessors had enjoyed.[30]

European planters and businessmen shared a marked antipathy toward Indian merchants. Charles Andrews accurately complained that Tanganyikan whites pursued "a deliberate campaign of vilification of the Indian in the eyes of the African native."[31] This view was propagandized to potential settler-sympathizers in Britain and Africa by the British jingoist F. S. Joelson, whose 1921 portrait of Dar es Salaam Indian merchants resonates with caricatures soon drawn by Africans:

> Each [shop] is kept by a Banyan, for the native retail trade of East Africa is almost exclusively in the hands of these grasping, unscrupulous Indians, who shun no methods of self-advancement once they have enmeshed the unsuspecting, trusting native in their toils. Living in squalor at the rear of the shop or in the very store itself, feeding on

rice and curry, hoarding every cent gained, with the exception of what he spends on finery for his wife and children, it is but a short while before the hitherto penniless trader finds himself in comfortable circumstances. Even then he does not put into circulation a large portion of his profits, and thus benefit in turn the country that has enriched him, but ships his hoarded wealth to the land of his birth, wither he means to follow it as soon as he has accumulated what he considers a sufficiency.[32]

Europeans consoled themselves that Indians were unbeatable rivals in certain commercial spheres because of their unnatural willingness to live at low standards. "What among the natives is a state of decent, primitive simplicity is squalor among the Indian immigrants," Evelyn Waugh reasoned a decade later. In a thinly veiled comparison with European Jewry, he explained that "because where the natives are bound by tribal loyalties and wedded to their surroundings by a profound system of natural sanctity, the East African Indians are without roots or piety."[33]

Such dire portraits notwithstanding, Tanganyika's Indian merchant community was well-capitalized, attuned to working with minimal government support, and well-disposed toward British imperial commerce. They exploited advantages of community and kinship to channel information, goods, and capital between villages, provincial towns, and trading centers in East Africa and India. By 1924, Indians owned all but two major retail businesses in Dar es Salaam. Capital either recirculated within distribution chains or was thought to have been repatriated to India—a subject that needs further research.[34] Currency speculation, long an important trading strategy, was neutralized between 1921 and 1939 by a stable exchange rate between the silver-based Indian rupee and the sterling-based East African shilling, following a brief but financially traumatic period of currency speculation between 1919 and 1921.[35] Financial capital was also repatriated through informal credit channels or simply smuggled onto ships. Alert to sordid detail, Joelson reported that Indian traders used friends and relatives to smuggle "large sums of silver rupees . . . concealed in consignments of ghee, or clarified butter, packed in petroleum tins!"[36] Whatever the scope and scale of capital repatriation was, significant amounts were reinvested locally, mainly in transportation, processing, small manufacturing, building construction, and land purchase. Successful merchants expanded and diversified their businesses while gravitating toward larger towns; failed merchants endured multiple bankruptcies while relocating to more-remote settlements. Out in the countryside, Tanganyika's Indian traders were ultimately "merchant-moneylenders," whose extension of credit was not for short-term usury but long-term indebtedness to ensure procurement of agricultural produce from African farmers.[37]

During the 1920s, a flourishing economy, rising immigration, and provocative journalism together produced a formidable Indian political diaspora. Tanganyika's Indian population more than doubled, from 10,209 in 1921 to 25,144 in 1931, with nearly one-third living in Dar es Salaam. Alert to rising commercial opportunities, the Aga Khan instructed Zanzibari Ismailis to gradually shift to Tanganyika in 1924. Dar es Salaam replaced Zanzibar as the main regional entrepôt outside Mombasa.[38] Tanganyika's internationalization through League of Nations mandate in 1922 empowered Indian nationals to petition a wider range of authorities to protest ham-fisted racial segregation. The London-based Indians Overseas Association quickly convinced Dar es Salaam to replace a blatantly segregationist railway passenger system.[39] Mass protest tactics that first blossomed in India were quickly embraced in Tanganyika. Following Gandhi's 1922 arrest for leading the noncooperation campaign, Indians in Dar es Salaam protested with a one-day *hartal*, or commercial strike, through shop closures.[40] Indian-owned newspapers in Tanganyika began publication in 1924, regularly lauding Indian National Congress progress in both English and Gujarati.[41] An India freed from colonial rule resounded strongly within East Africa's political diaspora, which linked itself to distant struggles by imagining a "Greater India." Visiting nationalist speakers typically linked local grievances to India liberation. V. R. Boal, editor of the *Tanganyika Herald*, appealed for political assistance from India by arguing that "the Greater India and Swaraj are inter-dependent."[42] Regional diasporic cooperation was particularly strong. The Dar es Salaam Indian Association replaced the Nairobi-based East Africa Indian National Congress as Tanganyika's chief Asian organization by the mid-1920s, but both worked closely to resist efforts to create an East African Union, which would plainly benefit white settlers at their expense.[43]

The apex of local protest occurred in 1923, when Indians throughout Tanganyika closed shop again, this time to protest a new law that imposed a 4 percent tax on profits and demands that accounts be kept in English or Swahili but not Gujarati. The German administration had earlier failed to enforce a similar system banning Gujarati account keeping in 1906, and instead conducted arbitrary profit assessments.[44] British Tanganyika's Chief Justice feared that accounting done in Gujarati would be unauditable and might lead to fraud in bankruptcy cases; others feared that permitting the hire of translators would also "open the door to corruption."[45] The legislation simultaneously attacked a comparatively unwritten system of commerce and the Gujarati language, wedding local economic concerns with Indian nationalist sentiments. A territory-wide *hartal* began on April 1, 1923, and lasted fifty-four days, bringing nearly all commerce to a halt in Dar es Salaam and to a lesser extent upcountry. Hindu and Muslim shopkeepers led the strike, eventually joined by

Goan and Arab traders.[46] The Dar es Salaam Indian Association enlisted support of both the Indian government and the Indian National Congress—the former pressured Britain to revise legislation; the latter called for a boycott of British goods in India.[47] The scale of the protest was ominous. According to his intelligence sources, Governor Horace Byatt claimed that local Indians were "acting very largely if not entirely under compulsion" from external actors.[48]

After striking for nearly two months, local traders had succeeded in securing a delay in the law's enforcement. In the face of stubborn local and international opposition, as well as meager revenue collections, the law was eventually abandoned in 1927 for a system of progressive license fees.[49] Subsequent protests, however, never matched the scope or success of the 1923 *hartal*, retrospectively memorialized as *Makkam* (adamant). V. R. Boal, a veteran of Bombay's Swadeshi movement, spent much of his subsequent career nostalgizing the 1923 *hartal* as Tanganyika's founding nationalist moment.[50] *Hartals* continued—to protest closer union proposals in 1929–1930, Gandhi's arrest in 1930, a non-native poll tax bill in 1932, and a produce marketing bill in 1937—but none were as remotely effective as the 1923 strike.[51] Indians instead exercised influence through institutional power. They gained representation in Tanganyika's Legislative Council upon its formation; wealthy Indian merchants joined the previously all-European Chamber of Commerce in the late 1920s; and Indians occupied key posts in territorial township authorities and economic control boards by the late 1930s.[52] Indian elites in particular feared that there was more to lose than there was to gain through high-stakes confrontation by the 1930s.

As we have seen, Tanganyika's laws and administrative policies generally categorized people by their autochthonous status (native, non-native); yet instances of continental categorization (African, Asiatic/Asian, European) stimulated Indian demands for equal privileges with Europeans. Indian education was initially self-financed and administered through communal religious schools, but state subsidies to private education began in 1925, and a state-run Indian Central School was formed in 1929. Although Europeans and Indians were taxed equally as "non-natives," Indians objected to inequitable expenditure that granted European pupils higher per capita subsidies.[53] Indian public health care was restricted to Sewa Hadji, the town's "native" hospital. The Indian Association and local Indian press loudly clamored for community access to the better-resourced European hospital.[54] The Indian Association also framed tax protests by attacking bloated European salaries and unnecessary military defense.[55] Asian civil servants had organized an association in 1922 to lobby for salary and benefit equality with Europeans; inequalities in housing, promotion opportunities, pensions, and passage assistance widened during the depression and became the key issues to protest racial discrimination.[56]

Cultural differences also sparked racial grievances. Dar es Salaam's Township Authority banned Hindu Mandal from using its beachside crematorium following a European's well-publicized complaint that his evening walk was ruined by burning corpse smells; after counterprotests and negotiations, the crematorium was grudgingly removed from the beach.[57]

Though bound together in diasporic protest and colonial categorization, Indian political unity declined amid growing class and communal antagonisms during the 1930s. The Indian Association, which claimed to also represent traders, had lost its pan-communal bona fides and political influence, and was seen to be simply a "Hindu" body by 1941, when small merchants bolted from the Indian Association to form the Indian Merchants Chamber.[58] Journalists such as V. R. Boal and M. O. Abbasi, the latter a Kachchhi Sunni and leading Muslim activist, attacked the Indian Association's patrician leadership for their unresponsiveness to the needs of workers and small merchants. Boal and Abbasi led the Dar es Salaam Tenants Committee, which represented poor Indian tenants pressured to pay higher rents or move out of distressed properties by wealthy Indian landlords.[59] The greatest sustained labor agitation in interwar Tanganyika involved Indian commercial assistants who formed Tanganyika's first registered trade union in 1933 to secure shorter shop hours in Indian shops. "Imagine," one worker pleaded after regulations proved unenforceable, "how miserably the shop assistants rot in the dark cellers [sic] of their employers. . . . Glaring instances of premature death and living skeletans [sic] can be found from the short and obscure annals of the poor shop assistants."[60] Lower-class entrepreneurs endured on slim margins. Small traders rented front and back rooms of shops to work and live; many artisans rented verandas for their businesses.[61] The Great Depression shrank or destroyed these margins, and forced a fundamental reorganization of Indian social and economic life.

Communalism was instantaneously appropriated in East Africa during the early 1930s, just as Gandhian nationalism had been in the early 1920s. A Muslim ex-serviceman explained in 1931:

> The Muslims and Hindus are internally hostile with each other because of communal discrimination in India. . . . The Hindus are religiously bound to crush a foreign Government. If there is a possibility of any danger to the Tanganyika Government it will be caused by those Hindus who belong to the Bombay Presidency.[62]

Yet the consequent weakening and abandonment of pan-communal institutions over the 1930s was not simply a diasporic response to Indian homeland politics, but also a pragmatic strategy to address economic depression and widening divisions of wealth among Indians. Schools, mosques, temples, dispensaries, and other confessional or caste-based institutions were reliable providers of social welfare to East African Indians, far more reliable than "Greater India" propagandists or Asian union organizers. Religion-based communities offered vertical umbrellas of credit, patronage, and social welfare that shielded differentiating confessional groups from forming disruptive horizontal linkages among Indian workers and poor shopkeepers. Seeking to better "umpire" trader-producer relations as world prices crashed, the colonial governments of Tanganyika, Kenya, and Uganda each adopted in 1932 a common marketing policy that confined trading to townships with scheduled markets, fixed produce prices, restricted the number of itinerant traders, and—most critically—conferred trading monopolies to a few select firms. Deeply resented upon introduction, the legislation had the practical effect of crystallizing trade channels, within which the profitability of small traders increasingly depended upon the patronage of large firms. Indian leaders feared that further protest might provoke more restrictive legislation. At the same time, a previous flood of *hundi* (wholesale remittance) credit dried up as cash-strapped importers called in margins, bankrupting small traders.[63] *Hundi* credit—which in Tanganyika was most often a promissory note between wholesaler and shopkeeper—had been the retailer's lifeblood, and originated with large Indian merchant houses that carried out importation and wholesale trading. After 1932, this system reconstituted itself along more exclusively communal lines. With formal bank credit similarly scarce, communal credit lines offered resurrection to growing numbers of failed entrepreneurs who suffered chronic bankruptcies. Nowhere was this trend clearer than in the Aga Khan's Ismaili community, which was the most influential model and "veritable pacemaker" for communal crystallizations among East African Asians.[64] Ismailis formalized communal lending patterns with the creation of two credit societies, the Nairobi-based Jubilee Insurance Company in 1937 and the Tanganyika Ismailia Co-operative Society in 1938—the former admitted non-Ismaili borrowers but overwhelmingly focused on expanding Ismaili capital and settlement; the latter provided seed money to small traders and expressly excluded non-Ismailis.[65] There was no commercial life without credit, and credit was increasingly communalized.

Social institutions and public space followed the communalizing path of credit. The wealthy industrialist Sheth Mathuradas Kalidas bemoaned "this growing communal spirit . . . separate schools, separate clubs, separate recreation grounds, separate rent houses and even separate libraries (misnamed Public Libraries) are cropping up everywhere like mushrooms, representing sectional and communal interests."[66] The Vande Mataram, roughly the Indian "national anthem" and celebration of "mother India," had been sung in Tanganyikan cinemas and other public forums since the 1920s. In 1937, the Muslim League boycotted its singing in India, which spread immediately to

Tanganyika. The *Tanganyika Opinion* lamented that the song's true meaning had not to do with a Hindu goddess but rather with the spirit of nationalism, as it became "associated in the minds of people with a fight against British Imperialism."[67] But not in everyone's mind—by 1940 a number of venomous *patrika* (anonymous Gujarati pamphlets) circulated to protest the playing of the Vande Mataram while showing a slide of a goddess in Dar es Salaam's cinemas. Owners were threatened with boycotts, vandalism, and arson. Hindus closed their accounts with Muslim merchants; Muslim boys were prohibited from playing at the *vyamshala* (gymnasium); "disrespectful words" were written on photographs of Muslim leaders. After cinema owners acquiesced, Hindu-penned *patrika* threatened their own boycotts.[68] Muslims in Dar es Salaam felt excluded from the town's dominant, Hindu-owned newspapers, the *Tanganyika Opinion* and the *Tanganyika Herald.*[69] Khoja Ismailia Council petitioned the government to censor the *Tanganyika Opinion* because it had published articles "deliberately calculated . . . to belittle His Highness [the Aga Khan] and to bring his name into ridicule."[70] Tanganyika's Indian Association was unable to pass a simple motion expressing sympathy with the Indian National Congress at its 1942 territorial conference. The organization was increasingly seen as a "Hindu" body that would later freely admit it did not represent "Pakistanis."[71] The effect of this thoroughgoing communalization by the early 1940s was not only the palpable antagonism between various Indian "communities," but a marked retreat from anticolonial politics that had previously united disparate classes, castes, and confessions during the 1920s.

Dar es Salaam's Indian community had grown to exercise tremendous economic power during the interwar years. Yet commercial wealth proved as compatible with the vituperative communalism of the 1930s as it had with the pan-communal activism of "Greater India" in the 1920s. Indian diasporic politics of equality offered a powerful but limited vision, which rarely looked upon Africans as anything more than fellow victims in need of an improved civilization. The enormous institutional strengths that Indians had developed over the interwar period imposed both an enviable model and a frustrating obstacle to Dar es Salaam's African population, to which we now turn.

AFRICAN IDENTITIES: FIRSTCOMERS, CULTURAL BROKERS, AND BUREAUCRATS

Even a cursory look at African identity in Dar es Salaam reveals striking heterogeneity that is at once cosmopolitan and parochial. John Iliffe offers a useful place to start with his overview of the town's major African population groups in the 1930s:

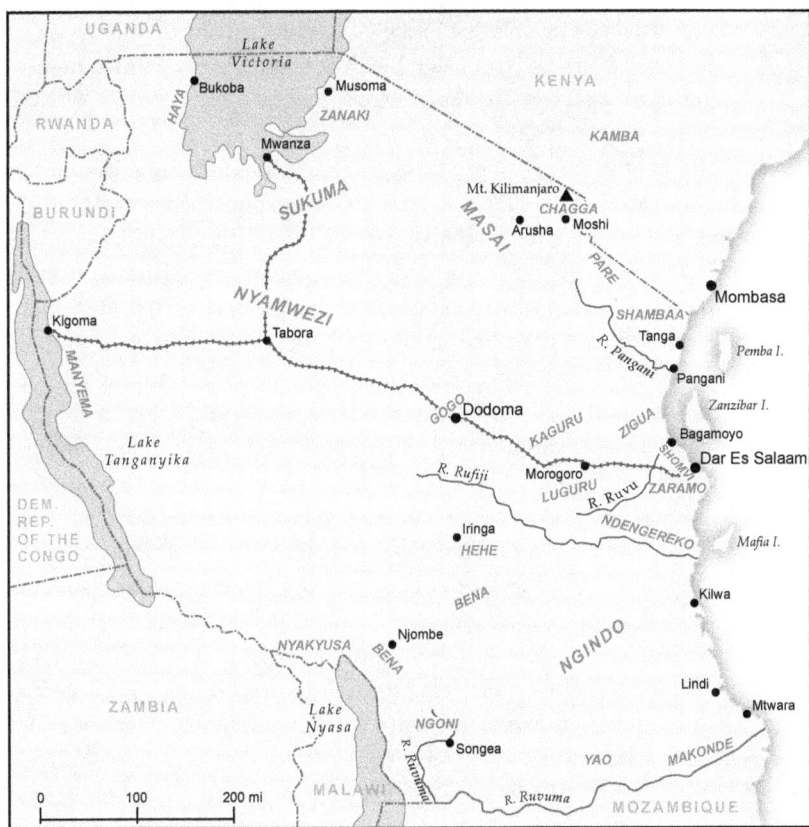

Map 3. Based on map of Tanganyika in John Iliffe, *A Modern History of Tanganyika* (1979), xvi.

The smallest was the original nucleus of fishermen and cultivators, usually calling themselves Shomvi. Their much more numerous neighbours, the Zaramo, whose tribal area surrounded the city, provided a floating population of short-term, unskilled workers, usually numbering more than a third of the inhabitants. The next to arrive had been the first fully permanent townsmen, among whom two groups had a special position. One was the small body of retired askari from the German forces, many of them Sudanese or Nguni in origin, who claimed the prestige of professional soldiers. The second was a rather larger group of people who called themselves Manyema and came ultimately from the slave-raiding regions around Lake Tanganyika. Settled, clannish, and strongly Muslim, the Manyema built their separate mosque, owned many houses, and became an important core of permanent residents. Finally, there were two types of

Identity and Social Structure in Interwar Dar es Salaam ⌐ 59

long-distance migrants: the unskilled labourers, many of whom were Nyamwezi, Yao, or Ngoni; and the small groups of skilled men from educational centres like Tanga, Moshi, and Bukoba.[72]

While useful as an overview, these tribal labels also obscure the earliest terms of debate over identity in Dar es Salaam, which concerned firstcomer status. As Igor Kopytoff argues, much of sub-Saharan African political culture is infused with the principles of precedence—by plausibly claiming to have first occupied the land, firstcomers act as relational "seniors" to latecomers, and enjoy forms of political, ritual, spiritual, or economic authority over more recent immigrants.[73] Firstcomer reckoning persevered in the minds of Dar es Salaam's "original inhabitants," even as outsiders moved into the colonial town and gained greater influence. The self-styled indigenes were the Shomvi and Zaramo, who claimed to be *wenye mji*, which translates from Swahili as "owners of the town." *Wenye* means "owners" but implies "freeborn" and was used to distance "town owners" from their social inferiors, who by not being "owners" implicitly bore the stigma of servile origins. Shomvi and Zaramo labeled other Africans as outsiders or *watu wa kuja* (immigrants). Although famously absorptive, the societies of the Swahili coast to which Shomvi and Zaramo belonged set great value on knowing who really "belonged," and expressed this status with the term *wenyeji*, which invoked firstcomer status and landownership over a given village or urban quarter. Outsiders were *wageni*, "guests" or "strangers" subject to *wenye mji* prerogatives in allocation of land and offices.[74] Although immigrants often participated in long-standing Swahili urban institutions, they made claims to colonial Dar es Salaam neither on aristocratic descent—as did Shomvi—nor on tribal custodianship like Zaramo. Rather, in the interwar period these immigrants appropriated Swahili institutions while also claiming modern colonial institutions on the basis of tribe and race.

The development of the ethnonyms "Shomvi" and "Zaramo" was a process of identification that emerged in the nineteenth century through different reckonings of descent, mutual assistance, and the politics of trade relations. "Shomvi" appears to have first referred to resident elites who occupied coastal areas between Bagamoyo and Mbwamaji during the eighteenth and nineteenth centuries.[75] One well-rehearsed account holds that Shomvi descended from the union between settlers from the Persian town of Shiraz ("Shirazi"), who founded Mzizima, and a coastal leader named Muhamed bin Shale El Hatimi, who lent the Shirazi salt to trade with neighboring Zaramo in exchange for Zaramo military assistance against Kamba invaders.[76] Like many ethnonyms of the Swahili coast, the term "Shomvi" fused office title with descent. It likely began as a status appellation but was appropriated by others asserting plausible claims to coastal citizenship, much like the neighboring "Shehe" or "Shaha" clan, a term derived from *sheikh* and a common title for village leader; or the far larger, Persia-originating "Shirazi" along the pre-colonial *Mrima* coast. Episodic fluidity between status and descent enabled someone like the author Mtoro bin Mwinyi Bakari to identify as a Zaramo Shirazi.[77] Regardless of these titular etymologies, Shomvi today understand themselves as a distinct descent group; many claim ancestral origins in the Yemeni Hadhramaut and trace their migration to Tanzania via the Somali town of Barawa. By claiming both overseas and local coastal ancestors, which together denote wider prestige, specific trading rights, and firstcomer status, the Shomvi represent typical processes of identification at work across the Swahili coast.

Where Shomvi locate their origins in Arabia or Persia, Zaramo locate theirs in the interior Uluguru Mountains and trace descent from a mainland *pazi* (chief) named Kilama.[78] Nearly all accounts agree that the Kamba invasion of Mzizima, which occurred around 1800, was the foundational event that estab-lished Zaramo-Shomvi relations. Zaramo gained the upper hand over Shomvi when Pazi Kilama relieved Shomvi villagers by driving out Kamba intruders. He demanded the Shomvi pay him annual tribute in return. Yet, decades later in the 1860s, when Zanzibar's Sultan Majid founded the new town of Dar es Salaam along the sheltering harbor just to the south of Mzizima, there was no longer a singular "Pazi" exercising authority; instead, Mzizima was politically fractured among a few Zaramo and Shomvi families.[79] Despite omnipresent elements of rivalry, the Shomvi-Zaramo relationship was at most tributary, never servile. Each exercised authority over different spheres of the nineteenth-century coastal economy. Through access to credit and prestige goods, Shomvi were better tied to Indian Ocean commerce, while Zaramo exercised greater suzerainty inland over export producers and trade routes.[80] Furthermore, the fluidity of Shomvi and Zaramo identities, underscored by regular intermarriage, indicates that neither remotely corresponded to the sociological category of "tribe."[81]

Local fortunes fell sharply after 1870, when Zanzibar abandoned Dar es Salaam following Sultan Majid's death. His successor, Barghash, partially dislodged *pazi* control by refusing to pay tribute and decisively defeating a Zaramo attack on Bagamoyo in 1875.[82] The 1888 Bushiri Rebellion marked all Shirazi as enemies of the new German government. Shomvi were stripped of offices carrying powers to tax and allocate land, while the precipitous de-cline of coastal slavery undermined the ability of Shomvi leaders—previously enthusiastic slave owners—to mobilize wealth and supporters.[83] German rule also imposed a system of direct rule through nonlocal agents (*akida*) upon defeated Zaramo chiefs. Long-resident Shomvi were forcibly removed from the center of Dar es Salaam, which became the only coastal town between Pangani and Rufiji to prosper under German rule.[84] The German capital attracted a heterogeneous population consisting of some 47 percent Zaramo in 1895; a later 1905 estimate claimed Zaramo made up only 26 percent, and were outnumbered by Nyamwezi migrants. Lutheran missionary Martin Klamroth characterized Dar es Salaam as a foreign enclave where Zaramo resided only as laborers.[85] By the First World War, the power and authority previously exercised by local Shomvi and Zaramo had been gutted, particularly within Dar es Salaam itself.

The British regime offered potential resuscitation. Its policy of indirect rule opened opportunities for ethnic construction grounded on historical reconstructions of African societies before German colonialism. British officials sought out potential African leaders who conformed to the normative notion of the tribe; when such chiefs and elders stepped forward, the effect was often to "create" new tribes.[86] Officials began to solicit Zaramo "tribal" histories in 1927, in order to recapture assumed pristine political structures that predated German rule. District officials concluded in 1930 that government by paramount chief "was a state unreached by the Wazaramu."[87] Yet lacking big chiefs did not doom indirect rule. Local Zaramo enthusiastically supported a new system that replaced direct-rule tax agents with a decentralized "Zaramo" authority based on nineteen separate Native Administrations.[88] The Zaramo Native Authority proved a massive disappointment—as one officer relates, it was "saturated with personal and family feuds which result in ceaseless attacks being made on those who dare to exercise authority."[89] Administrative disinterest in Zaramo subsequently grew; its ethnographic research materials were decidedly disorganized and third-rate.[90] Although Zaramo ranked as Tanganyika's ninth-largest "tribe" at 117,000 in 1930, local numerical predominance did not, according to Adolfo Mascarenhas, "correspond to Zaramo prestige, tenure of office or other deterrents to incoming alien tribes [sic]. . . . In fact the opposite is true."[91] Yet, despite these failures, indirect rule experiments had encouraged Zaramo to embrace the language of tribe—that bounded descent group in which kinship neatly maps to territory—in order to augment their own firstcomer claims over land, offices, and institutions in and around Dar es Salaam.

To the extent that indirect rule "created" the Zaramo tribe, it "dismantled" the Shomvi by classifying them as Zaramo. A 1928 census affirmed that Dar es Salaam town was a major Zaramo center, the district overwhelmingly so, while categories of Shomvi and Swahili identity officially disappeared.[92] Déclassé Shomvi aristocrats, who more closely resembled a deteriorating landowner class than a "tribe," were nonetheless rudely awakened to their official detribalization in Dar es Salaam and the Zaramo tribalization of the hinterland. Some Shomvi were likely counted as Arabs, which offered sensible legal attractions.[93] Yet "non-native" was also a category that extinguished the history of local authority and prestige that Shomvi desperately embraced. Outraged that recent Hadramaut arrivals were treated as Arabs while they were treated as natives, two Shomvi petitioners objected to being forced to labor for African *akidas*, "whose ancestors may in all probability have been the servants of your Petitioners' ancestors."[94] Mtumwa Msakara bin Jumbe Tambaza led Shomvi opposition to Zaramo claims over Dar es Salaam, asserting Shomvi indigeneity—"This land of Dar es Salaam belongs to Mashomvi and these Mashomvi are of '*Wamwambao*' [coastal people] and *wamwambao* are people of right here, nor have they came from any other place, and since over 400 years they stay here." Zaramo, Tambaza continued, would not have dared to come to the coast for fear that Shomvi would "sell them and kill them."[95] In a search for local nationalist heroes decades later, Zaramo historian Ramadhani Mwaruka ironically appropriated and celebrated Jumbe Tambaza as an early Zaramo resister to British colonialism for demanding that Uzaramo rule itself.[96]

Indirect rule had inverted traditional coastal hierarchies that valorized Middle Eastern descent. Tambaza, Dar es Salaam's leading "Shomvi" figure, was arguing in a language of self-identification that had become outmoded. The territorial model of tribe had displaced the aristocratic clan that most closely approximated Tambaza's Shomvi. The Shomvi could be accurately described as "Swahili," but this was never a term of respectable self-identity among high-status coastal peoples. Moreover, even as an identity category invoked by low-status peoples, "Swahili" had experienced a collapse in prestige across coastal East Africa over the 1920s. In Zanzibar, ex-slaves abandoned the designation "Swahili" for "Shirazi," not simply for material betterment conferred by the latter, but also because "Swahili" had been "but the first step up a ladder of social mobility" after slavery; yet its ranks were no longer being replenished following slavery's abolition in 1897.[97] In Mombasa, "Swahili" had initially facilitated freedom of movement, but lost its social cache shortly after slavery's abolition in 1907, when it came to signify the town's "anti-social dregs."[98] Discouraged by its elusiveness, officials in Tanganyika determined "Swahili" was an administratively useless category. Lacking both inclination and colonial recognition to exercise "Swahili" group identity, Shomvi could offer only an antique lineage. The town's district officer accepted Tambaza's version of Shomvi history but scathingly rejected his claims about the lineage's viability:

> The Washomvi of Persian descent have been so long settled on the
> East coast and have intermarried with the indigenous population

that their decendants [sic] of today are true Africans. As the result of intermarriage with Wazaramu women the so-called Washomvi of today are certainly in most cases not less than 90 per cent Wa-zaramu. . . . We might as well call the descendants of the Normans who came over to England with William the conqueror Normans or French as call the present day descendants of the early Shomvi set-tlers in this country "Washomvi."[99]

British officials had looked for tribes; Shomvi had stressed ancestral status.[100] They were speaking different languages of identity.

More widely significant to African identity formation within Dar es Salaam was the relational mode of identification that separated *wenye mji* (owners of the town) and *watu wa kuja* (immigrants). *Wenye mji* were generally, though not exclusively, Shomvi and Zaramo elders lacking Western education; *watu wa kuja* were generally, though not exclusively, younger and often Western-educated, yet lacked claims to local ethnic- or lineage-based authority. Other self-descriptions invoked by Shomvi and Zaramo stressed birthrights (*wazalendo*, original inhabitants or patriots) and land rights (*mawinyi*, land-lords).[101] *Watu wa kuja* is wholly imprecise as a sociological category, but it lies at the discursive heart of interwar urban divisions. It was an unsought label, a mild epithet used to call attention to someone's outsider status. In fact, many *watu wa kuja* had been settled within township limits longer than self-described *wenye mji*. What distinguished *watu wa kuja* was that they re-jected assimilation into local lineages, and instead selectively adopted aspects of coastal culture—most notably Islam—while simultaneously affirming a specific homeland or "tribal" identification. Many became urban success stories, growing wealthy through trading, home ownership, and careers in government service. E. C. Baker lamented in 1931 that "we are thus faced at the outset with an alien intelligentsia and a diehard aristocracy living on the memories of its past."[102] This "alien intelligentsia" had secured plumb positions within the urban economy through colonial educational institutions rather than lineage or local institutions of prestige. Another defining fault line that economically distinguished *wenye mji* from *watu wa kuja* was based on the former's waning ability to provide patronage to—and profit from—town newcomers in the form of housing. Home ownership in Dar es Salaam—the foundation of urban African wealth—became decisively dominated by *watu wa kuja* groups over the interwar period.[103] Yet *watu wa kuja* were themselves divided by geographical origin and more sharply by religion. Many had only modest secular educations, particularly among Manyema and Nyamwezi, whom the Shomvi and Zaramo would have agreed were less "outsiders" than mission-educated Christian clerks.

Manyema formed the largest and most successful of interwar *watu wa kuja* communities. A capacious ethnonym, the term "Manyema" initially signified outsiders who had confronted rather than acquiesced to local custom and authority around Lake Tanganyika during the late nineteenth and early twentieth centuries.[104] Along the Swahili coast, "Manyema" was a term invoked by slaves brought from Lake Tanganyika who loudly proclaimed their "free" and "civilized" status. The first Manyema in Dar es Salaam were possibly slaves of Sultan Majid himself. Manyema "freedmen" who came to Dar es Salaam during German rule were likely fugitive slaves fleeing coastal plantations and embracing a new urban identity. The stigma of slave origins lingered decades later, despite prospering in the capital as powerful landlords who had, according to Leslie, "got in on the ground floor."[105] The Batetera Union, one of several competing Manyema associations in town, included landlords who, according to the historian Mohamed Said, "owned about half of the houses built in Dar es Salaam between the two world wars."[106] Manyema townswomen similarly owned a disproportionately large number of houses, and formed an important landlord class in Kariakoo, allegedly—as elderly Kariakoo men expressed with casual misogyny and particular envy—through sharp business dealings with local Zaramo and via the accumulation of wages from male partners.[107] Unlike local Zaramo and Ndengereko women, as one Kariakoo resident explained, the *watu wa kuja* Manyema women understood that *nyumba ni mali* (i.e., a house is a source of wealth).[108] Manyema women were formidable rent collectors—one adopted the eccentric strategy of sitting in her rental property doorways in a detached automobile seat until tenants paid.[109] Kariakoo men drew distinctions between male-owned and female-owned buildings, implying that the latter carried the stigma of ill-gained wealth, often through prostitution.[110] Fiercely independent, Manyema women became widely associated with breaking coastal social taboos in the accumulation of wealth, reflecting not only a deep-seated male misogyny toward female financial independence, but also a larger lamentation about uncouth "immigrant" strategies to bypass previously hegemonic *wenye mji* customs and institutions in pursuit of power and authority.

Other immigrant groups varied tremendously in their rootedness within interwar Dar es Salaam. Among the most rooted were those who had arrived through German military service. Sudanese or "Nubian" mercenaries had established a firm presence in the capital during the 1890s; their wives and daughters were, like Manyema, prominent homeowners.[111] These "Wanubi" of Dar es Salaam had, according to Leslie, "no other home; nor any links outside"; he considered them, along with "the Shirazi and the coconut-owning Zaramo," to be Dar es Salaam's most permanent inhabitants.[112] A smaller group of Shagaan or "Zulu" *askari* (soldiers) recruited from Lourenço

Marques also settled in Dar es Salaam in the 1890s, but took greater advantage than the Sudanese of the German government's educational facilities. The early leader of this "Zulu" community was Effendi Plantan, whose adopted son Kleist Sykes Plantan emerged as a leading political figure among *watu wa kuja* of interwar Dar es Salaam, and was later head of Dar es Salaam's most prominent political family.[113] Although "outsiders" in the eyes of local Zaramo and Shomvi, these descendants of German mercenary troops had—like their Manyema neighbors—come to Dar es Salaam through a decisive rupture with their homeland, and had greater reason to invest their capital and labor within the town that was, for most, their only home. Groups with shallower roots relied more heavily on urban patrons and tribal associations. Transient Nyamwezi and Sukuma laborers enjoyed ethnic networks in Dar es Salaam that included cheap lodgings for ethnic affiliates. The undisputed Nyamwezi leader in town was Juma Sultani, who served as assistant *liwali* and was famous for letting out sleeping spaces at his Kariakoo residence to Nyamwezi clove workers.[114] Tribal associations usually began as burial societies, with smaller groups federating with others who shared common geographical origin or linguistic affinity.[115] Membership dues for the Kilwa African Union Association in Dar es Salaam were called *sanda*, literally "shroud," used to buy funerary items for deceased members.[116] Though nominally "tribal," a number of these societies appear not to have excluded members on grounds of ethnicity, and instead offered welfare and opportunity to individuals who themselves straddled multiple town organizations.[117]

Urban associational life was sharply animated by insider-outsider rivalries. Along the East African coast, the *chama*—a Swahili term capaciously translated as "group," "party," or "society"—took ingenious cultural forms, characterized by moiety-like rivalries between neighborhood groups based on indigeneity, ancestry, and status.[118] Although moiety-like in form, the significance of *chama* competitions was not in their ability to integrate outsiders and ultimately resolve disputes, as functionalist literature suggests,[119] but rather in providing realms of contestation where rivals demonstrated their abilities to provide social welfare and exercise local authority. Football and dance offer two revealing and intertwined examples of *chama* life. Dar es Salaam's first major team was Sunderland, originally the "Old Boys" and today known as Simba SC. Sunderland represented better-educated *watu wa kuja* as well as those of "Arab" descent, and found its great rival in 1938 in Young Africans FC, or "Yanga," whose supporters were mostly Zaramo, Ndengereko, and Shomvi. Sunderland supporters derided Yanga fans as uneducated fishmongers and coconut tree climbers; Yanga supporters in turn derided Sunderland as foreigners and slaves of Arabs and Europeans. Both clubs collected subscriptions, organized burials, and helped members find jobs, accommodation, and even arranged marriages.[120] Football and dance rivalries closely overlapped. Sunderland established formal relations with the higher-status, Arab-dominated Alwatan Musical Club, a *taarab* musical club founded in the early 1930s; Yanga established ties with the other major *taarab* club, the lower-status, Zaramo, Ndegereko, and Shomvi-dominated Egyptian Musical Club.[121] Indeed, *ngoma* or dance societies ranked among the most vital colonial-era organizations of urban associational life.[122] Characterized by elaborate internal hierarchies and rough external rivalries, *ngoma* were the *chama par excellence* of interwar Tanganyika. The most remarkable were Beni (Band) societies, characterized by appropriated military brass sounds, dress, and organization to form competitive welfare societies. Originating in coastal Kenya, Beni spread throughout East Africa during the war to provide competitive performances and funerary security. Among the most important Beni groups in Dar es Salaam were Marini and Arinoti—Marini represented higher-status clerks, much like Sunderland football fans, and Arinoti lower-status laborers, much like Yanga fans.[123] Perhaps the most vituperative struggle occurred over Islamic institutions. Led by Kleist Sykes, *watu wa kuja* figures established the Jamiatul Islamiyya in the early 1930s to coordinate Islamic education and welfare among African Muslims in Dar es Salaam, in part out of frustration with Indian-controlled Islamic societies (see below). Shortly following the establishment of the Jamiatul's successful primary school, however, *wenye mji* dissidents formally broke with its leadership in 1939. The immediate issues concerned *wenye mji* objections to religious control by "outside" figures like Sykes and a Comorian *sheikh*, Ali Saleh, as well as what they perceived as the Jamiatul's defiance of the *liwali*, whom they strongly supported. But also at issue was what *wenye mji* perceived as the blasphemous cosmopolitanism of Sykes and the Jamiatul leadership, who had suggested allowing young girls to sing at Islamic festivals, and renamed their club where men and women danced together as the "Tanganyika Muslim Jazz Band Club."[124] The organization split into two branches with separate primary schools, following a wider pattern then emerging among the town's political organizations in the late 1930s.

Political rivalry between *wenye mji* and *watu wa kuja* groups stymied organizational monopoly over African racial politics in interwar Dar es Salaam. In erratic fashion, district officers polled "town elders," a loosely defined group in which *wenye mji* figures constituted a majority, on questions of administrative personnel. Zaramo and Shomvi leaders scored a victory in 1930 when they ousted an outsider, Yusuf Kirumbi, from the position of *mwenyemzi*, the chief "native" court officer and tax collector for peri-urban Dar es Salaam; he was replaced by a Zaramo.[125] Far more significant to town life was the office of *liwali*, who was responsible for Dar es Salaam's native courts and tax collection. The *liwali* was uniquely empowered to carry out corporal punishment on "natives" in Dar es Salaam, whipping the convicted for "parental correction"[126] with no more than six strokes, "to deal summarily with the inevitable element of loafing boys and youths" who could "hardly be dealt with judicially by a European officer."[127] The office of *liwali* in Dar es Salaam was held exclusively by Arabs from its inception in 1921 until its abolition shortly before independence. Over most of this same period, many African residents protested that an Arab should not be given such powers over their lives. Men were particularly aggrieved that an Arab *liwali* had discretion to intervene in African marital affairs.[128] When another Arab was proposed to replace the retiring *liwali* in 1930, the recently formed African Association objected that "an Arab always looks down upon an African within or without, as a slave or putting it frankly an 'inferior' in all respects and therefore what justice and good treatment can the latter expect from the former."[129] Yet an officially convened *baraza ya wazee* (elders' forum), dominated by Shomvi and Zaramo leaders, ratified the proposal to appoint another Arab *liwali*, Sharif Salim bin Omar, a Sunni with deep family roots in Dar es Salaam.[130] Where the candidate's Arab identity had proved unacceptable among the *watu wa kuja* who dominated the African Association, it had reaffirmed the locally grounded authority of the *wenye mji*. The decision proved disastrous, and the new *liwali* was later dismissed for corruption in 1937.[131] That same year, the *baraza ya wazee* was deemed unrepresentative and dismantled, precipitating a wave of newly founded tribal societies,[132] the most significant of which was the Wazaramo Union, a welfare association registered in July 1938 to constitute "a society for all Wazaramo tribes in one unit, in Dar es Salaam and outside."[133] Thousands joined the Wazaramo Union, which had the effect of denying the African Association a broad base of support in and around Dar es Salaam, something that it would not enjoy until the 1950s.

The African Association had been founded not for "tribe or lineage [but] the entire race/nation [*taifa*] of the natives of Africa."[134] Yet realizing this goal of representing the African *taifa* was organizationally constricted by the ambitions and suspicions of Dar es Salaam's *wenye mji*. African Association leadership was overwhelmingly *watu wa kuja*, in particular "rehabilitated" German-era civil servants and clerks educated by missions in Zanzibar and Mombasa. Shortly after its formation in 1927, Baker reported that its leading personalities were "not natives of Dar-es-Salaam" and that "the local Wazaramo and Swahili elders appear somewhat biassed [sic] against it."[135] Moreover, had the latter become members or shown any enthusiasm, Baker suggested that the African Association would have had a far greater influence.[136] As small as its support was, the African Association exercised even less patronage—it ordered African tailors striking for higher wages to return to work for their Indian employers, "since the Association has no sufficient money to feed them."[137] It was eclipsed in vigor and even briefly taken over by the Tanganyika African Welfare and Commercial Association (TAWCA) during the late 1930s. TAWCA, formed in part to compete with Indian merchants, was not exclusively a *wenye mji* organization, but prominent Zaramo and Shomvi traders such as Makisi Mbwana, Ramadhani Ali, and H. P. Diwan did serve as president. Its founder and moving force was a sui generis figure, Erica Fiah. A Bugandan immigrant who had settled in Dar es Salaam after serving in the British military during the First World War, Fiah was a shopkeeper, farmer, and labor organizer who played a central role in Dar es Salaam's political and intellectual life in the late 1930s and 1940s by editing and publishing the independent newspaper *Kwetu* (Our Home). He excoriated educated English-speaking Africans who held themselves aloof from commercial and agricultural work.[138] TAWCA represented, according to Iliffe, the "traders and more radical civil servants" who opposed the elitism of the African Association. It took up the cause of African landowners who claimed that their properties had "wrongly been handed over to the injustice people [sic]"—likely in reference to contested property transfers from *wenye mji* to *watu wa kuja*, as TAWCA phrased the conflict in the following terms: "In Dar es Salaam the skilled Africans are robbing the unskilled ones."[139]

Yet it would be mistaken to read too much social history into these organizations by the late 1930s, when both the African Association and TAWCA had weak local support, and were becoming primarily vehicles for personal advancement and speculation.[140] It would be even more mistaken to read the rise of "tribal associations" and breakdown of the African Association's authority in the late 1930s as somehow presenting an obstacle to Pan-Africanist nationalism. The African Association's failure to monopolize racial politics, if anything, opened the issue to fruitful political competition. During the 1940s, when the African Association reached its nadir of influence in the capital, was also when African racial nationalism was acquiring mass popular support. Through its attacks on Indian produce buyers and land speculators, the Wazaramo Union did more to popularize anti-Asian sentiments in and around Dar es Salaam than the African Association had ever done. "Tribal" politics coexisted comfortably with those of race. What changed was the growing significance of race to people's daily lives in the capital. The relational mode of identification between *wenye mji* indigenes and *watu wa kuja* immigrants persisted throughout the 1940s over issues of local significance, particularly concerning control of peri-urban land and offices.[141] But it no longer predominated. The insider-outsider rivalry was steadily supplanted by race, a categorical mode of identification that achieved its categorical qualities during the interwar years within the texture of African-Indian relations.

"RACE RELATIONS"

The third layer of interwar identity formation emerged from the interactions between Africans and Indians. Zaramo and Shomvi had claimed Dar es Salaam as their birthright. More recent immigrants claimed Dar es Salaam through urban property, prestigious posts in the colonial economy, and selective appropriation of coastal social institutions. But the greatest challenge confronting African claims to independent urban life was the ever-rising cost of living, which was plainly mediated by a small but economically powerful Indian minority. As we saw in chapter 1, colonial urban planning, market regulation, and land administration divided Africans and Indians through the contradictory pursuits of "native" protection and "non-native" commercial encouragement. Africans and Indians in interwar Dar es Salaam also constructed corporate racial organizations, in part as a convenient mode of engagement to lobby the colonial state, but also to fulfill wider political ambitions—be it the "Greater India" of local Gujarati propagandists or the spectral Pan-Africanism of African civil servants and teachers. But it was in the texture of daily life, rather than in the petitions and decrees of political organizations, that race became a reflexive way to categorize humanity. In Dar es Salaam, this texture was constituted above all through the economic familiarity that joined—and the social distance that separated—Indians and Africans. The problem with casual analytical framings of "race relations," as Robert Miles reminds us, is that they often assume race is a real thing rather than just a mode of thought.[142] What is being examined in the following section is how "race relations" came to be naturalized through a series of social-economic processes that sustained racial modes of thought and caricature.

DAFTARI ECONOMICS: DUKAS, DEBTS, AND DOMESTICS

Pela lakh pachhi de.
(First write it down, then give the money.)

—Gujarati business maxim

The duka, Swahili for "shop," was where Africans and Indians most regularly met, and where guiding caricatures etched themselves into popular folklore and imagination. The Indian merchant represented the constricting structures of colonial commerce, and served to unify African imaginations across East Africa. His profit depended on combining produce buying with retail selling and credit extension. The economic effect of this, as Frederick Cooper has argued for Kenya, was the narrowing of commercial pathways and the creation of perpetual indebtedness, which created a closed financial circle that forced rural African producers to sell and buy all supplies from a single merchant.[143] The social effect of this was to highlight conflicting

interpretations of reciprocity. Future obligations were formed not in imprecise webs of kinship and patronage, but rather in the impersonal accounting
of monetary debt, typically written out in a *daftari*, Swahili for account book
or ledger. This process is reflected in the Swahili language itself, in which
a large percentage of "Indic" loanwords (Hindustani, Gujarati, Kachchhi)
concern instruments of commerce and contract.[144] More fundamentally,
different understandings of reciprocity also meant disagreement about what
constituted moral behavior. Indian virtues of thrift, savvy, and efficiency appeared to Africans as selfishness, dishonesty, and exploitation.

No event better illustrates the resulting gap between Indian self-
understanding and African understanding of Indians than the 1923 territorial
hartal, the touchstone of Tanganyika's "Greater India" politics (see above),
which protested colonial meddling with Gujarati account books. Although
shopkeepers had hoped to disrupt the colonial government, hit hardest were
urban African consumers, who saw prices of foodstuffs rise from 100 to 300
percent within two weeks.[145] Bukoba's Indian Association reported that "all
the Indians and Arabs were in danger of a riot from the natives who were on
the verge of starvation."[146] In Dar es Salaam, African traders refused to join
the strike; farmers transported large food quantities to town themselves, and
several residents took out native trading licenses to open small shops.[147] Where
Indians celebrated the episode as the successful flexing of nationalist muscle,
Africans ruminated bitterly on having their own commercial vulnerabilities
revealed. An unpublished letter from anonymous "Native Observers" of Dar
es Salaam wondered why "money and food which they [Indians] innocently
punished the natives with were from the natives themselves." Worse still, the
hartal occurred during Ramadan, leaving Africans to endure "the trial Rama-
than [sic], while the mothers of the Religion [sic] enjoyed peaceably in their
house. . . . *Such Party is not worth to claim itself as promoters of natives of
Africa*."[148] The Director of Education later invoked this episode to justify his
opposition to independent African newspapers, reasoning that "publication of
articles inspired by race hatred, as would certainly have happened at the time
of the Indian strike, might have led to most disastrous results."[149]

The seeming ease and regularity with which Indian immigrants moved
from poverty to prosperity appalled Africans, who understood this success to
come at their own expense. Indian domination over Tanganyika's retail and
wholesale trade—95 percent and 75 percent respectively, by one estimate—
seemed insurmountable to aspiring African traders.[150] An African resident
of Kariakoo complained to the Indian-owned *Tanganyika Herald* that "a
number of you arrived in Africa with little or no money [but] to-day you are
well up, buying our shambas for Shillings one hundred, and selling same
for £2,000."[151] Such prosperity evoked both admiration and resentment. A

lengthy meditation penned by an African on the methods and transformation of a typical Ismaili merchant is worth quoting at length:

> Many times we see Indians who come from their home in Bombay or somewhere, when he comes to Africa he is in deep poverty, but when he starts to do business he will start a small shop, and after several days he will look for a mason who does work and several unskilled laborers under him, [the Indian] will entice him and make a big friendship in order to get him to send all of those unskilled workers to buy on credit [*kopa*] at his place. If he doesn't find the mason he will look for another who is well-known to send his friends and neighbors to do a profitable business, well!, we did not know that we have made this poor person a man of status after a while, being called "MUKI" [*mukhi*, religious leader of a local Ismaili community], because of our money he will come to wear a beautiful gold-embroidered robe and hat, and become a famous person with a good reputation among his Indian friends, who when he first came they did not go to his shop to do business [*kopa*] in the way that those *washenzi* ["savages" or African customers] as they are later called, used to do.[152]

This account, which was censored for publication by the government, underscores the initial fragile dependence of Indian merchants on local Africans, and stresses not only Indian enrichment but also the growing social distance that accompanies success.

An arresting feature in the above account is the central place of the Swahili verb *kopa*, literally "borrow," but serving here as a term for buying on credit and doing business generally. All Indian businesses, as we have seen, relied heavily on credit systems. Supply-line credit from European and Indian merchant houses, often based on ninety-day terms, stretched from the docks of Dar es Salaam to the smallest rural shops. The system functioned on high turnover and small cash margins—often as little as 10 percent—offering higher profits but greater risks and frequent bankruptcies among small Indian traders.[153] Fast-moving product lines like sugar and rice carried razor-thin margins or were loss leaders subsidized by large profit margins on slow-moving lines such as imported tins.[154] Retail trade was a brutal endurance test in which only shopkeepers with large capital stocks or secure access to credit could prevail. And credit lay at the heart of economic relations between Indian merchants and African consumers. Credit was universally available at pawnshops, which in Dar es Salaam were owned entirely by Khoja Ismaili Indians, and intimately connected with most African household economies. Pledges peaked from the twentieth to the end of each month, during *siku za mwambo*, or "tight-stretched days." Upon wage payments on the first of the month, each pawnshop in town would attend to between three and four hundred customers who queued to redeem their goods.[155] All eighteen pawnbrokers in Dar es Salaam closed in 1930 to protest legislation that halved maximum chargeable interest rates from 6 percent to 3 percent per month. When stores reopened six weeks later, thousands of African residents had made a fire sale of their pawnable goods to other Africans, particularly visiting crop sellers who returned home with secondhand articles purchased at 10 percent of their value. It took six months for Africans to repurchase an equal quantity of goods, which soon recirculated once more through the town's reconstituted pawn credit system.[156]

As their popularity grew over the 1930s, pawnshops were blamed for attracting all things of value from African homes into Indian shops, insatiable maws that were "consuming the wealth of the resident African community; encouraging theft, burglary, and smuggling."[157] But such shops also provided the nexus for the distribution of basic necessities such as food and clothing to those living month-to-month on credit margins. As one longtime Kariakoo resident put it, *duka ya poni* was "our bank (*benki yetu*), because if a guest arrived and you had nothing, you took your shirt or embroidered *kanzu* and sent it to the shop, that should get three shillings—three shillings was enough for good food."[158] It was not unusual for African customers to use pawnshop credit six times per month, pawning clothes and jewelry in return for cash.[159] Although pawnshops were the only legal source of "non-native" credit available to Africans, most forms of "interracial" petty commerce functioned on informal credit. In one common practice known as *amana*, Indian retailers extended credit in return for offering safe deposit of African goods or money, usually accumulated from a dowry or crop sale, which would subsequently serve as a surety for monthly store credit.[160]

Dar es Salaam was only sporadically a cash economy; the bulk of transactions existed in the heads and account books (*daftari*) of borrowers and lenders. For most, having cash in hand was a short-lived moment between the birth of new loans and the retirement of old debts. As Erica Fiah explains, the first thing many Africans were obliged to do upon receipt of wages or harvest payment was "to go with all of our money to the shops of the European and Indian and hand over (*kumkabidhi*) our money."[161] Lending occurred in two spheres: among Africans themselves, most loans originating through kinship and patronage, and between African borrowers and Indian lenders. In terms of accounting and reciprocity these two spheres partially overlap, but they also occupy different positions on a continuum that Marshall Sahlins has typologized (for gift-giving) in Simmelian terms of intimacy and strangerhood. Forms of lending among Africans covered this entire continuum: from "generalized reciprocity," with relatively free lending without strict accounting, to the continuum's middle, of "balanced reciprocity" or tit-for-tat equivalency with strict accounting. In this middle also lay Indian-African lending. On the other end of this continuum was "negative reciprocity," characterized by getting "something for nothing" through haggling, deceit, or corruption.[162] Here lay the mistrust and wrecked relations of both Indian-African and African-African financial actors. Indian lenders rarely if ever occupied the position of "generalized reciprocity" with African borrowers, but were instead seen by Africans as "public strangers," widely recognized to inhabit the realm of strictly balanced reciprocity.

Collecting wages and renewing accounts constituted the financial rhythms of urban life. Traders and entrepreneurs extended credit to customers and employees respectively. When the African wage earner received his paycheck (nearly all were male), he would first pay off debts amounting to between one-third and one-half of his salary accumulated toward the end of the month.[163] He would then purchase, on credit, a supply of rice and cassava to last him the coming month, spend the remainder on perishable foodstuffs or luxuries such as tea, and exhaust his funds by the twentieth of each month; many went without food for the final two or three days. Although some purchased food directly from growers, many lacked the time and relied on retail food sales.[164] Far less is known about female indebtedness, except that women were more active in the informal economy and peri-urban farming than men, and thus slightly more shielded from wage rhythms or urban life.[165] Despite constant pleas from "sound money" advocates—mostly commercial bankers and large wholesalers—to restrict store credit because it generated inflation and greater default risks, the system had become thoroughly entrenched. Few shops could afford *not* to lend. An Indian trader showed a reporter a book of two hundred people who owed him money, with twenty names underscored in red for "urgent settlement." When asked why such a credit system persisted, he and another trader offered a number of reasons—housewives not trusting their African "boys" with cash for daily purchases, shop competition for credit-hungry customers, and lack of cash-on-delivery systems for up-country buyers.[166] Choosing not to lend also risked affronting African honor. After an African assistant medical officer was refused a six-shilling shop credit, an observer expressed outrage that, although the man "holds a good rank, it is still doubted that he is not a sort of man for whom a trader can legally accept for credit."[167] African customers proudly recalled that character was the main criterion used by Indian shopkeepers to gauge credit extension.[168]

Money's ghostly existence led African thinkers to question its circulation and utility. "Where does all the money which we get in salaries go to," a loyal *Kwetu* correspondent wrote, "does it not all find its way to the Indian shops, in bill settlements?" He continued:

What benefit does your African brother get out of your pay? If our money were circulated amongst the native population, it would greatly serve Tanganyika. Where do the Indians send their money? Supposing they were all ordered back to their Homeland, India, would they leave us their shops? Despite all we do to and for the Indians where is the gratitude? They simply say of us, "Fools, what does a black-skinned creature know?"[169]

Erica Fiah himself similarly excoriated Indian traders, cash and cloth in hand, who at harvesttime descended upon "unprotected villages" in order to fleece poor villagers; "With false balances and bellying spirit the wandering middlemen goes back with a fortune."[170] Money failed to circulate within virtuous African commercial circles, and instead drained away through non-African shops. Indians offered Africans no help at all, only "a wealth of insults."[171] Attacking Tanganyika's labor migration system that separated Africans from their "age-old friendship with the soil," Fiah despaired that Africans had come to regard money "as a god" while the African himself "is today an exile from home on transfer." Money had reduced Africans to "wage-slaves," who produced "temporary wealth but eternal moral as well as economic ruin." There was no returning to Eden, at least not until the government reversed territorial labor policies. "It is a wonder then," he concluded, "that the African is poorer today with the full knowledge of the power of money, but with very little of it, than without that knowledge and without the money in the past."[172] Yet for all its baleful effects, Fiah and others protested "native" lending restrictions that gifted Indians an insurmountable advantage. "Ninety out of every hundred African officials are allowed credits by Indians at the latter's risk," one writer explained, "and except in few cases the Indians have been getting their money all right." Removing this restriction would free African shopkeepers to deal more fully with Indian merchants, who "would not, of course, give credit to a person whom he knows he can never get the money out of in a civil court." Fiah agreed, but added that African shopkeepers were currently "compelled to await their doom at the hands of any non-native exploiter who may come round for a shop."[173] As a critique of capital's alienation of labor, Fiah and others understood the process in racial terms, and eagerly offered to replace Indian strangers with themselves as the true custodians of African money.

The second major meeting place of Indians and Africans was domestic service. The African male population of interwar Dar es Salaam was predominantly a wage-earning population; its two largest employers were non-African households and the colonial government.[174] Domestic work offered a reliable income, unlike the inherently seasonal rhythms attached to petty commercial work.[175] Low wages discouraged investment in laborsaving devices and encouraged a "one man, one job" domestic work system. In 1931, domestic servants, cooks, and washermen accounted for 3,643, or 26 percent, of African workers in "predominantly male" occupations in town working for non-African households, most of which were Indian.[176] African servants working in Indian households confronted intimate domestic settings in which racial boundaries were sharply demarcated. Prosperous Hindus boasted of having touched only food prepared by other Hindus, even after decades of living in Tanganyika.[177] African servants often found themselves prohibited from drinking water from the glasses of Indian homes. One man recalled that if an African were caught drinking from a glass—even if he washed it—the Indian employer would break the glass and perhaps fire the worker. He contrasted this with Arab households, where there was *glasi moja* (one glass) for employer and servant.[178] By the early 1940s, some 6,000 men and 1,000 children (presumably male) worked as domestic servants, together totaling 47 percent of town wage-laborers, while domestic service made up 12 percent of Tanganyika's entire wage-labor force.[179] More-prosperous African families and poorer Indian families employed juveniles as personal servants for a few shillings per month plus food.[180] Officials fretted that Asian households employed the youngest and most undernourished of available servants, contrasting this with their self-congratulatory assessment of superior conditions that prevailed in European households.[181] Young male servants, often runaways from nearby rural areas, received what food they could get and lived in the kitchens or compounds of their employers; the less fortunate slept at markets or under bridges. Their growing numbers stirred demographic fears that this class would become "potential fathers of a town-bred herd of citizens mentally and physically C. 3. [unfit]."[182] A servants association complained that Indian employers often accused servants of pilfering near the end of the month to drive them away to avoid paying a month's wages.[183] *Zaramo kuiba; Ndengereko kuficha* (Zaramo steal; Ndengereko hide) was a popular urban proverb likely created by Indians who tended to employ ethnic Zaramo and Ndengereko as domestic servants.[184] European households generally hired more servants—five on average—and paid better. Yet many African servants preferred Indian employers, who paid less but often demanded less and were more flexible about debt repayments and salary advances.[185] Like consumer credit, domestic service offered Africans limited access to wealth but denied social membership within the unit that extended wealth.

THE SELF-SEGREGATED CITY: SOCIABILITY, BUREAUCRACY, CRIME, AND HONOR

Beyond the working spaces of shops and households, social life in interwar Dar es Salaam was remarkably self-segregated. Indian social functions were organized along communal lines, and Indians rarely attended—let alone participated in—African *ngoma* or modern dance clubs. As one Kariakoo resident explained, the relationship between Indians and Africans was "not one of inviting one another into their homes to have a drink of water or tea."[186] As we have seen, sports like football united Africans in boisterous rivalries. African and Indian football teams did occasionally compete, but the most popular sport among Indians was cricket, a sport rarely played by Africans. English and Hindi language films were the most valued entertainment for "non-natives," and they were attended by Africans who could afford admission. However, a discriminatory rating system prohibited even educated Africans from attending some films, resulting in recurrent humiliation when, upon arrival, Africans learned the film was rated "non-natives only," and thus forced to leave. Even after a nondiscriminatory system was adopted in 1936, African filmgoers still suffered arbitrary admission refusals.[187] For non-African men, "life and norms were centered around a club."[188] Clubs were also raw expressions of colonial status. The most prestigious clubs were European-only—the Dar es Salaam Club rated the highest and occupied a prime position on the Azania waterfront; farther inland was the Gymkhana Club, which made up for its less enviable address, at least during the 1920s, by excluding all Europeans not born in England.[189] As social space, Uzunguni (European area) was rarely transgressed by non-Europeans except servants. Public processions to celebrate British imperial holidays did not enter Uzunguni.[190] Multiracial public venues were few, formalized, and awkward. The most prominent secular forum was the Dar es Salaam Cultural Society, which was "euphemistically named," as one-time acting secretary Andy Chande recalls, for culture "was rarely, if ever, on the agenda." As an appendage of the Dar es Salaam Museum, the Cultural Society hosted various European and Indian lectures and reading groups at the British Council, "because no hotel was willing to play host to such a mongrel grouping."[191] Directed by the town's leading European culture mavens—Clement Gillman, A. A. M. Isherwood, and J. P. Moffett—the Cultural Society's events featured lectures on literature, politics, and speeches by visiting celebrity figures such as the Aga Khan.[192] A small but dedicated group of Africans attended, yet its chairman later on regretted that the society had "little appeal for Africans."[193]

British officials happily indulged "multiracialism" in the soft realm of voluntary cultural activities, but attitudes hardened when it came to pay and pensions. The most racialized institution of interwar Tanganyika was without question the civil service. After the war, the new administration had sought the best strategy to staff trained clerks and artisans at the lowest expense. Asians from East Africa or India cost less than Europeans, required less training than Africans, and offered an expedient solution to immediate staffing problems; on the other hand,

African labor was cheaper, and training Africans for skilled jobs was closer in line with the mandate. Either strategy was unavoidably political. African civil servants in Tanga, who had earlier opposed political rule by India and soon formed the Tanganyika Territory African Civil Service Association (TTACSA), protested the "great distinction between Asiatic and Native Clerks" in salary, leave, and housing allowance.[194] The Maxwell Committee, headed by the railway director G. A. P. Maxwell, was appointed to answer the question, and concluded that there was an "almost unanimous wish to employ Africans in all branches of the service in preference to Asiatics." The committee planned to replace low-ranking Asian clerks with Africans within three years, completing replacement at all levels by 1932. Noting that telegraph services and printing presses were already staffed entirely by Africans under European supervision, the Maxwell Committee recommended that Africans be trained in school shops and not by personal apprenticeships because of "the strong Asiatic element already in the Government shops and their trade unionism, which will endeavour to keep the African in the position of a hewer of wood and drawer of water."[195] The Colonial Office accepted the recommendations with galling cynicism— "As soon as we have Africans qualified for the jobs, we shall be able to eliminate the Asiatics by offering salaries which only Africans could accept."[196]

The Maxwell Committee's vision of Africanization soon yielded, however, to pressing administrative needs for competent, affordable clerks and artisans. Only weeks after the committee's report was issued, the acting governor requested permission to recruit more Asian clerks, deeming their superior efficiency, compared to still-undertrained African clerks, essential.[197] Indian clerical staff responded by forming the Tanganyika Asian Civil Service Association (TACSA) to demand better terms for locally engaged Asian clerks and protection for those recruited abroad.[198] The Tanganyika Railways Asiatic Union, made up largely of First World War draftees, emphasized hardship to justify higher wages: "No one can conscientiously expect us to serve in this un-healthy country on the same pay as in India."[199] By 1925, the emerging enthusiasm for indirect rule dampened official enthusiasm for a highly trained and Westernized African clerical class. The Education Department embraced an "adaptive" curriculum to focus on more-"practical" skills. Such schooling would make, in the words of indirect rule's architect, Governor Donald Cameron, "a good African and not a cheap imitation of a European."[200] The department also championed separate schools for Indians and Africans. Rivers-Smith, Tanganyika's director of education, explained:

> With the knowledge of political development during the last few years in India, we cannot afford to ignore the possibility of an unfortunate African political repercussion in future years as a result of the

development of a closer liaison between the two races which might be a result of co-education. At present we have a healthy rivalry and a growing race-consciousness amongst the Africans and a certain feeling of resentment that the Asiatics get so many of the "plums." In my opinion co-education might conceivably weaken this healthy and natural rivalry and eventually lead to making common cause for political end.[201]

This "healthy and natural rivalry" would instead be fostered by subsequent colonial policies. Separate education ensured separate clerical services. Despite its earlier support of Maxwell Committee recommendations, the government ignored TTACSA petitions and African clerks labored without fixed scales until 1926.[202] TTACSA president Cecil Madalito lamented that "civilization requires us to live decently in every respect and since the Government has already agreed this privilege to one section of service [i.e., Asiatic Staff], it is obvious that it has to carry the same promise out in our case."[203] African clerks also invoked their autochthonous status when arguing their case. "If we are the children of the soil," Madalito asserted, "no doubt we deserve the same privileges if not more than those given to foreigners. . . . Who has better rights in the house, a child or a servant; aren't the foreigners like servants and we children in the house?"[204] Cheap but relatively well-educated, Asian civil servants—nearly all of whom were Indian, with many coming from Kerala and other parts of southern India—had presented a bargain for the government, but formed a stubborn obstacle to Tanganyika's emerging and resentful African bureaucratic elite.

Seeking savings to weather the depression, the government abolished its racialized civil service structure in 1933 in favor of a new system that separated expatriate Europeans from a cheaper "nonracial" local civil service, which would hire local Indians at lower wages instead of importing expensive Asian staff.[205] Tanganyika's Indians had fallen victim to their own success in education and population growth, having created a large pool of young, well-educated clerical talent that obviated the need to pay higher wages to attract recruits from abroad.[206] Local Indian press rejected government claims that Africans should now receive equal wages with Indians, for they "have not acquired that amount of efficiency and technical skill and sense of responsibility which an Asiatic clerk invariably has."[207] The local civil service nonetheless became law, immediately cutting junior Indian clerk pay. Police similarly integrated lower-ranking Asian and African appointments into a single subinspectorate in 1935.[208] Gaping disparities in quality of available education between Asians and Africans, however, ensured that disparity in grades and salaries, though no longer formal, would persist. By 1937, fourteen out of eighteen Secretariat clerks were "foreigners" (i.e., Asians); 100 of 119 Customs Department clerks, and 37 of 39 Treasury clerks.[209] Despite depression-era pay cuts, the Asian foothold over Tanganyika's mid-level civil service jobs seemed unshakable.

By contrast, widespread African unemployment provided the context for another intransigent feature of interwar Dar es Salaam: Asian fear of African crime. Indians perpetually demanded greater police protection for Uhindini, where protection compared poorly to that of the less-populated Uzunguni but quite favorably to that of the more populous African quarter.[210] Petty theft was so rampant that a visiting missionary quipped that "they practically have to roll up the sidewalks at night."[211] Perennial demands for improved street lighting and nighttime constabulary reflected the town's most pervasive criminal industry, nocturnal burglary, which could take most inventive forms. A Ceylonese man awoke one morning to find under his house wall a dug-out hole, which had taken several painstaking nights of silently removing and then concealing its gravel base, and through which burglars had climbed to steal the man's clothes.[212] Crime could be multiracial—such as the six-person band of Indian, Arab, and African armed robbers that terrorized shopkeepers in 1931, or the more systematic cooperation between African thieves and Indian receivers.[213] But Indian news reportage could be relied upon to stress the racial identities of African criminals and Indian victims. The *Tanganyika Herald* warned that a raid of an Indian restaurant by fifty hooligans was "just a specimen of the havoc a native mob can play in broad day-light."[214] Indian attitudes toward young African men living on the economic margins—popularly termed *wahuni*, or hooligans—visibly hardened over the 1930s, as reported thefts in town leaped from 443 cases in 1931 to 1,317 in 1939.[215] In 1932, the *Tanganyika Herald* had attacked the government's heavy-handed tactics involved in poll tax collection as "slavery in disguise"; by 1937 it called for the implementation of pass laws and forcible repatriations to reduce urban African unemployment and crime.[216] An association of two hundred Indian retailers in Kariakoo petitioned that, although they paid more than 20,000 shillings in taxes and license fees, the government nevertheless allowed "native and Shihiri [Arab] hawkers" to block entrance into their shops, as well as permitted "pilforage [sic], petty thefts, and house-breaking by native loafers."[217] Their appeals had gone unanswered by 1942, by which time "gangs of some undesirable natives" had developed sophisticated techniques to divert shopkeepers' attention while another stole shop goods.[218]

The specter of racial violence haunted Uhindini, where major riots had occurred in 1918, 1929, and 1937. Little is known about the 1918 riot other than that it occurred in the Indian bazaar.[219] The other two riots, as documented in police reports and fretful Indian newspapers, were ignited by relatively petty provocations. In 1929, a small group of intoxicated Africans had slapped

Indian children playing in the street; after parents stopped them, they turned their insults to the whole Indian community. Following more confrontation, a group of one hundred or more Africans were called, came to the area, and challenged Indians to fight; they attacked houses, injured five Indians, and were finally dispersed by police gunfire.[220] In 1937, an Indian shopkeeper gave chase to two African thieves who had stolen a shirt; a fight between Indians and Africans soon broke out. Indian children were "freely beaten by natives who had sticks in their hands," in one case raining sticks and stones on a shop where a child was seeking shelter.[221] But it was unsolved, unaccountable violence that most haunted Indian imaginations. Dar es Salaam was a large enough town—perhaps the only in Tanganyika—where criminals could rely on anonymity, and where multiple criminal cases would be left unsolved. Describing the nocturnal murder of an Indian "stabbed in the back with a spear by some natives in the Kisutu area," the *Tanganyika Herald* characterized community psychology: "On several occasions their memories bring before their eye that blood-boiling murderous act and compel them to find answers to several questions, such as, who killed him? Why was he killed? Is there any mystery about it?"[222] The paper was attempting not only to secure police attention but also to tame the crime's unaccountability by having its readers ask themselves questions about proper and cautious behavior in what seemed an insecure urban environment. Had the victim been careless, perhaps guilty of some unknown transgression, or simply attacked by chance? A wider siege mentality characterized daily routines of Indian households. Great precautions were taken regarding physical security of persons and lodgings; travel after sundown was avoided as much as possible, particularly through African areas. In the eyes of those being feared, the social and spatial self-segregation of Indians in Dar es Salaam was perhaps most objectionable as an affront to African honor.

Quotidian segregation made plain differing rights to respect. "They have separate toilets," one African noted about Indian-only lavatories, "and they have separate honor (*heshima*)."[223] Urban spatial hierarchies took vertical as well as horizontal form. Significant parts of Indian urban life occurred literally above the ground-level existence of Africans. The majority of Indian households lived in multistoried buildings, to which their African servants would haul food and water, while most African households lived in ground-level Swahili houses or *makuti* huts. Indians watched films from balconies, Africans from floor seating. Sharp feelings of honor and shame were never far from the surface, particularly when it came to social pressures on Indian men and women to avoid intermarriage with Africans. Interracial concubinage, by contrast, was not uncommon. Although little quantitative evidence and no official studies exist, anecdotal evidence indicates that it was fairly widespread, most frequently in the imbalanced relationships between lower-class Indian men and African female servants. In one case, Binti Burahim, an ethnic *mhiyao* girl and servant to an Indian in Kilwa, carried two of his daughters before moving to Dar es Salaam to live with her father; fifteen years later she cohabited with an Indian customs clerk in Kariakoo and carried his daughter; after he left, she moved into the house of a Goan man in Kisutu, who raised the daughter until his death.[224] But whereas an earlier, smaller and overwhelmingly male Indian population had endured only light scrutiny toward interracial liaisons, the shift to more gender-balanced immigration patterns during the 1930s—particularly as Hindu wives began to regularly accompany their husbands—sharpened social pressures to contract endogamous marriages.[225]

The firm linguistic persistence of Gujarati, Kachchhi, and Punjabi in Indian households reflected endogamous marital patterns. Although most Indians had at least a working knowledge of Swahili, full command of the language became an increasingly important marker of African identity in interwar Dar es Salaam. Miscommunication bespoke dishonor and mistrust. Mixing language identity politics with commercial motives, *Kwetu* warned that "it is known that Indians write Swahili poorly in their business advertisements. Africans now do not want their language to be ruined. If they want to write Swahili advertisements it behooves them to make them written by *Waswahili*."[226] African caricatures of Kiswahili cha Wahindi (Indian Swahili) flourished during this period, proving a durable feature of the Indian stereotype.[227] Though few Africans, excepting some domestic servants, had a speaking command of Gujarati, most readily understood the meaning of the Gujarati epithet *golo*, literally "slave," that was used like the acid Swahili epithet *mshenzi*, "barbarian." The Gujarati language itself could be an unpopular reminder of racial inequality. A Dar es Salaam crowd listening to speeches condemning Tanganyika's possible return to Germany in 1938 shouted down a speaker who began in Gujarati.[228] Cultural distance inspired resentment. "The Indian is not a good person," offered one bitter African poet. "He does not share his education."[229] But cultural resentment also inspired fascination and curiosity. Hindi films attracted large African audiences, and Hindi music filled the streets of Kariakoo as it did those of Uhindini. An African woman in Kariakoo was believed to have been bewitched by an evil Indian spirit (*shetani*) after having sung along to a popular Hindi gramophone record, giving her the ability to speak Hindi. Conversely, many Indian youths mastered Swahili, speaking it freely to each other in urban public spaces.[230]

Although cultural exchange was neither as limited nor as hopeless as some African critics would have it, Indian organizational politics and religion presented steep-to-impossible barriers of African participation. Indian nationalists in Tanganyika rarely engaged African political concerns. When they did, they employed a condescending language of civilization to compete with similar paternalist claims of Europeans. Both groups assumed that Africans were evolving toward civilization—"The non-native has to play the role of a trustee till it has reached an advanced stage," the *Tanganyika Herald* asserted, parroting the official language of interwar colonial policy.[231] African critics claimed that Arab and European education had brought self-evident material benefits—*kanzu* (robe) and *suti* (suit)—as well as religious foundations, but that Indian education offered nothing comparably useful, transferable, or spiritual.[232] Hinduism presented near-insurmountable barriers to African participation, while the three major Indian Shia communities—Bohoras, Ismaili Khojas, and Ithnasheri Khojas—conducted religious and social activities on a similarly caste-like endogamous basis.

Indian Sunni Muslims, led by M. O. Abbasi (see above), attempted to bridge the yawning social distances between Indian and African Muslims through the establishment in 1926 of the Anjuman Islamiyya, an interracial welfare society that organized Islamic festivals, hosted speakers, and raised funds for African Islamic education. During the 1930s, however, leading African Muslims broke away from the Anjuman Islamiyya, in part as a strategy to exercise more control over the town's main Islamic festivals, but mainly to protest the failure of Indian Muslims to share financial wealth for African Islamic education. Led by Kleist Sykes, a group of African Muslims instead founded the Jamiatul Islamiyya, which in 1936 established a primary school to prepare African Muslim children for competition to enter government secondary schools.[233] The school was located inside the Jamiatul Islamiyya headquarters, at the edge of Kariakoo on New Street, just down the road from the African Association headquarters. Standing exactly opposite the Jamiatul Islamiyya, across the "neutral zone" created to separate native and non-native, was the Anjuman Islamiyya headquarters at the edge of Uhindini, symmetrical yet distant.

CONCLUSIONS

Although race was already the defining feature of Dar es Salaam's urban layout and administrative categories, it was also becoming the defining identification of interwar social life. Voluntarily or involuntarily, urban life was largely segregated by race. Daily interaction inevitably lay within—more than between—racial groups. For Indians, religious-communal consciousness competed with, and at times overrode, racial considerations. Anticolonial protests from India fired diasporic imaginations, orienting politics as much toward India and the British Empire as toward Africa. Struggles between *wenye mji* and *watu wa kuja*—relational identities in which the former invoked firstcomer authority to brake the latter's growing economic and political strength—played at least as important a role in the daily lives of Africans as did struggles between Africans and non-Africans. Race mattered most in those commercial and domestic spaces where Africans and Indians met. Africans both admired and envied Indians' commercial and political success, while deeply resenting that such success appeared to come at their expense.

European colonial policies bear tremendous explanatory weight in historiographical accounts of the growth of ethnic consciousness in Africa. This is particularly true for interwar Tanganyika, where Iliffe's argument—that policies of indirect rule established the framework whereby Africans and administrators together "created" tribes—remains an exemplary case for instrumentalist explanations of identity formation. Dar es Salaam, however, came under a system of direct rule remarkable in both its inconsistencies and inattention to "subracial" urban identities. Fine gradations of ancestral prestige, so important to coastal Swahili culture and relational identities of *wenye mji*, had little purchase among urban administrators. Thus it was in debates among African colonial subjects themselves that the crucial dyad of interwar urban identity—indigene versus outsider—developed; terms deeply entrenched in African political culture but irrelevant to urban officials harnessed to the legal-administrative language of tribe and native/non-native. The economic and demographic revolutions brought about by the Second World War, however, rapidly overshadowed the salience of the dyad *wenye mji/watu wa kuja* by racializing urban distribution and consumption, while paradoxically accelerating the destruction of segregationist zoning. The racialization of Dar es Salaam's economy during the Second World War and the increasing power of racial nationalist thought and organization are the subjects of the following two chapters.

3 ⤺ Posing the Urban Question
War, State Intervention, and the Creation of Urban Entitlement

*Though the cost of living in Dar es Salaam is extremely high,
the standard of living is woefully low.*

—A. H. Pike, Dar es Salaam District Commissioner

The lack of money is the root of most evils.

—Erica Fiah, Editor of *Kwetu*

SOMETIME AROUND THE YEAR 1939, Dar es Salaam's rate of population growth leaped from its interwar pace of 2 percent to around 8 percent. This latter rate of growth has prevailed, more or less, up to the present.[1] Relevant "push" factors of rural taxation, communal labor requirements, and brittle chiefly power, as well as "pull" factors of better food security, employment opportunities, and educational facilities, had existed for decades, but were strengthened by sweeping wartime economic transformations and a postwar economic boom that sustained comparatively high urban wages into the 1950s and 1960s. This shift toward rapid urban population growth had many implications, but its immediate effect was to stress the town's fragile distributive economy. A sharp rise in demand for food, textiles, and housing in the early 1940s threatened the town's very political security. Urban distribution became too important to entrust to traders and markets alone. The ad hoc interwar system of urban growth management by separate administrative departments yielded to a fundamental reordering of Dar es Salaam's wartime economy by a more purposeful and coordinated colonial state. Racial identifications were built anew upon state intervention in the distribution of food, clothing, and housing.

The colonial state in Tanganyika grew immensely more ambitious during the 1940s, and stands as the major actor of this chapter. Nicholas J. Westcott offers a useful framework for understanding the state's new motivations and subsequent dilemmas. With the war-induced trend toward a closed economy, the colonial administration proved unable to cope with simultaneous demands made on it by Africans, on the one hand, and British national interests, on the other. The degree of control necessary to fulfill its development policies and manage the economy required Africans' minimal popular consent, which the state failed to secure.[2] Although it failed, scholars widely agree that the significance of the wartime colonial state lay in its novel efforts to secure consent. Frederick Cooper and others have argued that the relationship between imperial policy and local labor movements form the framework for understanding both urbanization and decolonization in sub-Saharan Africa during the 1940s and 1950s.[3] While labor was undoubtedly significant, this chapter argues that the city was first and foremost a site of consumption. The war became a time of ration cards across urban Africa. State control over access to that most basic of necessities, food, had the unintended consequence of sharpening claims on state resources, as well as on the identity categories that mediated access to resources.[4] It is access to the commoditized necessities of urban life that composed the lion's share of what Cooper terms the "labor question" (i.e., the colonial state's coming to terms with a large and settled urban African working class). Costs and availability of food, clothing, and housing—though relational to prevailing wages—warrant far more attention, both as primary subject of political debate and principal object of economic activity, than previous academic literature has suggested.[5] Urban transport workers undoubtedly played a key role. As Timothy Oberst argues, they took particular advantage of their "singularly strategic position within the colonial economy to extract allowances," while the prospect of rural revolt posed no analogous "convincing threat."[6] But as this chapter will demonstrate, the presence of transport workers only increased, rather than singularly defined, the political significance of urban space to wartime colonial regimes.

Urban population growth challenged state commitments to maintain minimal urban living standards, posing an "urban question" to both the state and its subjects. The origins of "urban appeasement"—those regulatory policies that reduced urban living costs, particularly that of food, at the cost of rural producers and subsequently distorted postcolonial Africa's agricultural policies[7]—are located in the wartime creation of what this chapter terms "urban entitlement." The term is defined here as a set of spatially defined legal rights to minimum necessities through the state regulation of market transactions.[8] This phenomenon emerged in Tanganyika during the Second World War as the creation of a new bundle of spatially defined entitlements for legal urban residents—universal food and clothing rations, rent controls, and employment-based government housing. For the colonial government, urban entitlement initially meant the right to a minimum standard of living in return for the obligation to pursue a transparent and fully employed working life. The subsequent political economy of Dar es Salaam formed a constellation of concerns within which residents identified themselves along racial lines, despite sharply growing class differentiation between renters and landlords, or between casual and full-time workers. African renters and workers drew attention to stark inequalities that separated Europeans, Asians, and Africans, recasting paternalist rhetoric of civilization and wartime sacrifice into more-confrontational language that emphasized racial unity and equality with unfairly privileged races. During the 1940s, firstcomer arguments of *wenye mji* indigenes, which had loomed large during the interwar decades in making claims and counterclaims to political authority, were supplanted by a racialized discourse of urban entitlement. Paradoxically, the language of urban entitlement initially represented a progressive policy shift that marked a partial abandonment of residential segregation as well as the paternalistic language of "native" and "non-native," and moreover explicitly recognized the permanency of African urban life. But in its implementation, urban entitlement served to racialize urban life far more than any interwar colonial policy.

WAR, POLICY, AND URBAN ENTITLEMENT

During the Second World War, cost-of-living regulations replaced segregationist town planning as the central feature of Tanganyika's urban policy. Food and manufactured commodity imports fell, while immigration from the countryside increased. In 1939, labor unrest at urban dockyards and charges that Indian shopkeepers were profiteering began forcing the government to reevaluate its commitments. Fearing the political instability that arises from sharp increases in urban living costs, the government increased the minimum wage for its own African employees in 1940. Subsequent charges from consumers of wartime profiteering by Asian middlemen begat further state intervention, which culminated in a full-blown rationing system for urban residents in 1943. Systematic regulatory controls were extended over food, textiles, and housing rents, as well as on "native" and "non-native" immigration in order to provide a minimal quality of life for those Africans deemed sufficiently productive (i.e., those who were visibly and fully employed) to warrant urban entitlement, while minimizing the presence of the "nonproductive" under- and unemployed.

Intensified regulatory control of basic necessities and immigration resulted from wartime decisions made by local officials. Focusing on Colonial Office initiatives, Cooper has argued that its Africa policy reached a critical juncture on the eve of the war:

> In 1939, the labor question was assimilated into the development question. And in those terms it remained. The development framework was elaborated in two contexts during the war years: the debate

over constitutional structures and political evolution and the debate over production and the standard of living.[9]

Through legislation such as the 1940 Colonial Development and Welfare Act, the Colonial Office sought control over urban African workers by improving their living standards and social services. But in Tanganyika, local officials sought development through regulation rather than expenditure. Moreover, the most striking disjuncture between London and Dar es Salaam was over the labor question. The Colonial Office's guiding principle was to maximize African labor output to meet wartime commodity demands. Tanganyikan administrators feared political and practical problems that zealous labor extraction—through closer conscription and tax enforcement—might produce. Instead of bringing the full brunt of state compulsion to bear on "unproductive" urban Africans to realize greater rural production, local officials more modestly sought to limit urban entitlement to a finite number of "productive" Africans through mobility controls and tax payment verification. Arguments for and commitments to these policies grew over the 1940s, but the initial template—rent controls, minimum wages, food rations, decasualization, and forcible repatriation—had already been laid out in the government's official inquiry into Tanga's port strikes in August 1939.[10]

The "labor question" of how best to create an urban working class consisting of fully employed permanent African residents was an important aspect, but only one aspect, of a looming *urban question*—how to create livable and manageable urban space through price and population controls. Ruinous wartime inflation in food, textiles, and housing had undoubtedly impoverished many urban workers in port cities like Mombasa.[11] Policymakers' decisions to decasualize transport and other urban jobs, to be accomplished in part through new urban immigration controls, was an answer that sought to ameliorate these impoverishing factors, but, in Cooper's view, was only a secondary consideration to the primary goal of creating a stable laboring class. "The bias of colonial states was not an urban bias per se," Cooper concludes in his foundational study on Mombasa dockworkers, "but a concern with creating a differentiated urban working class in contrast to the dangerous urban mass."[12] This chapter argues differently, that the colonial state was not *firstly* concerned with creating such a working class, though this certainly was *a* priority. Rather, it was first concerned with creating *a form of urban entitlement* that would enable it to manage critical variables of food, housing, consumer goods, and human mobility, upon which rested not simply worker impoverishment, but the very political security of a town beleaguered by threats and strikes not only from urban workers, but also from urban consumers and distributors. There was a "Manichaean tendency" in 1940s official thinking "to separate the domain of reform from the domain of backwardness,"[13] as Cooper argues. This chapter investigates the profound spatial implications of this thought as it was interpreted and implemented by officials on the ground.

MINIMUM GUARANTEES: POLITICAL SECURITY AND THE REGULATION OF FOOD, TEXTILES, AND HOUSING

A wariness born of present threats and future political uncertainty enveloped Dar es Salaam during the Second World War. Rumors had long circulated among Africans that Germans were determined to return. With much to fear from this eventuality, Tanganyikans of all races—although Ismailis and British settlers were the most keen—made effusive pledges of loyalty and generous contributions to war charities, amounting to £347,094 by 1945.[14] Security officials focused on internal threats from imprisoned Nazi Bund members and suspected spies who might foster "rebellion on the part of Tanganyika Africans."[15] Fears of external threats peaked after the fall of Singapore in February 1942, when a town defense organization that included twenty African sentinel groups was formed to coordinate responses to potential Japanese air raids. Public slit trenches were dug; blackouts and other civil defense drills became part of daily routine.[16] But the overwhelming fear among officials concerned urban political security. At the war's outbreak, one official predicted riots in Dar es Salaam, "because of the cost of food and lack of wages to pay for it."[17] The Dar es Salaam District was a net food importer, as was the surrounding Eastern Province.[18] Tanganyika's food import dependence had steadily increased over the 1930s, with little official encouragement given to grain production. Whether produced on town outskirts, hundreds of miles away, or imported from overseas, food in commodity form reached Dar es Salaam's urban consumers through a network dominated by Indian wholesalers and retailers. Indian merchant capital, only loosely regulated through trade licensing, coordinated most of Dar es Salaam's food provision, alongside local subsistence production.[19]

The urban question was first posed by a crisis in food distribution. Despite awareness that urban living costs outpaced wages, that many African workers subsisted on one meal a day, and that most relied on consumer credit to make ends meet, officials hardly addressed the problem of a living wage during the 1930s. Labor agitation on the docks of Tanga and Dar es Salaam in 1939 had forcibly raised the living wage issue, and impending war moved the government to arm itself with far-reaching regulatory powers.[20] Through these powers, administrators attempted to guarantee an urban living wage by exercising powers over each component of urban living costs, the most important of which was food. To meet the coming autarchy of war, maximum wholesale and retail prices were fixed on most foodstuffs, while wholesalers and retailers had to obtain official permission to sell controlled foods in townships. By 1940, nearly every food staple in Dar es Salaam District carried a maximum price, with sharp fines and long imprisonment for offenders.[21]

Tanganyika's wartime challenge was to maximize export revenues from rural production while maintaining minimally adequate urban living standards. Inflation proved the greatest enemy. The American entry into the war stimulated an international commodity boom, creating insatiable demand for Tanganyika's previously unwanted exports. Subservient to metropole commodity demands, the Tanganyikan state was, in Nicholas J. Westcott's words, "left chasing its tail in a downward spiral of enforcement and inflation, trying to increase production with an ever-diminishing supply of imports."[22] Exporting up to twice what it imported, Tanganyika ran large trade surpluses between 1938 and 1946, which lay credited as sterling balances in London. Across East Africa, currency in circulation more than doubled between 1940 and 1945, while availability of consumer goods like bicycles, hoes, and textiles dropped precipitously.[23] Inflation became the era's signature phenomenon — average prices of identical goods doubled between 1938/39 and 1945, and trebled between 1939 and 1949.[24] The stated purpose of Tanganyika's fiscal policy, embodied in customs duties, restricted producer prices, and taxation, was no longer to cover administration expenses but to contain inflation.[25] By 1942, Tanganyika was at last integrated into Britain's imperial economy through defense exchange controls, whose primary purpose was to protect the sterling area from draining away gold and dollars through imports from nonsterling countries.[26] Reckoning the pound overvalued, Asian investors fled from holding currency altogether, and instead embraced speculative land investment and valuable metals. By 1944, Indian merchants in Dar es Salaam had eschewed British war bonds, bid up gold to double its sovereign price in Britain and land to four times its prewar value, and expected the pound's buying power to drop "to eight or even five shillings."[27] Growing incomes chased dwindling consumer goods. Urban consumers, who depended more on market than subsistence production, bore the brunt of shortages and inflation. In April 1940, only eight months after a violent dockworker strike in town, Tanga's provincial commissioner estimated that the cost of living within those months had risen 40 percent, and considered it imperative that government raise unskilled worker wages by 33 percent, which it soon did for all its African laborers in Dar es Salaam and Tanga.[28] The potential for urban hunger and unrest was measurably rising.

Yet the specter of open-ended, inflationary fiscal commitments to urban centers acted as a brake on state initiatives to improve living standards. Officials responsible for large payrolls hesitated to endorse wage increases. The ensuing debate demonstrates that the labor question invoked a larger debate about colonial economics and coordinated administrative responses to war-time crises. The Tanganyika Railways manager argued that administrators' first duty was to raise "National Income," and that raising government wages would only encourage private enterprise to depress their wages to meet higher government costs.[29] The Director of Public Works concurred, and offered an argument that was appealingly pragmatic and frugal, which would guide much of Tanganyika's official approach to controlling living standards:

> Irrespective of the "market" cost of foodstuffs Tanganyika has a surplus—a surplus which it cannot just now encash—this is (if prop-erly handled) nothing less than money lying idle. . . . The contention is that the wages paid are insufficient to buy the food necessary for physical health and well being. Government in the country is faced with surplus products including foodstuffs. Why not then solve the problem by the enforced issue of rations. . . . Food control or no food control a rise in wages will inevitably result in the rise in the local "market price" of foodstuffs.[30]

Although long resisted by town employers, officials now came to agree that providing rationed food at the workplace was the most responsible and cost-effective means to ameliorate urban labor conditions.

The growing influence of the Labor Office entrenched government's theo-retical commitment to a living urban wage. The key figure was M. J. B. Molohan, who arrived in Dar es Salaam in mid-1941 as the town's labor officer. He car-ried with him two convictions about urban administration—that there must be a wage for unskilled labor commensurate with the cost of living, and that the mass of unemployed Africans should be confronted with augmented state powers to prevent further unwanted immigration and to repatriate the unpro-ductive.[31] When railway workers threatened to strike in late 1941, Tanganyika's Labor Board concluded that their demands were "not so much a demand for higher wages as a protest against the rise in the cost of necessities of life."[32] Of these necessities, food was the most critical—by the early 1940s, it accounted for between 44 and 52 percent of African household expenditures in Dar es Salaam. Food had become the most important issue on the docks of Dar es Salaam and Mombasa alike.[33] Fearful of a second wage increase and cynical about African budgetary discipline, the Labor Board agreed to provide rations to railway workers. Rations would not only avoid inflationary pressures created by wage increases, but would be cost-effective, buying in bulk food that cost twice as much at retail. Rations were extended to the lowest-paid government port laborers in Tanga and Dar es Salaam by mid-1942.[34] Molohan's report on Dar es Salaam living costs determined that 87 percent of the town's lowest-tier government employees were receiving less than a living wage. "Because of this lack of proper food," he appealed to other officials who would read his report, "a considerable portion of the population of Dar es Salaam are becoming unemployable."[35]

Political security first required food security. Located at a strategic regional transport nexus and potentially vulnerable to Axis attack, Dar es Salaam administrators could not afford to indulge themselves in the optimistic notion that unseen "family farms" would supply what urban wages could not. Retail distribution systems fell under closer scrutiny. The underweighing and adulteration of foodstuffs, long a complaint of African consumers, now posed an existential threat for administrators. Comprehensive price controls were enacted in late 1941 to avoid strikes. "The fires burning below should be damped with action," a district officer explained. "A general increase in wages followed by an efficient and adamant price control is essential—not only to Scotch the danger of inflation but to quell latent trouble."[36] In 1943, Tanganyika experienced a territory wide food shortage. In the short term, rain failures had reduced supplies; in the medium term, an unprecedented shift from subsistence to cash crops among price-sensitive cultivators and a newly conscripted wage labor force had reduced supply while greatly increasing demand.[37] To safeguard its urban living wage policy, the government responded by extending food rations to all its permanent employees in Dar es Salaam and Tanga.[38] Demands for ration entitlements spread among nongovernmental workers, who made up three-fourths of the capital's labor force.[39] Dockworkers employed by private firms complained that "we do not get any posho while we see that all kinds of employees are being provided with the ration, that is in the departments. . . . The government all gets rations, may we say that those who gets it are the Governments citizens?"[40] The principal protest of Dar es Salaam's dockworker strike that occurred in August 1943, a few months after the introduction of comprehensive urban rationing, concerned the poor quality and quantity of workplace food, which was, according to the subsequent tribunal, "not properly cooked, that is was not cleanly served and that, owing to the number of men crowding round the food containers, something in the nature of a scramble ensued with the result that on busy days those who arrived last for food got little."[41] Even small employers such as charcoal and copra manufacturers found it necessary to feed workers because of food shortages.[42] By attempting to provide a living wage to its own employees through manipulation of the urban economy, the government alerted other workers to their rights to state redistribution of basic necessities implicit in urban entitlement. A comprehensive ration scheme for Dar es Salaam was finally enacted in April 1943, in part to address severe shortages that enabled wholesalers— who had hitherto endured little scrutiny—to sell food and piece goods for prices higher than controlled retail prices.[43] Tanganyika's Economic Control Board, the unloved "great octopus of control" formed two years after the war's outbreak, initially oversaw the scheme's implementation by registering each town inhabitant and issuing ration cards to purchase food at selected sites in April 1943. Registration for the new scheme turned up nearly 45,000 Africans living in Dar es Salaam, when the number was thought to be only 33,000.[44]

By guaranteeing food access, the rationing scheme gave immediate and unprecedented material meaning to urban space. Both before and after the war, there was never a neat separation between rural and urban—rural ties were retained by most residents of Dar es Salaam for a host of reasons to do with security, welfare, affective relations, and opportunities in petty trade and in agriculture. What changed was the universal and abstract nature of entitlement, symbolized in official prices and ration coupons, and effectively mediated (as we shall see) through identity categories of race, rather than through interpersonal relations of patronage. Although controlled prices were not cheap and quality was often abysmal, comprehensive rationing entrenched a basic level of urban food security that had no rural counterpart. Africans flocked to the capital to take advantage of new state guarantees, particularly from the Rufiji and Morogoro areas. Whatever the town's many hardships, few if any ever starved in Dar es Salaam. By June 1943, just two months after the introduction of comprehensive rations, the government was issuing nearly five times as many weekly coupons as it had people officially registered to receive them. African ration cards thereafter required proof of residence in Dar es Salaam, further formalizing urban entitlement. Food consumption increased from 2,700 bags during harvest season in July 1943 to 7,000 bags by December, when food shortages had reduced neighboring rural Africans to digging up edible roots.[45] To meet overwhelming urban demand, officials abolished the decades-old auction system and gazetted all major food crops as "controlled produce," requiring producers to sell at fixed prices to licensed traders. Low fixed prices discouraged producers from bringing crops to market; most of the eight thousand farmers who came to Dar es Salaam weekly instead sold produce on the black market or directly to consumers. Sharp trading practices flourished. Fruits and fish had been left uncontrolled, but when officials found that fishmongers were making 100 percent profits, they took steps to regulate their sale.[46] Police found 71 percent of measuring weights inspected across Tanganyika were incorrect, and prosecuted thirty people for criminal offense.[47] Exhaustion and pessimism grew among regulators. In Tabora, a young Julius Nyerere worked as a government price inspector; he later recalled that both shopkeepers and the government ignored his price violation reports.[48] Yet frequent failures to attain regulatory compliance did not reduce the wide-ranging significance of the new regulatory regime. Urban rationing attracted rural immigrants seeking food security, rural producers seeking black market profits, and middlemen seeking to arbitrate within widening black market margins, with the effect of strengthening commercial linkages between town and countryside.

Food ensured survival. Clothing expressed honor and status. The common denominator surrounding consumer demand for clothing in coastal East Africa remained as it had a century earlier—clothing's ability to serve as a "visually immediate signifier of class and status" and "to bring recognition and envy"—as Laura Fair and Jeremy Prestholdt respectively argue.[49] For men, clothing not only reflected their own respectability, but demonstrated their wealth and ability to satisfy women's allegedly insatiable lust (*tamaa*) for fashion.[50] No wartime commodity proved more inflationary than textiles. This was partly attributable to the war itself: cheap Japanese cotton goods had flooded Tanganyika in the 1930s—increasing their market share from 17.6 percent in 1929 to 82.1 percent by 1936—at the direct expense of Indian and British manufacturers. Japanese imports enabled depression-era Tanganyikans to maintain or even slightly increase their clothing purchases despite greatly reduced incomes.[51] Following war's outbreak, however, more expensive and poorer-quality Bombay textiles replaced Japanese goods, removing what was in effect a consumer subsidy. Yet African sartorial demand was undeterred and proved inelastic in the face of reduced supplies, thus creating a lucrative realm for profiteering. Between 1939 and 1943, the quantity of cotton piece goods imported into Tanganyika fell by nearly one half, while the price per yard increased more than six times—foodstuffs by comparison generally rose only about 50 percent during the same period.[52] The Economic Control Board considered the chief offenders to be local wholesalers and the custom of "snowballing" price increases by retailers.[53] Wholesale merchants "deliberately and systematically" broke the law by issuing false receipts with controlled prices to retailers when transactions had been for much more; retailers rarely complained for fear of being cut off.[54] Price gouging inspired consumer strikes. When prices for *kaniki* and *kanga* (two popular textile styles) leaped 50 percent in 1942, consumers in the surrounding Uzaramo district boycotted shops until prices returned to near their original level.[55] By 1943, supplies had grown so scarce that textiles were unobtainable in Dar es Salaam as well as up-country; their absence was also noticeably discouraging local market production.[56] "The Indians are selling as they like," one African consumer complained, accusing them of concealing the most recent *kanga* designs in their homes and requiring advanced payments.[57] With maximum prices being ubiquitously ignored, textiles fell under a system of state rationing in 1944. Despite strong demand in rural Uzaramo, officials restricted textile rations to those consumers who could produce a food ration card or other proof of urban residency.[58] Textile entitlements delineated the city even further as a site of consumption by spatially differentiating the means to express social status.

Housing, scarce in ways similar to food and textiles, proved to affect political security such that the state committed itself to expand both its provision and its regulation. New economic and demographic pressures shifted administrative concern away from regulating housing growth through racial zoning and toward securing adequate housing for its urban residents. Regulation trumped expenditure once more as the favored response. Overcrowding had become so severe in Dar es Salaam that, in order to relieve housing pressures, the chief secretary begged the military to arrange special wartime passage to India for some three hundred Indian families living in town.[59] Sharp restrictions were also placed on Indian immigration to wartime Tanganyika, which dropped from an average of 1,110 immigrants per annum during 1930–1939 to 348 per annum during 1940–1945.[60] Indian tenants had been the first to push for rent controls by forming a Tenants Association in 1936, asking Tanganyika to adopt Kenyan legislation geared toward curbing "the increasing rapacity of our landlords."[61] The government agreed to rent controls in 1941 after relentless petitions from this association, despite protests from the similarly Indian-dominated Property Owners Association. Africans did not create a similar renters association during the war, distrusted the rent control board, and rarely sought its arbitration.[62] Finding implementation of any African rent control a "monumental task," Dar es Salaam's district officer, Dick Bone, urgently suggested that the government build more African housing, "supplemented by a subsidiary measure of some form of restriction of immigration into the Township."[63] Here, as elsewhere, regulating African mobility was viewed as the key to solving the colonial government's urban problem.

MOBILITY AND URBAN ENTITLEMENT

Part of the government's solution to its own "urban question"—how best to create livable and manageable urban space in order to maintain political security—was to reduce the number of casual workers and consumers by combating urban immigration. The irrefutable phenomena of rising urban population, skyrocketing urban costs, and declining real wages had fractured official consensus on labor policy in the late 1930s. Previous complacent assertions about equilibrium of supply and demand now clearly required revision. At the heart of the new labor policy debate was the suddenly inscrutable motives of the migrant African worker. Interwar labor officers and employers had shared the convenient conviction that migrant workers held strictly defined target cash incomes, with income elasticity of demand for wage goods approaching zero. In other words, wage increases would not result in any commensurate increases in worker production or consumer spending, but would instead simply shorten the stay of target-minded and homeward-bound migrant workers to their extended rural families.[64] While this conviction died hard among policy advisers obsessed with estate labor scarcity—in particular Granville St. John Orde-Brown[65]—officials in Dar es Salaam recognized that the town's swelling and underemployed population required new thinking. Extended families were no longer the mythical sources of rural security for underpaid and target-oriented bachelors, but rather visible consumers of urban resources that threatened political security. Focus instead shifted from labor scarcity to resource scarcity. Although there was no consensus over the specific range and methods of urban entitlements, officials unanimously agreed that they should be restricted to the "productive" African, envisioned as a full-time male laborer who headed a monogamous nuclear household of limited dependents. Except for limited military and railway housing, Dar es Salaam was never a "barracks" city that housed migrant adult male workers in compounds like interwar Nairobi or many industrial towns in southern Africa, and thus the transformation to household-based policies had fewer institutional impediments.[66] Eliminating the unemployed and casual workers on marginal wages, this new reasoning went, would conserve scarce urban resources for responsible employers and employees alike. "The old theory is that supply and demand automatically readjusted themselves," the town's district officer explained, "but that will not hold here as the supply is governed by other factors such as infant employment, the urge towards the town and a hard core of unemployable persons."[67] The ideal was to create a settled and well-paid urban workforce that would produce more than it consumed, and to eliminate the unemployed and casual workers who were immune to discipline because they had no permanent jobs to lose. But high wages carried the risk of creating extended families with multiplying unproductive members. E. C. Baker warned that "unless or until, the town can be purged of its unemployed a percentage of any increase of pay will be filched from the worker by his more needy relatives and tribesmen."[68] This fragile urban space of comparatively high wages and urban entitlements could be sustained only through a regimen of mobility control that targeted unproductive consumers.

Efforts to restrict African urban immigration, however, revealed deep legal and administrative incapacities. A short-lived identification system for urban residents had been introduced in 1938 based on African tax registration, but foundered on inefficiencies of the town's ramshackle native administration system.[69] It was an ironic strategy of urban control, as young men had long come to Dar es Salaam partly to escape more-efficient rural tax regimes. During the interwar years, tax collection had been, according to Andrew Burton, "an exercise of sovereign not disciplinary power," which, far from internalizing market discipline, was characterized by short bouts of heavy-handed enforcement by local headmen who were generally outmatched by savvy evaders. Up to three-quarters of the town's taxpayers were in default by 1934.[70] Annual October "tax wars," in which revenue officers chased defaulters through the backstreets of Kariakoo and Ilala, became a prominent feature of urban life during the Second World War, making it plain that Tanganyika's administrative capital was also its center of unorganized resistance to British fiscal impositions.[71] In response, the state took up the task of systematically repatriating the under- and unemployed *wahuni*.[72] In September 1940, the government enacted a statute that empowered officials to repatriate any "undesirable inhabitant or sojourner" living in a township. Repatriation was wildly popular among Eu-ropean and Indian residents. More prosperous Africans viewed it with mixed emotions—some celebrated the removal of would-be thieves and layabouts, but also expressed unease at the treatment meted out to defaulters, whom one writer described as being handled "as the Arabs were handling their slaves."[73] Yet, just as *wahuni* removals began in earnest in March 1941, a territorial jus-tice declared the statute *ultra vires* (outside the law) on grounds that it violated African civil liberties. The administration responded with makeshift legislation under wartime powers.[74] Most surprisingly, government departments began to think alike. The increase in visibly destitute Africans in Dar es Salaam who slept on open verandas and in public markets moved the Township Authority to pass a resolution eliminating casual labor, controlling immigration from the country, and organizing relief for the homeless.[75] The Economic Con-trol Board led an interdepartmental lobbying effort in early 1944 for greater migration controls, arguing that continued uncontrolled growth threatened urban food security.[76] Tanganyika's governor requested London's permission to introduce pass law legislation to control African movement, to ease "diffi-culties in connection with efficient distribution and rationing of foodstuffs."[77] Clinging to interwar assumptions about labor, the Colonial Office responded that "a more productive and satisfactory way of dealing with them would be to conscript them for work on sisal, rubber, food or other essential produc-tion," for such action would "probably have a salutary effect on the townward trend," and would be preferred to "merely driving them back to idleness in the tribal areas."[78] Massive labor conscription had long been territorial policy and not limited to military service—84,501 men were conscripted for production work and civil purposes between 1940 and 1945, at its peak amounting to 8.4 percent of the total wage force.[79] But Tanganyikan officials understood mass conscription was simply impractical. At the outbreak of war, only 10 percent of military service volunteers in Dar es Salaam were deemed healthy enough for service.[80] The Colonial Office overruled compulsory urban registration, fearing it might conflict with mandate terms, and the incipient pass law system was dropped entirely.[81]

The Tanganyika government responded as it always had, by improvising. Yet this particular improvisation marked a major departure from interwar urban statecraft. Not only did all departments fully agree on policy, but they directed untypical energy and resources toward its implementation. For Africans at the receiving end, the colonial state was for the first time reaching deep into their daily lives. Using the legal tools it had, the government embarked on its first major "de-spiving" campaign to remove tax defaulters and the otherwise unemployed in 1944.[82] The process was heavy-handed in the extreme. "Those who are of tax-paying age," as an officer later described it, "are rounded up daily by a team of tax clerks and a Jumbe but since the practice of tying their wrists together has dropped out, a good many fish get through the mesh."[83] Most repatriated *wahuni* originated from Eastern Province itself, and had little trouble in finding their way back to town. Yet, despite its Sisyphean absurdities, repatriation became a central feature of urban policy over the next four decades. Such corporal interventions, among the rawest of routinized state acts to occur in Tanganyika, did not simply result from colonial anxiety toward urban riffraff, but rather expressed a determined calculus that redefined urban space as a site of minimal entitlements. Such a calculus further immunized the fabric of urban space from the historical claims of firstcomers over land-ownership, tribal custodianship, and local office that had figured, however unevenly, in the political debates of the previous two decades. Urban space would now have to be claimed within the new terms of regulating economic exchange.

POLITICS OF THE MARKETPLACE

Tanganyika's interwar policymakers had prided themselves in resisting the legal-administrative entrenchment of sharply defined racial categories. Unlike neighboring Kenya and Zanzibar, Tanganyika had deftly avoided questions of racial representation in local government, arguing that it would "certainly not subscribe to the idea that Government, local or central, can be infinitely racialized or organized on a racial basis."[84] Yet increased state intervention in Dar es Salaam's wartime economy required more-rigorous categories of local administration, and new means to solicit consent. Wartime policies and subsequent "community" lobbying breathed bitter new life into debates over identity, urban space, and consumption. Most visible was the racialized system of food and goods rationing, which John Iliffe has argued "led to an increased categorisation which stimulated racial consciousness."[85] The statist urban economy of the 1940s raised the political stakes of group representation, placed racially hierarchical entitlements and their accompanying humiliations into public view, and further widened gaps in urban living standards along racial lines.

Food rations were a universal but unequal urban entitlement. Types and amounts differed according to "community needs." The resulting hierarchy was the product of colonial biases and vigorous political lobbying. When the program was launched in April 1943, the government contacted presidents of each Asian communal organization—but no African organizations—to ascertain population figures, and began what became negotiations over the size of communal ration allotments.[86] Subsequent lobbying for rations employed religious and regional differences within Dar es Salaam's Asian community; communal stereotypes were ruthlessly exploited to claim specific commodities. Punjabis secured large wheat ration allotments by arguing that they were strong-bodied artisans who needed more than one pound of wheat flour, a staple of their "traditional" diet. Gujaratis, Kachchhis, and Madrasis received differing proportions of wheat and rice in accordance with their diets.[87] The Ismaili-owned *Africa Sentinel* dramatized Ismaili dependence on atta and rice, and that it was "inhuman to deprive the community of its natural food."[88] Dar es Salaam's Hindus insisted that their children must have sugar candy as a "daily essential to life."[89] The Economic Control Board, staffed by European and Asian members but no Africans, determined that only Europeans and Asians would receive wheat flour—even though Africans had previously consumed three-quarters of the town's wheat—and that rice be rationed to Asians and to those Arabs and Africans who "customarily" consumed rice.[90] To secure rice and other highly sought commodities, Arabs and Africans stressed their immigrant origins. Recent Arab immigrants had themselves counted as "Asians" and were thus entitled to wheat, as well as to twice the sugar allotted to Africans; "local" Arabs, however, were treated as Africans.[91] *Watu wa kuja* "immigrants" claiming to originate from outside Tanganyika lobbied for separate food rights. The success of their claims depended on improvised colonial accounting. In order to stem a run on ghee, the Township Authority cut out "Zulus, Somalis, Nyasas and all sorts of other persons" who had registered as Arabs for superior rations, on the grounds that they had not paid non-native poll tax.[92] At the bottom was the ration category "African" or "native"—the latter was beginning to fall out of favor, but terms were used interchangeably and inconsistently. It was the lowest rung from which those who could climb out did.

Yet a powerful sense of aggrieved and defiant honor was nurtured at the lowest rung. Dar es Salaam's food rationing system generated petty and unceasing public humiliation. African ration cards required weekly renewal by queuing in person; non-African cards lasted a month and could be obtained by mail. Hours of queuing in the hot sun, first for cards and then for rations, led to physical collapse and sometimes even death among the old and infirm.[93] A district officer averted a riot by quickly procuring a ration card for a prominent elderly African Muslim, who had taken offense to having to queue while "young Asians of no prestige at all could get theirs in the mail by a written application."[94] Such racial humiliations also mocked rhetoric about shared wartime sacrifice. Why was it that only Africans had to queue, one *Kwetu* reader asked, when "Europeans and Asians and all of us fight for *uhuru*."[95] Indian food control supervisors entered African homes and seized ration cards on suspicion of fraud, inspiring profound antipathy.[96] Talk of food itself became racialized. While Indians enjoyed wheat bread appropriate to their brown-skinned privilege, Africans endured inferior products made of "soya, flour, maize, ten-year-old millet and cassava all mixed together" that produced a "hard loaf as black as he is."[97] The result was a marked increase in what the provincial commissioner termed "race-consciousness" among Africans in 1943; partly attributable to the "superior facilities which Asians, [Africans] consider, have of obtaining stocks of food when they, the Africans, are at times unable to obtain cereals even on production of coupons."[98] Employing the language of imperial loyalty, *wenye mji* elders opposed the appointment of an Indian to the presidency of Dar es Salaam's Township Authority, arguing that Indians already sell food and control its distribution as food control clerks, and therefore should not preside over the body that oversaw food distribution. "We are not Indian but British subjects; and we are under English masters," they appealed after ten months of food rationing. "We do not want to be ruled by Indians."[99]

Prolonged scarcity and racial inequity in food and housing formed the foundation of popular racial politics in Dar es Salaam. For urban consumers the immediate postwar years proved the most difficult in the town's history. Continued reliance on price controls in the face of robust black market sales, coupled with catastrophic rain failures led the provincial commissioner to declare that 1946 would be remembered "as being one of the bleakest in living memory."[100] Zaramo recalled this period as *njaa ya kadi*, or "card famine," associating the state control of food distribution with famine.[101] Textiles grew scarcer still—India's mills fell further behind demand, while demobilized soldiers and sisal workers were assigned priority for the receipt of imports. In 1946, territorial drought and locust attacks forced the government to reinstate wheat and butter rationing, as well as to reduce the size of maize and rice rations.[102] Accusations of Indian profiteering reached new heights. At least one rural branch of the African Association was founded with the primary goal of pressuring the district commissioner to arrest an Indian merchant who had hoarded textiles, rice, and sugar to sell on the black market.[103] Widespread charges of exploitation, sharper commodity shortages, and deep pockets of famine across the territory provided the contextual tinderbox in which a series of public events in Dar es Salaam would transform racial resentments into popular politics.

The year 1946, Tanganyika's *annus horribilis* of drought, famine, and commodity shortage, was also the fiftieth anniversary or "Diamond Jubilee" of the Aga Khan's reign as living Imam of East Africa's wealthiest Indian community, the Khoja Ismailis. To honor his Diamond Jubilee, twenty thousand Ismailis converged upon Dar es Salaam in August 1946 for an enormous feast on a hundred-acre site in Upanga, culminating in the weighing of the Aga Khan on a scale that matched his own hefty weight with an (apparent) equal weight of diamonds on the other side. Part of the celebration inaugurated the Diamond Jubilee Investment Trust, an Ismaili-only borrowing trust for businesses and properties to which the Aga Khan contributed one-quarter of the trust's capital to demonstrate long-term Ismaili investment in the country. The event placed enormous stress on already-scarce food and housing stocks. In the months leading up to the event, accusations of Ismaili food hoarding grew widespread and formal charges were made; African grain rations were reduced by 15 percent to manage pending territorial food shortages, and "non-African" counterfeit coupons accelerated the drawdown of bread and flour stocks.[104] Non-Africans consumed more; their impact on scarce supplies and manageable entitlements was increasingly called into question by Africans. "We have come to realize that the number of Asiatics in this town is very great," one African resident observed, asking that the government "see to it that the number of those Indians who lead a parasitic life in this town are sent back to India until the shortage is over."[105] Tensions ran high—in June 1946, an Indian who had refused to give alms to a beggar eventually hit him, upon which a crowd gathered, shouting, "Hit the Indians."[106] Sensitive to further violent reaction that conspicuous consumption might provoke, Ismaili organizers wisely reduced the feast to fairly austere meals of bread and vegetables for fifteen thousand Ismailis housed at camp "Diamondabad" in Upanga.[107] For Indians the event was a great success; for British officials it was a crisis averted; for Africans it was a stark reminder of their social distance from a community that appeared to thrive despite widespread territorial scarcity.

Although no food shortage occurred during the Diamond Jubilee, rice distributions were suspended three weeks later following territorial drought. Africans employed in various businesses laid plans for a general strike to protest the substituted and inedible mixed-meal rations. In early September 1946, thousands converged on the "open space" of Mnazi Mmoja to conduct the first African-led mass public protest rally in Dar es Salaam's history. The African Association prevented a general strike by extracting promises to replace mixed-meal with straight-meal rations immediately. At a later official *baraza*, however, several Africans demanded that they be first consulted on matters of purely African concern, and not Indians, Europeans, or even the African Association.[108] A popular issue, food distribution, was bringing large numbers of people into the streets without organizational mobilization. Local newspapers were flooded with angry commentary. "Why did the Government allow these thousands of Khojas to come here for their Diamond business," one writer complained, "in the light of our grave foodstuff shortage and how did it manage to feed them?"[109] Another decried the inedibility of African rations while Asian-only couponed bread sat unconsumed. "Frankly, I see the time is near," he threatened, "when the pure African-minded blackman will utter the regrettable word '*potelea mbali*' [get lost] at its proper cause and then the results would be seen."[110] By September 1946, one year before a successful, nationwide general strike (see below), the primary issues of popular racial politics in Dar es Salaam were already clear—racial inequity in ration distribution, black marketing abuses by Indians, and Indian influx into African residential neighborhoods. The Diamond Jubilee and subsequent events transformed urban entitlements into political issues for popular action.

As the reach of the urban colonial state expanded in the 1940s, its appearance seemed to weaken. Public health officials, who had exercised so much influence during the interwar years, appeared impotent to address food adulteration that grew widespread during the war. Ghee was often contaminated; milk was regularly watered down; simsim oil was mixed with cheaper coconut oil; melted candle wax was mixed with rice.[111] Shopkeepers in Kariakoo had disposed of arsenic by selling it as baking powder or white flour, poisoning hundreds of customers until they were finally caught by a health officer.[112] The lesson of wartime profiteering on African health was clear to one *Kwetu* reader: the rich had constructed buildings with their ill-gotten wealth, while "because of mixing rotten foods in the shops, now Africans die rottenly from diseases in the towns."[113] More important, the abundance of regulations and scarcity of commodities produced an enormous "parallel market," or illegal economy, in and around Dar es Salaam. Black market realities frequently mocked official pronouncements. In the darkest weeks of the 1946 famine, the provincial commissioner abandoned protocol and announced that the town's retail merchants were "holding a gun at Government's head" by refusing to accept fixed profit rates.[114] Such frustration was born of the effective monopolies that Indian wholesalers and large retailers had exercised over the urban economy. African town shopkeepers had made considerable progress—the African Retailers Association claimed forty-three African-owned shops by 1947—but their numbers were still dwarfed by the 240 Asian-owned shops.[115] Sustainable networks of trust among African retailers and between retailers and employees continued to prove evasive. Kleist Sykes opened "Sykes' Store" near Gerezani in 1942 selling textiles and food, but the shop failed because of "untrustworthy" associates.[116]

Trust itself was highly scarce, and endured within narrow and tested merchant circuits and their increasingly discreet activities with customers.

Black market sales required not only willing middlemen but willing producers and consumers. African farmers avoided official markets to get higher prices on the black market—either by falsely claiming that produce brought to town was for personal consumption, or by bringing it in covertly at night. Consumers sought greater amounts—particularly for rice—than legal rations allowed. They also grew impatient with the endless queues that surrounded official sale points and instead purchased food from unapproved shops, on the street, or at doorsteps.[117] Older Africans often chose to pay Indian boys to stand in queue for them to get a loaf or two of superior bread.[118] The black market for rice was so huge that it devalued ration coupons. Consumers spoke freely about illegal purchases:

> I get seven coupons from the Authority but I can only get rice at the controlled price on two of these coupons so I throw the other five coupons away. Indian duka owners will only give me enough rice for two coupons, and then not always. If I go to another duka I have to wait perhaps three hours in a queue and then I am told there is no more rice. If I say I will pay 1/- [four times the controlled price] for a pound of rice I can then get rice. Even then I don't get as much as I want and sometimes I have to wait two or three days.[119]

Textile scarcity led to black marketing and long queues that occasionally became disorderly—police often arrived to official sale sites to prevent fights before opening. Some six hundred Africans descended upon an Indian trader's stall in 1947 after an Economic Control Board officer discovered the trader had been illegally hoarding kangas beneath his counter. To restore order, the ECB took over direct supervision of all textile sales.[120] Controls were often ineffective and often seen to be ineffective, but inaction risked abandoning commitments to the larger framework of urban entitlement. Price control, however ignored in practice, carried with it a language of the just price and retained a fairly wide legitimacy among officials and residents alike. The 1951 Cost of Living Committee recommended "full physical control over price and distribution" by the state of key commodities that fell within the notional "African family budget."[121] The urban African family (see below) could not progress without this commitment to their entitlements.

Although entitlement replaced segregation as the main feature of urban policy, the segregationist zoning that had defined the interwar "native" quarter was popularly reinvented as an entitlement to African racial space. Severe housing scarcity and property speculation intensified the racial divisions of urban space, masking class conflict between a consolidating class of African landlords and a rapidly growing class of African renters. Dire building material shortages, particularly cement imports, practically halted construction.[122] Between 1939 and 1943, the number of African houses increased 11 percent while population rose from 33,000 to 45,000. As a result, the "native" area's population density rose from ten to nearly fifteen people per house.[123] Government housing construction came too little and too late to ameliorate overcrowded conditions.[124] Some public housing was available to Africans identified as "key workers," mainly civil servants who had not intended to settle but were serious about their careers. In the late 1940s they rented single-family, government-owned "quarters" houses in Ilala, Temeke, and Magomeni for submarket rates. But most of Dar es Salaam's African housing continued to be provided by private landlords, nearly all of whom owned "Swahili" houses, typically a compound on a rectangular surveyed plot with a six-roomed main house, a courtyard, and perhaps a few rooms in back. The majority (72 percent) of residents later surveyed in 1956 lived in "Swahili" houses, within which a large percentage of families (91 percent) occupied only one single room. Indian families who rented "Swahili" houses often took three rooms and created a separate access gate, kitchen, and latrine. Such sequestration eliminated the compound's public space where different African households would typically converse, cook, wash, fight, and share. As Indians either outbid African renters for rooms or took eventual ownership of "Swahili" houses through debt defaults, African renters loudly decried the paradoxical "failure" of urban segregation. Some African landlords in Kariakoo preferred Indian tenants because they paid higher rents and paid them reliably, but others preferred African tenants because Indians were not helpful in times of adversity and might eventually take over the house.[125] Seemingly insatiable demand for residential space created enormous opportunities in peri-urban land, which awaited harvest by largely African *rentiers* or place entrepreneurs able to trap "human activity at the sites of their pecuniary interests."[126] House ownership was, in Baker's words, the "great aim of the Urban African" as both investment and insurance in old age.[127] Building conditions improved in the early 1950s as construction materials became more easily available. By 1956 African landlords numbered 8,000, accounted for 19 percent of the town's African population, and owned 12,000 houses.[128]

For an increasingly vocal African population, urban entitlement meant holding the state accountable to its implicit promise of a "native" residential space presently encroached upon by non-Africans. Tremendous population increases created sharp competition for residential space. In Uhindini, landlords furiously subdivided existing properties, particularly joint commercial-residential buildings, to maximize numbers of rent-paying tenants.[129] Poorer

Indians moved in larger numbers to theoretically "native" Kariakoo, where residents had witnessed decades of official racial zoning contradicted by actual housing practice, in which no action was taken against the unauthorized erection of Asian-owned buildings. This Indian influx increased dramatically during the Second World War.[130] By 1947 there were 338 "non-native" households renting accommodations in the "native" Zone III, numbering perhaps more than one thousand people.[131] But such numbers were often guesswork—earlier estimates for rationing purposes placed up to twenty-five hundred "non-natives" living in the area.[132] High rents and horrendous housing conditions in Uhindini—where landlords were so contemptuous of maintenance that over one-quarter of surveyed houses had been officially condemned—pushed Indians toward Kariakoo. African tenants were subsequently turned out of rooms to make way for wealthier Asian tenants, so they moved either farther out of town or into one of a thousand-odd rented huts that African landlords had constructed in their backyards.[133] "The Asians occupying African houses have generally to pay fantastic rentals," an Indian civil servant explained, "*a room* in an African house for which a reasonable rent in 1939 would have been shs. 8/- . . . is being let to Asians at anything between shs. 40/- and shs. 100/- per month."[134] Even the cash-strapped African Association let out a room in its New Street headquarters to an Asian laundry business.[135] British officials concurred with popular African opinion that Indian "infiltration" was the principal cause of spiraling Kariakoo rents—the former just beginning to realize the political costs of its interwar gentrification policies; the latter just beginning to grasp the power of racial politics.[136]

The Indian "invasion" of Kariakoo provided a sturdy platform for racial polemics. The African independent newspaper *Dunia* located the source of housing exploitation in the transgression of established racial boundaries. Its editor, R. M. Plantan, observed that high rents were driving Indians out of Uhindini and into Uswahilini, depriving Africans of their now natural racial home. Appealing to British racialist sensibilities, Plantan rhetorically asked if the government would "agree to the mixture of your palm leave-roofed houses with those of Indians."[137] In a rare moment of class contemplation, Plantan did briefly consider African complicity in the housing crisis:

> The housing difficulties are caused through the greed of the *wenyeji* [natives]. They turn out their fellow natives who pay Shgs 6/- p.m. for a room in order to obtain large rents by leasing the whole house to Indians or whites, and so it continues, until many people are homeless, and the Indians have spread to every quarter of the native area. So let this Government take notice and remove the whites [i.e., non-Africans] from the houses in the native areas, returning them to the

Europeans or Indian quarters, for by living in the native area they avoid payment of high rents and their evasion damages the native.[138]

Racial invective, however, proved more attractive to Plantan and his readers than further investigating abuses carried out by African landlords. Indians' gentrifying encroachment into Kariakoo, Plantan argued, accomplished by using Swahili women and Arabs as straw purchasers, had tripled rental and housing prices, and imported a fundamental *fujo*, or disorder, into the area.[139] A government worker argued that wages should be raised "to pay house rents as an Indian can pay in African quarters," but also stressed that Indians should be removed from Kariakoo and "sent to the Indian quarters" to make room for Africans.[140] African landlords had the wind at their backs in the 1940s, enjoying both the rising rents generated by their Indian tenants and the political growth in racial solidarity generated by their aggrieved African tenants.

The popular solution was resegregation. If the government would only remove Indians from Uswahilini, then "Africans themselves would be able to live in comfort in their buildings."[141] Plantan later refused to publish a letter critical of both African landlords and the "agitating African" who sought to prevent landlords from realizing their investment by protesting higher rents.[142] The Tanganyika African Government Servants Association (TAGSA), representing those African salaried workers who were arguably hardest hit by inflation, interpreted the problem in exclusively racial terms by protesting that the government "should consider some way of reducing and/or expelling the number of Asians now residing and/or occupying houses in African quarters area."[143] *Dunia* implored its African readers to buy building plots to prevent further Indian expansion.[144] Few residents, landlords, or officials publicly took the cool view of Abdulwahid Sykes, the son of Kleist Sykes, who described rental increases as "a boon rather than a menace to house owners irrespective of race" because the increases raised needed capital for further housing construction.[145] Abdulwahid's daughter later explained that the Sykes family had long been property enthusiasts, and capitalized on the 1940s property boom by distributing building materials that she described as "not the highest quality ones but the medium ones to cater for African requirements"—in particular lime (*chokaa*), burnt coral rag used to make cement and whitewash.[146] What is perhaps most remarkable is how few critics directly attacked African landlords themselves—landlords who had colluded to rent rooms over legal maximum rates; who had backed up threats to silence tenants by once expelling some one hundred lodgers en masse after the latter complained to the *liwali*; and who, most efficiently, threatened tenants with witchcraft if they failed to pay higher rents.[147] Dar es Salaam's landlords did occasionally use statutory bodies such as the African Association to press for more-secure leases on their residential plots,[148] but in general employed little to no formal organization. They did not need to—African landlords had seized the *rentier* powers generated by rising population and demands for residential space, constituting themselves as the most powerful African economic group in Dar es Salaam, upon which later politicians would be highly reliant.

Spatial segregation flourished in popular politics just as it collapsed as urban policy. Officials were growing increasingly sympathetic toward popular African demands to resegregate Kariakoo, but had meager legal and economic resources with which to respond. Fundamental confusion remained concerning the legality of non-native tenancies on African property, intertwined as it was with poorly understood commercial zoning laws (see chapter 1). A compromise between nonracialism and "native" protection was struck in 1946, allowing natives three-year rights of occupancy over trading plots at standard rent, while "non-natives" had to pay rent determined at auction; for good measure, "natives" were prohibited from renting out houses or rooms in Ilala and most of Kariakoo to "non-natives."[149] But after the 1947 general strike, the labor commissioner recommended mass Asian evictions from Zone III; both the leasing and the sale of urban property from native to non-native was formally banned, though both continued in practice.[150] The town's district officer claimed that the "lure of high rentals paid by Asians has virtually meant that 90 percent of Kariakoo, once a purely African area, is now either owned or leased by Asians";[151] his successor reduced the figure to 60 percent.[152] Both were alarmist exaggerations, but a serious population shift had occurred. Kariakoo's 5,073 Indian residents accounted for 17 percent of the neighborhood's population in 1952, and also accounted for 26 percent of the entire town's 19,382 Indian residents.[153] Stricter enforcement of building codes had begun throughout Dar es Salaam in the early 1950s, leading to the more efficient removal of African squatters, as well as leaving "a general impression amongst African residents that there is a drive to oust them from the Municipality in favour of Asians and Europeans."[154] Popular rumors suggested that the purpose of new town planning proposals was to demolish African houses overnight to give the plots to Indians.[155] Reversing Indian-led gentrification became a central goal of incipient African racial populism in Dar es Salaam. Although not a material entitlement like food and clothing, urban space had been converted—through popular pressures and the wary decisions of British officials—into a psychological entitlement that had fairly wide official sympathy, if very little practical official action.

POLITICS OF THE WORKPLACE

Urban labor organizations in colonial Africa, particularly those of transport workers, played a large part in the development of popular anticolonial politics. At stake were competing visions of work and citizenship. Cooper argues that the struggle between business capital and the colonial state on the one hand and urban laborers on the other over control of work time, resulted in the "regularization" of transport work. At the heart of this struggle were efforts of business capital and the colonial state to eliminate casual labor and stabilize an urban class of full-time workers, imposing greater demands but affording greater rewards for this more reliable urban citizenry.[156] Conflict over the regularization of urban transport workers was indeed a major feature of Dar es Salaam's political history, but the chief issue for African workers was not control over their time. The chief issue was access to basic necessities, and the chief terms of debate were racial.

Transport and civil service were Dar es Salaam's largest employers. Both paid well, and both instituted a hierarchical division of labor by race. Norman Pearson, a visiting British Railways trade unionist, observed in Dar es Salaam that "practically everything was organised on a tri-racial basis."[157] One Kariakoo resident explained that the relationship between Indians and Africans foundered principally on different rankings given to workers on a racial basis.[158] Separate racial terms for civil servants had long haunted and united the African bureaucratic imagination. Differences in salaries and benefits were transparent, making public discourse open and heated. While many Indians and all Africans were a part of the Local Service, Africans resented the former's dominance of higher positions—"They get all the cream (quarters, bus traveling facilities, starting pays, etc.) and the African only a lemon."[159] The first question ever asked by an African member of the Legislative Council was why locally educated Asians received more than twice what locally educated Africans earned in civil service starting pay.[160] Africans, in the view of a *Kwetu* correspondent, were "impeded by a multitude of Asiatic employees both in Government and Companies, AND WHOSE INTENTION IS TO REJECT LIBERTIES OF AFRICANS."[161] The cruel fiction of a "color-blind" Local Service, whose higher positions were dominated by Indians, led one African staffer to threaten, "With the ruling of just freedom in view, we shall best tell what we think of Indians."[162] European civil service privileges were formally cemented by the East African Salary Commission (1947–1948), which recommended a "Three-Fifths Rule" in which non-Europeans would be paid three-fifths the salary paid to a European for the same position. The rule was thrown out in 1954 in favor of appealing for the need to use "inducements," a term used since the 1920s to justify higher salaries for recruited Europeans and Asians.[163] Although they lacked bargaining rights, TAGSA persistently pressured the government to reserve positions for Africans in the face of expanding postwar recruitment of Asians; its leader, Ally Sykes, was perhaps Tanganyika's loudest voice to oppose the hiring of Asian civil servants.[164]

Tensions were sharpest at Tanganyika Railways, which had created its own nonracial Local Service to reduce costs of hiring local Asians. But Indian youths had refused to accept local salaries; such lobbying, combined with generally higher educational qualifications, enabled them to secure higher wages than Africans for the same positions.[165] Subsequent politics turned on the question of training and skill transfers. In small business settings such as shoe-cobbling, skill transfers from Asian masters to African apprentices worked well.[166] But such transfers met far more resistance on factory floors. African locomotive shop apprentices complained that skilled Asian workers spoke no Swahili and taught no skills, while skilled African workers begrudged having to train Asian apprentices, enabling the latter to do the same work at higher pay.[167] Pearson observed staggering disparities between Asian and African railway craftsmen. A skilled Asian carpenter might make more than ten times what an African carpenter earned, though he might be even "deserving it less" because of his limited skills. Pearson met not one African apprentice, and discovered that those who had apprenticed left early for outside employment. He summarized his view of African attitudes by depicting a conversation with what he termed "a group of so-called craftsmen":

> Craftsmen: "Bwana, why do our masters give so much more to Indians than to us? We are craftsmen like they are."
> Myself: "But you are not such good craftsmen as they are."
> Craftsmen: "When it came to fighting for King George in the War we were better than they were. Why should we have been better men then and now?"
> Myself: "It is the skill and the products of your skill as a craftsmen which determines your wages, and your skill is low."
> Craftsmen: "But we are craftsmen the same as they are: What is the difference?"
> Myself: "The difference is mostly one of training. In Britain a man must serve at least a five-years lowly-paid apprenticeship before he can become a craftsman. What man among you has served such an apprenticeship?"
> Craftsmen: "Bwana, we are not Europeans, we are Africans. An African does not need to waste such a long time learning!"
> Myself: "Do you think yourselves better than Europeans?"
> Craftsmen: "Well it seems so Bwana!"[168]

"Always this question of making decent African craftsmen has haunted me," Pearson concluded.[169] Pressured by peers to maintain race-based pay premiums, Asian craftsmen were careful to protect their skills monopoly; aspiring

African craftsmen were impatiently awaiting transfers of skill promised to them in wartime rhetoric, confident that numbers were on their side.

African commercial workers—a diverse group ranging from hawkers and petty traders to shop assistants and shopkeepers—faced greater income insecurity than did civil servants or transport laborers, but enjoyed greater freedom from racially inscribed workplace hierarchies. Commercial work structures were racially segmented but more permeable to entrepreneurial innovation, particularly at the margins. African petty traders leveraged livelihoods by commercializing their mobility and claims to public space in order to extract maximum possible shares within commodity distribution chains. Itinerant hawking and stationary vending presented the lowest entry barriers of urban work for *wahuni*, underemployed young men filling Dar es Salaam's streets. Increasingly restrictive licensing schemes vainly attempted to limit petty commerce, primarily to address public health concerns about the wares of food vendors, and failed "to discriminate between the hawker who might be deserving and the rich man's agent."[170] The "rich men" were invariably Indian traders who paid African petty traders on commission. This system led to sharp contests over public space with stationary vendors. Rights to pavement stalls were formally nonexistent and informally tenuous. In a conflict that continues to the present day, African street vendors resisted orders in 1952 to leave their pavement stalls on Kariakoo's Swahili Street. They claimed that Indian shop owners were behind these complaints, and wanted to replace these semi-independent traders with their own African servants.[171] Self-employed mobile traders selling tea, produce, snacks, and water could generate the greatest incomes by pressing the limits of black market prices.[172] Fishmongers were particularly aggressive black market vendors, preferring to sell fish—one of the few urban trade items entirely controlled by Africans—off-market to maximize their cut. Fishing was a big business that employed some six hundred Africans in and around Dar es Salaam. Boat owners and fishermen took one quarter and three quarters of the takings, respectively, and either employed "boys" as agents to deliver catches directly to stalls, or sold to unlicensed middlemen who marketed fish at double the controlled price.[173] Successful traders invested profits in boats, bicycles, *hamali* carts, or other capital goods of urban commerce, and could aspire to that most desirable urban investment, a house.[174] The nucleus of this work was at the Kariakoo market, where networks and friendships among leading African traders like Dossa Aziz, fishmongers like Mshume Kiyate, and official market staff like Sharrif Atas and Abdulwahid Sykes met regularly; and was also where the African Association would be revived in the early 1950s.[175]

Women also were major actors in urban commerce, though they appear only in the margins of colonial documentation produced by British male officials, who received much of their information from often jaundiced African male informants. Women formed a minuscule 5.5 percent of Tanganyika's wage labor in 1956, four-fifths of whom were in agriculture, and were largely strangers to the formal colonial workplaces of Dar es Salaam.[176] Though men increasingly outnumbered women in Dar es Salaam during the 1940s, rising from a remarkably well-balanced 110:100 male:female ratio in 1940 to 141:100 by 1948, this was still far more balanced than comparable African colonial cities.[177] For the government, urban women figured mainly as expense lines in government cost-of-living budgets. Although East African governments did not promise a "breadwinner wage" to urban male workers until the 1950s,[178] officials in Tanganyika nonetheless worked with the ideal household unit—constituted by one wage-earning male, one female spouse, and children—to estimate living costs used to set official prices. In Tanganyika this was a widespread though little-discussed assumption, and there was no extensive debate about either the ideal of the monogamous nuclear "household" or the male breadwinner wage, unlike other colonies such as Nigeria.[179] Most women's working lives involved cultivating a nearby farm and caring for the children, food, and room of a male cash-earner. During the working hours, residential Dar es Salaam was "a city of women and children, with all adult males either away from home at work or seeking it."[180] Female commercial workers created marginal trading niches such as selling charcoal, firewood, and cooked food. But a minority of town women became powerful economic actors. A group of Manyema women who controlled the street sale of popular food such as *vitumbua* (pastries) and *dagaa* (small dried fish) parlayed earnings into building ownership.[181]

Because of the security it provided, home ownership was often an end in itself. The most accessible commercial means for women to achieve this end was in beer-brewing and prostitution. Elderly Zaramo women controlled Dar es Salaam's licensed and unlicensed *pombe* (traditional beer) markets, from which they could earn four times the median male wage. Female brewers struck in 1941 to protest government attempts to break their monopoly by establishing a rival *tembo* (palm wine) bar, which in sharp contrast to *pombe* was entirely controlled by African men. Over the 1940s, *tembo* displaced *pombe* as the African drink of choice, though female brewers found customers just outside the township limits.[182] Female Zaramo *pombe* brewers also operated a lucrative ferry service across the harbor to Kigamboni.[183] Haya women, immigrants from northwestern Tanganyika, dominated Dar es Salaam's *waziwazi*, or "open" prostitute profession, the "better class" of whom could earn up to ten shillings per evening. As with Zaramo *pombe* brewers, Zaramo prostitutes were pushed outward to work the town's margins. Successful prostitutes invested earnings in houses and formed a wealthy female landlord class who owned properties across Kariakoo and Kisutu, particularly along the "red-light" district of Kirk (now Lindi) Street and other locations in south

Kariakoo. The highest-earning prostitutes were Indian, Arab, and mixed-race women, whose customers were wealthy men of all races.[184] A visiting American medical officer noted that venereal disease infection rates in wartime Dar es Salaam were very high, and that prostitutes were "very numerous":

> Natives, Asiatics and all of the high yellows of the various religious affiliations are found in the prostitute group. The hybrids of lighter shade and more or less Arabic and European features make the most of European dress and appear to specialize in this profession. Contacts are made on the street, through taxi drivers and others. Licensed houses of prostitution are not in existence.[185]

Tanganyika's chief medical officer had proposed to license brothels, but was refused in favor of more rigorously removing town "undesirables."[186] Although there was an undeniable core of real professional prostitutes, unmarried urban women were often assumed to be "prostitutes"—a term that served as a male metaphor for growing female economic autonomy. In the reformist mind of African men, prostitution not only offended basic morality but created an urban fiscal crisis, for it diverted male wealth from paying *kodi*, or legitimate poll and house taxes, and instead redirected it to pay *honga*, also "tax" but a term that implies extortion, used to refer to extracted tolls, bribes, and payments used to seduce women. Prostitutes, these men argued, condemned male wealth to perpetual destruction in pawnshops.[187] Yet this same wealth was also employed to build much-needed housing. However arbitrary and discriminatory, urban legal mechanisms offered protections for female landlords to accumulate wealth unmatched by rural alternatives. One in five of all taxpaying African homeowners were women by 1952.[188]

Although landlords and commercial workers exercised significant autonomy, they could only envy the unique strategic position enjoyed by Dar es Salaam's all-male dock laborers, who could throttle Tanganyika's revenue nexus through strike action, and were thus afforded a natural leadership over urban workers. Iliffe locates the origins of Tanzania's popular labor organization in four major dockworker strikes that occurred during 1939–1950, events that awakened Africans to popular politics.[189] This chapter agrees that these actors and events played a critical role, but argues instead that popular politics emerged primarily from implementation, lobbying, and protest around urban entitlements. Dockworkers exercised leadership over other urban workers in large part by appealing to common complaints they shared as urban consumers. African dockworkers were united in demands for better pay, food, and housing, all of which were allotted along racial lines. Moreover, their workplace was highly stratified by race—Africans performed manual labor in crews led by an African head, or *serang*, who was supervised by mid-level Indian and top-level European managers. The first dockworker strike that occurred in 1939 was the first coastwide protest since the 1880s, spreading from Mombasa down to Lindi. The main issue of the strike, which in Tanganyika was centered in Tanga, was higher wages; its immediate spread deeply jarred officials' own sense of control and evoked deep anxieties about casual labor.[190] During the war, dockworker focus in Dar es Salaam had shifted firmly to workplace entitlements—workers had grown to see food as the critical feature of just compensation. By 1943, food rationing united African consumers to support the unprecedented possibility of a general strike.[191] In May, dockworkers complained above all about the poor qualities of workplace rations, and in August they organized a strike, principally over food and other unmanageable living costs.[192] During the strike, African workers directed anger against government officials, even physically threatening local administration headmen, or *majumbe*, who tried to convince them to return to work—one man had ominously threatened, "These are the coolies who are making trouble, next week you will have the cooks to deal with."[193] Entrepreneurial union organizers claiming to represent "All Native Servants" in town threatened a subsequent sympathy strike, and formed the African Cooks, Washermen, and House Servants Association.[194] A general strike never came off, and after ten days and several arrests, strikers returned to work after being awarded food ration gains from a tribunal. But a host of other African trade unions quickly formed along racial lines in the strike's wake.[195]

Postwar labor activity further entrenched the racialized nature of popular politics. Dar es Salaam's two great postwar strikes of 1947 and 1950 were fueled, respectively, by growing calls among African dockworkers to protest racial inequities in commodity distribution, and growing division between these same workers over labor regularization. In August 1947, African dockworkers demanded higher wages to meet rising living costs, and their chief complaint was lack of affordable housing. After demands went unanswered they struck, immediately receiving support from two thousand Railways African Association members. The general strike began early on September 1, coordinated in part by Dar es Salaam's reawakening African Association. Picket lines formed at town workshops and hotels manned by African civil servants and domestics, as well as along territorial railway lines and into sisal plantations, to become, in Iliffe's words, "the most widespread protest in Tanzanian history between the end of the Maji Maji rising and the formation of TANU."[196] The strike produced a potent mixture of radical optimism and racial intimidation. Pearson characterized the wage demands as "fantastically impossible," stating that in the strike's first two days "they lived in cloud cuckooland, and their imaginations seemed to visualize a fairy godmother or a genie."[197] Racial divisions of labor were made plain when only Africans honored the strike. Indian-owned ships unloaded cargo with their own crews, aided by nonstriking European and Indian dock employees. The *Tanganyika Opinion* reported that "armed African gangs banged the doors of Indian residents till they were answered and they searched houses for African boys," and luridly added that "husbands were in offices and women had to face the situation—if the Africans started looting there was nothing to stop them fulfilling their whims."[198] The subsequent tribunal award, with its generous wage and cost of living increases, confirmed the 1947 strike as the greatest labor victory in Dar es Salaam's history.

But this victory was achieved on the mistaken assumption that the urban labor force would agree to shed its part-timers. Three years later, Dar es Salaam's African labor movement collapsed under state pressures to regularize dockside and other urban work. In 1948, the newly formed Stevedore and Dock Workers Union ambivalently accepted Labor Department recommendations for worker registration as a means to reduce the large pool of unskilled casual workers. Shifting and ineffectual leadership, however, proved unable to slow the growing gap between permanent workers who supported registration and casual workers who opposed it. Despite plans to reduce casual dockworkers in Dar es Salaam, their numbers actually increased during 1949.[199] Union leaders and politicians, if such a distinction can be drawn, attempted to reap the whirlwind of rising expectations across employment sectors. African domestic servants provided the catalyst. Wartime inflation had particularly unsettled the largely unregulated market of domestic laborers, many of whom left multiyear employment in one household for higher wages in another without giving notice.[200] After years of negotiating with employers through the European Women's Service League, which had operated a domestic servant registry since the 1920s, African domestics successfully boycotted a short-lived official labor exchange, forcing its collapse in 1948.[201] Dar es Salaam households were now forced to hire staff directly through the Union of African Cooks, Washermen and House Servants, to their instant dissatisfaction and horror. The union was led by the charismatic Saleh bin Fundi, former leader of Arinoti *beni* and, according to Iliffe, "Tanganyika's first African labour leader," whose New Street office neighbored the African Association.[202] Union leaders competed with one another by employing increasingly confrontational tactics: for instance, special police were called out in April 1949 to arrest striking members of the Road Workers Union, who had brought city traffic to a standstill through the alleged intimidation of drivers.[203] Railway and municipal workers secretly met with the African Association in late 1949 to protest unequal employment terms with Indian workers and an increased "native" tax—participants adjourned to strike again, emboldened, allegedly, by recent successful strike action in England and other parts of the empire.[204]

This second general strike ended in disaster. On the morning of February 3, 1950, some 1,500 casual dockworkers surrounded the dockyard entrance in order to prevent government-recruited "volunteers" from entering via a new gate entrance built to ensure worker registration. Turned away from the gates, picketers marched to Kariakoo to gather up some 3,000 supporters for a return march back to the docks. A young British police officer unwisely followed and attempted to stop the mob; a small group of strikers responded by attacking a police truck, and police opened fire. Violence quickly spread to Mnazi Mmoja, where nineteen African constables and an Asian officer and a European officer were injured by a mob numbering between 400 and 600, many wielding machetes. Police gunfire killed two rioters and wounded five. Tanganyika's new Governor, Edward Twining, requested that a Kings African Rifles company remain deployed in town for several months. The registration system was eventually enacted, though later compromises were made to allow for a small casual workforce.[205] Iliffe suggests that the port authority's refusal to allow union participation to implement the registration scheme likely sparked the strike. Registration control was indeed the key issue, but this was not primarily a conflict between capital and labor. A Special Branch intelligence report claims that all parties had tolerated a corrupt system whereby dockworkers passed through an old gate guarded by "a gang of paid bullies," who permitted only dues-paying Stevedores and Dockworkers Union members to pass, while others paid fees to enrich certain union officials, one of whom was caught with six hundred shillings in his pocket. Resistance to the new scheme, claimed the report, had thus been led by those elements that had profited from the corrupt status quo.[206]

Urban entitlements were created to maintain political security through the regulation of the costs of living and human mobility. The entitlements instead generated spiraling material expectations and racial solidarities that legitimated employment of mass action to better negotiate levels of entitlement. Dysfunctional labor organizations could now threaten the wider public peace because they wielded the powerful discontent of the African urban consumer. "Inadequate housing (and lack of housing plots), high living costs, shortage of maize and other staple food, black marketing in food and goods and underemployment," the Special Branch concluded, provided sufficient troubled waters in which "political trouble-makers are busily fishing in an attempt to bring about more troubles."[207] And there certainly were troublemakers who preferred confrontation—the government purged its own ranks of subversives, arresting and deporting an appointed Industrial Relations officer, G. G. Hamilton, for having helped foment the strike and, allegedly, having Communist Party affiliations.[208] In the strike's aftermath, African trade unions rapidly disappeared, through either deregistration or financial collapse.[209] After the

African Tailors Union closed in 1951, there was not a single registered African trade union in Tanganyika. Others carried on illegally, most prominently the African Cooks Union, which claimed to be representing all urban Africans by demanding that the newly opened Arnautoglu Hall be reserved for use by Africans only. When it was made clear that the hall would be "multiracial" space, African Cooks responded; "Do you not know the enemies of Tanganyika? It is the European Council, especially Khoja Indians and Arabs."[210] The African Cooks Union also petitioned for house rent allowance to meet rising rents and reduce dependence on Indian employers' lodgings.[211] Others voiced a directionless, emasculated anger. "I want to rope [together] all the Europeans in Tanganyika," the leader of a marginal government union threatened to Queen Elizabeth, "so that I may show them African strength."[212] Rather than joining Tanganyika's only surviving union, the Asian Commercial Employees Association, African shopworkers attempted but failed to form the Dar es Salaam African Commercial Employees Association; the idea that Indian and African commercial workers might form a single union appears never to have occurred.[213] African unions later rebounded to become significant nationalist institutions after the formation of the Tanganyika Federation of Labor in 1956. But as with their predecessors, not one of Dar es Salaam's post-1954 trade unions would be multiracial in membership or character. The town's workforce had been too profoundly segmented by race, in both structure and protest, to become otherwise.

CONCLUSIONS

By committing to provide minimal living standards to all urban residents, the government had created a form of urban entitlement based on spatially defined cost-of-living regulations during the 1940s. The state's administrative and intellectual framework, however, proved reluctant and ultimately incapable of squaring the ideal of a fairly uniform and stable urban African workforce employed at living wages with the reality of a highly differentiated African population increasingly compromised by under- or unemployed migrants with modest skills but great mobility. The violence unleashed in the 1950 strike, led primarily by casual workers, served to crystallize official convictions that effective urban policy must rest on stabilization and full employment of urban Africans, a view later canonized in the 1955 East African Royal Commission report.[214] It remained a shibboleth among urban administrators that unless African immigration was curtailed, either accommodation standards would be reduced to "an impossibly low level," or ruinous tax levels would have to be imposed.[215] Housing, like food and other commodities, could be affordable only if it was restricted to the most productive and deserving of urban Africans; the nondeserving had to be removed.

Dar es Salaam underwent two interrelated revolutions during the 1940s: a demographic one where population growth rates leaped from 2 percent to 8 percent per annum; and a political one where the colonial state made unprecedented regulatory commitments to manage urban living costs. As a result, the state's wartime solution to the urban question dramatically raised the political and economic value of urban space; Africans for the first time were entitled to basic necessities by virtue of their spatial belonging. These spatially defined entitlements revealed and corroded interwar distinctions between native and rural and non-native and urban, and led both the state and its subjects to pursue and more sharply define continental categories of race as a substitute for native/non-native. Racial consciousness among Africans sharpened amid struggles for basic necessities such as food, clothing, and housing. The latter, the most obvious and tested path to urban wealth and power, starkly revealed the impotence of lingering "native" protections in the face of an expanding and gentrifying Indian population. Despite growing differentiation between African landlords and tenants, as well as between permanent and casual workers, the organizational and rhetorical responses of Africans attempting to carve out a livable urban existence were based increasingly on race. The intellectual and organizational elaboration of race that resulted in the political mobilization of a successful anticolonial nationalism is the subject to which we now turn.

4 ᔑ Continental Shift

Civilization, Racial Thought, and the Intellectual
Foundations of an African Nationalism

Ndugu zangu Mwafrika jivuneni kabisa kwa taifa letu.
(My African brothers take pride in our *taifa*.)

—*Kwetu* editorial, February 14, 1938

THE INTELLECTUAL TENETS of African nationalism in Tanganyika took firm shape during the 1940s. Black Tanganyikan thinkers—informed by urban experiences in Dar es Salaam and cosmopolitan ideas obtained from travel abroad—employed Pan-Africanist convictions to reforge colonial discursive themes of civilization and race. New terms of an exclusionary national categorical order based on race emerged out of long-standing discussions that addressed the relationship between civilization and uncivilized "natives." These thinkers appropriated civilization as a vehicle to realize an African nation, coherent in itself and distinct from European or Asian nations. They affirmed many popular tropes in European and Asian racial discourses, including the geographical determinism of continents, the duty to maintain racial purity and discourage interracial marriage, and the evolutionary development of families and tribes toward normative nations. But they also mobilized the idiom of patrilineal descent, itself profoundly embedded within normative Swahili notions of civilization, in order to invert unjust hierarchies imposed upon Africa by the imperial Indian Ocean world.

The African nationalist inversion of normative Swahili-language thought lies at the heart of this chapter. We begin by first tracing a history of nationalist key words and their employment within debates over civilization, continental descent, and interracial liaisons. This chapter next assesses how African travel to South Asia sharpened racial thought. Racial thought is understood here in the similar sense that Jonathon Glassman has mapped out in his pioneering study of colonial Zanzibar—not as the elaboration of genetic and biological differences, but instead as a discursive field in which people generally assume humanity to be divided into discrete natural categories, each with its own traits and characteristics.[1] This became newly important and newly explicit among African thinkers in the 1940s. Finally, this chapter demonstrates how intellectual convictions to realize the African *taifa* (race/nation) shaped the political history of Tanganyikan nationalism, both within the urban space of Dar es Salaam and the legal space of the country's national citizenship laws.

As we have seen in preceding chapters, contested legal rights, communalized social institutions, and burning economic resentments had made race central to colonial urban life. Africans readily appropriated urban administrative categories of "race" as an instrument to claim political space and acquire material benefits during the 1940s, just as "tribe" had been by interwar Africans confronting policies of indirect rule.[2] Yet "instrumentalist" literature on race in coastal East Africa has disallowed African intellectual production; instead, the sole agent of racial consciousness is the colonial state.[3] The production of African racial identity was intellectual work as well as instrumental response, and its leaders were the pamphleteers, letter writers, poets, and polemicists of colonial Africa's rich print public. Printed in newspapers like *Kwetu* and *Mambo Leo*, these were public arguments, written with the intent of being read aloud in the streets and cafés, in the forms of letters, articles, and *shairi* poetry, in order to be also consumed by Dar es Salaam's majority nonliterate African population.[4] As Benedict Anderson has argued more generally, nationalism was in major part a literary undertaking, in which print languages were the critical vessel—they created a unified field of exchange and gave a new fixity to language.[5] This literary undertaking, as Heather Sharkey reminds us for colonial Africa, "much like empire itself . . . was reliant on the power of the written word to affirm and eventually popularize its values."[6] This involved the appropriation of multiple discourses that not only contested colonial hierarchies, but created new intellectual communities. Rather than begin from conceptual definitions of race that typologize what it is and what it is not, we should instead investigate how the term "race" has been used at different times, what it has signified, and how it has served to articulate a conception of identity among its users. The English-language words "race" and "nation" emerged simultaneously in the late sixteenth century, and signify, as David Goldberg argues, "intersecting discourses of modernist anonymity." Race and nation as concepts are irreducibly political and "largely empty receptacles" through which population groups may be invented, interpreted, and imagined.[7] Such an approach, as Jonathon Glassman has argued, restores intellectual agency to colonial subjects whose sources of racial thought were both multiple and never fully "colonial," and who moreover actively appropriated those "colonial" elements of racial discourse into something oppositional.[8] The thinking and approach to the subject of race in this chapter plainly owes a great deal to the work of Jonathon Glassman, but it also differs in three important ways. First, although like Glassman this work does not seek to locate the "origins" of race, this chapter identifies the intellectual hardening of race as a popular identity category in the 1940s rather than in the *zama za siasa* or Zanzibar's "Time of Politics" in the later 1950s. Second, it argues that this earlier timing resulted from popular literary efforts that attempted to make sense of the categorization then enveloping urban life in Dar es Salaam. Finally, this chapter takes note of the important role of honor in defining categories of belonging. A shared experience of humiliation at the hands of Europeans and particularly Indians generated new needs to demonstrate African rights to respect. The category of race provided this, and became a political vehicle to realize the simple but powerful aphorism of colonial Africa's most influential Pan-Africanist, James Aggrey—"He who is not proud of his race is unfit to live."

This chapter investigates how interrelated concepts of race and nation, embodied in the Swahili term *taifa*, became the fulcrum of African nationalism in Tanganyika. To do so, it is vital to go beyond a priori definitions or singular translations that assume stable and discrete sociological categories, and to examine instead how historical actors adapted the inherited political terminology to fit changing needs. As we have seen, colonial-era Swahili categories of racial and national thought were imprecise and overlapping, but united in their concern with shared descent. Tribes, races, and nations in Swahili-speaking East Africa were primarily categories of descent, but they were not mutually discrete categories. *Kabila* and *taifa*, both Arabic loanwords conventionally translated from modern Swahili into English as "tribe" and "nation," respectively, were partially interchangeable, but *taifa* carried inflections of something larger, more settled, more cosmopolitan, and more associational than *kabila*. There was a sense among African writers that one *taifa* comprised multiple *kabila*,[9] but they rarely drew such distinctions before the 1950s. Colonial institutions rarely formalized a distinction between the two terms.[10] Coastal Kenya offers important comparisons. There, Swahili people more vigorously claimed Arab descent, and the various lines of descent claimed often retained specific geographical components, usually the name of original settlements. In this process, the Arabic *taifa* (literally "section") replaced the generic category for clans previously known by town (*mji*), in what Trimingham terms a "process of genealogical Arabization."[11] In coastal Kenya, as in coastal Tanganyika, *taifa* and *kabila* were largely interchangeable terms of clan membership that denoted location, kinship, and patrilineal descent.[12] To the extent that oral interviewees could be interested to speak about *taifa* or most other identity categories—with the important exception of *mwenye mji* and *watu wa kuja* discussed earlier—they mostly reinforced the postindependence, nationalist definitions I will discuss in chapter 5. The focus in this chapter is on the surviving letters, poems, petitions, and books that demonstrate how ideas of race and nation developed in the 1930s and 1940s. The materials available are overwhelmingly from male African writers. Women's voices are largely absent from the written record, and the male bias of the sources portrays women as dependent and auxiliary. However, as we shall see, the policing of female African purity was a touchstone in the development of Tanganyikan racial thought.

This chapter asserts that the discreteness and distinction between the group identity categories of race and nation, as they were understood by colonial-era historical actors, are in fact much weaker than historians and other academics have heretofore assumed. The terms were often, though not always, elidible; the Swahili word *taifa* could thus be translated in these contexts as "race-nation."[13] Evidence for this elide-ability lies in published literature and letters of Tanganyika's African writers. In the historical context examined below, usage of *taifa* invoked birth (*uzawa, mbegu*), descent (*ukoo, asili*), and skin color (*ngozi, rangi*)—ideas associated with contemporary understandings of "race"—along with ideas associated with contemporary understandings of "nation," such as language (*lugha*), culture (*utamaduni*), and tradition (*mila, desturi*). This blending is not extraordinary; distinctions between race and nation among Europeans were blurred beyond analytical coherence until the horrors of the Second World War induced a determined postwar clarity.[14] Contemporary distinctions between race and nation rest on the idea that "race" indicates a group bound by various factors, but above all by descent; "nation" may overlap with race, but the term also carries with it assimilative cultural characteristics, implying the potential realization for a nation-state that could theoretically house multiple races. Colonial government efforts to create a conservative "Tanganyikan" nationalism in the 1950s were grounded on "multiracialism" wherein three major races—European, Asian, and African—lived and worked implicitly apart. The steadfast rejection of "multi-racialism" by the Tanganyika African National Union (TANU), which formed in 1954 as the territory's major African nationalist party, draws our attention to vernacular terms that constituted race, nation, and nation-state. *Taifa* meant both race and nation; while *nchi* (land), with its greater emphasis on territory rather than descent, more closely approximated "nation-state," embodied in the geographical expression "Tanganyika." TANU's purpose was to recover the *nchi* for the *taifa*. To pursue this, we must shift analytical focus away from atemporal distinctions between race and nation, and toward historicizing the idea of *taifa* and how its *realization* became the principal concern of African (racial) nationalists.

The multiple origins of racial discourse for East Africa are particularly vexing. European conceptions of race and civilization, imported by colonial officials and missionaries and disseminated through schools, press, and colonial propaganda, are a major component. But earlier discourses had similarly elaborated racial thought in discussions of civilization. Although discourses of "civilization" and "barbarism" were certainly not unique to Africa, their ubiquity *within* Africa was remarkable—so common in oral traditions that they might be considered part of a continental political culture.[15] In Swahili, "civilization" best accords to the term *ustaarabu*, which etymologically means "to become Arab." The term *ustaarabu* first gained currency during struggles over cultural and political "Arabization" on the Swahili coast in the later nineteenth century when Omani power in Zanzibar challenged older forms of authority; it replaced *uungwana* (also "civilization") as the latter term lost its luster through promiscuous appropriation by ex-slaves seeking to assimilate into coastal culture. To assimilate into precolonial Swahili society and aspire to the high social status of Arab or Shirazi, or at least the *nouveau* title of *mwungwana* (free gentleman), one had to distance oneself from slave origins and claim deeper roots in both Islam and local patrilineages vis-à-vis more-recent newcomers.[16] *Ustaarabu* thus was a precolonial expression in which civilization meant social integration into a culture where one's acknowledged patrilineal ancestors came from the Middle East, and expressly did not come from "up-country." This long-standing assimilatory capacity of Swahili culture, combined with somatic diversity among Arabs themselves, reduced the centrality of somatic traits in coastal hierarchies of identity. According to Mazrui and Shariff, who define race in corporeal terms, the ideology of "cultural inferiority" was more prominent than that of "racial inferiority" under Arab rule in the nineteenth century.[17] Achieving high status required a plausible claim to proper lineage; one needed to be able to claim descent from prestigious coastal lineages, however fictive those claims might be. Use of the term *asili*, which first means "ancestry" or "origins" but also "temperament" or "essence," usually implied an ancestry worth having.[18] *Mtu wa asili* was a "man of noble lineage," while one without ancestry (*hana asili*) was "just a common man."[19] In the logic of patrician Swahili culture, one "assimilated" and became "civilized" by denying one's mainland African patrilineage, which is referenced in the caustic Swahili proverb "Mwacha asili ni mtumwa," meaning "He who disowns his ancestry is a slave." The term *ustaarabu* captures this cultural-lineage understanding of society, difference, and identity. Though still evoking past conflicts over slavery and belonging, *ustaarabu* had by the 1920s also come to signify a broader set of "civilized" values centering on accumulation of knowledge and wealth, and had become a key word of colonial public debate.[20] Furthermore, a specifically Zanzibari usage of *ustaarabu* was impressed upon a generation of Tanganyikan pupils, not only through the larger project of Swahili language standardization based on Zanzibari dialect, but more specifically through assignments based on *Milango ya Historia* (*Doors of History*, 1925–1931), a Zanzibar-centric history textbook that valorized Islam and Arab culture as well as Western civilization, for the reason that both had worked to take the African continent out of its darkness and into a universal history of civilization.[21]

Tanganyikan intellectuals had begun propounding racial-national groups as continental categories of descent during the interwar years. This mode of identification stemmed partly from wider Western ideas of race that divided humanity into continental categories—ideas that were "inescapably geographical."[22] But more immediately and vitally, local intellectuals were responding to Pan-Africanist inspirations generated by the 1924 tour of American-trained, Gold Coast educator James Aggrey. Despite visiting Tanganyika for only two weeks as a member of the Phelps-Stokes Commission, Aggrey left a profound impression on those he met.[23] Aggrey's definition of the African race made no reference to biological doctrine, and was wholly commonsensical—people who shared black skin and originated from the continent of Africa formed the African race. What was new was the contagious enthusiasm with which he ennobled African racial identity. Aggrey's aphorisms—in particular "He who is not proud of his color is not fit to live"—had a far-reaching influence on East Africa's intellectuals, who took away the more radical lesson of racial solidarity from Aggrey's pro-colonial politics and Tuskegee philosophy.[24] Such sentiments reached deeply into educated African households. The father of Chedieli Mgonja, the future minister of education in the 1960s, impressed upon the children of his Pare home Aggrey's homilies of racial pride and future African freedom.[25] Tanganyikan writers in turn connected descent-based idioms of identity with robust projects of improvement loosely termed "civilization." The African Association, progenitor to TANU, made civilization its principal goal. Its first president, Cecil Matola, informed the Colonial Office:

> It is the most sacred trust of His Majesty's Government to train and educate the African Native in East Africa and elsewhere, morally, socially, and economically in order to attain the Standard of Civilization which will enable him to stand for himself on the equality with the other Civilized Nations in the struggle for Civilization.[26]

Kleist Sykes encouraged African Association members to overcome petty internal rivalries and to struggle "with all our hearts towards the path of civilization just like other tribes are doing."[27] "Civilization" nominally transcended race, but was to be obtained on a racial rather than individual basis. Collective honor must precede individual advancement. The constitution of TAWCA, the African Association's chief rival, stated that no member could call any African *mshenzi* (savage), because a person could become *mshenzi* only by his actions.[28] *Kwetu*, the leading independent press forum for racial thought in colonial Tanganyika, discouraged readers from greeting one another with *ewaa*, an interjection of assent given by slaves to their masters, and instead encouraged using *bibi* or *bwana* to demonstrate respect (*heshima*).[29] Discouraging use of *ewaa* and *mshenzi* affirmed that civilization and barbarism were not ascribed by birth but products of how one lived. But subscribing to an idea of collective honor also meant honoring ancestors. Constructing a continental family tree required the flattening of genealogies and the genericizing of ancestors. Unlike "tribal" founding ancestors, all of whom had names, African racial ancestors were necessarily anonymous, apart from rare references to biblical Ham.[30] Though anonymous, they were, like tribal ancestors, singular parents. "We have one father and one mother," Ali Ponda lectured the African Association in 1937, "and that indeed is AFRICA."[31] Ancestral veneration focused on near-contemporary Pan-Africanist heroes, mainly Aggrey—whose name many East Africans bestowed upon their children—but also Booker T. Washington and Marcus Garvey. To identify oneself as *mbegu ya* (literally, "seed of") *Booker Washington* or *mbegu ya Aggrey* was a vivid metaphorical assertion of one's intellectual lineage.[32]

Systematic racial-national thought first required a standard terminology. Discarding the moniker of "native" and embracing instead that of "African" in both English and Swahili was the result of a deliberate campaign of African intellectuals during the Second World War. Earlier Tanganyikan writers had alternated between identifying themselves as "Africans" and "natives" in both English and Swahili. The Swahili term *mwenyeji* (native) carried powerful firstcomer overtones lacking in its English equivalent. "Indigenous" Shomvi of Dar es Salaam had rejected racial labeling and favored the term *mwenyeji* (see chapter 2) because "African" leveled distinctions between firstcomers and more-recent immigrants. But most other writers in Dar es Salaam vigorously adopted this leveling terminology over the 1940s. "Let's just remember that we are people of one skin [*ngozi*] and one *taifa*," a *Kwetu* reader explained, "Africans [Waafrika] are brothers, from Cape to Cairo all is Africa."[33] In its new usage, the moniker "African" wedded continental geography to a new emphasis on shared black skins. Another writer elaborated:

> The meaning of Dr. Aggrey's words is this: African, European, Asian *et cetera*, one has to be proud of his *taifa*, not proud only of his *kabila*

[tribe], African, you should be proud of your black color. He didn't just teach us to take pride in ourselves as individuals, but rather teaches us to share in our nation, all of us, so if you are intelligent and educated, help your nation as much as you are able, you, African, your *taifa* is the country of East Africa, South Africa, West Africa *et cetera*, all of these countries are people of one *taifa*, that is Africans.[34]

Colonial geographies affronted continental sensibilities. A resident of well-to-do New Street in Kariakoo attacked the *Tanganyika Standard* for identifying Africans as "Tanganyika-born" — "Never mind where the African was born, he is still an African."[35] The Indian-owned *Tanganyika Opinion* supported the replacement of "native" with "African" by reasoning that, just as the Gujarati epithet *golo* meant "a people destined for the condition of slavery for all times," "native" had become an epithet meaning "primitiveness, lack of culture and civilization, barbarism and subjectivity [sic] to slavery."[36] In 1942, *Kwetu* editor Erica Fiah loudly called for the rejection of the term "native," which "carries along with it, all the inferiority and social restrictions and divisions and colour-lines which are painfully suffered by all members of our race here." Yet he rejected "native" not only because it endorsed colonial hierarchy, but also because "native" was insufficiently rigid. Too many Africans wriggled free. Fiah was incensed at the bestowal of non-native status on those who shared African somatic traits: Comorians were categorized as non-natives to their undeserved advantage; Abyssinia was "purely African, barbaric and backward as we were or possibly are," yet politically independent and therefore "non-native"; the Somali has "succeeded in linking himself to a very doubtful ancestry with the Arab, black and backward as he may be or look." Fiah contrasted East Africans' ancestral artifices with the racial honesty of West Africans, who, though labeled natives, "like being Africans and being known as Africans of the best type, BUT FREE."[37] *Kwetu* readers similarly policed racial unity by decrying "Nubian" and "Zulu" exceptions to African wartime rations, and attempts by Nyasaland immigrants to distinguish themselves from Tanganyikans.[38] "Zulus" in Dar es Salaam who secured better rations and plot-lease terms as "non-natives" had traitorously "denied their African-ness" (Uafrika).[39] Youths learned the lesson. In 130 student papers read by a missionary for the 1950 Territorial Standard VIII examination in "History and Civics," every student had crossed out *watu weusi* (black people) in questions where it was used, replacing it with "Waafrika" (Africans).[40]

The deepest transformation of nationalist thought involved reconfiguring hegemonic notions of civilization embedded within Swahili language. The term *ustaarabu* lay at the root of most discussions concerning race and racial difference. Before European colonial rule, *ustaarabu* had been a central

Swahili concept that distinguished those who could claim some degree of Arab or Persian heritage and had adopted coastal cultural markers such as Islamic religion, food, and dress from those deemed uncivilized (*washenzi*). Like most civilizations, Swahili culture extended potential integration of outsiders through the adoption of coastal culture and intermarriage. This value-laden language thrived in the early twentieth century, when assumptions shared by interlocutors on race and civilization in Tanganyika's public sphere closely resembled those of Victorian anthropologists who understood humanity as being divided into discrete groups moving linearly from simplicity toward complexity and civilization—what Stocking terms "socio-cultural evolutionism."[41] For African thinkers, civilization both consecrated racial identities and moved discrete nations toward a common goal, necessitating separate cultural transformations that would destroy immoral atavisms but conserve positive ancestral inheritances. The point of *ustaarabu* was racial consciousness through self-recognition and self-improvement. "Let us become civilized like Europeans," one writer offered in this vein, "but we should not change our African names into European ones."[42] Harsh criticisms awaited those Africans who imitated British or Arabic culture in order to lord their higher social status over those they dismissed as *washenzi*—a danger, one activist thought, best represented by the Swahili proverb "Mvunja nchi ni mwana nchi," or "The destroyer of the country is a child of the country."[43] Suits, shirts, ties, *dansi*, and intoxication all formed a disagreeable cluster of European influence that compared unfavorably to the purity of the naked African who seeks only that "which is fitting for our *taifa*."[44] *Ustaarabu* required mastery over desires (*tamaa*), such as the pursuit of expensive and ruinous sartorial imitation, whetted by urban life.[45] Any *taifa* had to know farming and have intelligence and good customs; simply knowing English or Arabic languages or fashions "does not leave one filled with *ustaarabu*."[46] Particularly distressing were those educated Africans who scorned rather than exalted the Swahili language. Acquiring civilization necessitated mastery of language, and to accept a fellow African speaking one's language poorly was tantamount to a denial of one's *taifa*. Swahili, not English, should be the language of "intertribal" discourse; without this, Africans were condemned to futile imitation.[47]

Two self-improvement primers by Tanganyikan African authors addressed the relationship between civilization and race, and together reveal often-implicit bases of national categorical thought. The first was authored by Martin Kayamba, prewar Tanganyika's most accomplished African civil servant and English-language writer. He was, according to John Iliffe, "born an aristocrat, a fact which he was never to regret," and bitterly eulogized in *Kwetu* as a man "detached from [his] race" and "fond of singing his own praises."[48] Written in 1937 and published posthumously in 1948, Kayamba's *African Problems* addressed how one could remain "wholly African" while building toward an African future by "wise study and selection from all that the new forces of civilization had to offer."[49] Africans of his day, Kayamba argued, were in an artificial transitional period of "detribalisation" between the primeval tribal customs of their parents and those of modern civilization. Despite this transition, there were considerable African essences or attributes that persevered, and which must be respected in future progress toward civilization, such as the sacred connection to land—"As a Hindoo to his mother cow so is an African to his mother land."[50] Among attributes to be overcome, Kayamba identifies Africans' tribal life, which has "taught Africans to live in water-tight compartments," preventing them from being "capable to thinking of Africa as a whole."[51] Ever since the cash nexus of Indian traders supplanted the precolonial system of intertribal barter, Africans had esteemed Indian-sold goods over those sold by fellow African traders. Kayamba counters this reality with a racially autarchic vision wherein goods are purchased exclusively from African traders in order to "retain the circulation of money in the country," and the recovered wealth is used for "improvement of conditions in the country and the progress of its people." Anticipating Nyerere's *ujamaa* vision, Kayamba describes a future central village with brick houses containing locally produced tiles, a church, a mosque, a dispensary, a school, a council house, a central marketplace, and "a few shops owned entirely by Africans. . . . I think in this we have a nucleus for Africans' own civilization."[52] Africa's future "civilization" will thus be rural, self-sufficient, and exclusively African, reversing the anomie of detribalization.

The other African-penned primer was Salum Kombo's *Ustaarabu na Maendeleo ya Mwafrika* (*Civilization and Development of the African*). Published after winning the East African Inter-territorial Language Committee's writing contest in 1947, this book offers a rare glimpse into buried assumptions of racial difference. According to Kombo, a renowned *shairi* poet, civilization was a means to remove the shame (*aibu*) of Africa's backward customs and to build a *taifa* that would improve African conditions. *Shairi* poets hold a particularly esteemed place among Tanganyikan thinkers; they are those "divers who go deep into the sea."[53] Kombo's embrace of continental discourse in the 1940s represents a larger break of national-minded Swahili poets, such as Shaaban Robert, Saadani Abdu Kandoro, Mathias Mnyampala, and Sheikh Kaluta Amri Abedi, from the parochialism of older poets.[54] Employing classical sociocultural evolutionary categories, Kombo's prose explained how *ustaarabu* has enabled Africans to evolve into larger social units, the end of which was self-recognition and fulfillment of the African *taifa*. Kombo did not think of himself as "creating" race—like other African racial thinkers of his day, he saw race as being immanent in the order of things. It was only for others to recognize it as well:

The African of the day before yesterday did not know the value of tribe and therefore cared about nothing more than his family [*ukoo*]. The African of yesterday progressed a little by knowing the value of tribe [*kabila*] instead of family, and took some steps forward; the African of today cares greatly about *taifa* more than tribe or family, and this is a good sign that he has taken big steps forward in *ustaarabu* in connection with world affairs.[55]

In Kombo's account, evolution toward civilization ends at *taifa*. While each *taifa* had its particular forms of *ushenzi* (barbarism), each struggled against it by adopting universal mental tools of education and good sense bestowed by civilization. Kombo repeatedly cautioned readers not to confuse *ustaarabu* with merely imitating foreign styles of dress and behavior—African styles and names, like African elders, must be honored. Kombo even offered a definition of *taifa*, practically unique in Swahili literature—"'Taifa' ni jumla ya watu ambao asili yao walikuwa 'watoto' waliozaliwa na Baba na Mama zao"; or, "'*Taifa*' is the sum of people whose origins were 'children' born by their Father and Mother."[56] For Kondo, civilization enabled *conscious recognition* of extended familial bonds of descent, which in turn enables Africans to build the race/nation (*kujenga taifa*).

PATRILINEAL DESCENT AND THE PROBLEM OF INTERRACIAL LIAISONS

The sharpening of African racial thought in the 1940s turned on two developments—the intensification of African self-improvement rhetoric, which we have already seen, and the elaboration of a critique against interracial sexual relations. In Tanganyika's male-dominated, African public sphere, *taifa* was a moral question that for many began and ended with intimate relations between self-evident social groups. An exceptional debate in the government monthly *Mambo Leo* during 1945–1947 over interracial sexual relations demonstrates how the elaboration of racial thought drew upon local idioms of identity and morality, as well as on Pan-African sentiment generated by territorial and international travel. Civilization, for the mostly male debaters, depended on African women's fidelity to racial purity. Their *taifa* expressly conflated skin color and geographical origin into a self-evident social category. By equating sexual liaisons or marriage between races with savagery (*ushenzi*), these thinkers inverted conventional discursive and social practices of Swahili culture that equate becoming civilized with adopting Islamic coastal customs and ideally intermarrying with Arabs—or at least having the ability to claim Arab or Persian descent. This older cultural understanding, preserved in the word *ustaarabu* (becoming Arab), was decisively abandoned in the 1940s by

African male debaters who declared interracial liaisons a form of generational treason against (male) African elders.

Looming over these articulations of race and patrilineal descent in the 1940s was a deepening crisis in the institution of marriage throughout East Africa. Wartime inflation had sharply inflated regional prices of bridewealth, the core of patriarchy, which put marriage beyond the reach of many young African men, including returning soldiers. Elopements and informal co-habitations were some of the strategies young men and women employed to cope with an increasingly difficult situation.[57] Marriage crises threatened the normative family upon which political authority was ideally based. Discussions of chiefly authority in interwar Tanganyika had been nested in discourses of patrilineal clan hierarchies—normative units of "ancestors living in territorially discrete, patrilineal clans"—that coexisted messily alongside matrilineal relationships crucial to many people's daily lives.[58] The hopes and desires of young African men seeking to realize an honorable adulthood through marriage focused on what was most beyond their control—African women and the cash economy. The intellectual response to this crisis in the 1940s was to embrace the ideal of the patrilineal clan while continentalizing its principle. By having the children of men who did not belong to the continental clan, so this reasoning went, African women denied young African men their adulthoods and created children whose very existence defied the principle of racial-continental integrity.

At the heart of the print debate that most explicitly defined *taifa* was an angry lamentation against the perceived loss of African patriarchal rights over women. Male writers protested against the sinful and destructive nature of interracial liaisons and the alleged sexual usurpation of black women by "white" men that was destroying African ancestral lines—a particular resentment that also played a key role in the 1949 African-Indian race riots in Durban.[59] The debate in Tanganyika began in 1945 with an angry letter from an Education Department worker in Dar es Salaam who expressed his outrage at what he described as the habit of African women to disobey their parents and cohabitate with and bear children of *mbegu nyeupe*—literally "white seed" but also meaning white "stock" or "race"—the term "white" referring to Europeans, Indians, and Arabs indiscriminately. These women, he argued, should marry men of their own *taifa* to increase the African population, but they instead marry foreigners and give birth to savage children (*mtoto wa kishenzi*) who would become *chotara* (i.e., "mixed-race" or "half-caste").[60] Another writer claimed that such women brought shame by begetting non-African children, and that to do so was to enter into a state of slavery without knowing it, as whites would accept black women only to live in their homes as *ayahs*. "White" parents would never reciprocate and marry their daughters to an African, no matter what his wealth. By bearing children of *mbegu za makontineti mengine* (seeds/races of other continents), these women destroyed their ancestors' reputation and returned Africans to a state of savagery (*ushenzi*).[61]

African male advocates of racial purity tied their pronouncements on civilization with familiar anecdotes of racial mistreatment of African women by non-African men through a series of rhetorical questions. Another writer related the story of how an African woman living with an Indian man was kicked out of the house when her relatives visited, because the man feared these visitors would eat up his finances and never leave. The writer compared the woman unfavorably to the Indian's African *boi*, or servant, dwelling on her blindness to racial realities that were clear to the lowly domestic worker:

> The girl living with the Indian did not think herself to be like the *boi* but better than him, she considered herself the Indian's woman. But the truth is this, the *boi* was better and he did not leave that day, indeed he did all his work for [her] visiting relatives. Womenfolk who are able to figure this out could not agree to live with a white [*mbegu nyeupe*], but because of money, they no longer see it as a shameful thing.[62]

A Tanganyikan tailor serving in India blamed African men for allowing African women "to sell themselves without knowing themselves nor taking account of their own condition."[63] The tailor here refers obliquely to what all of these writers believed—that interracial sexual relations were necessarily a form of prostitution, which degraded African women, undermined racial unity, and was an affront to civilization. The prevailing double standard in which male African workers could be fired for joking with European women, while European men openly drank with African women in bars and then left together, understandably galled African men.[64] These male writers were writing to one another in the pages of *Mambo Leo*, confirming, through this lamentation of lost patriarchy, the need to build a race by imposing sexual discipline on wayward women.

We are not entirely without the viewpoint of African women, though these voices are sparse. Flowarose Salama binti Arubati argued in *Mambo Leo* that interracial coupling occurred because African men did not follow rules of marriage. When an African husband disliked his wife, Flowarose argued, he would trick her by behaving poorly until she divorced him and returned his bridewealth. She also contested the ubiquitous reasoning of male writers who argued that African women should "know themselves" and therefore avoid intimate relations with non-Africans—here she was addressing a rhetorical device derived from a widely held but mistaken understanding of Qur'anic verse

49:13: "We have made you into confederacies and tribes so that you may come to know one another."[65] Flowarose countered with another commonplace, that "there is not black or white in Islam, where black and white are people of one religion," and concluded that African women sought whites because Africans were not "strong of mind, wealth, or perseverance. . . . Therefore a poor African (man) cannot marry white."[66]

Flowarose's incendiary letter goaded the mainly male readership of *Mambo Leo*'s far-flung audience into a flurry of angry responses that continued for nearly two years. Many respondents had stayed in India and Ceylon during the Second World War (see below). At stake was the question of sexual reciprocity among races and nations. An *askari* (soldier) in the South East Asia Command rhetorically asked, "Why do Indian men marry African women, when African men do not marry the daughters of Indians? [Indian men] don't want their womenfolk to marry us, but just to marry our womenfolk." He continued:

> Why do other races/nations [*mataifa*] marry our women in our home, and we are ordered that we do not have permission to marry women of another *taif*? . . . Why do African women love those with money more than their own *taif*?[67]

An appended editorial note to this letter blamed African elders who had failed to instill discipline in their children, arguing that "no girl is taken by force; but those who live with foreigners do so by being attracted to self-indulgent things."[68] In one particularly hostile letter, an *askari* stationed in New Delhi attacked Flowarose's claims that African men were lazy by arguing that it was herself and African women who were lazy by living immorally:

> Civilization does not just come from sleeping and getting wealth without effort, or wealth from sinful means such as those you mentioned in the newspaper. God gives one intelligence and strength and hands in order that you should use them. It is up to you to do as you are able in order to civilize your country Tanganyika.[69]

The antidote to interracial moral debasement was the disciplined pursuit of civilization that would please the creator through maintenance of racial-national purity, and, more immediately, satisfy the honor of these writers, which had been traduced, in their minds, by wealthy non-African men pursuing morally weak African women.

African men also objected to the baleful effects that intimate interracial relations had on the ideal of the African family. An African veterinary worker lectured Flowarose that "husband, wife and children are a *chama* [club or society]," yet, "by your words you deter people who have no financial opportunity. . . . You encourage those people who bring shame and damage our *taifa*." Civilization and happiness, he explained, "are not brought by desire for money," and that "desire for worldly pleasures is emphatically the enemy of goodness and of all civilization." He countered Flowarose's pessimistic views on the natural qualities of African males with a theory of civilization-uplift acquired through mutual welfare, sublimation, and self-restraint:

> It is absolutely necessary that we differentiate between self-indulgence and CIVILIZATION, which are very different. Your [Flowarose's] argument depends on the desire for pleasure, and not on civilization particularly. . . . We younger people who have studied are blessed with the opportunity to marry our black friends, especially when they are poor, in order that our wives should be in a good state. If each one of us does this, after some years most of us will be in a good state. In this way a person marries one's own black person of one's tribe [*kabila*], this is the path that is the most practical.[70]

Flowarose responded by attacking detractors who had misrepresented her argument—for example, that she had sought to encourage African women to marry whites—yet failed to address her real complaints, such as the time African men wasted in bars shouting and getting drunk. African men, she argued, had failed to live up to civilization's promises and were quickly being surpassed by foreigners. She goaded:

> None of you has come to be motivated to seize upon a civilization of raising your condition to become higher and respectable. You all are surpassed by (foreigner) Indians who are too many in this country, while the affairs of the country deserve you instead. For this whole time you have not yet obtained enough progress, you are even unable to seize your right which is in the hands of the English, who want to give to you, but you refuse.[71]

Flowarose countered male objections to interracial marriage by citing examples of prominent, historical African men such as Muhammad's companion Bilal and James Aggrey, both of whom married "whites."[72]

The chief issue at stake in these print debates about interracial liaisons was the creation and fate of mixed-race offspring. This ultimate transgression of racial boundaries seemed self-evidently destructive and sinful to every African male intellectual, for it endangered continental patrilineages. Mixed-race children first posed problems of recognition and self-recognition. One man protested, "If you place them in the humanity of blacks they are not there, nor are they in European group, Indian group or Arab group, they are like a butterfly." Pluralizing the normatively nonracial phrase "sons of Adam" into racial-national terms, he rephrased a popular Swahili proverb by accusing Flowarose: "Lady of the sons of Adam *of this country*, you want to destroy this country."[73] The very existence of mixed-race offspring evinced sin. African fathers who gave their daughters to Indians and Arabs were condemned for contributing to the begetting of a *taifa la wanaharama*, or "race/nation of illegitimate offspring" who boast that they are better than Africans but ultimately marry one and live their lives without "knowing themselves." Africans, one writer explained, should stop expanding this *ukoo mwingine mpya*, or "new lineage," and should instead work to reduce this *kabila la haramu*, or "tribe of sin."[74] Another man asked Flowarose, "If you marry an Indian or any other white person and you bear his child, what tribe [*kabila*] will this child be called? We want every African to be pure, husband with wife should do his color proud, given to him by the Creator."[75] A female poet, or perhaps male using a female alias, composed a *shairi* verse titled "Mwafrika kwa weupe ni tamaa ya dunia," or "African with white is worldly lust." The poet ruminated on the confused identity of the mixed-race child:

> Akifika Afrika, twasema ni Indiani,
> India akishafika, asemwa Mwafrikani,
> Kabila atatajika, tumwite kabila gani?
> Mwafrika kwa mweupe, ni tamaa ya dunia.

> If he arrives in Africa, we say he is Indian,
> If he goes to India, he is reviled as an African,
> What tribe will he be called, what tribe should we call him?
> African with white, is worldly lust.[76]

Fiah had earlier warned African men about the dangers of marrying mixed-race women—such hectoring women ruined their husbands' honor (*heshima*) by reminding them that their fathers had been servants of these women's fathers.[77] *Machotara* were seen to hold themselves aloof from Africans. "Mpanda ngazi hushuka" (He who climbs the ladder comes down), one distressed African onlooker philosophized after having been snubbed by his mixed-race cousins and uncles on a visit to Iringa. He bitterly concluded that "mwafrika ni ngozi asili kwa baba na mama," or "The African is the skin color originating from father and mother"—an assertion that African identity was a somatic truth based upon pure descent, and also a play on the words *ngazi* (ladder) and *ngozi* (skin color).[78] The "ladder," or social hierarchy that externally defined East Africa's races, was unjust, but it was as authentic as one's own skin color; to attempt to deny this by "climbing" up another rung betrayed African racial authenticity. In the imagination of these male African print figures—as in that of many "whites"—the conflation of race, nation, and geography was self-evident and unambiguous. The sexual transgression of racial boundaries bespoke a failure of sublimation and surrender to base impulse.

The Flowarose debate coincided with heightened attention to the "problem" of mixed-race children. Progeny of interracial liaisons and marriages— inevitably between non-African fathers and African mothers—had long been keenly aware of their uncomfortable political and social status. Legally, a "half-caste" child belonged to the father's nationality in cases of legal marriage, and "native" where no marriage had occurred. Male children of European fathers were often educated in mission schools, and could aspire to European legal identity; daughters rarely received similar education, and tended to marry Indians or Arabs. The offspring of Indian fathers were usually educated at Government Central School or Indian schools.[79] Mixed-race children of legal marriages, Dar es Salaam's provincial commissioner observed, tended to suffer greater discrimination, as they were "looked down on and neglected by their non-native relations . . . the exceptions being the Ithnashiri, the Mohammedan Punjabis and, generally speaking, Arabs."[80] Untold numbers were conceived but never born. *Kwetu* reported that non-African men—particularly Europeans—gave African women medicine to induce abortion.[81]

Tanganyika never created a separate legal or administrative category for "half-caste" or "coloured" populations, and instead followed Colonial Office declarations that legal status of mixed-race people "should depend primarily upon the standard and mode of their life," and thus not place obstacles in the way of "native half-castes being classified among members of a higher civilization."[82] Yet a growing "mixed-race" population—whose legal invisibility makes it difficult to guess at their numbers—only further steeled officials' resolution to address their legal identities on a case-by-case rather than a categorical basis.[83] Impetus to create a special status came from Europeans concerned with the fate of mixed offspring—particularly that of mixed-race daughters, who, one self-styled European altruist argued, often ended up as prostitutes or abused wives of Africans.[84] For male African thinkers, the tragedy of *machotara* was their abandonment by non-African fathers, who left them to "be thrown to us, their *wajomba* [maternal male kin]."[85] These writers were horrified at suggestions that Africans abused "half-castes," and that they innately deserved better government treatment, such as being given separate schools. Such a proposal, J. A. Zimba argued, maligned the natural geography of racial-national continents—"There is no land for half-castes in the whole world so far. . . . The only good way to avoid such hereditary problems is to avoid intermarriage or cross intercourse."[86] The African who marries a "half-caste," another writer suggested, does so only out of generosity and pity, in order that this lost child enjoys "things which she could not otherwise possess and without which no 'pure race' can exist. . . . If his African mother won't have him he has no one else in the world."[87] In practice there was only limited truth to this latter assertion; but within Tanganyika's racial discourse in the 1940s, the "mixed-race" child increasingly had no home.

Increased sensitivity to the fate of "mixed-race" children, together with the Flowarose debate, raised political consciousness among mixed-race Tanganyikans. A few mixed-race associations had existed before the war—such as the "Half-Caste Dancing Club" in 1930s Dar es Salaam—but more formally political ones now emerged.[88] M. M. Abushiri wa Mbwana, a mixed-race worker at Amboni sisal plantation near Tanga, founded the Association of Masuriama and Machotara, an organization that recruited males born of an African mother and an Arab or Indian father. Each, according to Abushiri, faced dilemmas—a *suriama* would not have equal rank (*hadhi*) with Arabs of Arabia-born Arabs, while *chotara* could not marry an Indian girl of Indian parentage, and would still be called *golo* (Gujarati, "slave")—yet both were refused admission into the African Association. Abushiri appealed:

> I'm not saying that you should be called Africans, no way! follow your tribe of *mataifa* [race-nations]. . . . Not to claim that you are an Arab although it is true, but that you are our compatriot because of how we have mixed blood. . . . The essence of this advice, don't think that we will be defeated by the African Association.[89]

But Abushiri was making appeals in the face of an African Association that now steadfastly held intermarriage to be utterly destructive, in which "the African is always the loser." Noting that Africans had "been convicted or even suffered death on account of sheer love affairs with the fair sex of other races," the African Association resolved in 1947: "If it is considered an insult for a male native to marry a female foreigner . . . a law needs be framed against a male foreigner to marry a female native."[90] Amid this lobbying and political posturing, the colonial government felt compelled to take at least limited action regarding the welfare of *machotara*, and passed the Maintenance of Illegitimate Children Act, which required men to pay child support if mothers brought suit—clearly aimed at mixed-race offspring because it did not apply to cases where both father and mother were "natives."[91] During the bill's reading, the Legislative Council's three African members agreed that the real value of the law would be to discourage interracial liaisons and their consequent "rapidly growing population of illegitimate half-caste children."[92]

The "problem" of mixed-race children sharpened ideas about race by high-lighting moral responsibilities fulfilled or unfulfilled by the mostly Indian and Arab fathers. Some took offense to Abushiri's overt methods of political recruitment, decrying *chotara* and *suriama* as pejoratives, their very invocation insulting Africans and mixed-race people alike.[93] Most important, the general assumptions revealed in these debates demonstrate that a wide intellectual consensus had now been reached, one that understood race to be both a natural product of continental descent but also the means to self-improvement. One was born African but only remained so by acquiring civilization and embodying a specific kind of moral living. Among the leading proponents of this vision were veterans of the Burma campaign. For them, race not only provided a portable identity to fix continental claims, but also the grounds for a bitter act of comparison that served to evaluate the profound inequalities that structured the imperial Indian Ocean world.

HESHIMA: HONOR, SHAME, AND THE COMPARATIVE IMAGINATION OF AFRICAN ASKARI IN SOUTH ASIA

> *Hindi ndiko kwenye nguo na wendao tupu wako!*
> (India is the country of clothes, yet there are naked, poor
> people there!)[94]

In 1945 the initials "TANU," standing for "Tanganyika African National Union," were scratched, for the very first time, into the diary Abdulwahid Sykes was carrying while stationed as a soldier in Bombay. Whether or not this means that the future ruling party was thus first invented by Abdulwahid Sykes and his brother Ally, as they later claimed, Bombay and the rest of war-time South Asia were undoubtedly sites of fertile comparative imagination for future African nationalists. Few East Africans had previously enjoyed the luxury to reflect on the meaning of homeland, travel, and identity in other Indian Ocean countries before the Second World War. From 1943 to 1946, sections of Tanganyika's Sixth King's African Rifles (KAR) trained in Ceylon, fought in Burma, and traveled extensively through British India, providing a rich comparative experience for *askari* or African soldiers.[95] Some *askari* returned inspired by a wider vision of anticolonial nationalism. One veteran signaler advocated for an "African Continental Union" to transcend Tanganyika's territorial boundaries by observing India's relative unity and their advancement in the country's civil service.[96] Doing oral research in 1971, the historian Lorne Larson was struck by "the marked impact of the Indian experience on *askari*, particularly on modifying the stereotypes of Indians derived from the Indian merchant class of East Africa."[97] Waruhiu Itote, a Kenyan better known by his Mau Mau nom de guerre "General

China," had served in Tanganyika's 3/6 KAR where he learned the political lesson of unity and trust from Indian nationalists he met in Calcutta. But such positive impressions were, by and large, exceptional. When Itote himself returned to Kenya, outraged to find that Asian "guests" had "stifled us economically," he asked, "Was this not Africa, our Africa, and were we not Africans?"[98] For Itote and most of the Tanganyikan *askari* whom he had served alongside, this imperative to reclaim racial-national birthrights from the exploitative grasp of foreigners overshadowed ecumenical anticolonialisms of the Indian Ocean.

KAR *askari* spent most of their time in South Asia performing physically demanding, dull, and routine work, confined to segregated camps that suffered from "disabilities of separation and strangeness."[99] Amenities were practically nonexistent—entertainment facilities located on the ill-named "Slave Island" in Colombo were not, unsurprisingly, well-patronized by KAR troops.[100] Isolation bred alienation and contempt, but also a fleeting sense of ethnographic wonder. An ethnic Kamba *askari* found water plentiful, food cheap, and that he and his fellow soldiers were respected more in Ceylon than in Africa; but he also found it easier to fall into local debt, and that soldiers were not as warmly welcomed as they had been in Abyssinia.[101] Ceylonese dowry practices provided soldiers with a fascinating if incredible alternative to East African bridewealth traditions; local Ceylonese were in turn fascinated with *askari* skin color.[102] Such mutual interest bred official anxiety. A social welfare officer posited that African *askari* in Ceylon, experiencing first contact with a new culture and separation from Africa, now faced the possibilities of "complete orientalisation," "complete segregation," or "partial fusion, adaptation." He elaborated:

> For instance, the payment of a dowry by the bride's father is in direct opposition to the African system where the dowry is payable by the bridegroom. Any attempt to introduce the Eastern order in to Africa will lead to disastrous results. . . . On the whole the evidence is in favour of "avoidance" as far as possible with Oriental culture.[103]

The officer concluded by advocating "exploitation of African games, amusements, and recreation, camp firesides, story telling, proverb sessions, and so on," in order to "Africanise askari camp life in Ceylon."[104] Combat in Burma was as vicious as any in the entire war; violence between encamped *askari* and South Asian locals was rare but not unknown—a KAR camp outside Calcutta was relocated following a riot, cause unknown, between *askari* and local Indians.[105] Camp life not only segregated Africans from larger Indian and Ceylonese populations, it also sharpened identities based on colonial territory through social activities such as football. More than ethnicity, "Tanganyikan" territorial identity emerged as a defining feature among Tanganyikan 6 KAR soldiers serving abroad.[106]

Honor (*heshima*), minimally defined as the individual's right to respect, loomed large in how Africans perceived their new environments, and became their principal idiom to frame interactions with South Asians. In its Swahili conception, *heshima* means not only "honor" but also attention to status and reputation; "*the maintenance of the position in which respect or honor is due.*"[107] Yet *heshima* required not only positive external recognition, but also confidence that unspoken recognition could be mutually sustained. As John Middleton argues:

> It is not a quality of an isolated individual, but an aspect of relations of communication and exchange. By behaving with courtesy, sensitivity, and goodness toward someone else, a person both acquires heshima himself and bestows it on the person addressed, who, by responding seemingly and graciously, in turn affirms his own heshima and emphasizes its possession by the original giver.[108]

Experience of travel, war, and wages vastly accelerated these relations of communication and exchange. *Heshima* during the 1940s was ultimately a quest for "due recognition," as Tom McCaskie terms it, something powerfully felt among African soldiers abroad. It was an "agitated interrogation of self," sustained by mobility and money, that valorized an "interiority that might command and secure acknowledgement from others similarly engaged."[109]

Military recruitment appeals to male honor—"Join the K.A.R. and lead a man's life"—had proven powerfully effective in East Africa.[110] *Heshima*, title of the KAR thrice-monthly, Swahili/Chichewa newspaper launched in Ceylon, was saturated with items stressing the importance of maintaining *askari* honor. Much of its content was disciplinary.[111] As its first editorial instructs, "The *heshima* of our [East African] Army is high. . . . As strangers in Ceylon let us see that we do nothing to spoil our good name."[112] A *shairi* verse concurred, noting that *askari* arrived at Ceylon with *heshima*, and exhorted, "Let's not damage our honor, for they will then call us idiots."[113] This flourishing *askari* print culture also reflected that part of *heshima* included mastery of basic literacy in Swahili, a necessary tool of instruction and command for East African military recruits; English literacy was more scarce, but also far more sought after.[114] It was, in short, a transplanted venue to acquire *ustaarabu*. In one case, roughly 85 percent of an African artillery battery in Burma had to become literate within six months. Gerald Hanley captured the ensuing excitement in his classic account of the Burma campaign, *Monsoon Victory*:

The passion for writing and reading had gripped them and every man had learned even a few words. In their spare moments they sat down with stubs of pencils, pushed out their tongues, and with much labour wrote a letter to Africa.[115]

Back home, a class of professional letter writers were busily employed replying to soldier correspondence on behalf of illiterate family and friends.[116] Literate expression of honor and related concepts were explored by the numerous African *askari* flooding *Heshima* and East African newspapers with the products of their newfound literacy in letters, reports, and poetry.

Askari in Asia were both comparative ethnographers and literary introspects attempting to make sense of a radically different culture through a vocabulary of honor. The enemy of *heshima* was *aibu* (shame). One clerk complained at feeling shame when local Ceylonese ran away at the sight of African *askari*.[117] Another warned that soldiers brought *aibu* upon themselves through incontinent living, in particular by spending hard-earned wages on local prostitutes rather than on their wives and families back home.[118] Soldiers' impressions upon reaching mainland India were often marked by shock and wonderment. Arriving in Calcutta, a corporal concluded that all Indians were *washenzi* after watching them remove the teeth of snakes and fish; others leaped at the opportunity to buy gold teeth and snakebite medicines from traveling Indian salesmen.[119] Still others were appalled, observing that Hindus worshipped (*kuabudu*) idols rather than simply honored them (*kuheshimu*) as Christians did.[120] The concept of *aibu* could also be used to launch institutional criticisms against the army's own racial structure, to point out the lack of African officers or humiliating racial restrictions to the attendance of certain army cinema showings.[121]

"One perquisite that every soldier could expect," Iliffe argues, "was a woman"[122]—but such perquisites posed sharp problems for African soldiers stationed in South Asia. Camp anxieties fastened upon the obvious and potent sexual frustrations of KAR *askari* abroad, particularly those who frequented or attempted to frequent South Asian prostitutes.[123] Darrell Bates, a KAR officer who created a brothel in Abyssinia to control venereal disease infections, observed that African *askari* in Ceylon, Burma, and India "used to wander round the villages, smiling at the girls, and knocking on the doors as they had done with impunity, and more, in Abyssinia."[124] Military brothels serving KAR *askari* were widespread during the war—in Southeast Asia, *askari* acquired prostitutes through either Indian pimps or British officers.[125] Engaging local prostitutes exploded racial hierarchies while cementing racial stereotypes. In one disastrous case, during a 3/6 KAR training exercise near Trincomalee, a Ceylonese man agreed to offer "his woman" to an *askari*, but on the night of the meeting not one but three *askari* arrived. When the man tried to back out of the deal, he was shot. The woman was badly cut and was raped when the commanding officer entered the hut. The man died, and the three *askari* escaped without being identified.[126] African soldiers living in close proximity to European women provoked "black scare" responses. Rumors that *askari* sexually assaulted European nursing sisters in India Command military hospitals led to an ordered reduction of female nursing staff in hospitals treating East and West Africans, replacement of sisters' African personal servants with British or Indian orderlies, and restriction against sisters doing night duty in African hospitals.[127] "Once away from his native land," the commanding staff officer opined, without any reference to factual cases, "it would appear that the African's attitude towards women changes considerably, and it is necessary in some African hospitals to have flares burning and guards posted around the Sisters' Messes at night."[128] Such sexual humiliation only intensified the more systematized affronts to *askari* honor. Veteran *askari* seethed at the superior rations, amenities, and pay given to Indian troops of the same rank. In one case, an injured *askari* was flown from Burma to India for emergency treatment but quickly transferred from the "Indian" hospital to one "only for Africans" to recover.[129] Sartorial humiliation rankled the African rank-and-file, one of whom bitterly asked why Indians wore the same clothes as Europeans, but Africans did not.[130]

Askari experience in the eastern theater particularly crystallized Tanganyikan nationalist racial sentiment within the Sykes family, the leading African family of Dar es Salaam. Abdulwahid Sykes, eldest son of Kleist Sykes, had been conscripted in KAR in 1941 or 1942, which prevented him from attending Makerere College.[131] His young brother Ally, who joined KAR at age fifteen in 1943, understood the experience of traveling to South Asia as an awakening to racial inequality. After briefly serving in Somalia, Sykes found himself shipped out to Ceylon, where onboard mess was allocated by race. Ally demanded equal rations with Europeans and Indians, and through an organized protest managed to secure Tanganyikan soldiers an "Arab" diet.[132] Shortly after the war, the two Sykes brothers and James Mkande made a pact—on Christmas Day in 1945 at Kalieni Camp near Bombay, where homeward-bound KAR from Tanganyika had regrouped—to form a political party upon returning home, working with fellow Kenyan nationalists, to address general injustice (*udhalimu*) and particular discriminatory restrictions against Africans traveling first class, entering hotels, and being served drinks. So in Abdulwahid's diary on that day was recorded the name of this new party, the Tanganyika African National Union or TANU, which eventually formed in 1954.[133]

The lesson learned by most KAR *askari* in South Asia was not Indian tutelary nationalism, but outrage at India's comparative squalor. Fifty years later,

Ally Sykes—who worked as a teacher instructor because of his excellent English—recalled that he spent no time speaking with Indians about Indian nationalism; indeed, he categorically denied that Indian nationalists influenced Tanganyikan veterans at all.[134] South Asia's profound poverty made Sykes bitterly reflect on why such peoples should be given political opportunities, yet comparatively more-prosperous Africans had been denied such opportunities in their own home.[135] India opened his eyes:

> We were still thinking that the white man was a demi-god, who had blue blood and the Asian had cream blood, and we believed that. But after seeing what the Asians are in Asia, they're more primitive, poor condition of life, very unhygienic. How can whites who ruled here and Asians who come from here rule over us?[136]

India was then on the verge of independence; Indians in East Africa continued to dominate the region's economy, yet African *askari* saw something very different. Randal Sadleir, serving as KAR officer in 1945, recalled "thousands of human scarecrows" who stormed railway stations to fight over scraps left behind from soldiers' meals as they made their way from Dhanaskodi opposite Ceylon to Calcutta *en route* to the Burmese front. "The *askaris*," Sadleir witnessed, "amazed by the spectacle of the broken-down brothers of the prosperous Asian merchants in East Africa, announced that they would never again allow themselves to be exploited by such miserable creatures."[137] Unpublished letters to *Heshima* indicated that "color consciousness" was sharply rising in 1945, not only concerning discrimination between British and African troops, but also the desire "to end the Indian's monopoly of trade in East Africa."[138] The historian Kevin Brown discovered these same sentiments during interviews he conducted for his doctoral thesis. Many of these retired KAR veterans were appalled by the poverty they encountered in Calcutta, Ceylon, and other areas. One veteran told Brown that "here [Tanzania] the Indians controlled many things, but when we went there [India], they were nothing. They were beggars. They were the poorest and dirtiest people I have ever seen in my life. They had nothing."[139] One official report narrates this shifting *askari* viewpoint:

> The askari had not had an opportunity of meeting the better class Indian, and his opinions of the race have been based on observations of the poorer classes. He is therefore firmly convinced that India consists of ragged beggars and undernourished peasants. Consequently he has begun to despise the Indian civilian, and wonders why Indians are considered superior to Africans in Africa. One pointed out that, in Africa, the Indian is addressed as "Bwana" by the African, whereas

in India the Indian calls the African "Sahib" and is glad to beg from him. The result has been growing resentment against the Indians domiciled in East Africa and their grip on trade there.[140]

One *askari* wrote that all Indians in East Africa should be sent home; another violently ruminated that Indians in India were "horrible," and that he had never seen "such filthy beggars as these Indians." "Mind you," he concluded, "in future we will wring their necks."[141]

Generic anticolonial nationalism thus did not neatly diffuse from a radicalized India to receptive African soldiers who subsequently proselytized upon their return. Excluding the Sykes brothers and a few others, *askari* veterans played a minute role in subsequent nationalist politics in Tanganyika, much as they did elsewhere in Africa, despite persistent historiographical myths that ex-soldiers played key roles in Africa's independence movements.[142] But a new and powerful comparative vision had been seen, quickly communicated through word of mouth and in print. African *askari* felt that there was a political debt owed to them, but it was rudely mocked with the final appearance of outright Indian initiatives for "subimperialism" in the Second World War's aftermath. Led by Hradayanath Kunzru, politicians in New Delhi proposed to transfer the mandate of Tanganyika to India in April 1946, primarily for the benefit of Asians in South Africa.[143] Some Indians in Tanganyika greeted this proposal warmly, justifying the takeover by citing India's history as a free, non-enslaving nation, its role in the First World War, and the commercial and administrative contributions of its nationals.[144] More circumspect Indian writers distanced themselves from the proposal and instead attacked disingenuous European talk of eventual African self-government.[145] African writers vigorously challenged the arguments favoring Indian trusteeship. One compared the Indian proposal to the camel that stuck his nose and then his head into the poor man's tent, "the poor man being too kind agreed until he was lastly forced out of the tent to suffer the cold."[146] Others considered Kunzru's proposal "most fabulous, humiliating and fantastic."[147] Another correspondent elaborated on the proposal's injustices:

> The exported slaves from this country are now living where they have been sent. They cannot demand any country in those parts as they are not the natives of the country. The Tanganyikans who remained are not slaves nor have they any trace of slavish blood. But the Indians are the direct descendants of the imported coolies and therefore have no right to claim anything. . . . Had there been plenty to eat in India the imported coolies would have not agreed to settle in a foreign land, forgetting all about their motherland. . . . Africans fought in Burma,

and saved India from the claws of a hungry Japan. Now have they any right to claim a portion of India as a reward for the war? Of course not, that is not what they fought for. Similarly the Indians have no right to claim any territorial reward. The era of colonisation has already passed. . . . What profit the Indians have made from this country is immense and they give nothing in return. This seems to be unsatisfactory to them and now they claim to dominate the whole country. Therefore we have nothing to say to them but—quit.[148]

Abdulwahid Sykes, who had reached the highest obtainable African military rank, that of Regimental Sergeant Major, advised Indian leaders interested in obtaining a subcolonial mandate "to mind their own business and stop taking an upper hand into things that have nothing to do with them."[149] Other African writers in Dar es Salaam similarly inverted Gandhian slogans—"Indians are squealing for the British to quit India, similarly the Africans are eagerly reciprocating for Indians to quit Africa."[150] Compensation for African military sacrifice in South Asia would not be further Indian tutelage, but instead African racial autarchy. Only a political reordering of society along the "natural" lines of racial continents could restore African *heshima*.

KUJENGA TAIFA (BUILDING THE *TAIFA*) TANU, INDIANS, AND RACIAL RECRUITMENT IN DAR ES SALAAM

Tanzania's nationalist metanarrative of a pan-ethnic, pan-religious, and triumphant response to colonialism—manifested in a single political party, TANU—emerged shortly after independence in 1961 and continues to influence academic and popular understandings of the events and dynamics of the 1950s. Revisionist works fault this metanarrative for its exclusions of gender and religion but ironically reconfirm many of its core elements by focusing exclusively on TANU and its elites.[151] Yet all these works leave unanswered the questions of how and why nationalist elites adopted and propagated racial rhetoric so thoroughly and with such great success over the 1950s. This section investigates how the exclusionary categorical order of *taifa*, forged in the urban experiences and racial thinking of the 1940s, shaped the nationalist political mobilization of supporters based on racial grievance and promised vindication—or what I term here "racial recruitment"—in Dar es Salaam during the 1950s. The African Association—after 1948, the Tanganyika African Association (TAA); and in 1954, the Tanganyika African National Union (TANU)—became the key institution to coordinate racial recruitment as a means to acquire political power, though its successful assertion of an organizational monopoly over racial politics was secured only in the mid-1950s. Rather than renarrate the often-told story of TANU's rise to power,[152] this section will instead map how racial-national convictions shaped political mobilization within the urban space of Dar es Salaam, and how this raised difficult questions about the role of Indians in the country's political future.

The postwar government offered numerous political initiatives to increase African involvement in local administration, encouraging formation of a professional class of racial recruiters. Dar es Salaam's township ward council was established just after the war to afford urban Africans a "constitutional" mode of expressing views, awakening the African Association to its nominal role as both town and territorial representative of the African *taifa*.[153] The Association responded by calling into question the legitimacy by which stubborn *wenye mji* elders, the Wazaramo Union, and other "tribal" associations were laying claim to representative institutions, and decreed that it was the duty of Africans first to remove differences, for

> Africans are first Africans. It is only after that that they are or may be any other things. Unless this sense of complete brotherhood and unity thoroughly pervades the thought of all Africans, no true unity can be achieved. . . . Africa is one country, and Africans are one nation, no matter where they live or where they are born.[154]

The African Association grew increasingly urban-minded, strengthening organizational ties with local municipal and railway workers, but also overstating the significance of urban issues to the "average" Tanganyikan.[155] Its longstanding extraterritorial ambitions were never realized—it had separated from its Zanzibar branch in 1948 after long-standing organizational frustrations; a planned 1949 union with the Kenya African Union to coordinate regional politics never occurred.[156] The two principal demands of the TAA were abstractly rural and parochially urban—to stop further alienation of land to immigrants, and to abolish "imposition of Arab Liwalis" and replace them with African *kadhis* or Muslim judges.[157]

As the African Association awoke from its slumber in the late 1940s, Indian nationalists in Dar es Salaam sought to influence and direct African nationalists toward a generic critique of European privilege and the injustices and unaccountability of colonial rule. In April 1947, in what might have been a pivotal political moment of African-Indian unity, two Asian members of the Legislative Council offered a spirited argument against "closer union" legislation (Colonial Paper 210) that favored European representation, and voted against the bill; all European members voted for it. The council's two African members, Chiefs Abdiel Shangali and Kidaha Makwaia, both abstained, and instantly discredited themselves in the eyes of aspiring African nationalists. The nays of Indian members V. M. Nazerali and I. C. Chopra were met with embarrassed silence by African nationalists in Dar es Salaam, who instead diverted their hostility onto the chiefly stooges.[158] The (Tanganyika) African Association began accepting financial assistance from sympathetic Indian benefactors from the late 1940s while simultaneously vocalizing African resentment of Indian racial privilege embodied in segregated medical care, unequal wages, and ongoing Indian expansion into African residential areas.[159] Speaking to the East African Indian National Congress in Nairobi, Abdulwahid Sykes declared Indo-African relations in Tanganyika "far better" than African-European relations, and that a "united front of Indians and Africans in Dar-es-Salaam" would be possible in the near future.[160] Yet political unity proved elusive, stymied not only by African resentment toward Indian privilege but also by Indian fears about crime and violence at the hands of Africans. Riots in Durban, South Africa, in 1949 had resulted in the deaths of several Indians, followed by a smaller but similar racial disturbance in Uganda. Security fears weighed heavily on the minds of most Indians in Dar es Salaam, and the town's Indian press grew even more alarmist in its reporting of African robberies, provocations, and insults to Indians.[161]

Tanganyika's Indian diaspora deepened its East African roots over the 1940s and 1950s as it grew less dependent on India as a source for commodities, capital, and peoples. Tanganyika's Asian population had risen from 25,000 in the 1930s to 45,000 in 1948; much of the growth was internal, from a new generation of South Asians raised in Tanganyika.[162] Jawaharlal Nehru urged East African Indians to identify themselves first with East Africa, and to acquire British rather than Indian nationality to better integrate themselves politically within the colonies. Heeding Nehru's call, the Asian Association—which formed in February 1951 to succeed the Indian Association—presented itself as an auxiliary movement to Tanganyika's African nationalist organizations.[163] Several thousand Indians in Tanganyika applied for British citizenship—and only a few for Indian or Pakistani citizenship—after passage of the 1948 British Nationality Act, in what was then an indication of their intention to stay in East Africa.[164] Governor Edward Twining (1949–1958) was relatively sympathetic to Tanganyika's Indians, whom he recognized were a long-settled diverse community increasingly cut off from India. His ultimately self-destructive embrace of "multiracialism" (see below) owed much to his conviction that Indian wealth and commercial skills were irreplaceable.[165] Significant internal population growth and greater independence from India-based business firms had lessened material dependence on diasporic networks. The Indian "family" in East Africa grew less transoceanic and extended, and became more nuclear by the 1940s; "family businesses" were increasingly owned by individuals. Indian men preferred to marry local Indian women. Indian capital, though still warily mobile, was increasingly invested locally.[166]

One such critical Indian investment was in Dar es Salaam's African nationalists. Just after TANU's formation in 1954, support from Dar es Salaam-based Indians to finance party-building far outstripped amounts raised by all other branches. The Asian Association, the Nationals of India Association, and the Muslim School Association supported TANU activities by subsidizing party newspapers and funding travel expenses. While eschewing formal politics, the Indian Merchants Chamber publicly welcomed the rising number of African retail traders and encouraged its own members to diversify into agricultural activities. Hindu Mandal hosted TANU's first annual conference in 1955, and Amir Jamal helped to finance Julius Nyerere's reputation-making visit to the United Nations later that year.[167] Nyerere continued to work closely, if discreetly, with the Asian Association to secure Asian financial and electoral support for both TANU and non-African, TANU-sympathetic candidates.[168] He explained that Indians who welcomed Africans as their friends had nothing to fear, but if they ignored advice of their leaders and regarded "Tanganyika as a country primarily to be exploited by them for their own benefit or for the benefit of their brethren in India, then it would be easy to see why they should be frightened of the Africans and African nationalism."[169] Sensitive to accusations that Indian financing of TANU implied political control, Nyerere courted Indian votes by proclaiming:

> We do not want your wealth. We do not want the salt and pepper that you sell in your shops. We only want one thing—your knowledge of fighting for independence peacefully without shedding blood. We want small Gandhis and Nehrus in this country.[170]

But rising African political strength, palpable on the streets of Dar es Salaam during the late 1950s, quickly altered customary relationships with Indians. Asian creditors grew reluctant to press TANU provincial offices for debt repayments, fearing to offend the party; some made personal contributions to help branches repay urgent debts.[171] Most important, it became bad politics for African politicians to be seen courting financial support from Indians—such donations could not be given, it was widely believed, without an opaque quid pro quo.

Coinciding with this shift in political power was a shift in political vocabulary. The quasi-religious language of civilization and self-improvement yielded to a more secularist discourse of development and political representation, as *maendeleo* (development) became the new watchword of public discourse, eclipsing *ustaarabu* but still directed toward constructing *taifa*. "Development" promised to deliver material benefits through government-driven schemes for agricultural and industrial education and exhorted others to labor for public improvement. TANU embraced the discourse of *maendeleo* by recasting race/nation in secular terms with the same end of *kujenga taifa* (building the race/nation) through modern means, while also drawing on antimodern but popular discursive themes like bloodsucking (*unyonyaji*) to popularize promises to eliminate exploitation. These themes had become part of earlier TAA rhetoric through the leadership of Stephen Mhando, an ethnic Bondei teacher whose energetic if divisive TAA presidency at last cohered around a political message that systematically criticized racial discrimination, called for education, loans, Africanization of civil service, and opposed any form of registration.[172] Mhando also pursued a bold concept in nationalist thought—that TAA's objective was "the removal of all injustices towards Africans," which they suffered.[173] This formulation of politics as *removal* would become a touchstone for popularizing African nationalism.

TANU party leaders wedded appeals of racial-national exclusivity with promises to deliver extrastatist welfare.[174] It was in 1955—the year Governor Twining declared "nationhood" the aim of Tanganyika—that TANU managed to secure widespread support in the town of Dar es Salaam and the surrounding peri-urban areas that served as the party's territorial springboard. The rapidity of its success was striking. Just one year later, J. A. K. Leslie explained that "it should be understood from the first that African Dar es Salaam is almost 100 per cent. a Tanganyika African National Union (TANU) town."[175] TANU's local competition had included the Wazaramo Union, which self-destructed through embezzlement scandals, and the "Bantu Group," whose followers decried both Christianity and Islam as foreign religions to be rejected by authentic Africans—leaders of the former joined TANU Elders, while those from the latter became the nucleus of TANU Youth League.[176] TANU closely followed trails blazed by the Wazaramo Union in the late 1940s by appealing to resentment against Indian traders and promising to short-circuit these middlemen through African cooperatives and shops.[177] African development was becoming popularly interpreted as African self-sufficiency and freedom from non-African economic forces. As a self-styled "modern" party, TANU had to be seen to deliver welfare but also avoid becoming too closely identified with thoroughly "unmodern" figures such as witchcraft eradicators.[178] A "son" of Nguvumali Mpangile had practiced witchcraft eradication, like many before and after him, on the town's outskirts in 1955–1956 with great success. Nguvumali circled peri-urban areas, not only removing the spells of other witches, but also selling medicines to prevent crop theft.[179] But eradicators generated dangerously large amounts of wealth and influence, challenging secular authorities of all sorts. The town's district commissioner repatriated Nguvumali to Kilwa shortly after for "embarrassing" the District Office; Nyerere very publicly refused numerous requests to intervene and reverse Nguvumali's deportation.[180]

As *maendeleo* became the new pole of public discourse over the 1950s, its discursive antonym was not *ushenzi* (barbarism), the long-standing antonym to *ustaarabu*, but rather *fujo*, or "disorder." Preventing *fujo* became the central concern for both TANU urban nationalists and the colonial government.[181] As membership exploded in 1955, Nyerere asked TANU's executive council to protect the party from the inevitable "bad people" (*watu wabaya*) in the new membership who would lie and cause discord (*fitina*) in the party's name. He recommended dividing Dar es Salaam into several small, closely administered units—explaining that "the life of our party depends mostly on how Dar es Salaam will be handled."[182] Nyerere rebuked those who interpreted his words as calls for racial expulsions.[183] Tanganyikan politics were "thoroughly peaceful," as Iliffe has judged, even though "TANU's language was often that of war."[184] Most TANU public meetings in Dar es Salaam were remarkable for their order—a very few were marred by bouts of petty racial violence. Yet, despite this, the government attitudes toward TANU hardened in early 1957, after Nyerere gave a speech in Dar es Salaam emphasizing that Africans were "habitually insulted by Europeans and Indians and nothing is done about it."[185] Governor Twining worried that he was appealing to the dangerous *wahuni* population, and countered by intensifying police action against "hooliganism" through more intense "de-spiving" campaigns (i.e., forced repatriation of the urban unemployed).[186] This confrontational stance, which identified TANU above all as the creator of *fujo* among "the gullible and idle" Africans, resulted in Nyerere's ban from public speaking in April 1957, and subsequently colored state strategy until Twining was replaced in mid-1958 by Richard Turnbull.[187] Despite this conflict between TANU and the colonial state, which stands at the center of most historical accounts, TANU largely adopted the state's commitment to bring *maendeleo* and prevent *fujo* when it took up state power after scoring electoral victories in 1958–1959. Party discipline increasingly turned on the implementation of bureaucratic structures and office etiquette. Punctuality, politeness, and procedure became the dominant themes of intraparty correspondence and circulars.[188]

TANU's "language of war" was directed against colonial rule in general and against Governor Twining's policy of "multiracialism" in particular. "Multiracialism" was an improvised and highly malleable term employed across East and Central Africa to describe various race-based approaches to constitutional reform. In Twining's Tanganyika, multiracialism signified a tripartite approach to constitutional development in which Europeans, Asians, and Africans would each be entitled to separate representation but would be voted in through a single common electorate. It was intended as a gradualist bulwark against Nyerere's demand for nonracial universal suffrage, which the paternalist Twining deemed as "racialism disguised in idealistic language."[189]

The settler- and chief-friendly United Tanganyika Party (UTP) hoisted its unfortunate flag to multiracialism; TANU rejected it as mere rationalization to delay universal suffrage, which it was. Nyerere controversially agreed to participate in two rounds of "multiracial" elections; after decisively winning the second round in 1960, multiracialism was formally abandoned by the government. Like its political work, the conceptual work of multiracialism was inelegant and pragmatic—to provide a veneer of "civic" territorial nationalism that would insulate political debate from logical conclusions latent within exclusive racial-national categories. Nyerere himself opposed Twining's multiracialism on grounds that it delayed independence and secured minority privilege, but countered not with an outright rejection but a soothing prevarication: "Although Tanganyika is multi-racial in population, it is primarily African."[190] A white settler from Njombe stripped away this veneer and laid bare the underlying discursive assumptions by asking:

> What is multiracialism really? A nation is not something artificial. You cannot just build it up like a ship. Nation, as the word itself suggests, is a natural group of people who have common interests, customs, traditions, beliefs, and history. It is born of a natural urge, not of mere political reasons. Now, is multiracialism anything of the sort? Will such a nation be born, exist and live? Does anyone honestly and really believe in the practicability of the idea of multiracialism? Everyone knows for certain that multiracialism is an excellent and clever device to confuse the public and mislead the unenlightened. Recently, and only recently, we have introduced the technical term "Tanganyikan" for all born or domiciled in this country. Well why not, right out, call them all natives or Africans? Don't you like it? And then we should also call all the Africans born or domiciled in Britain "Europeans."[191]

For Tanganyika's Indians, "multiracialism" posed a vexing dilemma. TANU remained "uniracial" from the time of its founding as the African Association in 1927 until it opened its doors to non-Africans in November 1962.[192] With a political empathy rarely seen among African nationalist leaders of his time, Nyerere personally regretted this exclusion and understood it to be a temporary political necessity. He worked closely with non-African politicians and once famously attempted to reframe the racial-national question as one of "Tanganyikan" nationalism by stating that the path to democracy was "to say we have 123 tribes in Tanganyika, the youngest and relatively the most educated being the European and Asian tribes."[193] In his booklet *Barriers to Democracy*, Nyerere strategically stripped Asians of their political volition to explain their privileged status in Tanganyika. The Asian, Nyerere argued, "is essentially a businessman and does not govern the country"; he has been "pushed into a position of artificial political privilege which he had never asked for, and, almost bewildered with this gift from the blue, he hangs on it, as if it were some magic charm that would safeguard his economic interest against impending African competition."[194] For its part, not only had the Asian Association quickly dissociated itself from any connection to multiracial "Tanganyikan" nationalism by the late 1950s; it also questioned its own existence. Its president, Mohamed Rattansey, asked Asians to welcome the end of multiracial parity so that the country would be governed "on democratic lines." Others implored Asians to simply await the opening of TANU's doors to non-Africans.[195] The Aga Khan had gone out of step by instructing his followers to quit the Asian Association in 1952 and to remain neutral or support UTP. His grandson and successor, Aga Khan IV (1957–present), made a quick and unconvincing turn from imperial loyalist to TANU supporter, leaving Ismailis particularly vulnerable to charges of bad political faith.[196]

But the discursive logic behind TANU's racial exclusivity, based on racial imagination of continental origins and "homelands," was too powerful to be directly challenged by Nyerere, who was himself dogged by criticisms from potential challengers that he was too "multiracial." Territorial expressions had always had to contend with more politically durable racial categories now fixed deeply within popular thought.[197] To the question, "Are not all Tanganyikans Africans, because this country Tanganyika is situated in the continent of Africa?"[198] a nationalist responded:

> The African in Tanganyika is the only person belonging to Tanganyika and is the only person called Tanganyikan and the rest are self-calling Tanganyikans to suit themselves. We always read in the papers that somebody has gone on home leave or so, if you are Tanganyikans and Africans at the same time, why go to England or Asia for your home leave? while you belong to Tanganyika as your motherland? Have you got two motherlands? . . . How can you nationalise three different races of which each has got her motherland?[199]

The categories of race and nation themselves were rarely interrogated during TANU's rise to power. *Taifa* (nation/race) and *nchi* (territory/country) did not carry with them their abstractions into any national public discourse during the 1950s: *utaifa* (nationalism) was and remains an unused academic abstraction in Swahili; *ukabila* (tribalism) was popularized only in the 1960s to describe a political evil to be avoided. The position and future of interracial offspring, either figurative or real, continued to provide the sharpest political definitions of race. E. B. M. Barongo, then a TANU publicity secretary who would later author a semiofficial history of Tanganyika, declared his opposition to multi-racialism in the following terms—"Do you, my reader, favour a future Tang-anyikan to be a Coloured? If a multi-racial government is to be introduced, then inter-marriage is apt to be practicable along with other achievements. It is queer, isn't it?"[200] The existence of *machotara*, or "half-castes," continued to bespeak a moral failure of national will. "As an half-caste," one Dar es Salaam resident suggested, "it is certainly very difficult for him to maintain a full love for the country generally"; thus it was the nationalists' task to combat "the subversive element of inter-racial marriage and stamp it out if possible in our young and progressive country."[201] Politically, *machotara* were at last permit-ted to join TANU in September 1955 on the condition that they legally classify themselves as "Africans."[202] Nyerere later explained that this decision followed adamant lobbying by African women, "who said that after all they were their children!"[203] The Tanganyika Coloured People National Society—a party that claimed to represent the country's *machotara*—banned its members from joining TANU, but anxiously distanced itself from those *machotara* who had joined TANU only to develop a reputation for high-handed elitism.[204] When the government finally announced in 1961 that, legally, an African was any-one of African racial descent, the society welcomed the pronouncement and dropped its lingering opposition to TANU.[205]

By this time, TANU had fully monopolized the politics of racial recruitment in Tanganyika. The most important component in this effort was the TANU Youth League, which by 1960 had taken up state functions such as issuing cer-tificates of ownership to traders, detaining those without certificates, arresting and interrogating suspected criminal offenders, holding courts, and patrolling townships. No African group in Dar es Salaam was more race-conscious—its members searched Asian shops suspected of purchasing produce illegally, and detained non-Africans consorting with African women. As part of the party's shadow state, the Youth League exercised occasional "vigilante" police powers during the late colonial years in order to shape national spaces in ways that honored popular racial sensibilities.[206] Young men in Dar es Salaam competed to join the Youth League because it extended the promise of future work and patronage in a city with few jobs. The two answers that Africans gave to the question "What is the worst feature of town life?" in 1956 were "hunger" and "unemployment."[207] Repatriations of the unemployed dramatically increased over the decade, but so, too, did Dar es Salaam's African population, nearly doubling from 51,231 in 1948 to 93,363 in 1957.[208] TANU's rapid domination over African political life also emboldened the resurrection of African trade unions. A fresh wave of urban strikes in late 1956, when Domestic and Hotel Workers Union launched an abortive national strike; workers across industries in Dar es Salaam struck briefly in sympathy. The strike, combined with the weight of the newly established trade union umbrella, the Tanganyika Federation of Labour, moved the government to at last establish a minimum wage rate for hourly work in Dar es Salaam in April 1957.[209] The relatively high wages that accompanied local labor stabilization, however, also moved urban employers to reduce workforces in order to increase productivity, paradoxically ensuring structural urban unemployment.[210] The victories of TANU and its affiliated trade unions raised general expectations but delivered uneven material benefits. The potential for violence seemed great.

The *duka* became a site increasingly fraught with racial tension in the late 1950s. Desired goods lay in plain sight but out of reach, taunting would-be consumers while enriching foreign merchants. Most instances of racial violence in late colonial Dar es Salaam involved African crowds and broadly "Asian" shopkeepers, the latter of whom were increasingly Arabs. Locals labeled the Arabs who came to fill the town's postwar petty retail sector as *washihiri*, in a not-always-accurate reference to Hadhramaut Arabs who notionally departed from the port town of al-Shihir. Between two and three hundred Arabs immigrated to Tanganyika each year by the mid-1950s, most flouting immigration laws.[211] Peddling textiles on deferred payment terms or taking over retail trade in newly planned African suburban neighborhoods, *washihiri* traders exploded across peri-urban Dar es Salaam. African-owned houses frequently passed into the hands of Arab tenants with better financial resources.[212] Successful *washihiri* vendors in Kariakoo would later serve as models for *machinga* (informal street traders) in the 1970s,[213] but during the 1950s, Africans viewed their displacement from the petty end of retail commerce by Arab shopkeepers and hawkers within the aura of revived memories of slavery—or, more accurately, the political reconstruction of such "memories" then being popularized by Afro-Shirazi Party rhetoricians in nearby Zanzibar. Should Tanganyika receive self-government prematurely, one female African writer warned, then Arabs "will be the first people to take up their daggers in order to renew their long dormant slavery trade and try to rule the black."[214] Stabbings figured prominently, by both thieves and vengeful shopkeepers. Combustible resentments also led to peculiarly symbolic or "nonutilitarian" forms of violence.[215] After an Arab shopkeeper slapped an African in Kariakoo, he and his business partner were beaten with sticks, in mock sword fashion, by an angry mob of more than one hundred Africans while police looked on impotently. Throwing rocks on roofs and then setting fire to the rafters of Arab shops became a recurrent tactic of African criminal gangs working Dar es Salaam's peri-urban locations. No less than eleven Arab shopkeepers were attacked—many were stabbed while their shop roofs were set on fire—by African gangs in the town's outskirts within a period of six weeks in 1960.[216]

Indian shopkeepers, by comparison, kept their heads low. Although sometimes victims of robbery and small bouts of violence, they were never systematically targeted like Dar es Salaam's Arab traders; nor had they earned a reputation of reaching for daggers in response. Political neutrality had its benefits. Indians could not be associated with an ambitious political movement like the Zanzibar National Party (ZNP), which was widely viewed in Dar es Salaam as an aggressive "Arab" party that threatened to roll back African political gains. Social distance similarly had its benefits. Indians had been acquiring large swaths of freehold land in Dar es Salaam's peri-urban areas since the 1920s, often acting as absentee landlords to African squatter-tenants. As the land's residential value skyrocketed in the 1950s, the number of conflicts between rent-hungry landowners and their recalcitrant tenants also increased, provoking occasional racial violence. The most dramatic of such instances occurred in February 1959 in the then-peri-urban neighborhood of Buguruni, where an African police officer was killed and an Arab shop destroyed following rumors that police were abducting residents to make a magical medicine known as *mumiani* from their victims' blood. An absentee Indian landlord, Suleiman Daya, was alleged to be the unseen force behind these abductions—he had been having increasingly bitter disputes with his squatting tenants over rents. Although his Buguruni house was symbolically torched, Daya had spent that evening as he spent most evenings—in the safety of his main Uhindini residence. Instead, it was neighboring Arab shopkeepers who bore the racial brunt of the night's violence.[217] Although the keeping of low profiles is not a subject well-suited to historical documentation, the historical fiction of Moyez G. Vassanji offers a glimpse into what those Indian strategies were shortly before independence. His novel *The Gunny Sack* illustrates the period's wary political pragmatism: "Watch the green colour [the color of TANU]. . . . There lies safety," advised one of Vassanji's characters. "Buy flags, buy badges, pay the fundis day to day, make them sign for everything."[218] A pall of fear had enveloped Dar es Salaam's Indian population, several of whom recalled the relief that they felt after independence passed on December 9, 1961, without any major incidents. Many had stayed indoors, fearing riots in the capital.[219]

RACE, NATION, AND CITIZENSHIP IN INDEPENDENT TANGANYIKA

Formal African opposition to TANU revealed the success with which TANU had already realized and controlled the politics of *taifa*.[220] The first African-led party to oppose TANU was the African National Congress (ANC), created by Zuberi Mtemvu in January 1958, with the aim of forcing TANU to abandon its "moderate" policy of agreeing to participate in multiracial elections. Mtemvu had threatened to lead a walkout of TANU members aiming to form a party advocating "Africa for Africans only"; Nyerere immediately expelled him from TANU. Mtemvu attacked Nyerere for wishing Tanganyika to be declared "primarily an African state," but significantly not *wholly* an African state, thereby seeking to maintain unjust minority protections.[221] But so complete was the triumph of racial-continental thought in Tanganyika's public sphere that there was little intellectual room left for ANC to elaborate racial or national ideas. Mtemvu sought to exploit African resentment of Europeans and Indians for political gain, but did so neither more frequently nor more effectively than several of his TANU opponents. ANC racial ideology attracted few supporters because racial polemicizing had become too universal to use it to distinguish any Tanganyikan political party by 1959. Those who did join ANC did so out of specific disaffections with TANU, which itself was a very big tent that housed not only antiracialists like Julius Nyerere but also members who held anti-European and particularly anti-Asian views, such as Bibi Titi Mohamed, Oscar Kambona, and countless middle-level figures who subscribed to the views of TANU's racialist Swahili newspaper, *Uhuru*. TANU officials were sensitive to their potential vulnerability on race. In private they criticized Nyerere for his close cooperation with Europeans and Asians, particularly Derek Bryceson and Amir Jamal.[222] But TANU enjoyed the luxury of being a racially exclusive organization that concurrently supported a nonracial citizenship to be enjoyed by all in the near future, and began preparing its followers to accept the idea. "Although many citizens (*raia*) of Tanganyika are Africans in truth citizenship (*uraia*) is not color (*rangi*)," TANU's publicity secretary explained, further analogizing that "the Negro of America is an American and not African, even if his grandparents are from Ugogo."[223]

The National Assembly debate over the Tanganyika Citizenship Bill on the eve of independence entwined many of the above strands of racial thought and ideas about national belonging. Nyerere, in consultation with soon-departing Secretariat officials, had already secretly negotiated the bill's details with the Colonial Office as a critical legal piece in the decolonization process. British officials in both Dar es Salaam and London had initiated the process in March 1961, using citizenship legislation from Nigeria and Sierra Leone as templates after earlier files were misplaced. Long-standing but vague discussions about citizenship within a system of East African federalism were superseded by Tanganyika's quickly impending independence.[224] The TANU-dominated government committee that drafted Tanganyika's citizenship bill accepted Britain's insistence on Commonwealth citizenship, but declined Britain's insistence to allow for dual citizenship. The committee also redefined descent in explicitly patrilineal legal terms.[225] Fearing an exodus of stateless Indians and property-stripped Europeans, the Colonial Office attempted to browbeat

Nyerere into accepting dual citizenship, but failed.[226] The late colonial government presciently feared that a large portion of the more than twenty thousand Asians who had registered or been naturalized as citizens of the United Kingdom since 1951 would choose British rather than Tanganyikan citizenship.[227] After dual citizenship was rejected, Whitehall pressed Dar es Salaam to expand provisions that would automatically qualify people for Tanganyikan citizenship, fearing the responsibility and political embarrassment that would accompany so many Asians falling through legal cracks.[228] This, too, failed. The final bill offered citizenship, in order of ascending restrictions, on basis of birth, descent, marriage, registration, and naturalization; a two-year grace period was allowed for those who did not take citizenship at independence. Indians, who had been spoiled for choice in 1950 with both India and Pakistan permitting dual citizenship, as well as with Britain extending the possibility of citizenship or at least residency through its 1948 Nationality Act, now faced in 1961 an India, Pakistan, and Tanganyika that each insisted upon single citizenship, as well as increasingly restrictive interpretations of what entitlements "British Subjects"—and, more severely, "British Protected Persons"—held in Britain.[229] Yet nearly all of the one hundred thousand or so Indians resident in Tanganyika in 1961 either automatically qualified for citizenship or could register for it within two years.

The ensuing legislative debate in October 1961, less than two months before independence, determined whether or not citizenship would be granted on a territorial or racial basis. African legislators had already doubted the authenticity of a "Tanganyikan" identity in earlier debates that turned on distinguishing between "Africanization" and "localization" of the civil service. "Everyone here knows who is an African," M. R. Kundya ponderously explained, "and the word Africanisation is derived from the word African, and Asianisation would concern Asians. . . . But I think Africanisation concerns only Africans."[230] Annoyed at the prospect that non-African civil servants might quickly embrace being "Tanganyikan" but deny being "African," R. S. Wamburga asked, "How does Tanganyika exist before Africa? . . . How can a man recognize the name of his father and reject the name of his grandfather."[231] Opponents of the bill objected to granting automatic citizenship to Europeans and Asians by virtue of birth and descent in Tanganyika, arguing that all non-Africans should instead undergo a five-year waiting period to demonstrate loyalty and fitness as a condition of citizenship. Otherwise, a new round of racial domination by outsiders flocking to Tanganyika would be inevitable. Supporters countered that imposing any racial criteria would undo the hard work of TANU's opposition to multiracialism; moreover, it would open the door to other forms of exclusion by identity. Describing his opponents as "race-glorifying Hitlers," Nyerere rose to argue, "in a voice cold with suppressed anger," that the principle of equality was at stake. If "we in Tanganyika are going to divorce citizenship from loyalty and marry it to colour, we won't stop there. . . . A day will come when we will say all people were created equal except the Masai, except the Wagogo, except the Waha, except the polygamists, except the Muslims, etc."[232] He concluded by threatening to instruct the entire government to resign should the bill not pass. The bill passed.

At stake were not only short-term concerns about the Africanization of the civil service and indigenous land rights, but also the viability of long-debated categories of political identity. Christopher Tumbo, a leading railway trade unionist who was the bill's most prominent critic, seized upon its language of multiracialism, which recognized that Tanganyika had "several different races."[233] Such a phrase, he argued, conveys the impression that "Tanganyika is a multi-racial State and similar to the West Indies where the native people of those islands have lost identity." Tumbo instead suggested changing the language to "immigrant races" to show that "we the natives have not lost identity."[234] To Tumbo's mind, identity was a strict matter of parentage. He insisted that "half-castes" be forced to call themselves Africans, or otherwise be forced to undergo naturalization along with Indians and Europeans. Such mixed-race people, he thought, should have to "be at the mercy of the Council of Chiefs," who, as guardians of native identity and traditional authority, should be empowered to make final decisions regarding citizenship of non-Africans.[235] The bill's supporters countered that any conditional qualification of citizenship should be based on one's politics rather than one's ancestry. Sheikh Amri Abedi argued that citizenship is principally about loyalty, which was "a condition of the mind" rather than function of race.[236] Michael Kamaliza concurred, stating that "the common man in the streets of Dar es Salaam" also supported this bill because they wanted to know "who are the real Tanganyikans," and did not want people with one foot in Tanganyika and another in Bombay.[237]

As a piece of political drama, the citizenship bill debate marked an important symbolic victory for Nyerere's vision of a nonracial Tanganyika in the face of small but not insignificant resistance. A visiting official opined that the "extremists" had "some support for their views in the country at large, and a good deal more could no doubt be whipped up by demagogues without too much difficulty."[238] Nyerere had yet to deliver the other half of his prevarication, that Tanganyika was "primarily African." He subsequently adopted a strategy of governance that alternated between making similar public stands against the grubby racism of shortsighted opponents, wrapping policies with sharp racialist effects in the language of socialism, or using surrogates to voice politically necessary racialist policies that could not be explained in the language of socialism.[239] But if "racialism" had lost, citizenship was nonetheless defined in the patrilineal racial language formed out of the inversion of *usta-arabu*. Few members challenged two of the bill's provisions that remain today the most heated issues of Tanzania's citizenship laws—the exclusion of dual citizenship and exclusive legitimacy of patrilineal descent. George Kahama, Minister of Home Affairs, who formally introduced the bill, justified the ban on dual citizenship as a necessary forcible display of loyalty. "We do not want any half-hearted Tanganyikans in the future," Kahama said, "nor do we want any 'fair-weather' Tanganyikans" who would make use of citizenship rights in good times, but "deny their obligations to Tanganyika when they are called upon to make some sacrifice."[240] The Tanganyikan "native-born" had to prove indigeneity in patrilineal terms in order to be recognized. "The fact that one's father was born in Tanganyika," Kahama argued, "demonstrates at least a long-standing family connection with Tanganyika."[241] Children born outside of Tanganyika, but whose *fathers* had been born in Tanganyika, "therefore should be considered as 100 per cent Tanganyikans despite their accident of birth somewhere else."[242] Neither the bill nor Kahama even mentioned, let alone recognized, the rights of people to acquire citizenship through Tanganyikan women. Only one eccentric member proposed that male terms of qualification be made gender-neutral. Patrilineal mainland ancestry proved a nonnegotiable legal provision, as well as a principal intellectual fulcrum, for defining citizenship in the new nation.

CONCLUSIONS

African elaborations on race and racial difference were rarely explicit; they instead lay encrusted within enduring discussions of civilization (*ustaarabu*) and development (*maendeleo*). The racial imagination of many African intellectuals accorded with that of several European and Asian thinkers on a constellation of commonsense points—the existence of a common descent bounded by a shared continental origin and, less explicitly, shared somatic traits such as skin color. Civilization and development provided a simultaneously historical and programmatic intellectual framework to explain current differences among people and provide discrete groups with a plan for the future. An older Tanganyikan identity paradigm that understood the reasons and remedies of difference in terms of integration into a superior, Arab-Islamic-centered coastal civilization yielded during the 1940s to an identity paradigm that understood the history and future of human difference in terms of fidelity to and realization of one's racial-continental identity. The political epiphanies and searing humiliations experienced by Tanganyika's most cosmopolitan writers, veteran *askari* who traveled the Indian Ocean during the Second World War, ensured that popular conceptions of *heshima* (honor) would entail recovering a continent from foreign predations on the basis of *taifa*, an African race-nation. This race-centered identity paradigm satisfied desires of male African intellectuals to assert economic control over trade, political control over the government, and social control over African women and their children—all while honoring African male ancestors.

In Dar es Salaam, postwar state initiatives to encourage African participation in local and territorial government enabled a young urban class of African politicians to become professional racial-national recruiters. The success of the African Association and its successors hinged on their ability to popularize the racial-continental identity paradigm by championing both the modern idea of development as well as the "unmodern" concern of fighting against the exploitation (*unyonyaji*, literally "bloodsucking") of non-Africans. Indian nationalists attempted to guide African postwar politics toward a generic critique of European colonial unaccountability but frequently found themselves targets of African racial polemicists. Nationalist leaders, however, had to temper these popular criticisms in light of the potential for racial violence as TANU took power and became increasingly accountable for maintaining urban order. TANU gained its popular and electoral victories by guaranteeing further development while monopolizing discourses of difference in what had become the now commonsensical paradigm of Tanganyika's status as a "primarily African nation," realized with some compromise in its patrilineal citizenship laws.

The structure of racial difference had long been inscribed into Tanganyika's colonial laws, urban geography, educational system, and divisions of labor. African racial-national thought did not merely reflect racialized structure, but rather engaged with and ultimately transformed that structure. Discussions centered on *ustaarabu* demonstrate the limits of the imaginable as well as the independent appropriation of a paternalist understanding of the world that plainly ranked Africans at the bottom. Tanganyika's African intellectuals divined that the world's racial-continental division—a view implied in *ustaarabu* and *maendeleo* and long championed by a handful of influential Pan-Africanists—provided the strongest case upon which to assert control over society. Unleashed in the political realization of these racial-national ideals was not only heightened racial consciousness, but a new national political discourse that placed ideas of exploitation and its eradication at the center of public debate and policy. The development of postcolonial Dar es Salaam turned on the implementation of racial and social leveling policies designed to reverse exploitation, or *unyonyaji*.

5 ↜ Nationalist Thought, Racial Caricature, and Urban Citizenship in Postcolonial Tanzania

THIS CHAPTER EXAMINES how the language and politics of national citizenship transformed material meanings of urban entitlement. Dar es Salaam continued to grow rapidly during the 1960s, and wealth continued to concentrate in commercial networks and urban properties. Yet such concentrations flew in the face of Tanzania's political goal of *ujamaa*, "African socialism" or "familyhood," which condemned capitalism and urban divisions of labor as exploitation (*unyonyaji*) and located legitimate wealth and virtue in rural agriculture. Postcolonial nationalist rhetoric retained and elaborated the exclusionary racial-national idea of *taifa*, despite Nyerere's consistent antiracialist exhortations and the presence of non-Africans in major political offices. A popular urban nationalist sensibility emerged, manifested in a new vocabulary that supported the broad aims of *ujamaa* while empowering urban residents to claim a legitimate role in the new nation, and to critique the excesses and unaccountability of nationalist leaders. This rhetoric particularly targeted the behavior and intent of *ote dugu moja*, a caricature of the poorly adjusted urban Indian who remained socially aloof from the African *taifa* and politically opposed to the goals of *ujamaa*. The economic logic of accumulation, which had enriched Indian and African *rentier* landlords alike for decades, was confronted by the political logic of urban *ujamaa*. Postcolonial urban policies preserved key elements of colonial-era urban entitlement, but also sought to secure postcolonial populist consent by leveling urban wealth, most dramatically through the nationalization of buildings in 1971.

Academic studies of African nationalism have generally concentrated on organizational aspects to the neglect of intellectual content. This tendency is reflected in literature on Tanzanian nationalism, which locates its intellectual substance as either descending from generic African and Asian anticolonialism, ascending out of experiences of local resistance to European colonial rule, or being identical to the intellectual development of Tanzania's first president, Julius Nyerere. In these treatments, the victorious Tanganyika African National Union (TANU) serves as both primary source and teleological subject of nationalist thought.[1] The late Susan Geiger summarized the historiographical impasse when she observed that even John Iliffe's magisterial national history mistakenly "conflates nationalism and the nationalist movements such as TANU."[2] Using her criticism as a point of departure, this chapter argues that TANU exercised no monopoly over nationalist rhetoric, but rather worked within a shifting discursive field consisting of international and indigenous concepts and terms. TANU and the TANU-led government were not unmoved movers of nationalist discourse, but conduits and translators of popular dissatisfaction, sharply limited by commitments to maintain public order. In Dar es Salaam, a popular nationalist vocabulary developed, directed primarily toward claiming a livable urban existence for Africans who faced steep economic and political obstacles. TANU crafted and coined much of this vocabulary, but it never dictated its shifting content and meanings.

The work of the thinkers under consideration here was to elaborate what nationalism meant. Isaiah Berlin memorably defined nationalism as "the straightening of bent backs." Pursuing Berlin's insight, this chapter contends that African nationalists throughout this period understood nationalism first and foremost to mean the elimination of exploitation. Although the dominance of this discursive theme is partially beholden to international socialist ideologies, in Dar es Salaam the discussions of exploitation emerged equally out of idioms of parasitism and witchcraft eradication. Defining exploitation was also a way to define who was a good citizen and who belonged to the nation. At its root, the ideal national citizen was someone who was "African"; someone who was an urban laborer or preferably a rural farmer; and someone who not only refrained from but actively fought exploitation. The postcolonial state's general hostility toward—and failure to cope with—urban growth moved urban residents to develop an alternative vocabulary to make sense of postcolonial social change and lampoon self-serious official rhetoric. But despite occasional discord, Tanzanian nationalists widely agreed that membership in the new nation depended on each citizen's commitment to combat exploitation.

THE NATIONALIST VOCABULARY OF *UJAMAA*

The intellectual landscape of postcolonial Tanzania was transformed by state and party efforts to standardize political language. The terms *taifa* and *kabila* had served semi-interchangeably as foundational markers of ethnicity and race during the 1950s, most obviously in the titles of *mila na desturi* (customs and traditions) ethnohistories in which Gogo, Nyamwezi, and others were each celebrated as a prestigious *taifa*. As TANU began to win government offices in early 1959, however, ethnic associations and vernacular languages suddenly faced sharp political discouragement. Just before independence, tribal associations in Dar es Salaam "seemed to disappear overnight," many being absorbed by other political organizations.[3] By 1961, the specter of secessionist violence then engulfing Congo and threatening Kenya and Uganda darkened TANU's already dim view of "tribal" associations. Rashidi Kawawa announced that TANU's official policy was "to suppress any tribal or religious societies with a political background," and named the All-Muslim National Union of Tanganyika (AMNUT), the Hehe and Chagga Democratic Parties, and the Masasi African Democratic Union as threats to national unity.[4] In June of that year, the party's executive committee asked all tribal parties to voluntarily disband or face proscription within two months.[5] Three months later, Nyerere informed the Chiefs' Convention, a postwar venue created to discuss questions of "native administration" policy, that the office of chief was incompatible with modern democratic government, and that all chiefs would be replaced eventually by executive officers.[6] Shortly after independence, existing ethnic associations across Tanganyika fell under close government surveillance, and new ones found it difficult to secure registration. An official in Tanga Region instructed that tribal societies "of a political nature" not be registered, as "their existences are against the declared intention of the Government to unite all small tribes of the Territory into one big nation."[7] Long opposed in principle to hereditary authority, believing it incompatible with an equal citizenry, Nyerere eliminated all chiefly offices with abolition of the Native Authority system by early 1963.[8] Usage of "tribal" vernaculars in local public forums was rigorously discouraged, as were registrations of "tribal" mutual aid or burial societies, particularly following the January 1964 army mutiny.[9] In less than five years, TANU and the TANU-controlled postcolonial government had more or less eliminated alternative institutional sources of ethnic authority and welfare.

The TANU government[10] systematically downgraded the term *kabila* to fit the subnational sense of "tribe." In official rhetoric, *kabila* became one of several dependent, nonsovereign appendages of the sovereign and singular Tanganyikan *taifa*. The titles of ethnohistories republished after independence replaced the word *taifa* with the subnational *kabila*.[11] Aspiring party leaders learned to make this substitution. Among the primary self-identifications given by 656 Kivukoni College applicants at this time, specific tribal names (21 percent) lagged well behind both race ("African," 46 percent) and geography ("Tanganyikan," 26 percent).[12] "Tribes" could still thrive, for a while at least, as a source of national entertainment. With Nyerere's endorsement,

Tanzania's Ministry of National Culture enthusiastically reproduced "tribal" cultural forms, in which cultural production revolved around, as Kelly Askew argues, "the reconstruction and collection of local traditions and customs."[13] But such "traditional" forms of cultural content soon ran afoul of an even greater state enthusiasm for modernization. The Ministry of National Culture's significance quickly faded in the later 1960s, after which an increasingly instrumentalist national cultural policy encouraged tribal cultures to develop into a singular national culture.[14] Tanzanian attempts to nationalize its own history were marked by similar tensions between cosmopolitan modernization and local tribal particularity. National Heroes Day (Sikukuu ya Mashujaa), first celebrated on September 1, 1969, comprised a dreary recitation of "colonial" epochs and homage paid to a pastiche of resisting heroes, including long-dead "Tanzanians" such as Mirambo, Mkwawa, and Kinjikitile, along with living Lusophone leaders such as Machel, Neto, and Cabral. None of the Tanzanian heroes honored had lived past 1905, and all were stripped of their ethnic and geographical context.[15] Tanzania's composite tribal parts, having first been depoliticized and downgraded in the political realm, were now seen as national hindrances in the cultural realm, as postcolonial efforts to define the nation displaced *kabila* in every sense.

But standardization of political language also involved the work of independent, self-styled grammarians who took aim at the unwieldy vocabulary of urban coastal life. K. K. Kondo stripped away the maddening imprecision and multiple referents accorded to the term *mswahili*, which stood for descent (*mshirazi*, *mngazija*, etc.), religion (Muslim), served as a descriptor of urban cunning, and as a residual category of the "detribalized." Its true meaning, Kondo argued, followed its grammatical derivation—*mswahili* is simply a person who speaks Swahili, the national language of Tanzania—"a sovereign State with its own ethics." Completing the syllogism, Kondo argued that "the present pertinent definition of 'Mswahili' is a person who speaks Swahili as his national language and he is ethically homogenous [sic] with the other nationals," and optimistically added that "he may be a European, an Asian, an Arab or an African."[16] Few of Kondo's contemporary readers would have agreed with his last point, but most would have understood that *mswahili*'s coastal and religious associations posed a potential problem for nationalists. This anxiety was particularly clear in published Swahili poetry, whose production centers were moving away from the *baraza* of coastal sheikhs and into the offices of young professionals who were quick to discard antique coastal hierarchies and elaborate a national identity based on utilitarian language. The stigma of the ex-slave who had been stripped of his ancestry, which had rendered "Swahili" a wholly unfashionable identity during colonial rule, was now being embraced by modern urban writers. "Don't call me by name, I am *Mswahili*," one nationalist *shairi* asserted. "I disown my lineage, I don't care about my origins."[17] Nationalist thinkers rehabilitated *mswahili* from its earlier dubious connotations into one that connoted a respectable figure who followed Tanzania's ethical imperatives. By contrast, "Asian" fully replaced "Indian" as the English-language referent, and widely served as an antonym to "citizen" and "Tanzanian" in discursive practice. A. Y. A. Karimjee, a well-known businessman, former Legislative Council speaker, and first "Asian" to acquire Tanzanian citizenship, ended a published interview by testily observing, "From the questions you have put to me, you also seem to think I am an Asian and not a Tanzanian."[18]

The concept behind *ujamaa*—Tanzania's policy of African socialism, which roughly translates as "familyhood"—was the proposal to undo the damages wrought by colonial rule by restoring the familial relationships of authentic African society. "The foundation, and the objective, of African socialism," Nyerere wrote in 1962, "is the extended family." *Ujamaa* rejected modern capitalist development, which had been brought to Africa through European imperialism, and instead called for a return to African traditional society where previously there had been "hardly any room for parasitism." True socialism was an "attitude of the mind," in which people fought the acquisitive impulse that led individuals or groups within the "tribe" to exploit one another.[19] In *Ujamaa—The Basis of African Socialism*, Nyerere does not pillory Indians or other national groups but emphasizes instead the need for a specifically "African" self-liberation. Combating parasitism, preventing income differentiation, mobilizing people to fight poverty, and encouraging (some) political criticism became the hallmarks of Nyerere's early postcolonial writings.[20] He was particularly concerned with combating the parasitism of *rentier* activity. *Makabaila* (landlords) lived off the work of others without having added significant value to the land themselves, an unforgivable affront. As these ideas permeated and developed in the country's public sphere after 1962, however, the intellectual content of *ujamaa* became much more than the background and trajectory of Julius Nyerere's thought.[21] It became a popular national language. Many of Nyerere's ideals, particularly the need to remove "parasitism," resounded with the public, but neither he nor they really sought to return to the deeply romanticized "African traditional society" that undergirded Nyerere's theory. Much subsequent political debate instead turned on who did or did not belong to the new *ujamaa* family, and how this could be determined.

At the center of popular *ujamaa* rhetoric stood the idea of *unyonyaji*, which translates literally as "sucking" and was often used in reference to the sucking of blood. Nationalists translated *unyonyaji* in English as the conventional socialist term "exploitation," but the core understandings of *unyonyaji* were grounded on distinct regional beliefs and metaphors. In one popular and long-standing campaign, nationalists pronounced *ujamaa* to be *dawa ya unyonyaji*, or medicine to combat and protect against "sucking," which appealed to widely held beliefs that people needed medical protection from evil spirits and treatment for those already bewitched. Eradication of *uchawi* (witchcraft) had long been a popular concern across East Africa, upon which itinerant *waganga* (traditional healers) could build enormous medical/exorcist practices. These beliefs flourished in colonial and postcolonial Dar es Salaam, where people from most classes and backgrounds feared bewitching by evil spirits or malevolent sorcerers (*wachawi*, purveyors of *uchawi*)—particularly so in peri-urban areas such as Buguruni, site of the 1959 *mumiani* abduction scare.[22] Residents in Dar es Salaam's outer neighborhoods patronized a famous *mganga* (healer) named Hamedi Said Matoroka to administer medicine to them. Unlike their colonial predecessors, the regional commissioner and neighborhood TANU officers not only welcomed Matoroka—who stood in a long line of Ngindo-trained *waganga* who took their lucrative practice to Dar es Salaam[23]—but asked that local residents cooperate rather than hinder his work. Fear of bewitching, urban officials believed, had discouraged local residents from investing in modern buildings and style of dress, and hoped that Matoroka's *dawa* would bring *maendeleo* (development) to the area. Those who refused to purchase medicine faced accusations of *uchawi*. Matoroka was in effect taxing peri-urban populations, and he shared his revenues with party and state officials.[24] The oft-used metaphor of *ujamaa* as *dawa* against *unyonyaji* demonstrates how local engagement required grafting local discourses to the Fabian sensibilities underlying Nyerere's vision of *ujamaa*.

Unyonyaji fast became central to nationalist discourse, within which fantastic beliefs about *mumiani* bloodletting stood at the edge of a wide spectrum. Accusations of figurative bloodsucking had been a staple of TANU speechmakers such as Bibi Titi Mohamed, who decried Africans "who sell their blood of their fellows"; and John Mwakangale, who claimed whites had "sucked our blood for too long, it cannot be tolerated. . . . We have been quiet under the yoke because we have only just begun to realise how much we were being exploited."[25] Nyerere himself, speaking to a crowd during Dar es Salaam's beer factory strike in 1958, warned that to drink foreign beer was to drink the blood of the three hundred striking African workers.[26] The official party watchword, however, was *uhuru* (freedom). Fearing that radical interpretations of what *uhuru* meant might spread—rioters in Buguruni had chanted the word amid their attacks on African police officers and Arab shopkeepers; others were taking it to mean freedom from taxation—the colonial government enjoined TANU to explain that the term ought to be understood as "Uhuru ni Jasho" (Freedom Is Sweat), and encouraged TANU to spread its new slogan, "Uhuru na Kazi" (Freedom and Work).[27] The rhetoric of many party nationalists met the popular understanding of urban Africans with arguments that *uhuru* meant freedom from exploitation (*unyonyaji*).

The British colonial state had dismissed witchcraft eradication discourses and prohibited *waganga* from selecting sorcerers (*wachawi*) to eradicate. The Tanzanian postcolonial state, in contrast, fully embraced the removal of evil as a metaphor of governance, and jealously guarded for itself the task of selecting the nation's enemies who required elimination. *Removal* had been one of the colonial government's chief legitimating activities—abolition or "removal" of slavery was widely understood to have been the primary justification for the colonial government's existence well into the 1940s. TANU's first promise to its Kariakoo supporters was to remove poverty so that Africans could become landowners.[28] Nyerere stated in 1965 that the purpose of revolution was not simply to remove the colonial government but to remove exploitation and bring justice in its place.[29] With this common goal, a nationalist and socialist language grew quickly in the early years of independence. The term *unyonyaji* invoked obviously biological forms of parasitism. "Usiwe kupe," or "Don't be a tick," was a popular *ujamaa* slogan that tapped into familiar frustrations, with local parasites seen to be as useless and harmful to an individual's life as social *makupe* (ticks) were to the nation. The three types of historical, wealth-sucking *makupe* endured by Africans, according to the newspaper *Uhuru*, were nineteenth-century Arab traders, twentieth-century Indian "coolies" and shopkeepers, and European colonialists.[30]

Alongside a vocabulary evoking biological parasites emerged a sociological terminology that translated local social strata into a more conventionally socialist vocabulary of enemies. *Bwanyenye*, deriving from the Bantu root *-enye* indicating ownership, translates as "bourgeoisie" and was used in reference to urban exploiters. The Arabic loanword *kabaila*, which referred unambiguously to sociopolitical status, translates as "feudalist" and references rural landowning exploiters as well as urban *rentier* landlords. *Bepari*, deriving from Gujarati, means "merchant," and rather appropriately served as the Swahili gloss for "capitalist."[31] Several words nicely bridged the chasm between socialist terminology and popular usage and meaning. The pejorative *mhuni* (hooligan)—considered yet another enemy of *ujamaa*—took on a rich array of meanings that referenced public anxiety toward young, unemployed African men. The word *mhuni* captured the unease experienced by established urban residents about crime and the breakdown of social order. It served as a discursive antonym for *mwananchi* or "citizen," who was distinguished by employment, marriage, and implied loyalty to the nation. The many colorful embodiments of the *wanyonyaji* (exploiters) of Tanzania—*kupe, mhuni, kabaila, bwanyenye, bepari*—together made up the purge categories of postcolonial nationalist discourse. These terms were employed more intensively after 1963, and particularly after the 1967 Arusha Declaration, when TANU published a political primer defining these terms.[32] Fluency in this new terminology armed citizens to confront colonialist propaganda or *kasumba* (opium), a term frequently invoked to describe hegemonic colonialist, antisocialist thought.

Amid these refined categories and rich epithets stood the image that justified *ujamaa*—the problem of *unyonyaji na mirija*, or "sucking by straws." The image had two manifestations: the first is of African men sitting around a jug sucking alcoholic drink with straws; the second is of non-Africans or "exploiter" Africans standing around a poor African and sucking either his sweat or blood with straws. The first image acts to reproach Africans who prefer indolence and intoxication to doing the nation's work; the second image links and deliberately confuses literal fears of bloodsucking by foreigners with the idiom of parasites who profit from the sweat of others. The first image caricatures Malawian dictator Hastings Kamuzu Banda sitting on a stool and sucking through a straw labeled "South Africa—Rhodesia," with the fluids contained in two jugs labeled "Malawi" and "Africa." The second, more explosive image depicts a slim young African wearing only a hat and shorts, surrounded by four corpulent *wanyonyaji*, or exploiters—a European, an Arab, an Indian (with passport in pocket), and an African—who are sucking blood from straws inserted into the African's body. In the following cartoon, his expression turns from pain to joy as black hands holding scissors cut the straws. The caption reads "Mirija imekatika" (The straws have been cut)—the decisive act of *ujamaa*—which ends the young man's suffering. He now has strength to farm with his hoe and strike the *wanyonyaji* surrounding him. The exploited consumer of retail textiles, for instance, could now expect the impending elimination of these unproductive middlemen. Nyerere himself enters subsequent cartoons as *fagio la ujamaa* or "broom of *ujamaa*," sweeping away the insect-like *wanyonyaji*; next Nyerere fuels the fire burning the exploiters, who are held together in a sack called *ubepari* (capitalism), with wood labeled *taifa*. Eradication of blood- or sweat-sucking is now nearing completion, thanks to Nyerere's war against exploiters.[33]

The ubiquitous language of battling *unyonyaji* transformed national citizenship from passive legal right to conscious political act. Yet lines between rhetoric and action remained unclear. Literal-minded shopkeepers in Kariakoo at first refused to keep soda straws in stock, "since Tanu and the Government are preaching that all types of straws must be cut off."[34] To help guide popular interpretation, the government produced a didactic pamphlet for its civil servants explaining how self-reliance (*kujitegemea*) applies to the workplace, defining *mnyonyaji* (exploiter) as "one who lives without working; lives off of the sweat of others." The pamphlet's goal was to make civil servants reflect on their role in *ujamaa* by instructing them to ask whether their actions would exploit others (*huku ni kunyonya?*), and covering such matters as arriving late to work and backbiting to secure a promotion.[35] If *kunyonya* could now be appropriated to express office-place politicking, the inflated propagandistic uses of the term were leading skeptics to question the ability of party leaders to communicate or even interpret *ujamaa* policy correctly.[36] But the literal meaning still held a place in public rhetoric. Among state-supported artists who dutifully applied this language to their work, one *shairi* poet represented *ujamaa*'s enemies:

> What punishment should we give, to those guilty of sucking
> Who suck like a tick, until they clot and die from sucking
> They don't let go even when burned with a wick, how will we warn
>   them
> What punishment should we give, to the exploiters of Tanzania?[37]

The nationalist elaboration of *unyonyaji* bridged popular metaphors of extraction with international socialist prescriptions for economic justice, enabling the government to signify who belonged to the new nation and, more important, who did not.

FROM ENTITLEMENT TO CITIZENSHIP: THE PARADOX OF URBAN BIAS IN TANZANIA

Postcolonial policies that differentiated between rural and urban activities represent a sharp paradox. In terms of real incentives and practical results, Tanzania represents a textbook case of "urban bias," in which currency overvaluation and low commodity pricing generally raised urban living standards, encouraged urban migration, and discouraged export-oriented rural production.[38] In other words, what this book has termed "urban entitlement"—those regulations established during the war that effectively subsidized, however modestly, food and other commodities not similarly guaranteed in rural areas—continued to be part of what attracted urban immigrants to Dar es Salaam and other cities after independence. Yet in terms of specific urban policies and stated national goals, Tanzania represents one of Africa's most anti-urban postcolonial states. Urban growth rate reached 8.9 percent per annum between 1967 and 1978—and 9.7 percent in Dar es Salaam—but urban centers, particularly after decentralization in 1972, were deliberately starved of infrastructural investment.[39] *Ujamaa* rhetoric and policy alike stressed that the nation's primary activity was agriculture and implied that cities themselves, particularly Dar es Salaam, were parasites benefiting from the nation's agricultural sweat. Nyerere framed the problem as one of potential class conflict—"If we are not careful we might get to the position where the real exploitation

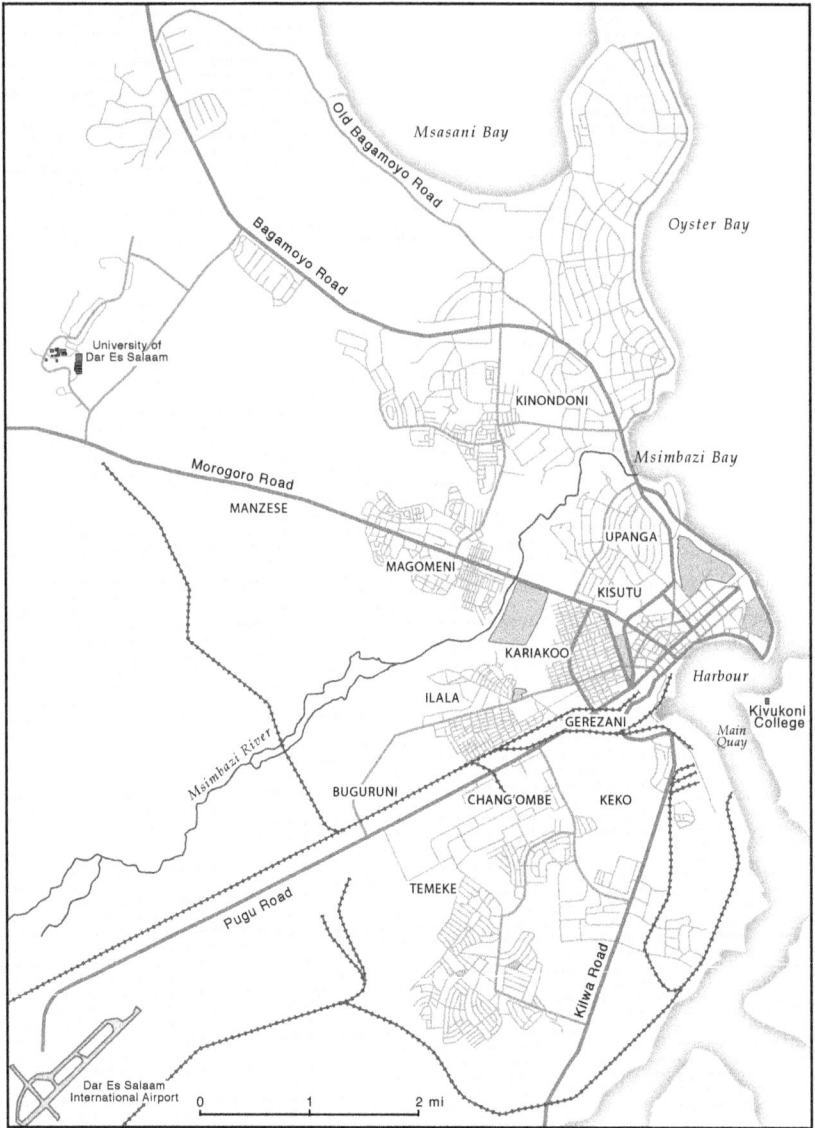

Map 4. Based on 1976 map of Surveys and Mapping Division, Ministry of Lands.

in Tanzania is that of the town dwellers exploiting the peasants."[40] Such was official anti-urban prejudice that trade unionists felt compelled to hold public meetings to state that urban workers did not exploit farmers, but joined with them in their struggle against capitalists.[41] The Arusha Declaration stated that rural development was to be the nation's primary goal. This resolution was considerably bolstered by an ILO report that criticized deteriorating terms of trade between rural farmers and urban workers: "The wage earners' improvement has thus occurred partly at the smallholders' expense."[42] The TANU government embraced the International Labor Organization report with alacrity and adopted a more equitable incomes policy in 1967 to reverse disparities between urban and rural incomes.[43] By 1972, however, rural incomes continued to stagnate because foodstuff prices had been artificially depressed to stabilize urban wages, thus placing the burden of rising urban inflation on peasant farmers.[44] The equitable incomes policy was abandoned in 1973, encouraging still greater urban migration just when villagization — the forced resettlement of Tanzanian farmers onto socialist villages — became national policy. Tanzania's disastrous and Orwellian "decentralization" policy (1972–1978) — nominally a reform strategy aimed at increasing decision-making capacity at local administrative levels — in practice removed several productive activities from Dar es Salaam, stripped the city of its municipal status, disbanded the city council, divided Dar es Salaam into the three districts of Temeke, Ilala, and Kinondoni, and culminated in the transfer of the capital to Dodoma in 1974.[45] Decentralization replaced local councils with regional and district committees whose first task was to increase rural production. Committee finance was entirely controlled by central government, and committees were staffed by central government officials.[46] Staffs grew in size but not in expertise, while material and equipment procurements fell. Roads, public transport, water provision, garbage collection, latrine pit emptying, and other public services all sharply deteriorated over the 1970s.[47]

Yet urban space remained exclusive and retained material value, owing to comparatively high wages, on the one hand, and the provision of minimal living standards secured through cost controls and mobility regulations, on the other. "High and downwardly inflexible urban wages"[48] continued to pull people into Dar es Salaam, while the practice of repatriating under- and unemployed *wahuni* sharpened considerably during the first two decades of independence. Based on an optimistic calculus of unrealized labor productivity, postcolonial repatriation campaigns to rural villages were accorded militarized titles.[49] Those unable to prove local residence were removed in "Operation Idlers Round-up," also titled "Kifagio Songambele" (Songambele's Broom, named after the regional commissioner), in which more than 600 of the town's estimated 4,000 jobless were arrested, placed on trucks, and "returned" to the countryside. Fresh roundups targeting the unlicensed self-employed immediately followed the Arusha Declaration.[50] This included a ban on water selling, a service for which there was great urban demand — the ban struck at the heart of both unregulated employment and "unproductive" labor. "Because our parents carried water on their heads in the villages," one official explained, "people in Ilala and

Magomeni should do the same."[51] The water-selling ban was never fully implemented, nor was the city's ambitious new pass system, wherein urban citizenship was obtained by an identity card confirming full employment.[52] Despite promises that surprise roundups of "the unemployed people and indecently-dressed women" would continue "for ever,"[53] enduring economic incentives steadily overwhelmed the zeal and resources of the *ujamaa* state by the 1980s.

In other words, the basic policy calculus of what this book has termed "urban entitlement"—the regulation of scarce urban resources that were reserved for the productive African worker and guarded by mobility restrictions— had not significantly altered after independence. What had changed was the public and performative nature of what it now meant to be productive. It was no longer enough to be fully employed in a way that was transparent and acceptable to colonial officials. One now had to be seen performing the tasks of a citizen (*mwananchi*) in front of one's fellow nationalists, namely by combating exploitation or *unyonyaji*, particularly when the nation's rural work was being left undone. As others have emphasized, national citizenship ideals in postcolonial Tanzania concerned public performance at least as much as they did legal status.[54] If full-time jobs were not available, people could create their own urban "nation-building" work—no group was better at this than the TANU Youth League, whose often unemployed young male members justified their presence by policing urban space to combat anti-national behavior.[55] Thus the term "urban citizenship," which entails the visible performance of nation-building activities, better captures how postcolonial urban space was defined than the term "entitlement."

Because cities were primarily sites of consumption that generated unwholesome divisions of labor, the ideal urban citizen was also someone who held urban life in contempt. A sharp anti-urban populism thrived in Dar es Salaam amid mass urban migration, juxtaposing associations of rural African virtue with urban non-African indulgence. Nodes of urban density embodied in the image of Indians closely clustered in commercial shops and high-rise residences should yield to an Africanized landscape of evenly distributed, low-density *ujamaa* villages. Counterposing Asian and European "naturalized citizens" against African *wananchi*, the *Nationalist* declared in 1968 that de facto racial zoning must now end, putting blame for its persistence squarely on *wananchi*:

> Up to now, we have failed to dismantle the myth of "uhindini," "uzunguni" and "uswahilini." As a result, negative attitudes of judging people according to the "racial zones" they live in still persist. In this way no person can be respected in a shop situated in "uzunguni"

unless he is white. No person can be respected in an "uhindini" area unless he is brown!! To rectify the situation all naturalised citizens must be called to order. They must behave. The myth of zoned living which is in some ways responsible for the arrogance of some naturalised citizens must be destroyed.[56]

Cartoons addressed the unwillingness of urban residents to do the nation's work on farms—one depicted a hoe chasing an unwilling farmer with the caption "Don't fear the hoe"; another showed an urban water carrier being handed a hoe by a black arm inscribed with the word *taifa*, accompanied by the caption "You will build with the hoe, not with the water can." Nyerere himself bulldozed a skyscraper being supported by his regional foe Hastings Kamuzu Banda, the antisocialist, antiliberationist president of Malawi—the building standing in as the foe of dense urbanization and capital accumulation.[57] For Nyerere, provincial cities at least facilitated rural production; the capital city seemed only to produce rumor and intrigue. He harangued a large audience in the capital: "If you are in TABORA you talk about tobacco and its price, if you are in MWANZA you talk about cotton and what its price will be, if you are in MTWARA you talk about cashew nuts . . . but in DAR ES SALAAM they talk about people," and added that "when we began TANU here in 1954 I told my companions that our country will not flourish if the headquarters is DAR ES SALAAM and DAR ES SALAAM is rotten. . . . If the headquarters is rotten it will corrupt people from other parts."[58]

The state employed a host of media to convince urban residents that life on *ujamaa* cooperative villages was far superior to the uncertainties and immoralities of a town existence.[59] *Fimbo ya Mnyonge (The Poor Man's Stick*, 1976), the first and only feature-length film produced by the state-owned Tanzania Film Company, was primarily designed to discourage urban immigration.[60] Nationalist rhetoricians considered *wahuni* to be among the greatest of Tanzania's exploiters. A *shairi* poet offered the following verse in regard to the country's lazy:

> The lazy are a hindrance, to our development
> They don't like work, they don't grin when they work
> To deceive is their work, our home is a broken heart
> The lazy are the enemy, we must keep our eye on them[61]

Vilifying *wahuni* resounded among many Dar es Salaam residents frustrated with thieves and crime. *Wahuni* repatriations attained an important postcolonial popularity.[62] The volunteer policing zeal among Dar es Salaam's male youth, usually directed through the TANU Youth League, found an independent existence in the "Tata Kabwera Foola Union" of Ilala, a short-lived vigilante organization that took up the task of expelling the urban unemployed to "remove this shame" from town.[63] Another revolutionary suffering in the fleshpots of Manzese asked that this "Village of the Witch" be purified by implementing the Arusha Declaration to abolish "all this rubbish" of *waganga*, prostitutes, and criminals.[64]

The urban public sphere, like urban public space, remained aggressively male under *ujamaa*. The increasing participation of women in Dar es Salaam's formal workplace—their share rose from 4 percent in 1961 to 20 percent in 1980—challenged the wage monopoly of men, who felt that such public female presence brought shame. Men expressed their resentment and sense of victimhood through vigilante campaigns to control women's dress.[65] Praiseful nationalist descriptions of women were reserved for those in rural areas; "virtuous" urban women had little place in nationalist rhetoric. Male-to-female ratios in Dar es Salaam had grown gradually more balanced, from 141:100 in 1948 to 123:100 in 1967—yet only one-third of all men were married upon their arrival in 1967, compared to two-thirds of all women.[66] Not only were too many single men competing for too few unmarried women, but both faced sharp difficulties in securing their own housing. Landlords often denied rooms to unmarried men and women—fearing the former were transients and the latter prostitutes.[67] Single women were suspected—by virtue of their being single—of being prostitutes, around which a rich language developed—*guberi*, a term for colonialist or imperialist, also meant "prostitute." Men came to use the graphic term *kupe* (tick) to describe women, allegedly because they relied on men to provide everything.[68] Such insults could be read as expressions of nostalgia, for women were exercising a growing degree of economic independence in postcolonial Dar es Salaam. By the early 1970s, women were participating in revolving credit societies where cloths and food were pooled, and 70 percent of self-employed women were by then controlling their own earnings. They were also becoming landlords in fast-growing and gritty peri-urban neighborhoods like Manzese and Buguruni, which was the home of the period's great urban male personification, *kabwela*.[69]

KABWELA AND *NAIZESHENI*: CLASS, LANGUAGE, AND URBAN CITIZENSHIP IN *UJAMAA* TANZANIA

Male residents of Dar es Salaam crafted their own language to navigate and legitimate their presence in a rapidly changing urban landscape, even though the larger terms of debate were set by political elites. In his 1962 pamphlet *Ujamaa—The Basis of African Socialism*, Nyerere argues that *ujamaa* does not start from the existence of conflicting classes in society, and even doubts that a word for "class" exists in any African language.[70] This proposition is famous for its idealization of Africa's past; it also demonstrates the chasm between Nyerere's idealization of Africa's present and the reality of a robust urban language of class. While the reality of class conflict under *ujamaa* socialism has certainly not passed unnoticed by researchers,[71] the popular language of class that constituted a central element of postcolonial urban life largely has. This language inevitably developed within the values and constraints of *ujamaa* ideology. The postcolonial Tanzanian nationalism of *ujamaa* depended on an active citizenry willing to partake in nation-building exercises and not only refrain from exploitation of fellow citizens, but to fight it. There were two legitimate "classes" within this national conception of citizenship—the peasant (*mkulima*), the ideal citizen who lived and farmed in rural districts; and the worker (*mfanyakazi*), the urban citizen necessary for certain aspects of national development but whose activities warranted closer scrutiny. Nationalists demanded that *wahuni*, those Africans living unproductive lives in cities and thus failing to live up to the demands of national citizenship, should—together with "immodest" women and exploitative Indians—be removed and sent to work in the countryside. In all cases, nationalist categories of citizenship derived their legitimacy by combating *unyonyaji*.

Official *ujamaa* rhetoric never defined the ideal African urban citizen in positive terms. He—the basic categories were male—was known rather by the exploitation he suffered from the costs and dangers of city living. But African residents of Dar es Salaam offered their own terms. The term *kabwela* signified someone who was poor and exploited, and became the common denominator of urban nationalist frustrations; a Tanzanian Everyman or John Bull. The origins of the term *kabwela* are rather obscure— originally the title of a popular song and slogan hailing Nyerere's return from the United Nations in 1957, by the early 1960s it had become the ubiquitous term to describe the loyal urban citizen who deserved sympathy and assistance.[72] Other popular terms for the urban poor carried disagreeable connotations—*mhuni* was plainly pejorative and officially condemned; *mmatumbi*, another "everyman," was a "tribal" name. Its imprecise origins and usage enabled *kabwela* to become the popular term to make sense of the towndweller's plight, especially among residents of Dar es Salaam. *Kabwela* was a rhetorical personage who, despite working hard and (somewhat) honestly, found himself exploited by rack-renting landlords, cheating shopkeepers, and abusive employers—and also provided a new language that enabled TANU government and its undesired but intractable urban population to negotiate with one another.

The popular discursive antonym to *kabwela*, roughly "urban poor," was *naizesheni*, or *naizi* for short. *Naizesheni* referred to those urban Africans who, with relatively little effort, had come to enjoy the lion's share of the fruits of independence by inheriting the privileges of departing colonialists. The term clearly derives from "nationalization" and less directly from "Africanization," both processes very much in the public eye in the early 1960s. *Naizi* were seen as exploitative and often taken to task for abusing the spirit of *ujamaa*, such as paying domestic servants subminimum, "relative-to-relative" wages by persuading their employees that they were "relatives."[73] Alongside the term *naizi* emerged a related moral vocabulary to assess the easy success that some Africans enjoyed. *Nyeupe*, literally meaning "white," was slang for "easy to get"; in this vein, *mweusi mzungu*, or "black European," refers to the easy life enjoyed by certain Africans after independence. The popular antonym to *nyeupe* was not "black" (*nyeusi*) but *kienyeji*, meaning "local" or "native"; to travel as a stowaway on a train was *chukua safari kienyeji*, or "take a trip local-style," in contrast to how those who could afford tickets would travel. The word *jengesha*—from *jenga* (to build), which referred to those who "built the nation"—meant "to grow fat," a bodily metaphor ubiquitous across sub-Saharan-Africa political discourse linked to easy success and inattention to others' welfare.

Kabwela and *naizi* were popular class terms that enabled urban residents to speak about social realities of economic differentiation beyond the Manichaean categories of *wananchi* and *wanyonyaji* prescribed in official nationalist discourse. The terms were sociologically imprecise—a *kabwela* could be a recently arrived water carrier or an old dockworker who had lived his whole life in Dar es Salaam; a *naizi* was most frequently a civil servant, although the definition could include a successful trader or a landlord—because their purpose was both to make sense of rapid social changes and to pronounce moral judgments on their effects. Both were characters who spoke and were spoken about on the public stage. The general dynamic in public discussion of these terms was for a *kabwela* to bemoan a *naizi*'s easy life, which he believed came at his exploitation. *Kabwela* expressed anxiety over how and where the urban poor fit in postcolonial society. One asked, if there being two "names" or classes, *kabwela* and *naizesheni*, why was it that only *kabwela* had to pay one-third of his income on rent alone? Others asked where *kabwela* would live, for the same gentrifying forces of African landlords and their affluent African tenants, the *naizi*, were now driving *kabwela* even out of down-at-heel Manzese as they earlier had from Magomeni.[74] Class resentment often punctured the spirit of humor in which these terms were cast. *Ngurumo*'s serial "Ala! Kumbe" narrated the story of Mzegamzega, who took violent offense to being called *kabwela*. A friend explained that Mzegamzea should not be offended by *kabwela*, because the term merely signified the endless gradations of material inequality in Dar es Salaam:

If it's like this, then even those who own cars are *kabwelas*. Because the Volkswagen owner is the *kabwela* of the Peugot owner, and the Peugot owner is *kabwela* of the Benz owner, and the Benz owner is the *kabwela* of the lorry, and the lorry owner is the *kabwela* of the bus owner.[75]

In his rather humorless novel *Zika Mwenyewe*, Alex Banzi portrays a young official in Dar es Salaam who falls out with his lower-class Zaramo neighbors. During a heated argument, the protagonist disparages his poorer neighbors by calling them *makabwela*; they respond angrily by calling him *naizi* and harangue him with militant *ujamaa* slogans, "Wazalendo oyeee, vibaraka zii!" or "Patriots hurrah, down with puppet-lackeys!"[76] Mid- to upper-level African civil servants, the most easily identifiable *naizi*, were sharply sensitive to class reproach. After *Civil Service Magazine* published a *shairi* criticizing *naizi* for their selfishness and irresponsibility, several responded with their own *shairi* to defend *naizi* behavior, or to call on *naizi* to behave better.[77]

Kabwela and *naizesheni* carried humorous, sometimes self-deprecating overtones far removed from the somber pronouncements of state-party propaganda. People publicly joked in asking, "Where are you going, citizen?" (Unakwenda wapi, mwananchi?), and the other would respond, "I'm going to build the nation" (Nakwenda kujenga taifa).[78] Mocking *ujamaa* rhetorical excesses became a popular sport. Just after the "straws of exploitation" were declared cut with the Arusha Declaration, people in Dar es Salaam joked that someone drinking a Fanta soda should stop because "the straws have been cut." *Mpinduzi wa serikali* (or government revolutionary) became a slang term for an adulterer.[79] The decidedly unhumorous Thaabit Kombo demanded that union government outlaw usage of *kabwela* on the same grounds that the Zanzibar government had banned public usage of *mhuni*—because under *ujamaa*, all people should be equal, and such words made light of irresponsible youth.[80] Yet most government officials, by definition *naizi*, ultimately if grudgingly accepted these terms, even lending their imprimatur by granting them official definitions in *ujamaa* literature. Government represented itself as benefactor of *kabwela*, appropriating the personification as a convenient foil to *wahuni*.[81] Although often prone to heavy-handed censorship, the government generally tolerated more-subtle criticisms embodied by the humor in the popular press.

It would be mistaken to draw too firm a distinction between official and popular nationalist vocabularies of postcolonial Tanzania. The purge categories of party-state official discourse set limits on what could be argued in popular press. To be *mhuni* (hooligan) remained anathema. Urban males who identified with *kabwela* asserted that *mhuni* was an unnatural state, an

unfortunate condition that they struggled to overcome. Many traced this condition to the dilemma of being single and without good housing. Not only
did landlords often refuse to rent to single men, women refused to marry
men without a home or room.[82] Urban residents in Tanzania used official
terms like *unyonyaji* and unofficial ones like *naizi* and *kabwela* to address the
concerns that urban Africans had faced since the 1940s. They made moral
claims hoping to secure the basic necessities to which the urban citizen was
due, but were still mediated through racially inequitable economic structures.
Unyonyaji and its English equivalent, the word "exploitation," provided ways
to debate the morality of impossibly high prices of food, clothing, and rents.
But the employment of domestic servants, that most unseemly reminder of
class differentiation, proved far less amenable to personification and, therefore, public scrutiny.[83] The personification of *naizi* served as a means of moral
surveillance on wealthy urban Africans to constantly remind them of their
responsibilities to the new nation. The personification of *kabwela* enabled
poor urban Africans to lay claim to an urban existence otherwise ignored or
forbidden by *ujamaa* policy, and eventually to demand that government remove the exploitative conditions endured by those labeled as *kabwela*.

OTE DUGU MOJA: NATION BUILDING, RACIAL
DISTANCE, AND THE INDIAN CARICATURE

Nyerere's ideal of cultural assimilation into the new Tanzanian *taifa* via socialist behavior was an important development, but one that never displaced, or
even reached parity with, earlier descent-based notions that conflated nation
and race in urban public discourse. For many in Dar es Salaam, what was
labeled patently antisocialist behavior by the authorities instead only stressed
underlying continental incompatibilities long identified by previous African
thinkers. Days after the Arusha Declaration, Nyerere released an essay titled
"Socialism Is Not Racialism," which defined socialism as rejection of those
who judge people by race. It was instead a philosophy of human equality
that began with the fundamental distinction between "those who stand for
the interests of the workers and peasants" and those who do not.[84] But as we
have seen, Indians were long unpopular figures in the political and economic
imagination of Africans, widely held to be the primary obstacles to development and African self-improvement. In the 1960s, Indians had—at least in
African popular perception—responded to TANU's success by ridiculing
African competence to self-rule. The independent newspaper *Zuhra* warned
that Indians would soon no longer call on African prostitutes, use the widely
understood Gujarati epithet *golo* (slave), or dismiss nationalist ambitions
with the question "How will he get ability to rule?" (Ataweza wapi kuupata
utawala?), "Indianized" as "Weja wapi?"[85] Discouraging political words

spoken in poor Swahili left a bitter impression on Kariakoo residents—one such resident clearly recalled Indians taunting him by asking "Wapi nyie pata huru? Uhuru chejo?" (Where get *huru*? Is *Uhuru* a dance?).[86] Language revealed the deep divides on both sides. *Golo, shenzi*, and other casual terms of abuse had become unacceptable affronts to African honor.[87] The name Patel became common slang to refer to all Indians, while the term *mwananchi*, meaning "citizen," with strong connotations of patriotism (literally "child of the land"), was exclusively used to describe Africans. The terms *mwananchi* and *Patel* became self-evidently antonymic in urban discourse. Indians were widely considered "paper citizens"—the TANU newspaper *Uhuru* demanded the expulsion of Indians who had not chosen a citizenship within the two-year window after independence; others called on TANU to vet all Indian passport applications; still others called on Indians who held Tanzanian citizenship to reapply and be accepted only if they offered qualifications.[88] One *mwananchi* proposed that all Asians "MUST on their own initiative participate actively in the day-to-day Tanzanian way of living. . . . A sign of arrogance noticed by 50 per cent of his/her neighbours/workmates deprives his/her citizenship."[89]

Bitter sarcasm directed at the disparity between postcolonial ideals of equality and persisting realities of racial inequality was captured in the phrase *ote dugu moja*, a reference to the distinctly Indian pronunciation of the nationalist mantra "Sisi wote undugu mmoja," or "We are all one family." Africans long complained that Indians used this phrase only when needing to get something from Africans.[90] African writers in turn imbued the phrase *ote dugu moja* with dark humor and cynical relish, using it to create another postcolonial personification in order to criticize racial inequalities persisting within the "family" of postcolonial Tanzania:

> One day at a Sundowner, Patel was there with his tie, Smith sauntering around with his glass of beer, everyone saying we are one family [*sisi wote dugu moja*] in front of *manaizesheni* [successful Africans], tomorrow he [Patel] will see his servant and disregard this *Mwananchi*, in fact he lords it over him and bullies him and continues to suck his blood. For the same work Kabwela receives 150/- and Patel receives 300/-; Juma carries heavy luggage, and Patel carries light luggage. . . . Oh friend what kind of family is this?[91]

Indian failure to fully join the *ujamaa* family was underscored by a lack of participation in "nation-building" activities. Aloof Indian households defied national integration. A university student insisted that the problem rested with the Indian family, where innocent children grew up "in the homes of those speculators, racketeers and plunderous [sic] capitalists," and thus matured differently than "citizens who are Africans by birth."[92] The nation of India stood ambiguously not only as a model of peaceful socialist liberation, but also as a symbol of enormous inequality. "Is this India?" one writer warningly asked, in a diatribe against emerging inequalities in Tanganyika.[93] Africans befriended by Indians often viewed themselves as being used like a ladder (*ngazi*) for Indians hoping to secure necessary political contacts.[94] Others encouraged arrest of *dugu moja* if they were caught staring out windows rather than joining political marches or parade receptions of foreign dignitaries.[95] All Indian shops in Morogoro were briefly closed to punish Indians' failure to publicly protest an alleged Western plot to overthrow Nyerere in 1964.[96] District officials in Dar es Salaam ordered Indians to attend meetings, parades, and other public functions on short notice and at peak business hours, exhausting businessmen's patience and exacerbating popular anger.[97] Some writers confronted anti-Asian populism by drawing distinctions between socialism, economic nationalism, and racialism, but such debates were rare and rarely sustained.[98]

Unlike 1940s debates over intermarriage, which defined the meaning and direction of *taifa*, postcolonial debates attempted to diagnose the stubborn persistence of racial distance and find solutions to create a single nation. Marriage between Africans and Indians remained extraordinarily rare after independence, but its rarity was now more sharply noticed. Speaking at Zanzibar's *diwali* festival in 1965, President Abeid Karume urged Indians to intermarry with Africans to break down colonial hierarchies, warning that there "was great danger ahead if the Indians refrained from mixed marriage."[99] Across the water in Dar es Salaam, a male university student agreed with Karume's instructions, welcoming intermarriage as a means to dilute non-Africans into one African race. "Nations of East Africa encourage national cultures," he argued, "and discourage racial, tribal or group or minority cultures. . . . As the Indians are a minority they must swallow their cultures and follow the majority."[100] In 1970, Karume went further by supporting the forced marriage of four Parsi girls, ages between fourteen and twenty, to senior Zanzibari government officials; their protesting fathers and brothers were caned and imprisoned. "It was the Arabs and Asians who in the past were allowed to keep African concubines," Karume explained. "The revolution brought to an end this feudal injustice and now it is time for all the people of the islands to inter-marry."[101] He later clarified that marital consent should be based on three principles — "The in-law should not have a prison record, not be a lunatic or have suffered from leprosy."[102]

Most Dar es Salaam residents were horrified at Karume's actions; many demanded the union government intervene.[103] Despite international condemnation, Karume stood firm, asking, "How can we achieve our unity if we cannot marry one another?"[104] Onlookers debated the wider problem of integration—one decried Asian endogamy, particularly cousin-marriage, as a cynical strategy to preserve wealth within family circles; another declared intermarriage a solution to the problem of "inferior-superior race" belief; still another argued that classes cannot be eliminated through intermarriage, but only "by being expropriated by being educated and cleansed with an [anti-class] ideology."[105] An African woman from Dar es Salaam named Linda Wabuliba asked, "What do my brothers gain by marrying Indians?" and answered her own question, saying that nothing would be gained, for such marriages would force Tanzania

> to accommodate a completely new tribe of neither Asians nor Africans; a tribe of neither Sukumas nor Punjabis! Pity us who have to introduce in our family, completely, new values—un-African and un-Asian! We may console ourselves by calling them Tanzanians but is Tanzania not formed of tribes and are they not enough already? What reason have we to create others? I know why some of my brothers would want to plunge our family into such a state of affairs. It is a question of long years of slavery. I am sure if my brothers were to be in India, they would never dare marry these next-to-useless souls.[106]

Such actions, she concluded, were motivated by base motives to "dislodge" Indians from their continued feelings of superiority over Africans.[107] Mrs. B. Munduli, an Indian Shia who had married a Maasai man, found the debate absurd—Asian families who had lived for decades in Africa had already adopted much African culture; the real problem lay in how Asian fathers spoiled daughters with riches, making them unfit for any marriage.[108] Although the women in the controversy itself were pawns in male political machinations, there were now finally significant numbers of female voices debating the virtues of racial endogamy.

Tanzania's popular press eagerly demonstrated how Indians continuously transgressed the norms and spirit of *ujamaa*. One illustration of this point of view was the popular press's portrayal of *Kiswahili cha Kihindi*, or "Indianized" Swahili, the distinctive pidgin spoken by many Indians and widely felt to communicate disrespect toward nation-building.[109] One writer, upset that Indians seemed unable to give the patriotic citizen his due honor (*kumpa mwananchi kheshima zake*), wrote of the dismissive treatment African women received in Indian shops. He underscored his argument that Indians avoided nation-building work (*kazi za kujenga taifa*) by proposing their theoretical response to this criticism—*hii tavesa vapi kazi hiyo*. This pidgin response is difficult to translate, but it captures both the bad faith (asking where exactly one can find this "work") and poor Swahili (*utaweza* becomes *tavesa*) that Indians were widely assumed to exercise. The author concluded by writing, "Now is not the time to disrespect the African."[110] *Uhuru* was a particularly ebullient vehicle for voicing anti-Asian criticism.[111] In the late 1960s, *Uhuru* launched a column titled "Miye"—the pseudonym for a sort of "everyman" writer who engaged a recurring set of characters in fictional dialogues about issues of the day. Miye never joked about *ujamaa*, and his attempts at political humor regularly came at the expense of Indians, though Arabs and Europeans were also occasionally mocked. In his representation of fictional Indian characters, Miye contrasted his own correct Swahili with the tortuous *Kiswahili cha Kihindi* of Indian characters.

A major purpose of Miye was to demonstrate how out of touch Indians were with *ujamaa* and the basic tenets of Tanzanian nationalism. Miye, an apparently earnest African nationalist and *ujamaa* supporter, repeatedly engaged in didactic conversation with a caricatured Indian shopkeeper named Mamujee—whose scorn of African businessmen, reluctance to perform agricultural work, and belief that his TANU card exempted him from nation-building activities—represented the bad political faith widely attributed to Tanzania's Indians.[112] The pseudonymous author played on familial meanings of nationalist terms such as *ndugu* and *taifa*, both to exhort Indians to behave better and to highlight the implicitly unbridgeable racial differences that stood between Indians and Africans. In one typical column, Miye demonstrates how Indians retain colonial attitudes about "multiracial" society rather than heeding calls to "build the nation." This fictional conversation followed a real speech by India's President Varahagiri Venkata Giri, who had urged Indians in Dar es Salaam to respect *ujamaa* and help build the nation by taking up farmwork:

> Miye: And you, Bwana Mamujee, when a guest of the nation arrives, quit that game of peeping through the window. You have to line up on the streets with other Tanzanians to receive him.
> Mamujee: Yes friend, big man already say, All Indians agree, Hindus, Arabs, Swahili all one family [*ote dugu moja*]. Giri already say.
> Miye: And in the work of building the *taifa*, don't lag behind.
> Mamujee: Friend, if all Indians build *taifa*, who sell curry powder?
> Mama Mamujee: If all Indians close shop, where get bread?
> Miye: The honorable Giri has already said, you now have to wind up your shops and begin the work of building the *taifa*.
> Mama Mamujee: If all Indian go build *taifa*, where Swahili get rice?
> Miye: At the cooperative shops.
> Mamujee: If all Indian close shop, where Swahili get . . .
> Miye: Get lost!
> Mamujee: Friend, you smoke *goro* [marijuana]? Say what now? God

divide people three part: White rule, Indian build shop, Swahili dance. Don't you know?[113]

Following this conversation, Miye bitterly ruminates on how the Indian president's call was being received by *hawa ndugu zetu*, or "our family members."[114] In a visit to Mwanza, Mamujee complains to Miye that everyone was using the word *taifisha* (nationalize), when the only word he could find in his dictionary was *taifa*.[115] Mamujee, a caricature of the exploitative Indian merchant, could grasp neither the language nor the ideas of the new nation in which he now lived. Miye later addresses two Indians distraught about the recent nationalization of buildings by greeting them with *hamjambo wananchi*. The address conveys bitter irony, for *wananchi* sharply contrasts with what for Miye are plainly "unpatriotic," noncitizen Indians. One replies defensively, "We are not citizens. Will TANU card work?"[116] Such cards, which had been restricted to Africans during the years of colonial struggle, were now available for purchase regardless of race or citizenship.

AFRICANIZING URBAN LIFE

Dar es Salaam grew more "African" over the 1960s—not only as a public space in which to express national culture but also as its Asian population share fell from 29 percent in 1961 to 11 percent in 1969.[117] Nationalists grew impatient with the lingering elements of Indian culture in public institutions. A writer calling himself *mwananchi* demanded that East African Airways terminate the practice of its Asian stewardesses wearing saris on flights to Karachi and Bombay.[118] Indian social clubs quickly changed names—Goan Institute became Dar es Salaam Institute; Hindu Sports Club became Upanga Sports Club, Patel Brotherhood became Dar es Salaam Brotherhood.[119] But intent also mattered. Indian, Arab, and Somali shop owners were criticized for playing Radio Tanzania only to attract business, while having no interest in the political educational programming or even understanding of Swahili broadcasts.[120] In response to Indian complaints regarding termination of Hindustani programming on Radio Tanzania, TANU's *Nationalist* produced an instructive rant encapsulating the spectrum of African resentments toward Indians:

> What disturbs us most is the obnoxious attitude of many people of Indian origin in this country who think that because they contribute "colossal" amounts of money to this or that fund, they can get favours even at the expense of the whole nation. We wish to be very frank with them today. By contributing to this or that fund, these people actually do nothing but merely reimburse the country the wealth they have exploited out of its labour and natural resources. . . . Let

it be said frankly that Wananchi have tolerated enough of the abuses of these people. Indeed, these are the same people who during our struggle for Uhuru used to tell us "weja wapi." These are the people who have refused to learn our national language, Kiswahili. These are the same people who, when there is a national function or meeting go to the beaches instead of attending. These are the people who have failed to offer any substantial Africanisation in their businesses. These are the people who have refused to take part physically in nation building work. These are the people who hoard foodstuffs. These are the people who increase prices unilaterally whenever there is a call for national sacrifice!! These are the people who threaten us with imaginary inflations and all sorts of dangers in order to hold back our nation building spirit! These are the same people who are prepared to exploit Wananchi remorselessly under the guise of "dugu moja." These are the people who are prepared to call themselves Tanzanians only as long as they remain a privileged group! It is imperative this claim for special privilege should stop. It is incompatible with our attitude to citizenship and nation-building and cannot be tolerated.[121]

Indian wealth, social life, and entertainment remained walled off from the wider city, still patterned by multistoried urban density and cosmopolitan mobility. Agehananda Bharati counted 80 out of 100 cars on Dar es Salaam's streets as driven by Asians; movie houses had more than 50 percent Indian attendance during English-language film screenings, and more than 70 percent Indian attendance for Hindi films. "All of this is known and resented by the Africans," Bharati observed, "and the resentment is universal."[122] One Dar es Salaam resident simply refused to accept that Asians were anything but foreigners. "Do they not still call him 'goro' [slave]?" he asked. "Do they not still live in exclusive communities and meet in temples only to backbite the African? . . . Do they not use all sorts of deplorable means to make sure they drain the country of its hard earned currency?"[123] Visible persistence of wealth and endogamy posed an inescapable political problem. "As long as the Asian community remains conspicuously rich comparative to the rest of the community—and is also an immigrant community—the problem remains," Nyerere explained to a newspaper reporter, concluding, "I wish I knew an easy answer—I would use it at once."[124]

Nationalists juxtaposed crimes of Asian cosmopolitan mobility with the virtue of rooted African citizenry. Asian expulsions from Tanzania, usually on grounds of bribery or failure to observe immigration laws, were touted in the press and celebrated in editorials, particularly after tight restrictions on exporting currency were imposed in 1965.[125] Dar es Salaam *baraza* meetings became didactic nationalist spectacles. Mustafa Songambele warned a *baraza* of Indian leaders to stop scorning TANU leaders and "to not use their citizenship like a shield" in order to avoid nation-building work—should we ever go to war with India, he explained, all Tanzanian citizens will fight on the side of their country.[126] *Uhuru* decried the moneyed spirit of Indian responses to urban nation-building work—Hindus had offered to lend money to the city council, while Ismailis encouraged their members to buy Tanzanian national bonds.[127] Revelations that Indians would own national bonds were met with outrage. "They separate from us in private," one Dar resident explained, "but when they meet with our leaders, they make themselves liked with *sisi dugu moja*."[128] The area's regional commissioner later instructed an audience in Uhindini to teach their children to mix with other races, to share their houses with Africans, and demanded that they not collect donations without his office's permission.[129]

The Arusha Declaration had declared that money was the "wrong weapon" for Tanzania's development struggle. Its mysterious movements came under increasing public scrutiny. Asian religious leaders had long faced accusations of illegally expatriating money from East Africa beneath the guise of religious pilgrimages.[130] In late 1968, the *dai* (leader) of the global Bohora community was arrested while departing Dar es Salaam airport on charges of contravening foreign exchange regulations.[131] The Patel "Kanti Brothers," whose family had founded the *Tanganyika Opinion*, were arrested at the airport in 1969 on charges of tax evasion, defrauding the government, and illegally repatriating money to India. After a highly publicized trial, they were fined, deported, and their book store liquidated.[132] That same year, prosecution of an Indian-led criminal ring that forged passports led the Home Minister to attack "big businessmen" who were trying "to sabotage the national economy."[133] Questioning the relationship between foreigners and food, nationalist rhetoricians regularly attacked Indians and Arabs for hoarding foodstuffs—the *Nationalist* reported that "fortune-hunters of foreign origin in their attempts to ruin the national institutions were turning to black marketing of rice, flour, and other foodstuffs essential to the workers and peasants."[134] In 1972, hoarding became a crime punishable by up to fourteen years' imprisonment and a hundred-thousand-shilling fine. State commitments to higher education had become thoroughly racialized, in both policy and family choice. In the 1960s, almost every Asian studying overseas was financed by his or her family, while almost every African studying overseas was either sponsored by a foreign government or contracted to serve the Tanzanian government.[135] Feverish "integration" rhetoric notwithstanding, pluralist governing strategies established during colonial years proved institutionally resilient in socialist Tanzania. Local government bodies had neither the will nor the ability to adjudicate internal disputes within Dar es Salaam's tightly knit Indian communities. Communal bodies founded in the colonial period continued to play an important role in administering and policing these private spheres. Most significantly, the 1971 Law of Marriage Act empowered communal organizations—governing *jamaats* among Indian Muslims and Hindu Mandal among Tanzanian Hindus—to perform marital rites, issue certificates, and settle marital disputes.[136]

Africanization of municipal offices had been instantaneous and complete—all Indian and European town councilors in Dar es Salaam resigned at independence, replaced by newly elected, all-African councillors.[137] But the scope and pace of the Africanization of civil service and commercial economy was the central political debate of the 1960s. Tanganyika's wage hierarchy at independence—when Europeans averaged annual salaries of £1,547, Asians £586, and Africans £106—could not stand, and was quickly transformed. Two years after independence, the African share of middle- and senior-ranking civil servant jobs had risen from 26 percent to 49 percent.[138] Government leaders, particularly Rashidi Kawawa, deftly managed to Africanize civil servant posts without precipitating a mass exodus of expatriate workers. Yet the process was widely seen to be moving too slowly—"*Akina* Nair, Patel, De Souza," and other Indians, one writer suggested, should all be fired instantly.[139] Frustrated with the self-seeking and often racist spirit behind populist demands to hasten Africanization, Nyerere released a circular in early 1964 that replaced Africanization with "localization" as the new guiding policy for government hiring, and formally abolished hiring distinctions between African and non-African citizens, arguing that "we cannot allow for the growth of first and second class citizenship."[140] Five days later, the Zanzibar Revolution broke, followed one week later by an army mutiny in Dar es Salaam that drove Nyerere into hiding—the latter was in essence a strike to protest the slow pace of officer Africanization within the military.[141] After Nyerere reemerged, Africanization quickly resumed its place as official policy. Yet, compared to most neighboring countries, the policy's implementation was gradual—five years later, nearly 20 percent of middle- and senior-ranking civil servants remained non-Tanzanian, mainly owing to educational qualification requirements.[142]

Asian domination over Tanganyika's wholesale and retail trade (80 percent) and import-export trade (more than 50 percent) at independence was also unsustainable in the eyes of African politicians.[143] Pressure to Africanize non-African businesses, already strong, was significantly bolstered by a 1962 report that criticized Tanganyika's wholesale traders for being inefficient, deceptive, utterly opaque, and "chronically addicted" to bargaining and overtrading at the expense of regularizing commodity flows through fixed prices. Widely aired and discussed, the report was used to justify rapid expansion of state cooperatives, though the report had also stated that Tanganyika's distribution system was "one of the most competitive on price of any system in the world."[144] In a bracing 1963 speech to the Dar es Salaam Merchants Chamber—formerly the Indian Merchants Chamber until 1960, and still overwhelmingly Indian in membership—Minister of Commerce George Kahama accused up-country Asian traders of refusing to rent properties to African businessmen, of thwarting the state marketing board by overpaying producers, and finally of plotting to drive African traders out of business through a secret "defense fund" to subsidize temporary subwholesale pricing in strategic Indian shops. *"We demand that they cease NOW!"* he shouted at his audience, warning that danger of racial conflict "is a very real one," and that Indians must "go to the land and produce."[145] The Merchants Chamber responded by launching an "Identification with Africanisation" program, which sought to accelerate the Africanization of staff in shops, banks, and industries in Dar es Salaam. Businesses changed names from obviously Indian to more "national" ones, and sought the chamber's recommendations for African staff.[146] *Mwafrika* endorsed the initiative, but reminded readers that *taifa* could still mean separate racial groups as well as a new nation—"Building this country (*nchi*), does not concern simply one race (*taifa*), but every person who lives here."[147] High urban food prices and opaque distribution networks, an explosive political issue dating back to the 1940s, became explainable through the public hunt for Asian food hoarders. Such hunts had occasional success, such as the discovery of one hundred tons of foodstuffs hidden by an Indian businessman in four godowns in Dar es Salaam. Remarkably, fraudulent commercial weights and scales remained common throughout Tanganyika in the 1960s.[148] Some took matters into their own hands. Members of Dar es Salaam's African Charcoal Dealers Union precipitated a major brawl by throwing bags of charcoal from Indian shops to protest their refusal to join the union—one shop owner was ordered out of his store, told "it is not your property but ours."[149]

Yet African urban households continued to rely on Indian credit. The average Dar es Salaam household in 1956–1957 was estimated to have taken in shs. 120/- per month but to have spent shs. 140/- per month. With food representing nearly 60 percent of this budget, many households either negotiated credit or went hungry at the end of pay periods.[150] Kichwele Street had been renamed Uhuru Street, but its pawnshops still attracted enormous queues each morning, signaling the seeming permanency of African consumer debt. TANU ministers pronounced it a disgrace, and demanded that African credit unions take their place.[151] Seeking to break the Asian grip on petty consumer credit, the government outlawed pawnbroking in March 1965, in hopes that state credit unions would fill the need.[152] Not all urban consumers rejoiced. One resident explained that government removal of pawnshops was a giant blow to "us *Kabwela*," arguing that these shops were "our great shield" in managing urban lives of low wages and indifferent high prices—people "are not asked at shops whether or not if they are *kabwela* or *naizesheni,* the price is the same."[153] There was a growing if still-muted skepticism toward the government's utopian promises to revolutionize entrenched urban economic structures. Moreover, unregulated store credit constituted nearly three times the amount of pawnshop credit in terms of gross average borrowing. It was in the realm of finance where African debtors negotiated the unaccountable discretion of Indian shopkeepers.[154] Aspiring African shopkeepers found themselves vulnerable to shorter and more-expensive terms of supplier credit than Indian shops, with smaller shops seldom acquiring any credit. But their greatest vulnerability was customer default on store credit. One Ilala shopkeeper explained, "Sometimes, out of 50 debtors, only 12 will be able to pay you. . . . My shelves are now empty just because I have given out goods on credit."[155] Successful careers in shopkeeping and other businesses were built on carefully husbanding credit relations, minimizing familial monetary obligations, and employing effective traditional medicines.[156]

Tanzanian nationalists worked to dissolve colonial divisions of labor through socialism and self-reliance. Indians were implored to integrate with Africans by working on farms—Nyerere himself exhorted Asians and Arabs to give up urban life, grab a hoe, and farm.[157] As Dar es Salaam's schools desegregated, the institutional routines of youth were nationalized within a Leninist/Maoist tradition. Asian and African children alike marched off to school with brooms over their shoulders. "Learning how to wield a *jembe* (hoe) and maintain a *shamba* (farm) growing one's own vegetables," the Asian writer May Joseph recalls from her youth, "was a crucial component of the curriculum in many high schools."[158] Other Indians viewed this replacement of academic subjects with "self-reliance" as a disastrous waste of valuable learning time.[159] Several Asians had joined TANU after the party's racial membership restriction ended in December 1962—by 1968, 10 percent of TANU cell-leaders in Dar es Salaam were Asian.[160] Yet prominent Indian presence in the party—from Amir Jamal, the first non-African TANU member and Nyerere's Minister of Treasury, down to Mohamed Baker Somji, who in 1966 became the first Indian to hold the post of TANU ward chairman in Dar es Salaam—scarcely affected the contours of public debate.[161] Most Indians quietly disagreed with the *ujamaa* objective of labor despecialization, particularly after Indian companies were ostentatiously placed under African control within days of the Arusha Declaration.[162] Tanzanian parliamentarians made frequent calls to expel Asians, even those who had already acquired citizenship.[163] Zanzibar president Abeid Karume, the second-highest official in Tanzania, gave official notice in 1970 and again in 1971 to all noncitizen Indians to quit the country within one year. About half of Tanzania's Indian population did leave by 1973, not in response to Karume's order, but following state expropriation of that most valuable and symbolic investment: urban property.

FROM *TAIFA* TO *TAIFISHA*: RENTIERS, LANDLORDISM, AND TANZANIA'S BUILDING NATIONALIZATION

The groundwork for the Arusha Declaration was laid in the selective repeal and preservation of paternalist colonial laws. Just months after independence, Nyerere proclaimed that *ujamaa* was Tanganyika's aim, that there was "no room for land parasites" in independent Tanganyika, and that individual ownership of land was unacceptable.[164] The 1963 Freehold Titles Act effectively nationalized all freehold properties by transforming them into ninety-nine-year rights-of-occupancy leases, fully reversing late-colonial proposals to eliminate distinctions between "native" and "non-native" land rights by transforming customary tenure into individual freeholds.[165] The 1923 Credit to Natives Act was repealed in early 1961, following four years of consultation with chiefs and native authorities who feared that lifting restrictions would result in land transfers to non-Africans; they were satisfied that retaining the 1923 Conveyancing Act, in which mandatory governor approval was required for all land transfers from Africans to non-Africans, would prevent racial proletarianization.[166] Saidi Maswanya, Minister for Lands, later clarified that the Land Ordinance clearly preserved African lands "for their own development and for their children," and that Europeans and Asians "could only occupy land according to other land regulations and could not take land in the tribal way without being members of a tribe."[167] Tanganyika's semi-reformed land laws thus discouraged commercialization by partially preserving the paternalist colonial legacy of "native" protections from "non-native" land predations, as well as wholly preserving the governor/president's untrammeled discretionary power as final arbiter and allocator of land.

The high cost and low availability of housing became the greatest economic concern of Dar es Salaam's rapidly growing citizenry. State-constructed housing fell ever further behind population growth. The early postcolonial government established the National Housing Corporation in 1962, and by 1973 it had constructed 13,000 houses. Yet its housing allocations regularly went to the politically connected, and its capital allocations from the government declined after the Arusha Declaration, ceasing entirely in 1973 when national policy took a decisively antiurban turn. High-density allocation for private construction reached 6,000–7,000 plots annually by the early 1970s, but was again largely restricted to the politically connected and fell well short of overall demand.[168] Rising rents and unworkable regulations inexorably followed. Rent restriction legislation had been allowed to expire in 1960 in hopes that a free market would encourage investment in housing construction;

when investors failed to materialize, restrictions were reintroduced limiting annual rents to 11 percent of 1959 building costs or value, raised to 14 percent in 1966. Enforcement of maximum rents remained difficult to impossible, just as widely publicized arrests of Asians for demanding "key money" belied that problem's intractability.[169]

Illegal supply from unplanned settlements met most of the rising demand. Squatter building skyrocketed from 5,000 illegal houses in 1960 to nearly 28,000 by 1972, partly encouraged by party and governmental exhortations of "self-reliance" that valorized urban agriculture and discounted legal processes.[170] Population growth rates within Dar es Salaam city boundaries actually declined between 1967 and 1971, while rates just outside the boundaries in Mzizima District exploded.[171] The sprawling squatter population of working-class Manzese numbered 93,000 people living in 7,600 dwellings in 1974, outnumbering Tanzania's second-largest city of Tanga. By the late 1970s, more than 60 percent of Dar es Salaam's population lived in unplanned settlements.[172] Legal plot acquisition entailed interminable waiting lists and formidable bureaucratic hurdles to secure a simple right-of-occupancy. Residents more commonly obtained plots illegally through "a local landlord (self-appointed), a Tanu party leader, or community headman." Such plots were informally secured by payment of urban house tax and building construction. Although they were illegal tenants, many demanded a house number in return for tax payment in order to acquire further recognition.[173] In 1973, a newcomer to Dar es Salaam's outskirts could expect to purchase informal rights to a plot from a clan *mzee* (elder) for shs. 150/-. Although this transaction was strictly illegal, this purchaser enjoyed the security of neighbor recognition and right to compensation for any building or crop destruction that state squat-razing might bring; and overall enjoyed a preferable trade-off to the endless wait for legal and cheaper right-of-occupancy plots.[174] Finance was largely a matter of piecemeal construction through individual savings, as state and commercial loans played an even smaller role in Dar es Salaam's postcolonial housing expansion than they had in the 1950s.[175] On the one hand, the state made it clear that squatters would not stand in the way of urban and industrial development. Yet squatting had been paradoxically encouraged since the late 1950s, when the late colonial government generously compensated dislocated squatters—excepting those on freehold land—to placate nationalist critics. The postcolonial government continued on this path, even having to guard against speculative squatters who built in areas about to receive compensation.[176]

A *rentier* class of African squatter-landlords grew wealthy serving Dar es Salaam's starved rental market, navigating a lax and confused regulatory regime lent to rare but brutal interventions. Calamitous confusion over land authority emerged in peri-urban areas, where three institutions—Ministry of Lands, *ujamaa* village authorities, and City Council—could each give "first" registration to the same plot.[177] Official Land Division policy in 1967 had stated that "land shall be developed by whoever holds it for the time being," yet illegal settlements in prime urban locations risked being razed, as happened in Mwananyamala in 1968 and Kisutu in 1974–1975.[178] Despite these hazards, illegal settlements offered semisecure home ownership with handsome rental incomes, and remained the urban African's best investment. In 1971, when the waiting list for national housing stood at 18,000 people, a fully rented, four-bedroom Swahili house could generate 23 percent gross annual return on investment. Only 7 percent of adults in planned areas were homeowners; in unplanned areas the figure was 17 percent, slightly lower than the 1956 overall figure of 19 percent.[179]

Survival of de facto racial segregation was an affront to popular understandings of *ujamaa*. However, despite wider Africanization, Uhindini remained overwhelmingly Indian during the 1960s, when most new multistoried residential buildings had been built by and for Indians. Unlike Uzunguni, which became home to powerful African politicians, very few Africans moved to Uhindini after independence. A frustrated Ilala resident asked if the Indian practice of renting buildings exclusively to Indians was really *ujamaa*, and demanded that government do all it could to "remove (*kuondoa*) this problem." Indian landlords largely continued their colonial-era patterns of renting accommodation primarily to Indians. A popular saying emerged—"Kama wewe si Patel hupati chumba" (If you are not Indian, you won't get a room). One rumor held that an Indian landlord had denied a flat to a *mwananchi*, arguing that it was built by an Indian, and thus had to be occupied by an Indian. The *mwananchi* responded that, as the town's food was grown by Africans, it should therefore be eaten only by Africans; and as the country was African, it should therefore be occupied only by Africans.[180] Africans phoning for rental accommodation complained that they were declined after not being able to answer questions in Gujarati.[181]

Nyerere's government felt pressured to take dramatic action to keep urban development within the spirit of *ujamaa*. In 1965, shortly after Zanzibar's revolutionary government nationalized housing, Nyerere led a parade and a mass meeting of forty thousand, promising a "housing revolution" and warning that the state would confiscate properties from landlords who exploited their tenants.[182] Such *rentiers* were fully in the public eye, effortlessly capturing economic rents that accompanied rising demand for well-located properties. "*Makabaila* (rentiers/ landlords) who build houses early in these areas," an *Uhuru* editorial observed, "now collect enormous rents."[183] Seven weeks after Nyerere's promise, more than six hundred plots were nationalized without owner compensation—including freehold land in Buguruni where the 1959 *mumiani* riot had occurred, which had long been zoned for residential occupation but lay undeveloped while its Indian owners held out for higher prices.[184] Landlordism had been diagnosed as the principal evil of urban capitalism, yet it was also the principal source of income for key TANU constituents. Coastal African landowners in peri-urban Dar es Salaam were bitterly disappointed at the failure of parliamentary efforts to exclude them from land acquisitions for national development, despite pleas that they—unlike wealthier Indian and Arab landowners—relied upon farm income as their primary retirement security.[185] In 1967, the Arusha Declaration's leadership code barred TANU and government leaders from earning income on rental properties—a prohibition that led to a few resignations, most notably Bibi Titi Mohammed's exit from the TANU central committee.[186] Shortly after the Arusha Declaration, Nyerere explained:

> One little house—when you built the first house then your intention was to live in it yourself, and then suddenly you said, "why not rent it out?" And now you are making plans for a second one. This is not good but it is the temptation we have stopped. It was really a lot more temptation than fulfillment. . . . This was the right time. Had we delayed, you would discover two years from now that our leadership has become rather entrenched in the accumulation of personal property.[187]

Restrictions imposed by the leadership code generated additional resentment among some TANU elite because they did not apply to Afro-Shirazi Party leaders, who invested in Dar es Salaam's post-Arusha property market with alacrity. In early 1971, a group of African elders from Kariakoo upbraided John Mhaville, Minister of Housing, for condemning their *makuti* houses to construct large office complexes. They argued that rental incomes from these houses had financed their retirements, and that they should be thus entitled to flats in the new buildings, in keeping with the Arusha Declaration's promise, as they saw it, to house Tanzania's elderly for free.[188] Removing "landlordism," widely popular in principle, rapidly became poor politics when it threatened the pensions and incomes of core TANU supporters and leaders.

Nyerere's own political position had weakened noticeably in early 1971 following Idi Amin's coup in Uganda, a severe balance of payments crisis, and a surge in Asian capital flight.[189] Rumors of Nyerere's impending fall circulated widely: he had lost control of government; he had retreated to Kigoma to recover from physical and mental illness; he had lost the support of the army; Chagga farmers planned to secede and join Kenya; Karume stood ready to seize power from Zanzibar, as did Oscar Kambona from his London exile. The British high commissioner observed that there was now "a greater national uncertainty than at any time since the Arusha Declaration."[190] A Tanzanian "cultural revolution" seemed in the offing. TANU party militants had pressured Nyerere to issue *Mwongozo* (Guidelines), a pronouncement of party supremacy and set of radical democratic axioms that were in turn appropriated as a Maoist "red book" (only this one was green) with which to scold, judge, and justify all ranges of political behavior in the name of revolution. In April 1971, a group of organized workers attacked NHC executives and Mhaville at a public meeting for their failure to provide sufficient, affordable housing, and for allocating new flats according to wealth and connection rather than by waiting list. Angry speakers suggested "revolutionary methods of acquiring more houses in Dar es Salaam" to meet this crying demand.[191]

Two weeks later, on April 22, 1971, Mhaville introduced a bill to nationalize all buildings worth more than 100,000 shillings and not entirely occupied by the owner, handing over their control to NHC. Everyone knew this to mean the expropriation of what was overwhelmingly Indian-owned residential and business property. It quickly passed the National Assembly to great celebration. Stephen Mhando recalled that the bill "was handled with as much secrecy as any that he could remember."[192] Building nationalization had been earlier ratified behind closed doors by the TANU National Executive Committee in Kigoma. Proclaiming that *makabaila* (or rent-seeking "feudalists") had been overthrown, Mhaville explained, "We must make a distinction between our enemies, who include all those who own buildings for exploitation, and their tenants who are among the people who are being exploited."[193] Nyerere told a crowd of more than sixty thousand assembled at TANU headquarters that "landlordism is theft," and explained that poverty could now be eliminated with this crucial step of ridding Tanzania of its exploiters:

> A country which wishes to eradicate poverty has two things to do: the eradication of wealth and of the aspiration to acquire wealth. Wealth is not the result of work by the wealthy; it is acquired through exploitation. . . . Exploitation is a kind of theft, legalised theft. . . . We are eradicating exploitation so that all people shall start to live by their own sweat, so that we advance to a stage when our country will deserve the name of a proletarian state, a country where the exploited and exploiters—those who reap what they did not plant—just don't exist.[194]

Then followed an exuberant eight-mile march, mostly through the newly nationalized Uhindini. J. D. Namfua, Tanzania's Minister of Information, explained that the housing nationalization was "to erase *unyonyaji* and to increase *uhuru* of the Tanzanian."[195] Kawawa calmed nervous African landlords by promising that smaller buildings—those "dog-ribbed" houses in Uswahilini such as those located in Buguruni and Magomeni that were owned by *wananchi*— would not be nationalized.[196] Kariakoo residents recall the government boasting loudly and repeatedly that European and Asian houses were being seized by TANU to become "our buildings."[197] An Asian emigrant recalled that Radio Tanzania editorials during the building nationalization "attacked South Asians and called them 'bloodsucking capitalists,' often inserting names like Patels, Meralis, and Khanjibhais."[198] The *Nationalist* prominently featured a picture of one nationalized building, which happened to be the Air India office.[199] An effort by a Mwanza Indian named Habibu Mohamed Thaki to rally against nationalization precipitated a far larger counterrally, including many Indians, which denounced Thaki as an "economic saboteur."[200]

Tanzania's housing nationalization in April 1971 was the postcolonial government's most aggressive urban act. A total of 2,482 buildings worth five hundred million shillings were acquired nationwide between 1971 and 1974; in Dar es Salaam, 1,363 buildings housing a total of 8,178 residents were ultimately acquired.[201] While roughly 98 percent of those homeowners were Asians, a handful of major African landlords—Ally Sykes, Abdallah Fundikira, John Rupia—lost considerable wealth. Sykes, who went on to a spectacularly successful career as an international property investor, declared that the 1971 housing nationalization was the moment when the "spirit of discipline, hard work and of personal initiative and the urge for one to improve the quality of life was lost" in Tanzania.[202] Socialism in Tanzania for the middle class, an American embassy employee reported, "is becoming less of an abstract ideology and more of an actuality—and it hurts."[203]

The 1971 act permanently alienated large numbers of Indians who had invested their life savings in housing, in part to demonstrate their long-term commitment to the independent nation. Despite nationalization, many premises were still transferred between Asians, moving NHC to form a Dar es Salaam Housing Allocation Committee in 1974 to identify all vacant buildings through intelligence from TANU branches, and to then allocate houses "to the people who need them."[204] Pressures to emigrate increased further with Idi Amin's expulsion of all Indians from Uganda in August 1972—an expulsion that inspired spontaneous celebrations across Tanzania.[205] Such was Asian unpopularity at the time that Nyerere's government refused to accept any Ugandan Asian refugees, turning away eighty-three who were stranded at sea without a country.[206] Those who remained were vulnerable to the whims and designs of corrupt authorities. The head of Coast C.I.D., colluding with two Indian businessmen, systematically extorted money from dozens of Dar es Salaam businessmen using threats of arrest, imprisonment, and deportation.[207] National Assembly members urged the government to have its C.I.D.

and security personnel take Gujarati language instruction to better investigate "unscrupulous activities done by Asians."[208]

Although precise numbers of Tanzania's Asian exodus are unavailable, emigration certainly peaked in 1971–1973. Between 10,000 and 15,000 Asians left within seven months after the buildings acquisition.[209] Building nationalization, in the words of one Ismaili who remained, "killed the future of those who wanted to own their own homes."[210] The total Asian population declined by nearly one half from 1962 to 1973, roughly 112,000 to 60,000, by which time less than half of those remaining had taken Tanzanian citizenship.[211] But Ismailis were hardest hit—90 percent of Ismailis had followed the Aga Khan's instructions to take out Tanzanian citizenship by the mid-1960s. Having invested so heavily in property and citizenship, Ismaili Khojas now emigrated in droves from Dar es Salaam, many to Canada; Ithnasheri Khojas by contrast immigrated in droves to Dar es Salaam from the countryside, growing in number from 3,000 in 1971 to 12,000 by 2005.[212] As the Asian population decreased, the likelihood of arbitrary arrest increased, as did ingenious schemes to smuggle out wealth. Within a few weeks after the nationalization, nearly US$20 million had been legally repatriated, at a time when the country had only US$66 million in reserves; meanwhile, the black market rate jumped from 9 to 14 shillings to the dollar.[213] African cynics were richly rewarded in late 1971 when 690 Asians were caught preparing to illegally export their valuables on a Karachi-bound ship—upon which the *Nationalist* gratuitously speculated that it was "almost certain that the 'brothers' [*dugu*] from India and Pakistan would have returned to Tanzania only to repeat the same practice over and over again."[214] Vassanji narrates the episode:

> One day before departure, at about eleven in the morning, an old Ignis refrigerator hung suspended from a crane making its way into the hold of the saviour ship. But some silly passenger had secured the door of the fridge with a tape . . . which snapped at one point and then rapidly at several others and the door swung open. Out dropped manna for the dock workers below, notes in several currencies, and jewellery. The police were called, impounded the ship and found: fridges overflowing with currency, iceboxes stashed with dollars and pounds and rupees, butter and cheese compartments containing jewellery.[215]

Well-intentioned schemes such as the Ismaili Diamond Jubilee Investment Trust stopped giving loans, and quickly teetered toward insolvency as mortgage repayment rates collapsed.[216] The state by this time had introduced price controls on more than one thousand consumer items, designating wholesale and retail profit margins for each item—wholesale profits not to exceed 10 percent and retail 25 percent.[217] Those Indian traders who remained, however, profited from numerous gray or black-market opportunities, and found themselves ideally placed to take advantage of liberalization policies initiated in the mid-1980s.[218] Urban wealth would be rebuilt within parallel informal markets by an even more wary and cosmopolitan Indian commercial community. Indian-African relations remained characterized by social distance and economic familiarity. Uhindini residents recall a sharp racial solidarity among rich and poor Indians following the 1971 nationalization, during which time new African renters were discouraged from renting newly nationalized flats, or bribed to leave after taking possession. Most Africans who did secure these prized properties were well-placed in government and politics.[219] Although done in the name of *kabwela*, it had been a victory by and for *naizi*.

CONCLUSIONS

The rhetorical success of Tanzanian nationalism and *ujamaa*—the two are inseparable—depended on politicians' ability to marry regional discourses of extraction and eradication with global ideas of anticolonialism and socialism. By claiming to be the nation's diviner and eradicator of *unyonyaji*, the TANU government positioned itself as the nation's sole legitimate authority. It found itself, however, confronted with many of the same problems that had faced its colonial predecessor. In urban areas like Dar es Salaam, the postcolonial state chose to continue its predecessor's urban policies of relying on price regulations and movement restrictions rather than committing the necessary investments to manage urban growth. Nationalist politicians also shared the colonial calculus that Africans, excepting themselves, could best serve the country by engaging in agricultural production on rural farms, to which the *wahuni* were dispatched. They introduced a host of other purge categories that served to explain present difficulties and justify aggressive government programs. At the level of *ujamaa* ideology, urban problems were identified as ones brought by *wanyonyaji*, and the government's solutions were accordingly predicated on removal of these enemies.

Material entitlements of urban citizenship had grown torn and frayed over the 1960s, just as rhetorical entitlements of national citizenship had reached dizzying heights. Indians were the most visible accumulators of urban wealth across Dar es Salaam's history, particularly via the acquisition of urban properties, although collecting rents had also been a successful economic strategy for African residents. Julius Nyerere had balanced the pursuit of his twin convictions to fight capitalist accumulation and racialism with much success over this period, but had also developed a tactical style that combined pragmatic savvy with a weakness for political drama. Popular pressures to make national citizenship meaningful to urban citizens moved Nyerere to lance the boil of landlordism by instituting a policy of building nationalization, which, for a time at least, did the expedient political work of satisfying popular anti-Asian resentment without destroying the wealth of rank-and-file African *rentiers*. But Nyerere's "housing revolution," of course, did not fundamentally alter the urban patterns of those seeking rooms and those seeking rents; it only reduced the scales of investment. Among African residents of Kariakoo, housing nationalization was still viewed as deeply unwise three decades later. Although they had not personally been affected, they viewed the subsequent distribution of houses as benefiting only those with strong government connections. Cynics also point out that well-connected wealthy Africans such as John Rupia quickly regained their properties on legal appeal. Other Kariakoo residents disagreed with the underlying philosophy, and thought that those who built the houses themselves should be its owners.[220] "Many false words were said," one resident recalled. "They said that landlords exploit people, but I did not see exploitation (*kunyonya*), people just worked and deserved to own the house that they built."[221] The biggest regret among this population was not to have built or bought a house of one's own.[222]

Newcomers to Dar es Salaam were generally unwelcome in the 1960s as they had been during the colonial period. At best, they were left alone to navigate an urban terrain dominated by "bloodsuckers" of all sorts. With humor and savvy, urban Africans made sense out of fast-moving changes, seemingly beyond the government's discursive and coercive controls, by crafting their own urban vocabulary. Urban class differentiation was understood not through the government's purge categories but through rhetorical personages created by towndwellers themselves. The twin concepts of *kabwela* and *naizi* opened discursive space that enabled poor Africans to live legitimate lives in cities, and called into question the morality of wealthier Africans who enjoyed the lion's share of the fruits of *uhuru*. Perhaps the only thing unambiguous for urban Africans and the state was their shared attitude toward Indians, the urban *wanyonyaji par excellence* who remained socially aloof despite the ubiquitous rhetorical admonishments to join the nation in its work. A decisive majority of African politicians and their urban supporters concluded that even the generous offer of *ujamaa* could not, to their mind, induce Indians to join the new Tanzanian *taifa*.

Afterword

This book has been a study of identity and its categories in urban Tanzania, told through multiple lenses of social, economic, political, and intellectual history. Besides presenting a history of what might be termed "race relations" between Africans and Indians in Dar es Salaam, I also seek to demonstrate in this book how the very categories of race and nation had been constructed by historical actors themselves, and in the process undermine notions of their a priori existences. *Taifa*, a nation or race, lies at the center of African intellectual work during latter decades of colonial rule to construct a naturalized category of social and political community that transcends local ethnic divisions, challenges colonial racial inequalities, and finally inverts East Africa's hitherto subordinate relationship with the wider Indian Ocean world.

This book also brings into more prominent view two understudied processes of urbanization in twentieth-century Africa. The first is the sustained attempt by the colonial state, subsequently the postcolonial state, to ensure political stability by instituting what I term urban entitlements that provided urban dwellers with the barest necessities and services. This development not only explained the dramatic demographic urban shift that occurred across the continent after the 1930s, but it also implicitly indicated that urban citizens (and by proxy all citizens) were entitled to food, clothing, and housing. This transformed relationships between the urban individual, the state, and the distributive economy. The second understudied process of urbanization is the *rentier* strategy of accumulation on the part of landlords, which for coastal East Africa and surely farther afield was a fundamental economic strategy upon which sustained claims to African urban residencies as well as to local political authority were based.

I have sought to render more unambiguously the ways in which the colonial state influenced processes of identity formulation. British administrators untenably separated urban citizens into two legal identities, "native" and "non-native," in order to pursue two contradicting sets of policy commitments: to protect "natives" from "non-native" predations by prohibiting Africans' access to credit and individual land tenure, and to encourage "non-native" urban development through investments secured by access to credit and individual land tenure. The spatial proximity and daily interactions between African "natives" and Indian "non-natives" brought the ineffectiveness and injustice of this dithering urban policy into stark relief. The dramatic increase in urban population growth during the Second World War shook the colonial state out of its ambivalence and toward a tighter urban administration through cost controls and entitlement guarantees. New categories of urban entitlements were not necessarily racialized until colonial officials started using racial categories as the basis for determining entitlement amounts, a decision that soon undermined the state's own legitimacy in the face of rising African popular protests. By the mid-1950s, when the East Africa Royal Commission recommended that racial distinction in law should be abandoned, decades of colonial ambivalence toward African urbanization, as well as the administration of urban growth along racial lines, had indelibly structured Dar es Salaam's urban space and its networks of distribution.

Continuities between colonial and postcolonial urban policies are striking. Unaccountable discretion by government officials to decide on land disputes continues to characterize urban administration and to render both customary and lease tenures weak protections for the urban poor.[1] Postcolonial urban planning has continued for decades after independence to rely on housing density as a major zoning feature, a clear legacy of colonial segregationist thinking.[2] But urban planning generally and "master plans" in particular have been most notable for their irrelevance in Dar es Salaam's subsequent urban growth. Eager to protect the spoils of urban citizenship and maximize rural production, the postcolonial government has continued into the new millennium pursuing its predecessor's notorious forced removals of under- and unemployed Africans. The nationalization of buildings worth more than 100,000 shillings in 1971 did not end racial segregation in Uhindini, although it did significantly integrate the newer neighborhood of Upanga. A substantial number of nationalized flats remained occupied by their original owners or tenants for years, even decades; many of those flats allocated to African tenants were later taken over by Indian tenants, who often bribed the former to vacate in return for a large lump sum.[3] Meanwhile, Zone II—Uhindini—reversed its very modest desegregation sometime in the 1980s, as state controls wavered under liberalization and Asians simply bribed Africans to move out of their state-owned flats.[4] Uhindini today remains mostly segregated and predominantly Indian, just as Kariakoo remains Dar es Salaam's most racially and ethnically diverse and vital neighborhood. Both areas still form the city's commercial center, yet unlike during the colonial period, they now constitute only a very small slice of Dar es Salaam's total population.

Dar es Salaam has continued its exponential growth since independence, rising from a population of 128,742 in 1957 to nearly four million today. The city's urban infrastructure of roads, water, and sewage, as well as of plot demarcation and land titling, has not remotely kept pace. The disbandment of the city council in 1974 proved an unmitigated disaster, directly resulting in the collapse of basic urban services such as garbage and cesspit disposal. Although fortunes were made in urban and peri-urban property markets during the *ujamaa* years, Dar es Salaam since the 1980s has known the scramble for land rights long experienced in many postcolonial African cities. Such a scramble draws in an array of government officials, as Tom McCaskie has observed for Kumasi, as well as "armies of businessmen, entrepreneurs, speculators, fraudsters and dreamers into struggles of unprecedentedly intense kind over rights in land."[5] Public works projects such as slum clearances, national housing construction, and urban land development were ambitious and partially effective during the 1960s and early 1970s. Yet because of falling revenues and an antiurban ideological orientation, the state stopped these projects by 1975, the same year that the number of squatters surpassed the number of legal residents in Dar es Salaam. Uncontrolled and illegal urban growth has been the rule ever since.[6] Dar es Salaam's population grows exponentially; its urban plot allocation grows geometrically. Between 1979 and 1992, the government received 261,668 plot applications, but allocated only 17,751 plots, or 7 percent of demand; by 1998, only 3 percent of the city's total residential land was obtained legally through state allocation.[7] The popularity of "Swahili" houses faded after the 1970s, while that of single-household structures grew; home ownership rates soared to more than 50 percent by the late 1980s.[8] National land reform in 1999 terminated the problem of multiple land allocating bodies by centralizing authority in the office of the Commissioner for Lands, which has full discretion to regularize Dar es Salaam's many irregular settlements and landowners. Yet potential housing finance institutions remain reluctant to lend, and complain that the 1999 Land Act favors borrowers at the expense of lenders by eliminating earlier foreclosure laws. Infrastructure remains abysmal—in the 1990s, 10 percent of the city's waste was collected for disposal, and 5 percent of residences were connected to a central sewer system.[9] Aside from a few major public works, many financed by foreign aid, urban public development in Dar es Salaam during the relatively prosperous 1990s and 2000s was practically nil. Investments instead have flowed into individual property such as houses and durable vehicles, while roads, sewage, and city water supply fall into further disrepair, or more often are simply not created for new residents. Random and heavy-handed squatter clearances to make way for these few major public works have become a deeply unpopular routine.

The political success of Tanzanian nationalism has been stunning. Few doubt that the economic policies and development programs of *ujamaa* socialism have unfavorably affected the country's postcolonial economic growth. Even fewer doubt that *ujamaa* positively contributed to a sturdy national identity that is relatively free of ethnic tension, blessed with a genuinely national language, and generally averse to political confrontation and violence. This is particularly poignant in light of the postcolonial trajectories of its contiguous neighbors—Uganda, Rwanda, Burundi, Congo, Kenya, and Mozambique—who have experienced horrific civil war, genocide, and more recently harrowing electoral violence.

Tanganyikan/Tanzanian nationalism, as manifested in the success of TANU, has been the conception and realization of a *taifa* or race/nation in which Indians were popularly appointed the most proximate and persistent of national "exploiters." The success of TANU/CCM has been its ability to deliver a primarily "African" nation while maintaining order over racial and religious resentments. In 1997, Julius Nyerere admitted that he had had no choice but to nationalize buildings and businesses, for fear that otherwise the private sector would be entirely dominated by Asians and produce unacceptable racial conflicts.[10] In this light, *ujamaa* socialism must be seen as an extension of Tanzanian nationalism. To decry the work of racial polemicists who reduced *ujamaa* to an East African "socialism of fools" would be to apply international socialist criteria to a debate that was primarily about defining and preserving a new nation.

Identifying Indians as the nation's main enemy did not end in 1971. The darkest moment for Tanzania's Indian population was the government's war on "economic saboteurs" in March 1983, when consumer goods shortages brought the nation to the brink of economic collapse. By the end of April, 4,216 saboteurs were held in detention without legal recourse, more than half of whom were South Asian, charged with hoarding, smuggling, and profiteering.[11] Fearing arrest, many people hid or destroyed their illegal radios, video recorders, and even toothpaste and soap, prompting Nyerere to announce that people should cease throwing away their goods and simply surrender them to police.[12] Racial polemicizing against Indians gained new currency in the 1990s, with legalization of formal political opposition. Oppositionist politicians began championing "indigenous" control over emerging business opportunities in the wake of economic liberalization policies that were plainly benefiting Indian businessmen. They called for a policy of *uzawa* (literally "birth-ness") or "indigenization" of the economy—now directed toward capitalist development—in order to benefit Tanzania's "indigenous" African population—even though, by the 1990s, many Indians had lived longer in the country than many African businessmen. The great racial polemicist of the period was Christopher Mtikila, a clergyman and head of the unregistered Democratic Party who called for expulsions of Indians and Arabs from Tanzania. Mtikila crafted a richly racist political language, replacing the implicitly racial African term for citizen, *wananchi*, with the explicitly racial African term, *wazawa*; he also identified Asians as *magabacholi*, a vivid epithet—ironically Gujarati in origin—that refers to large parasites. Mtikila himself did not succeed politically, but other prominent oppositionists have taken notice of his rhetorical successes.[13] Racial invective retains power to generate considerable political support, even though Indians in Tanzania today—well over half of whom live in Dar es Salaam—number perhaps only 60,000 out of a national total now exceeding 40,000,000.

Explicit public definitions of what races or nations actually are remain rare in postcolonial Tanzania. In a notable and recent exception, Tanzania's Prime Minister Mizengo Pinda declared to the Zanzibar Parliament in 2008, that, while Zanzibar does form its own *taifa* (nation), it was not an *nchi* (country). Pinda drew this distinction in part to preserve one of Nyerere's most prominent political legacies, the 1964 union between Tanganyika and Zanzibar. Pinda was allowing Zanzibaris to enjoy their separate identity but not their separate sovereignty. The statement drew enormous criticism from both CCM and CUF party leaders, who both agreed that Zanzibar was very much an *nchi* (i.e., they were insisting upon Zanzibar's latent sovereignty within the union). But there was an even greater, indeed unquestioned consensus that Zanzibar forms its own separate *taifa*, a consensus that captures the postcolonial success and limitations of Nyerere's national project. Tanzania, the last surviving constitutional success of continental Pan-Africanism undertaken during the 1960s, had been formed in order to create a new larger African nation. Yet, by the 2000s, leading politicians on both Zanzibar and mainland Tanzania could agree that the two in fact constituted natural and discrete nations. The continental imagination of Tanganyikan thinkers, who had not seen any utility in accepting the territorial boundaries of colonial rule and instead boldly conflated race and nation into *taifa*, had been eclipsed by the durable, politically successful, and territorially defined realities of the Tanzanian nation-state.

Notes

INTRODUCTION

1. For most of this book's period, Dar es Salaam lay in Tanganyika (1920–1964), the name the British gave to the conquered territory of German East Africa. In 1964, Tanganyika joined with the islands of Zanzibar to form the United Republic of Tanzania.

2. Jonathon Glassman, *War of Words, War of Stones: Racial Thought and Violence in Colonial Zanzibar* (Bloomington: Indiana University Press, 2011), 302.

3. *Uhuru*, 24 April 1971, original in Swahili. Unless otherwise noted, all translations are by the author.

4. Noorali Velji, interview by author, Dar es Salaam, 31 July 1999; Lois Lobo, *They Came to Africa: 200 Years of the Asian Presence in Tanzania* (Dar es Salaam: Tanzania Printers, 2000), 56.

5. Moyez G. Vassanji, *The Gunny Sack* (Portsmouth, NH: Heinemann, 1989), 242.

6. Bashir Punja and Badru Velji, interviews by author, Dar es Salaam, 1 August 1999.

7. Of the 2,908 buildings acquired by the government by November 1972, 97 belonged to Africans, and most of the rest to what Nagar terms the "Asian commercial bourgeoisie." Richa Nagar, "The South Asian Diaspora in Tanzania: A History Retold," *Comparative Studies of South Asia, Africa and the Middle East* 16 (1996): 70. See also surnames of acquired property listings in *Nationalist*, April–July 1971.

8. *Majadiliano ya Bunge (Hansard)*, 22–27 April 1971, col. 46.

9. Nagar, "The South Asian Diaspora," 70.

10. Major works conducted in this vein include Frederick Cooper, *On the African Waterfront: Urban Disorder and the Transformation of Work in Colonial Mombasa* (New Haven, CT: Yale University Press, 1987); Luise White, *The Comforts of Home: Prostitution in Colonial Nairobi* (Chicago: University of Chicago Press, 1990); Charles Van Onselen, *Studies in the Social and Economic History of the Witwatersrand, 1886–1914*, vols. 1–2 (London: Longman, 1982); and Teresa Barnes, *"We Women Worked So Hard": Gender, Urbanization and Social Reproduction in Colonial Harare, Zimbabwe, 1930–1956* (Portsmouth, NH: Heinemann, 1999).

11. The best examples of this approach are Gyanendra Pandey, "Peasant Revolt and Indian Nationalism," and Shahid Amin, "Gandhi as Mahatma: Gorakhpur

District, Eastern UP, 1921–2," both in *Selected Subaltern Studies*, ed. Ranajit Guha and Gayatri Spivak, 233–87 and 288–349, respectively (Delhi: Oxford University Press, 1988).

12. Sana Aiyar, "Nation, Race, and Politics amongst the South Asian Diaspora: From Colonial Kenya to Multicultural Britain" (PhD diss., Harvard University, 2009), 45, 180. See also Isabel Hofmeyr, "The Idea of 'Africa' in Indian Nationalism: Reporting the Diaspora in *The Modern Review* 1907–1929," *South African Historical Journal* 57 (2007): 60–81.

13. Sugata Bose, *A Hundred Horizons: The Indian Ocean in the Age of Global Empire* (Cambridge, MA: Harvard University Press, 2006), 151.

14. Thomas R. Metcalf, *Imperial Connections: India in the Indian Ocean Arena, 1860–1920* (Berkeley: University of California Press, 2007).

15. Jon Soske, "Navigating Difference: Gender, Miscegenation and Indian Domestic Space in Twentieth-Century Durban," in *Eyes Across the Water: Navigating the Indian Ocean*, ed. Pamila Gupta, Isabel Hofmeyr, and Michael Pearson (Pretoria: University of South Africa Press, 2010), 207.

16. J. S. Furnivall, *Colonial Policy and Practice: A Comparative Study of Burma and Netherlands India* (Cambridge: Cambridge University Press, 1948), 304.

17. William A. Shack and Elliott P. Skinner, eds., *Strangers in African Societies* (Berkeley: University of California Press, 1979), 1–17; Pierre L. van den Berghe, *The Ethnic Phenomenon* (New York: Elsevier, 1981), 137–56; and Carmen Voigt-Graf, *Asian Communities in Tanzania: A Journey Through Past and Present Times* (Hamburg: Institute for African Affairs, 1998), 15–26.

18. Van den Berghe, *The Ethnic Phenomenon*, 153, quoted in Voigt-Graf, *Asian Communities*, 76.

19. Bill Freund, *The African City: A History* (Cambridge: Cambridge University Press, 2007), 68. Freund's study is the best up-to-date survey on the history of African urbanization.

20. Frederick Cooper, *From Slaves to Squatters: Plantation Labor and Agriculture in Zanzibar and Coastal Kenya, 1890–1925* (New Haven, CT: Yale University Press, 1980); Cooper, "Urban Space, Industrial Time, and Wage Labor in Africa," in *Struggle for the City: Migrant Labor, Capital, and the State in Urban Africa* (Beverly Hills: Sage Publications, 1983), ed. Cooper, 7–50; Cooper, *African Waterfront*; Cooper, *Decolonization and African Society: The Labor Question in French and British Africa* (Cambridge: Cambridge University Press, 1996).

21. This comes from David Warsh's discussion of Jane Jacobs and Robert Lucas in *Knowledge and the Wealth of Nations: A Story of Economic Discovery* (New York: W.W. Norton, 2006), 245–46.

22. The term *rentier* is used broadly here to include landlords, rather than its more limited usage by many economists and historians of Europe that refers only to bondholders.

23. Or, as Gareth Austin elaborates, "the difference between the return actually obtained for the supply of a resource and the minimum return necessary to elicit the supply of the resource in its current use." Austin, *Labour, Land and Capital in*

Ghana: From Slavery to Free Labour in Asante, 1807–1956 (Rochester: University of Rochester Press, 2005), 10.

24. See Donald N. McCloskey, "The Economics of Choice: Neoclassical Supply and Demand," in *Economics and the Historian*, ed. Thomas G. Rawski et al. (Berkeley: University of California Press, 1996), 133–38.

25. Jeremy Prestholdt, *Domesticating the World: African Consumerism and the Genealogies of Globalization* (Berkeley: University of California Press, 2008), 48–49.

26. John Lonsdale and Bruce Berman, "Coping with the Contradictions: The Development of the Colonial State in Kenya, 1895–1914," *Journal of African History* 20 (1979): 491.

27. The classic statement of this view is Michael Lipton, *Why Poor People Stay Poor: A Study of Urban Bias in World Development* (London: Temple Smith, 1977).

28. Ann Laura Stoler, *Carnal Knowledge and Imperial Power: Race and the Intimate in Colonial Rule* (Berkeley: University of California Press, 2002), 206–13.

29. Justin Willis, *Mombasa, the Swahili, and the Making of the Mijikenda* (Oxford: Clarendon Press, 1993), 201.

30. Cooper, *From Slaves to Squatters*, 158–67; quotation on 164.

31. Laura Fair, *Pastimes and Politics: Culture, Community, and Identity in Post-Abolition Urban Zanzibar, 1890–1945* (Athens: Ohio University Press, 2001), 46–52. For censuses, see ibid., 30–31.

32. Jonathon Glassman, "Sorting out the Tribes: The Creation of Racial Identities in Colonial Zanzibar's Newspaper Wars," *Journal of African History* 41 (2000): 405. Rather than relitigate the debate between "primordialists" and "instrumentalists" or "constructivists," I refer readers to Glassman's insightful critique of this very framing in *War of Words*, chapter 1.

33. The standard account remains Philip D. Curtin, *The Image of Africa: British Ideas and Action, 1780–1850* (Madison: University of Wisconsin Press, 1964).

34. James Sidbury, *Becoming African in America: Race and Nation in the Early Black Atlantic* (Oxford: Oxford University Press, 2007), 7.

35. Robin Fox, *Kinship and Marriage: An Anthropological Perspective* (Hammersworth: Penguin, 1967), 13.

36. Benedict Anderson, *Imagined Communities: Reflections on the Origin and Spread of Nationalism* (New York: Verso, 1991).

37. John D. Kelly and Martha Kaplan, *Represented Communities: Fiji and World Decolonization* (Chicago: University of Chicago Press, 2001), ix, 15, 32, 36–41.

38. Robert H. Jackson, *Quasi-States: Sovereignty, International Relations and the Third World* (Cambridge: Cambridge University Press, 1993). This view is pursued for East Africa in James R. Brennan, "Lowering the Sultan's Flag: Sovereignty and Decolonization in Coastal Kenya," *Comparative Studies and Society in History* 50 (2008): 831–61.

39. Rogers Brubaker and Frederick Cooper, "Beyond 'Identity,'" *Theory and Society* 29 (2000): 1–47.

40. This understanding owes much to the insights expressed in Glassman, *War of Words*, 11.

41. For a comprehensive history of Tanzania's newspapers and other media, see Martin Sturmer, *The Media History of Tanzania* (Ndanda: Ndanda Mission Press, 1998).

42. Karin Barber, *The Anthropology of Texts, Persons and Publics: Oral and Written Culture in Africa and Beyond* (Cambridge: Cambridge University Press, 2007), 139–40.

43. Only 8 percent of men and 2 percent of women were literate in English. J. A. K. Leslie, "A Survey of Dar es Salaam" (1957), appendix A/8.

44. Glassman, *War of Words*, 150; Andrew Ivaska, *Cultured States: Youth, Gender, and Modern Style in 1960s Dar es Salaam* (Durham, NC: Duke University Press, 2011), 28–34.

45. John Iliffe, *Honour in African History* (Cambridge: Cambridge University Press, 2005), 1.

CHAPTER 1: NATIVE AND NON-NATIVE

1. Mahmood Mamdani, *When Victims Become Killers: Colonialism, Nativism, and the Genocide in Rwanda* (Princeton, NJ: Princeton University Press, 2001), 20.

2. Ibid., 14. Emphasis in original.

3. Jon E. Wilson, "Agency, Narrative, and Resistance," in *The British Empire: Themes and Perspectives*, ed. Sarah E. Stockwell (Oxford: Blackwell, 2008), 260–61.

4. "British Mandate for East Africa," Article 6.

5. John Iliffe, *A Modern History of Tanganyika* (Cambridge: Cambridge University Press, 1979), 262.

6. Michael D. Callahan, *Mandates and Empire: The League of Nations and Africa, 1914–1931* (Brighton: Sussex Academic Press, 1999), 81; minute of Strachey to Read, 5 August 1921, CO 691/45/f.166.

7. Law of Property and Conveyancing Ordinance, 1923; Land Ordinance, 1923; Credit to Natives Ordinance, 1923; D.M.P. McCarthy, *Colonial Bureaucracy and Creating Underdevelopment: Tanganyika, 1919–1940* (Ames: Iowa State University Press, 1982), 39.

8. Byatt to Churchill, 25 May 1921, CO 691/44/f.546.

9. John Iliffe, *Tanganyika under German Rule, 1905–1912* (Cambridge: Cambridge University Press, 1969), 94.

10. Byatt to Churchill, 25 May 1921, CO 691/44/f.546.

11. *Dar es Salaam Times*, 17 March 1923.

12. In the town's 1929 census, I group British Indians and Goans together as "Indians," who totaled 8,060; Europeans totaled 1,334; "Arabs," "Other Asiatics," and "Other Races" account for the remaining 964 "non-natives." E. C. Baker, "Memorandum on the Social Conditions of Dar es Salaam, 4 June 1931," SOAS Library, 78.

13. A. I. Salim, "Native or Non-native?: The Problem of Identity and Social

Stratification of the Arab-Swahili of Kenya," *Hadith* 6 (1976): 65–85; Margaret Strobel, *Muslim Women in Mombasa, 1890–1975* (New Haven: Yale University Press, 1979), 39–41.

14. CS Zanzibar to Secretary, East African Governors Conference, 10 September 1931, TNA 18675/I/f.53. This same dispatch noted that mixed-race children in Zanzibar were classified as "non-African" because it was felt that grouping the large numbers of Arab-African descendants as "African" would have been "politically undesirable." But compare also with Jonathon Glassman, *War of Words, War of Stones: Racial Thought and Violence in Colonial Zanzibar* (Bloomington: Indiana University Press, 2011), 53.

15. Minute of PC Eastern to CS, 12 September 1942, TNA 18675/III/f.2.

16. Christopher Lee, "The 'Native' Undefined: Colonial Categories, Anglo-African Status and the Politics of Kinship in British Central Africa," *Journal of African History* 46 (2005): 455–78.

17. "Native Administration in Townships" by F. W. Brett, 13 July 1929, TNA 13723/f.2.

18. Memorandum on meeting held 30 January 1931, CO 822/36/16/f.58.

19. "Definition of Native and Position to Be Assigned to Half-Castes" by P. E. Mitchell, 22 January 1932, TNA 18675/I/f.86.

20. Ibid. Mitchell later argued that what was needed was not "a new definition of native but an unqualified definition of person," because most racial legislation "is matter of habit rather than need." Mitchell to Perham, 20 November 1932, Perham Papers, RH MSS Perham 491/2/f.57.

21. "Attitude of Tanganyika Government towards Racial Discrimination in Legislation," Secretariat, 20 February 1933, TNA 18675/I/f.148, emphasis in original. See also Freeston to CS Nyasaland, 9 February 1938, CO 822/91/12/f.6. The Tanganyika Bill became a model for other regional governments to either adopt or ignore. Lee, "The Native Undefined," 470–73.

22. William C. Bissell, *Urban Design, Chaos, and Colonial Power in Zanzibar* (Bloomington: Indiana University Press, 2011), 1.

23. Compare Allen Armstrong, "Colonial Planning and Neocolonial Urban Planning: Three Generations of Master Plans for Dar es Salaam, Tanzania," *Utafiti* 8 (1986): 44–53; with A. M. Hayuma, *Economic and Financial Constraints in the Implementation of the 1968 Dar es Salaam City Master Plan from 1969 to 1979* (Dar es Salaam: Ardhi Instiute, 1984). See also Bissell, *Urban Design*, 267–309.

24. Clement Gilman, "Dar es Salaam, 1860 to 1940," *Tanganyika Notes and Records* 20 (1945): 16.

25. Stack to Churchill, 27 June 1922, CO 691/55/f.721.

26. Deborah F. Bryceson, "A Century of Food Supply in Dar es Salaam," in *Feeding African Cities: Studies in Regional Social History*, ed. Jane I. Guyer (Manchester: Manchester University Press, 1987), 162–63.

27. 1919/20 Dar es Salaam DAR, TNA 1733/1.

28. R. R. Scott, "Public Health Services in Dar es Salaam in the 'Twenties," *East African Medical Journal* 40 (1963): 351.

29. Infection rates ranged between 14 percent and 21 percent during 1907–1913. Heinrich Ollvig, "Dar es Salaam from a Health Point of View," *Medical Journal of South Africa* (July 1916): 214; and A. J. Orenstein, "Contribution to the Study of the Value of Quininization in the Eradication of Malaria," *Journal of American Medical Association* 63 (1914): 1932.

30. 1927 Dar es Salaam DAR, TNA library.

31. 1921 Dar es Salaam DAR; memorandum by R. R. Scott, 1 October 1919, TNA 450/39/10. "Chafukoga" roughly coincides with today's Morogoro Road, Bibi Titi Road, Uhuru Street, and Samora Avenue. See map enclosed in Scott to Devonshire, 11 December 1922, CO 691/61/f.332.

32. Roderick Mackay, *Work Done at Dar es Salaam, January 1932–January 1934* (Dar es Salaam: Government Printers, 1935).

33. *Annual Reports of Principal Medical Office and Senior Sanitary Office, 1918-1920*, 48, CO 736/1.

34. Prashant Kidambi, *The Making of an Indian Metropolis: Colonial Governance and Public Culture in Bombay, 1890–1920* (Aldershot: Ashgate, 2007), 39–40, 52–54; *Kwetu*, 20 November 1941.

35. 1921 *Tanganyika Annual Medical Report*, 74–75, 105, CO 736/1.

36. 1922 Dar es Salaam DAR, TNA 1733/f.22; correspondence in TNA 61/250.

37. Cameron to Passfield, 6 July 1929, CO 691/105/2/f.1.

38. Franck Raimbault, "Dar-es-Salaam: Histoire d'une societe urbaine coloniale en Afrique Orientale Allemande (1891–1914)" (PhD diss., Universite Paris I, 2007), vol. 1, 457–62; LO to CS, 25 March 1924, TNA 3088; "Notes on Building Plots," EO, DSM TA, 18 May 1931, TNA 12589/I/f.133. German medical authorities had earlier published a racially zoned city plan in 1904. Philip Curtin, "Medical Knowledge and Urban Planning in Tropical Africa," *American Historical Review* 90 (1985): 608.

39. Minute of Hollis to Byatt, 22 December 1920, TNA 3152.

40. Minute of Byatt to CS, 22 December 1920, TNA 3152.

41. Allen to CS, 15 October 1920, TNA 3152/f.1.

42. "Rules for Dar es Salaam Township," *Occupied Territory of German East Africa, Official Gazette*, 15 October 1919, 50–51; Andrew Burton, *African Underclass: Urbanisation, Crime and Colonial Order in Dar es Salaam, Tanzania* (Oxford: James Currey, 2005), 165.

43. J. M. L. Kironde, "The Evolution of the Land Use Structure of Dar es Salaam 1890–1990: A Study in the Effects of Land Policy" (PhD diss., University of Nairobi, 1994), 190, 210.

44. Senior Sanitation Officer to Principal Medical Officer, 16 October 1920, TNA 3088.

45. The key law was the 1924 Building Areas for Dar es Salaam. Kironde, "The Evolution," 161.

46. Webster to CS, 15 April 1926, TNA 3088.

47. Baker, "Memorandum," 9–10.

48. "Notes on Building Plots" by EO, DSM TA, 18 May 1931, TNA 12589/I/f.136;

Baker, "Memorandum," 10; 1923 *Annual Land Department Report*, 4, CO 736/2; DSM TA minute book, 18 May 1928.

49. Baker, "Memorandum," 15; Kironde, "The Evolution," 181; Wilkin to Helps, 22 November 1935, TNA 61/250/f.234; PC Eastern to CS, 16 December 1935, TNA 12589/II/f.171.

50. Helps to DSM TA, 30 November 1935, TNA 61/250/f.239.

51. Petition of Mwinyi Waziri bin Mwinshehe et al., 16 May 1931, TNA 12589/I/f.102; Kironde, "The Evolution," 184.

52. Kironde, "The Evolution," 175; Baker Memorandum, 10; Helps to EO, DSM TA, 22 November 1935, TNA 61/250/f.244.

53. PC Eastern to CS, 3 April 1936, TNA 23547/f.12; minute of Treasurer to CS, 14 April 1936, TNA 23457/f.19; CS to PC Eastern, 15 May 1936, TNA 23547/f.23; DO Dar es Salaam to CS, 5 August 1937, TNA 61/626/f.132.

54. LO to CS, 25 March 1924, TNA 3088.

55. *Dar es Salaam Times*, 12 February 1921; *Nationalist*, 9 July 1966; Brett to CS, 10 February 1922, TNA 3088/f.14.

56. Ronayne to PC Eastern, 2 April 1929, TNA 61/250/f.45. EO, DSM TA to CS, 19 September 1930, TNA 12227/I/f.13; 1930 Dar es Salaam DAR, TNA library.

57. "Extract from revised draft circular by Honourable Attorney General," n.d. [*ca.* 1923–1924], TNA 3125B/f.3.

58. "Extract from Sayers' comments on House Tax, 4 July 1923," TNA 3125A/f.3; "The Kiwanja Tax and indigenous Natives" by Keeper of German Records, 22 January 1923, TNA 3125A/f.6.

59. In 1914, the German administration had begun surveying the townships of Dar es Salaam, Tanga, and Tabora to create a "Grundbuch," a type of "domesday" book, but in Dar es Salaam, the land officers had fully surveyed only the European and Asian areas when war intervened. "Notes on German Land System—Acquisition of Land," n.a., 29 January 1919, TNA 2689; Baker, "Memorandum," 10; Ag. LO to PC Eastern, 4 May 1936, TNA 61/250/f.288; "Notes on Building Plots" by EO, DSM TA, 18 May 1931, TNA 12589/I/f.136.

60. R. W. James, *Land Tenure and Policy in Tanzania* (Dar es Salaam: EALB, 1971), 100; Kironde, "The Evolution," 173; minute of Treasurer, 19 August 1927, TNA 3944/f.18; Ag LO to CS, 4 October 1928, TNA 3944/f.23.

61. Griffith to CS, 19 October 1930, TNA 61/94/A/f.93.

62. Laird Jones, "The District Town and the Articulation of Colonial Rule: The Case of Mwanza, Tanzania, 1890–1945" (PhD diss., Michigan State University, 1992), 141, 273–74, 287–88.

63. 1924 Dar es Salaam, TNA 1733/f.26.

64. *Tanganyika Herald*, 12 March 1932; Acting PC Eastern to CS, 2 July 1930, TNA 61/250/f.113.

65. Kironde, "The Evolution," 174–75; Indian Association to DO Dar es Salaam, 17 October 1931, TNA 61/250/f.185; *Tanganyika Opinion*, 1 April 1932.

66. DSM TA minutes, 3 January 1936.

67. Eastern PAR 1927, TNA 11676/I/f.5; Owen to CS, 7 December 1927, TNA 7841/f.187.

68. Siggins to Evans, 21 September 1927, CO 691/91/f.10.

69. See Ag. LO to CS, 12 November 1928, TNA 10063/II/f.34/1; LO to CS, 18 November 1929, TNA 10063/II/f.62; *Tanganyika Herald*, 18 August 1934.

70. Lois Lobo, *They Came to Africa: 200 Years of the Asian Presence in Tanzania* (Dar es Salaam: Tanzania Printers, 2000), 38; George Delf, *Asians in East Africa* (London: Oxford University Press, 1963), 52.

71. Evelyn Waugh, *Remote People* (London: Duckworth, 1931), 172.

72. Pashen to Baker, 29 October 1935, TNA 23806.

73. Gerezani lies to the south of Kariakoo; Kisutu refers to a sprawling area lying to the northeast of Kariakoo that was bisected by Zone II.

74. Mohamed Said, *Life and Times of Abdulwahid Sykes (1924–1968): The Untold Story of the Muslim Struggle against British Colonialism in Tanganyika* (London: Minerva Press, 1998), 29; Lawrence Mbogoni, *The Cross versus the Crescent: Religion and Politics in Tanzania from the 1880s to the 1990s* (Dar es Salaam: Mkuki na Nyota, 2004), 58; David Henry Anthony, "Culture and Society in a Town in Transition: A People's History of Dar es Salaam, 1865–1939" (PhD diss., University of Wisconsin-Madison, 1983), 225–26.

75. Dar es Salaam DAR, 1929, TNA library.

76. Baker, "Memorandum," 15.

77. Ibid., 14–17; Baker, Amendments to "Memorandum," op. cit.

78. Anthony, "Culture and Society," 97.

79. See Anne Phillips, *The Enigma of Colonialism: British Policy in West Africa* (London: James Currey, 1989); and Penelope Hetherington, *British Paternalism and Africa, 1920–1940* (London: Cass, 1978).

80. Bruce Berman and John Lonsdale, *Unhappy Valley: Conflict in Kenya and Africa* (Athens: Ohio University Press, 1992), 95.

81. Brett to CS, 16 January 1923, TNA 7016/f.5.

82. Richarde to CS, 9 February 1923, TNA 7016/f.18.

83. AO Morogoro to CS, 30 January 1923, TNA 7016/f.12; AO Rufiji District to CS, 2 June 1923, TNA 7016/f.14.

84. Webster to CS, 18 November 1925, TNA 7016/f.51.

85. Helps to CS, 17 April 1931, TNA 61/403/I/f.1; DO Dar es Salaam to PC Eastern, 27 June 1931, TNA 61/63A/f.34.

86. Dar es Salaam DAR 1921, TNA 1733/f.7.

87. Ibid.; minute of Jardine to ACS, n.d., TNA 2618.

88. McCarthy, *Colonial Bureaucracy*, 39–34; minute of Mitchell to CS, 6 May 1930, TNA 18858/f.9.

89. Buckley to CS, 30 August 1923, TNA 2712; "Notes on Building Plots."

90. "Notes on Building Plots."

91. DSM TA minutes, 30 January 1929; minute of Helps to CS, 16 November 1932, TNA 10849/188/f.4.

92. Baker, Amendments.

93. Brett to CS, 5 May 1928, TNA 61/286/f.1; PC Eastern to CS, 3 August 1929, TNA 61/286/f.20.

94. Orde-Brown to CS, 14 March 1928, TNA 61/295/f.45.

95. "Good Old Kariakoo" by Abdul Baker, *Sunday News*, 17 November 1974.

96. Brett, Dar es Salaam DAR 1921, TNA 1733/f.7; Scott to E.E., 12 April 1920, TNA 2712; Scott to CS, 6 May 1920, TNA 2712/f.6; Adolfo Mascarenhas, "Urban Development in Dar es Salaam" (MA thesis, UCLA, 1966), 97.

97. "Notes on Building Plots"; Skelton to CS, 18 November 1920, TNA 3088.

98. Eastern PAR, 1927, TNA 11676/I/f.53.

99. Baker, "Memorandum," 16, quotation from 11–12.

100. "Notes on Building Plots."

101. Town Planning Secretary, DSM TA to CS, 28 September 1932, TNA 11150/II/f.285; Hartnoll to CS, 6 October 1932, TNA 11150/II/f.287.

102. Minute of I.L.L. to CS, 6 October 1932, TNA 11150/II/f.289.

103. CS to Town Planning Secretary, DSM TA, 13 October 1932, TNA 11150/II/f.290; Kironde, "The Evolution," 161; circular 10063/403 of 4 July 1934, DSM TA minutes, 16 September 1940.

104. Ronayne to LO, 30 July 1929, TNA 61/324/I/f.46.

105. DSM TA minutes, 8 June 1932.

106. CS to EO DSM TA, 4 July 1934, TNA 12589/II/f.148.

107. DO Dar es Salaam to PC Eastern, 28 March 1939, TNA 26862/f.2A; DSM TA minutes, 5 January 1939; Pike to PC Eastern, 2 June 1939, TNA 61/490/f.363.

108. "Report on Native Affairs in Dar es Salaam" by A. H. Pike, 5 June 1939, TNA 61/207/II/f.222.

109. Raimbault, "Dar-es-Salaam," vol. 2, 77–80, 100–102, 113.

110. Yahaya Mwaruka, interview by author, 10 August 1999.

111. Iliffe, *A Modern History*, 387.

112. Frederick Cooper, *On the African Waterfront: Urban Disorder and the Transformation of Work in Colonial Mombasa* (New Haven, CT: Yale University Press, 1987), 52.

113. Luise White, *The Comforts of Home: Prostitution in Colonial Nairobi* (Chicago: University of Chicago Press, 1990), 146.

114. Baker memorandum on housing conditions, 5 October 1943, TNA 61/4/3/f.46.

115. *1925 Annual Medical Report*, 26, CO 736/4.

116. 1931 Dar es Salaam DAR, TNA library.

117. Baker, "Memorandum," 25. Baker estimated minimum cost for materials alone at shs. 1,200.

118. Helps, 1934 DSM TA Report, TNA 61/625/f.7; Helps to PC Eastern, 8 July 1935, TNA 61/27A/f.15; Helps to PC Eastern, 27 August 1936, TNA 61/534/f.3; Hugh Hamilton McCleery, "Extent and Conditions under Which Some Natives Are Occupying Land on the Outskirts of Dar es Salaam," June 1939, RH MSS Afr.s.870, 4.

119. Mama Nurdini to CS, 21 August 1931, TNA 10849/1.

120. Baker, "Memorandum," 17.

121. Baker, "Memorandum," 16–17.

122. Helps to PC Eastern, 29 September 1938, TNA 61/490/f.300.

123. Ibid.

124. H. M. Kanji, Tenants Association to CS, 20 June 1941, TNA 27313/I/f.6.

125. McCleery, "Extent and Conditions," 6–13.

126. For Burma, see Sugata Bose, *A Hundred Horizons: The Indian Ocean in the Age of Global Empire* (Cambridge, MA: Harvard University Press, 2006), 116–17; for Zanzibar, see Michael F. Lofchie, *Zanzibar: Background to Revolution* (Princeton, NJ: Princeton University Press, 1965), 104–26.

127. For analyses of the immense discretionary power given to governors, see Andrew Lyall, "Land Law and Policy in Tanganyika, 1919–1932" (MLL thesis, University of Dar es Salaam, 1973), 1–103; and Issa Shivji, *Not Yet Democracy: Reforming Land Tenure in Tanzania* (Dar es Salaam: IIED, 1998), 1–7.

128. Charles Strachey, "Land Policy in Tanganyika," 4 August 1921, CO 691/52/f.262; Lyall, "Land Law and Policy," 39–64.

129. Gerald F. Sayers, ed., *The Handbook of Tanganyika* (London: Macmillan, 1930), 243.

130. McCleery, "Extent and Conditions," 53; "Notes on German Land System."

131. McCleery, "Extent and Conditions," 14–15; LO, "Note on Flurbuch," 22 April 1939, in McCleery, ibid., 54n1.

132. Minute of McCleery to PC Eastern, 20 May 1931, TNA 61/63A/f.31.

133. Hutchinson, "Memorandum on Freeholding of Land by Adverse Possession," 30 September 1944, enclosed in Jackson to Stanley, 19 December 1944, CO 691/192/2/f.1.

134. Minutes of Permanent Mandates Commission, 28 June–6 July 1927, 84, in CO 691/89.

135. Elizabeth Colson, "The Impact of the Colonial Period on the Definition of Land Rights," in *Colonialism in Africa, 1870–1960*, ed. Peter Duignan and L. H. Gann, 194–211, vol. 3 (Cambridge: Cambridge University Press, 1971).

136. "Notes on Land Tenure in Temeke District," 28 April 1928, DSM District Book, TNA; Greig to PC Eastern, 5 November 1935, TNA 61/63/A/f.112.

137. Colson, "The Impact of the Colonial Period," 195.

138. 1927 Dar es Salaam DAR, TNA library.

139. McCleery, "Extent and Conditions," 10.

140. Hartnoll to PC Eastern, 15 January 1936, TNA 61/382/f.18.

141. McCleery, "Extent and Conditions," 15–17.

142. "Notes on Mr. McCleery's Report," n.a., n.d. [*ca.* 1939], 18, TNA 26177.

143. Ronayne to PC Eastern, 29 March 1935, TNA 10849/265/f.6; James R. Brennan, "Nation, Race and Urbanization in Dar es Salaam, Tanzania, 1916–1976" (PhD diss., Northwestern University, 2002), 67–68.

144. Susan Geiger, *TANU Women: Gender and Culture in the Making of Tanganyikan Nationalism* (Portsmouth, NH: Heinemann, 1997), 21; Richa Nagar,

"Communal Places and the Politics of Multiple Identities: The Case of Tanzanian Asians," *Ecumene* 4 (1997): 6.

CHAPTER 2: IDENTITY AND SOCIAL STRUCTURE IN INTERWAR DAR ES SALAAM

1. Although I do not systematically adopt their awkward term "identification" here, I do strive to minimize the reifying tendencies of "identity," which—as Brubaker and Cooper note—in common usage conflates categories of practice and analysis. Rogers Brubaker and Frederick Cooper, "Beyond 'Identity,'" *Theory and Society* 29 (2000): 1–47.

2. Craig Calhoun, ed., *Social Theory and the Politics of Identity* (Oxford: Blackwell, 1994), 26.

3. As representative of this view, see Stephen Cornell and Douglas Hartmann, *Ethnicity and Race: Making Identities in a Changing World* (Thousand Oaks, CA: Pine Forge Press, 1998); and Jyoti Puri, *Encountering Nationalism* (Oxford: Blackwell, 2004). "Ethnicity" is consistently the most poorly defined of the three terms, serving either as a residual category or as a euphemism for "tribe."

4. Max Weber, "Ethnic Groups," in *Economy and Society: An Outline of Interpretive Sociology*, ed. Guenther Roth and Claus Wittich (Berkeley: University of California Press, 1978), 385-398. Weber defines "ethnic groups" as "those human groups that entertain a subjective belief in their common descent because of similarities of physical type or of customs or both, or because of memories of colonization and migration; this belief must be important for the propagation of group formation; conversely, it does not matter whether or not an objective blood relationship exists." Ibid., 389.

5. Dar es Salaam's 1921 population was 600 Europeans (2.4 percent), 4,000 Asians (16.3 percent), 20,000 Africans (81.3 percent); in 1931: 1,334 Europeans (4 percent), 8,865 Asians (27 percent), 22,716 Africans (69 percent); in 1943: 1,100 Europeans (2.4 percent), 11,000 Asians (24.4 percent), 33,000 Africans (73.2 percent). Clement Gilman, "Dar es Salaam, 1860 to 1940," *Tanganyika Notes and Records* 20 (1945): 22; E. C. Baker, "Memorandum on the Social Conditions of Dar es Salaam, 4 June 1931," 78; Dar es Salaam DAR, 1931, TNA library.

6. J. S. Mangat, *A History of the Asians in East Africa, c. 1886 to 1945* (Oxford: Oxford University Press, 1969), 1–26; M. Reda Bhacker, *Trade and Empire in Muscat and Zanzibar* (London: Routledge, 1992), 67–76.

7. Only 15 percent of colonial Gujarat was under direct British rule, coinciding roughly with the cities of Ahmedabad and Surat. Achyut Yagnik and Suchitra Sheth, *The Shaping of Modern Gujarat: Plurality, Hindutva and Beyond* (New York: Penguin, 2005), 64.

8. Sugata Bose, *A Hundred Horizons: The Indian Ocean in the Age of Global Empire* (Cambridge: Harvard University Press, 2006), 29, 99–100.

9. Franck Raimbault, "Dar-es-Salaam: Histoire d'une societe urbaine coloniale en Afrique Orientale Allemande (1891-1914)," vol. 2 (PhD thesis, Universite Paris I, 2007), 7–9; John Iliffe, *Tanganyika under German Rule, 1905–1912* (Cambridge: Cambridge University Press, 1969), 94.

10. Martha Honey, "A History of Indian Merchant Capital and Class Formation in Tanganyika, c. 1840–1940" (PhD diss., University of Dar es Salaam, 1982), 297.

11. Carmen Voigt-Graf, *Asian Communities in Tanzania: A Journey Through Past and Present Times* (Hamburg: Institute of African Affairs, 1998), 57–61; Richa Nagar, "The Making of Hindu communal Organizations, Places, and Identities in Postcolonial Dar es Salaam," *Environment and Planning* 15 (1997): 711–14; Raimbault, "Dar-es-Salaam," 148–51, 217–24.

12. Voigt-Graf, *Asian Communities*, 68–70.

13. The Hindu Mandal (est. 1919) represented territorial Hindus regardless of caste, and the Ismailia Council represented territorial Ismailis. Ismailis formed 40 percent and Hindus 33 percent of Dar es Salaam's Indian community in 1944. N. G. Mehta, "The Hindu Mandal: Its Changing Role," in *Hindu Mandal Golden Jubilee Souvenir, 1919–1969* (Dar es Salaam, 1969); Singh to Baker, 7 March 1944, TNA 61/617/f.397. Tanganyika's largest *jati* associations were Lohana Mahajan and Patel Brotherhood.

14. A 1934 linguistic survey found 56 percent of Indians in Tanganyika surveyed were literate, of whom 1,174 were literate in Gujarati, 908 in English, 284 in Punjabi, 161 in Hindi, 128 in Arabic, 125 in Marathi, 85 in Tamil, 83 in "foreign" languages, 53 in Malayalam, 28 in Sindhi, 20 in Bengali, 10 in Telegu, 5 in Kanarese, 4 in Konkani, and 119 in "other." S. Waiz, *Indians Abroad Directory* (Bombay: Imperial Indian Citizenship Association, 1934), 408.

15. Honey, "A History," 289.

16. For general accounts, see Robert J. Blyth, *Empire of the Raj: Eastern Africa and the Middle East, 1858–1947* (Basingstoke: Palgrave Macmillan, 2003), 96–119; and Thomas Metcalf, *Imperial Connections: India in the Indian Ocean Arena, 1860–1920* (Berkeley: University of California Press, 2007), 182–87; for the Aga Khan's campaign, see Honey, "A History," 225–30; on India's role, see Robert Gregory, *India and East Africa: a History of Race Relations within the British Empire, 1890–1939* (Oxford: Clarendon Press, 1971), 162–68.

17. Honey, "A History," 230–33; Jadab to Desai, 13 November 1918, CO 691/16/f.544.

18. Morison to Montagu, 19 August 1917, CO 691/2/f.368.

19. Theodore Morison, *A Colony for India*, July 1918, in CO 691/2/f.353-6.

20. Hussein Suleman Virjes to Long, 17 November 1918, IOR L/E/7/1206/5183/1918, India Office, British Library.

21. Indian Association Dar es Salaam to Gandhi, enclosed in Jadab to Desai, 13 November 1918, CO 691/16/f.545.

22. Ali Diwani et al. to Byatt, 17 December 1918, CO 691/16/f.546.

23. Cranworth to Long, 21 October 1918, CO 691/18/f.53. Andrews insisted that only a few Indians supported subcolonization. C. F. Andrews, *The Indian Question in East Africa* (Nairobi: Swift Press, 1921), 14. This was true only by 1920, however, with new fears of losing rights in British East Africa (Kenya). Honey, "A History," 240–44.

24. Byatt to Long, 18 August 1920, CO 691/33/f.425.

25. British Vice-Consul to Bonar Law, 11 September 1916, CO 691/1/f.312.

26. Indian nationals spent £445,241, and British nationals spent £705,434, out of £1,344,604 total paid for enemy properties. Honey, "A History," 463; Nanji Kalidas Mehta, *Dream Half-Expressed* (Bombay: Vakils, Feffer, and Simons, 1966), 147–55; Gerald F. Sayers, ed., *The Handbook of Tanganyika* (London: Macmillan, 1930), 100–101, 193.

27. Charlotte Leubuscher, *Tanganyika Territory* (London: Oxford University Press, 1944), 35, 203.

28. Franck Raimbault, "Les stratégies de reclassement des élites arabes et indiennes à Dar-es-Salaam durant la colonisation allemande (1891–1914), *Hypothèses* 5 (2001): 114.

29. Byatt to Milner, 11 May 1920, CO 691/31/f.542.

30. Honey, "A History," 424.

31. Andrews, *The Indian Question*, 38.

32. F. S. Joelson, *Tanganyika Territory* (New York: Appleton, 1921), 28.

33. Evelyn Waugh, *Remote People* (London: Duckworth, 1931), 166–67.

34. Shirin Walji, "History of the Ismaili Community in Tanzania" (PhD diss., University of Wisconsin, 1974), 153. Gregory argues—with optimistic logic and anecdote—that capital repatriation could not have been significant until the 1950s, but offers no evidence relating to capital flows. Robert Gregory, *South Asians in East Africa: an Economic and Social History, 1890–1980* (Boulder, CO: Westview Press, 1993), 329–46.

35. 1921 Dar es Salaam DAR; Byatt to Milner, 6 February 1920, CO 691/30/f.202; Byatt to Milner, 7 July 1920, CO 691/33/f.16; Sayers, *The Handbook of Tanganyika*, 192; Gilchrist Alexander, *Tanganyika Memories* (London: Blackie and Sons, 1936), 113–14; Gregory, *South Asians*, 88. The rupee exchange rate stood at 1s 4d before 1919, rose as high as 2s 10d in early 1920, then crashed below a guaranteed 2s exchange rate until the rupee ceased being legal tender in East Africa in mid-1921. The rate subsequently settled at 1s 6d until 1939.

36. Joelson, *Tanganyika Territory*, 29.

37. Stella Bendera, "Industrial Growth, 1920–1967: A Study of Medium Size Industries in Dar es Salaam" (MA thesis, University of Dar es Salaam, 1976), 52; Honey, "A History," 485–520; Gregory, *South Asians*, 275–85; H. S. Morris, *Indians in Uganda* (Chicago: University of Chicago Press, 1968), 135. Cf. Claude Markovits, *Global World of Indian Merchants, 1750–1947* (Cambridge: Cambridge University Press, 2000), 51–52, 82.

38. Robert Gregory, *Quest for Equality: Asian Politics in East Africa, 1900–1967* (Hyderabad: Orient Longman), 4; Abdulla Tejpar, interview by Martha Honey, 2 November 1973; and Alibhai Bhatia, interview by Martha Honey, 19 September 1973.

39. Michael Callahan, *Mandates and Empire: The League of Nations and Africa, 1914–1931* (Brighton: Sussex University Press, 1999), 100–101.

40. *Dar es Salaam Times*, 18 March 1922.

41. *Tanganyika Opinion* and *Tanganyika Herald* were launched in 1924 and 1929, respectively.

42. *Tanganyika Herald*, 4 March 1933.

43. Ibid., 1 September 1931; Gregory, *India and East Africa*, 386, 390–91; Gregory, *Quest for Equality*, 34, 58–66.

44. Gijsbert Oonk, "'We Lost Our gift of Expression': Loss of the Mother Tongue among Indians in East Africa, 1880–2000," in *Global Indian Diasporas*, ed. Gijsbert Oonk (Amsterdam: Amsterdam University Press, 2007), 72–73; Byatt to Devonshire, 2 April 1923, CO 691/62/f.392.

45. Byatt to Devonshire, 28 May 1923, CO 691/63/f.96.

46. Walji, "History of the Ismaili Community," 151–52; *Dar es Salaam Times*, 7 and 14 April 1923.

47. Honey, "A History," 333–34.

48. Byatt to Devonshire, 2 April 1923, CO 691/62/f.390.

49. Treasurer to CS, 21 May 1925, TNA 7596/f.26; Scott to Amery, 16 June 1927, CO 691/92/f.55; Honey, "A History," 345–53.

50. "MAKKUM 1st April 1923," *Tanganyika Herald*, 6 May 1935.

51. John Iliffe, *A Modern History of Tanganyika* (Cambridge: Cambridge University Press, 1979), 346; Gregory, *India and East Africa*, 390; *Tanganyika Opinion*, 22 January 1932.

52. Kenneth Ingham, *History of East Africa* (New York: Praeger, 1965), 295–96, 403; Honey, "A History," 305.

53. Daya to CS, 12 March 1925, TNA 7017/f.6; K. S. Bajwa, "Indian Education," *Tanganyika Herald*, 6 May 1935; *Tanganyika Herald*, 2 November 1935.

54. Sheth to CS, 27 June 1930, TNA 11521/f.43; Indian Association to CS, 15 August 1930, TNA 25574/f.1; *Tanganyika Opinion*, 7 and 22 May 1928; *Tanganyika Herald*, 31 January 1938.

55. Indian Association to CS, 25 January 1932, TNA 20673/f.20.

56. Satthiadhas to CS, 6 March 1922, TNA 3236; *Tanganyika Opinion*, 8 May 1931 and 27 April 1934.

57. Brett to CS, 23 September 1921, TNA 3543/f.1; *Dar es Salaam Times*, 28 March 1925; Webster to Hindu Mandal, 8 October 1925, TNA 3543.

58. Honey, "A History," 440–47; Dar es Salaam Merchants Chamber, *Silver Jubilee Souvenir*, 1941–1966 (Dar es Salaam: self-published, 1966), 14.

59. *Tanganyika Herald*, 18 February 1939; *Jolly Joker*, n.d. (*ca.* 1931), in TNA 10818/If.37A; DSM TA minutes, 8 July 1936.

60. Unpublished letter to *Tanganyika Standard* by "Victim," 19 February 1934, in TNA 21226/I/f.23.

61. Minute of PC Eastern to CS, 20 August 1942, TNA 27313/I.

62. Abdul Hakim Jan to CS, 30 September 1931, TNA 19495/f.34.

63. Gregory, *South Asians*, 70–73; Walji, "History of the Ismaili Community," 173; Mangat, *A History of the Asians*, 136–38; *Tanganyika Herald*, 13 February 1932 & 3 March 1934; *Tanganyika Opinion*, 3 November 1933; Stewart Symes, *Tour of Duty* (London: Collins, 1946), 172–74; and especially Honey, "A History," 360–430. In 1930, Philip Mitchell described commerce in East Africa as being "carried on under a load of credit which it cannot hope to stand for long."

Mitchell to Vischer, 2 August 1930, J. H. Oldham papers, RH MSS Afr.s.1829 Box 6/8/f.36.

64. Michael Twaddle, "East African Asians through a Hundred Years," in *South Asians Overseas: Migration and Ethnicity*, ed. Colin Clarke, Ceri Peach, and Steven Vertovec (Cambridge: Cambridge University Press, 1990), 154. See also Morris, *Indians in Uganda*, 25–44.

65. Walji, "History of the Ismaili Community," 167–70; Moledina to Battershill, 26 February 1948, TNA 10849/1392/f.1a.

66. *Tanganyika Opinion*, Special Number, September 1937.

67. *Tanganyika Opinion*, 22 October 1937.

68. "Translations of Some Leaflets Circulated in Dar es Salaam," n.d. [*ca.* August 1940], TNA 28974/f.3A.

69. See *Ismaili Voice*, 19 August 1936, TNA 12915/f.96.

70. Honorary Secretary, Shia Imami Ismailia Council to CS, 21 June 1935, TNA 19588/f.12.

71. Freeston to Stanley, 28 January 1943, CO 691/185/42420/f.2; James R. Brennan, "South Asian Nationalism in an East African Context: The Case of Tanganyika, 1914–1956," *Comparative Studies of South Asia, Africa and the Middle East* 19 (1999): 30.

72. John Iliffe, "The Age of Improvement and Differentiation," in *History of Tanzania*, ed. I. N. Kimambo and A. J. Temu (Dar es Salaam: EAPH, 1969), 143–44.

73. Igor Kopytoff, "The Internal African Frontier: The Making of an African Political Culture," in *The African Frontier: The Reproduction of Traditional African Societies*, ed. Igor Kopytoff (Bloomington: Indiana University Press, 1987), 52–61.

74. August Nimtz, *Islam and Politics in East Africa: The Sufi Order in Tanzania* (Minneapolis: University of Minnesota Press, 1980), 29–32; Hasani bin Ismail, *The Medicine Man: Swifa ya Nguvumali*, ed. Peter Lienhardt (Oxford: Clarendon Press, 1968), 13.

75. On Shomvi origins and history, see especially Geoffrey Ross Owens, "On the Edge of a City: An Historical Ethnography of Urban Identity in the Northwestern Suburbs of Dar es Salaam, Tanzania" (PhD diss., University of Wisconsin, 2004), 56–100.

76. See E. C. Baker, "A Note on the Washomvi of Dar es Salaam," *Tanganyika Notes and Records* 23 (1947): 47–48, for the account of Mwinyiheri bin Akida. Also see David Henry Anthony, "Culture and Society in a Town in Transition: A People's History of Dar es Salaam, 1865–1939" (PhD diss., University of Wisconsin, 1983), 23–25; Mohamedi Mkasi, interview by author, 6 August 1999.

77. Jonathon Glassman, *Feasts and Riot: Revelry, Rebellion and Popular Consciousness on the Swahili Coast, 1856–1888* (Portsmouth, NH: Heinemann, 1995), 117–20, 146–58.

78. On Zaramo origins, see Owens, "On the Edge," 101–35; and Ramadhani Mwaruka, *Masimulizi juu ya Uzaramo* (London: Macmillan, 1965), 1–18. Pazi

Kilama figures in most accounts of Zaramo settlement in Dar es Salaam. Anthony, "Culture and Society," 32; Dawkins, Dar es Salaam DAR 1927, TNA library; Geoffrey Ross Owens, "The Shomvi: A Precursor to Global Ethnoscapes and Indigenization in Precolonial East Africa," *Ethnohistory* 53 (2006): 731–33.

79. "History According to Kitambaa Kirakara," recorded by J. A. K. Leslie, 1 November 1956, Kisarawe District Book, TNA; account of Saidi Chaurembo, 16 March 1955, DSM District Book vol. 2, TNA.

80. Anthony, "Culture and Society," 42–47; Owens, "On the Edge," 133.

81. Few in Africa ever did. See Aidan Southall, "The Illusion of Tribe," *Journal of Asian and African Studies* 5 (1970): 28–50.

82. J. E. G. Sutton, "Dar es Salaam, a Sketch of a Hundred Years," *Tanzania Notes and Records* 71 (1970): 1–19; Walter Brown, "Bagamoyo: An Historical Introduction," *ibid.*, 71 (1970): 73. Cf. Owens, "On the Edge," 136–73.

83. Nimtz, *Islam and Politics*, 47; Jan-Georg Deutsch, *Emancipation without Abolition in German East Africa*, c. 1884–1914 (Oxford: James Currey, 2006), 228–30.

84. Iliffe, "Age of Improvement," 134.

85. Iliffe, *A Modern History*, 161; Anthony, "Culture and Society," 75–76. The 1895 estimate stated Dar es Salaam was 47 percent Zaramo, 23 percent "Swahili," 10 percent Sagara, 7 percent Nyamwezi, 5 percent Shambaa, 3 percent Maasai, 2 percent Gogo, 2 percent Mahenge, and 1 percent Manyema.

86. Iliffe, *A Modern History*, 318–41.

87. Kisarawe District Book excerpt titled "Wazaramo, etc." by Fryer, 29 July 1931. Cf. Dawkins, Dar es Salaam DAR 1927, TNA library; Griffith to CS, 23 June 1930, TNA 12801/I/f.168; Fryer to PC Eastern, 11 April 1930, TNA 12801/I/f.172. But see also Owens, "On the Edge," 189, which claims that Pazi Mazongera was appointed paramount chief for Uzaramo and stationed at Yombo.

88. 1929 Dar es Salaam DAR; Margaret Bates, "Tanganyika Under British Administration, 1920–1955" (DPhil diss., Oxford University, 1957), 260.

89. 1936 Dar es Salaam DAR.

90. T. O. Beidelman, *The Matrilineal Peoples of Eastern Tanzania* (London: International African Institute, 1967), 15.

91. Sayers, *The Handbook of Tanganyika*, 38; Adolfo Mascarenhas, "Urban Development in Dar es Salaam" (MA thesis, UCLA, 1966), 42–43. The eight largest "tribes" of Tanganyika in descending order of size were Sukuma, Nyamwezi, Gogo, Chaga, Turu, Ha, Makonde, and Irangi.

92. In 1928, Zaramo made up the overwhelming plurality of township African population, numbering roughly a third (7,074 of 21,930) and followed distantly by Manyema (1,495), Yao (1,232), and Rufiji (1,147). In Dar es Salaam District, Zaramo accounted for over half (99,971 of 164,422), and only Ndengereko (17,389) numbered over 10,000. Dar es Salaam Township Census 1928, TNA 61/167/A/f.6; Native census Dar-es-Salaam District, TNA 61/167/A/f.7.

93. Eastern PAR 1928, TNA 11676/II/f.81.

94. Petition of Mahomed bin Diwani Hatemi and Hija bin Shomaril Hatemi to Cameron, 7 November 1927, TNA 10849/I/12/2/f.2.

95. Tambaza to CS, 5 March 1930, TNA 10849/10/f.1.

96. Mwaruka, *Masimulizi*, 118.

97. Jonathon Glassman, *War of Words, War of Stones: Racial Thought and Violence in Colonial Zanzibar* (Bloomington: Indiana University Press, 2011), 55. Cf. Laura Fair, *Pastimes and Politics: Culture, Community, and Identity in Post-Abolition Urban Zanzibar, 1890–1945* (Athens: Ohio University Press, 2001), 28–55.

98. Justin Willis, *Mombasa, the Swahili, and the Making of the Mijikenda* (Oxford: Oxford University Press, 1993), 110–11, 188–90. See also A. H. J. Prins, *Swahili-Speaking Peoples of Zanzibar and the East African Coast* (London: International African Institute, 1961), 11–14.

99. Fryer to PC Eastern, 28 March 1930, TNA 61/207/I/f.10.

100. Ibid.; Tambaza to Mitchell, 23 February 1931, TNA 10849/10/f.10.

101. Anthony, "Culture and Society," 119.

102. Baker, "Memorandum," 7.

103. Only a handful of prominent *wenye mji* — Tambaza, Abdallah Chaurembo, Abbasi Makisi, and Mshumi Kiatu — had wielded rental housing as patronage. Alhaji Iddi Sungura, interview by author, 28 September 1998. In 1956, 78 percent of Manyema heads of households owned their houses, easily the highest percentage among Dar es Salaam Africans. J. A. K. Leslie, unpublished 1956 survey appendix A/1, 21, SOAS library

104. Sheryl McCurdy, "Transforming Associations: Fertility, Therapy and the Manyema Diaspora in Urban Kigoma, Tanzania, c. 1850–1993" (PhD diss., Columbia University, 2000), 73–74, 108–11.

105. J. A. K. Leslie, *A Survey of Dar es Salaam* (London: Oxford University Press, 1963), 47; Raimbault, "Dar-es-Salaam," vol. 2, 308–9; Iliffe, *A Modern History*, 390; Baker, "Memorandum," 74; Baker to CS, 15 September 1941, TNA 10849/696/f.13; Deutsch, *Emancipation*, 217; Alhaji Iddi Sungura, interview by author, 28 September 1998. Quotation is from Leslie, *A Survey*, 50.

106. Mohamed Said, *The Life and Times of Abdulwahid Sykes (1924–1968): The Untold Story of the Muslim Struggle against British Colonialism in Tanganyika* (London: Minerva, 1998), 169.

107. Ahmed Salum Abdallah, interview by author, 14 August 1999; Juma Manjenga, interview by author, 12 August 1999; and Iddi Said Gude, interview by author, 2 January 1999. Leslie found in 1956 that 82 percent of Manyema women surveyed owned one or more houses, compared to average female home ownership of 47 percent, and average male home ownership of 19 percent. Of surveyed Manyema households, 38 percent were headed by women, nearly three times the city's 13 percent average of female-headed households. Leslie, unpublished survey, appendix A/1, 20–21.

108. Mtoro Seif, interview by author, 4 January 1999.

109. Ahmed Seifu Salum Mponda, interview by author, 22 September 1998.

110. Shabani Gonga, interview by author, 5 October 1998.

111. Leslie, *A Survey*, 47–48; Ahmed Salum Abdala, interview by author, 14 August 1999. In 1928 there were 892 Manyema women to 603 Manyema men,

and 109 Nubian women to 89 Nubian men; all other "tribe" gender ratios favored men. Dar es Salaam Township Census, 1928, TNA 61/167/A/f.6.

112. Leslie, *A Survey*, 15, 260.

113. Daisy Sykes Buruku, "The Townsman: Kleist Sykes," in *Modern Tanzanians*, ed. John Iliffe (Dar es Salaam: EAPH, 1973), 96–97.

114. Baker, "Memorandum," 89; Leslie, *A Survey*, 43–44; letter of Rashidi Mlewa, *Kwetu*, 2 August 1938; Ahmed Seifu Salum Mponda, interview by author, 22 September 1998; and Yunus Daud Mwinyikambi, interview by author, 29 December 1998.

115. Ukami Union, for example, formed in 1938 following the visit of Chief Kingaro of Kinyori to unite Kwere, Luguru, Kutu, Zigua, and Kami. Iliffe, "Age of Improvement," 146; Leslie, *A Survey*, 41.

116. Tadasu Tsuruta, "Urban-Rural Relationships in Colonial Dar es Salaam: Some Notes on Ethnic Associations and Recreations, 1930s–1950s," *Memoirs of the Faculty of Agriculture of Kinki University* 36 (2003): 62.

117. Mohamed Hassan Kiswagala, interview by author, 13 January 1999.

118. The literature is vast—see especially Glassman, *Feasts and Riot*, 158–65; T. O. Ranger, *Dance and Society in Eastern Africa 1890–1970: The Beni "Ngoma"* (London: Heinemann, 1975); Kelly Askew, *Performing the Nation: Swahili Music and Cultural Politics in Tanzania* (Chicago: University of Chicago Press, 2002), 75–85; Margaret Strobel, *Muslim Women in Mombasa, 1890–1975* (New Haven, CT: Yale University Press, 1979), 12–19, 156–70; and Fair, *Pastimes and Politics*, 103–8, 226–64.

119. For a functionalist view on the role of moieties along the Swahili coast, see John Middleton, *The World of the Swahili: An African Mercantile Civilization* (New Haven, CT: Yale University Press, 1992), 80, 98, 169.

120. Tadasu Tsuruta, "Simba or Yanga?: Football and Urbanization in Dar es Salaam," in *Dar es Salaam: Histories from an Emerging African Metropolis*, ed. James R. Brennan, Andrew Burton, and Yusuf Lawi (Dar es Salaam/Nairobi: Mkuki na Nyota/BIEA, 2007), 199–203.

121. Tadasu Tsuruta, "Popular Music, Sports, and Politics: A Development of Urban Cultural Movements in Dar es Salaam, 1930s–1960s," *African Study Monographs* 24 (2003): 201–3; Werner Graebner, "The *Ngoma* Impulse: From Club to Nightclub in Dar es Salaam," in Brennan, Burton, and Lawi, *Dar es Salaam*, 180–82; *Sunday News*, 6 June 1976.

122. The principal work is Ranger, *Dance and Society*.

123. West to DPO Dar es Salaam, 8 October 1919, TNA SMP 075; Ranger, *Dance and Society*, 41. I thank John Iliffe for lending me his notes on this important file, which apparently survives only in microfilm copy held at Seeley Library, University of Cambridge.

124. James R. Brennan, "Nation, Race and Urbanization in Dar es Salaam, Tanzania, 1916–1976" (PhD diss., Northwestern University, 2002), 144–50.

125. Fryer to PC Eastern, 25 November 1930, TNA 26150/f.13; Baker, "Memorandum," 71–72.

126. 1921 Dar es Salaam DAR.

127. Byatt to Devonshire, 23 April 1923, CO 691/62/f.533.

128. Dar es Salaam DAR 1927.

129. Matola to CS, 22 April 1930, TNA 61/207/I/f.12.

130. Fryer to PC Eastern, 23 April 1930, TNA 61/207/I/f.15; Fryer to PC Eastern, 15 May 1930, TNA 61/207/I/f.19.

131. Juma bin Alimasi to Dawkins et al., 10 November 1932, TNA 10849/190/f.3; Hassan Omari to Symes, 5 August 1933, TNA 26079/f.5; Kennedy to Ormsby-Gore, 25 September 1937, CO 691/159/16/f.4.

132. Hartnoll to Helps, 12 January 1937, TNA 61/207/I/f.74. See also *Tanganyika Standard*, 6 August 1938; *Mambo Leo*, November 1938.

133. Mohamed Omari et al. to PC Eastern, 31 March 1937, TNA 61/207/I/f.124.

134. *Mambo Leo*, September 1931. Original reads *Chama hiki maana yake si kabila wala ukoo ila ni taifa zima la wenyeji wa Afrika*.

135. Baker, "Memorandum," 75. The African Association's founding date is usually placed in late 1929. Iliffe, *A Modern History*, 406, citing *Mambo Leo*, September 1931. The date seems more likely 1927, or even 1926. One administrator wrote in 1930 that the African Association formed "three or four years ago." Minute of A.E.K. to CS, 18 August 1930, TNA 11601/I/f.129. A 1933 newspaper item states that it "has been in existence for some six years." *Tanganyika Standard*, 30 December 1933. Finally, Governor Cameron wrote in 1930 that it "was formed 3 or 4 years ago by some of the better educated natives." Cameron to Passfield, 22 August 1930, TNA 19325/f.5.

136. Baker, "Memorandum," 69. Although two prominent Zaramo men were active in the African Association—Ramadhani Ali, an important trader; and Ali Saidi, a building inspector—few other Zaramo followed. Ranger, *Dance and Society*, 95; Iliffe, *A Modern History*, 408–10; *Tanganyika Standard*, 6 August 1938.

137. *Tanganyika Herald*, 20 June 1936.

138. Makisi Mbwana to EO, Dar es Salaam, 11 September 1934, TNA 22444/f.1; Fiah to PC Eastern, 13 January 1936, TNA 22444/f.42; Diwan to CS, 9 April 1938, TNA 22444/f.138; *Kwetu*, February 1945. On Fiah's life, see Nicholas J. Westcott, "An East African Radical: The Life of Erica Fiah," *Journal of African History* 22 (1981): 85–101; and Fiah's own "Maisha ya Mvumbuzi wa Kwetu," *Kwetu*, February 1945.

139. Idi Salim to CS, 9 August 1936, TNA 22444/f.96.

140. Especially following treasurer Ali Saidi's alleged embezzlement of African Association funds in 1936. Mirambo to Assistant DO, Dar es Salaam, 8 October 1936, TNA 61/385/f.38; Assistant DO Dar es Salaam to PC Eastern, 8 October 1936, TNA 61/385/f.37.

141. Brennan, "Nation, Race and Urbanization," chapter 4.

142. Robert Miles, *Racism after "Race Relations"* (London: Routledge, 1993).

143. Frederick Cooper, *From Slaves to Squatters: Plantation Labour and Agriculture in Zanzibar and Coastal Kenya, 1890–1925* (New Haven, CT: Yale University Press, 1981), 263.

144. Examples include *ankra* (invoice), *bepari* (capitalist), *bima* (insurance), *gabacholi* (swindler), *gari* (vehicle), and *hundi* (bank draft). Abdulaziz Lodhi, *Ori-*

ental Influences in Swahili (Göteborg: Acta Universitatis Gothoburgensis, 2000), 134, 142-143, 162-163, 169.

145. *Dar es Salaam Times*, 14 April 1923. Orde-Brown later claimed that "little actual hardship or privation occurred" to African townspeople. Dar es Salaam DAR 1923, TNA 1733/f.26.

146. Indian Association files, 1920s, quoted in Honey, "A History," 339.

147. Honey, "A History," 336; Dar es Salaam DAR 1923, TNA 1733/f.26; Buckley to CS, 30 August 1923, TNA 2712.

148. Anonymous letter titled "Scene from the Day of April 1923," TNA 2712.

149. Director of Education to CS, 4 December 1925, TNA 3806/f.99.

150. Touchette to Secretary of State, 29 May 1944, NARA RG 59 862S.52/5.

151. Letter of Bakari bin Kambi, *Tanganyika Herald*, 28 October 1930, in TNA 61/385/f.8.

152. Unpublished letter of Sulemani Bajuma to Editor, *Mambo Leo*, n.d. [*ca.* January 1936], TNA 13038/II/f.503.

153. Andy Chande, interview by author, 15 August 2009; M. M. Devani, interview by Martha Honey, 9 March 1974; Bates, "Tanganyika under British Administration," 276; Gijsbert Oonk, "'After Shaking his Hand, Start Counting your Fingers': Trust and Images in Indian Business Networks, East Africa, 1900–2000," *Itinerario* 27 (2004): 75, 80; H. C. G. Hawkins, *Wholesale and Retail Trade in Tanganyika* (New York: Praeger, 1965), 107. For a similar account of Mombasa, see Karim Janmohamed, "A History of Mombasa, c. 1895–1939" (PhD diss., Northwestern University, 1978), 143–62.

154. Hawkins, *Wholesale and Retail Trade*, 110–13.

155. Leslie, *A Survey*, 143–47; Dharsee to CS, 31 March 1930, TNA 12230/I/f.85.

156. PC Eastern to CS, 3 August 1929, TNA 61/286/f.20; *Tanganyika Standard*, 12 May 1953. The 1930 Pawnbrokers Ordinance restricted pawn loans to maximum shs. 400/-; extended redemption periods to six months (shs. 15/- or less) or twelve months (over shs. 15/-); extended powers to inspect premises for stolen property; required loan terms be made explicit on the premises; and redemption tickets printed in English or Swahili.

157. Letter of Mary Margaret Mkambe, *Tanganyika Standard*, 18 November 1944, quoted in Burton, *African Underclass: Urbanisation, Crime and Colonial Order in Dar es Salaam, Tanzania* (Oxford: James Currey, 2005), 141.

158. Ibrahim Chande, interview by author, 20 September 1998.

159. Shabani Gonga, interview by author, 5 October 1998; Saidi Majaliwa, interview by author, 8 January, 1999; and Yahaya Mwaruka, interview by author, 10 August 1999.

160. The *amana* system began with the storage of goods by traders for *hajj* pilgrims, but had transformed in late nineteenth-century East Africa into a banking system where the store was responsible for any damages, but also retained rights to charge or invest the goods in return for this service. F. O. Karstedt, "Beiträge zur Inderfrage in Deutsch-Ostafrika," *Koloniale Monatsblätter* (August 1913): 344–45. Africans in Dar es Salaam, particularly those from up-country, deposited boxes of

clothing at Indian shops for safekeeping and credit. Loss of paperwork or death of depositor led to bitter complaints by Africans, but this informal arrangement continued throughout the interwar period, despite efforts to regulate the practice. *Kwetu*, June 1944; Orde-Brown to CS, 1 April 1931, TNA 19620/f.1; Brett to CS, 31 March 1933, TNA 19620/f.34; Leslie, *A Survey*, 142–43.

161. *Kwetu*, 25 June 1942. *Kumkabidhi* implies handing over through obligation, used in context of debt repayment.

162. Marshall Sahlins, *Stone Age Economics* (New York: Aldine, 1974), 193–96, cited in Parker Shipton, *The Nature of Entrustment: Intimacy, Exchange, and the Sacred in Africa* (New Haven, CT: Yale University Press, 2007), 26–27.

163. Prins, *Swahili-Speaking Peoples of Zanzibar*, 70; Baker, "Memorandum," 53–56.

164. It is unclear what role women had in food procurement—some participated in producing crops in peri-urban Dar es Salaam, but Baker also states that there was "a tendency on the part of the local housewife to disassociate herself entirely from financial matters and merely to demand that her husband shall feed and clothe her adequately." Baker, "Memorandum," 53–56.

165. African women unfortunately appear only as backward, clothes-hungry, and divorce-inclined parasites in the otherwise-rich social data of Baker's 1931 "Memorandum"; see especially 82–85.

166. *Tanganyika Standard*, 26 February 1949.

167. *Kwetu*, 31 July 1943.

168. Habib Omari Musa, interview by author, 16 August 1999.

169. Elias Amos Kisenge, "African Progress Is Retarded Because of Lack of Money," *Kwetu*, November 1941, English translation by T. L. M. Marealle.

170. *Kwetu*, November 1941. See also Westcott, "East African Radical," 96–97. Fiah warmed to Indians after the war, seeking their patronage to keep *Kwetu* afloat. *Kwetu*, May 1946 and January–February 1947.

171. Elias Amos Kisenge, "Tulalamike mpaka tusikiwe," *Kwetu*, 26 December 1941.

172. "Money and Its Effects upon the African," *Kwetu*, 7 September 1941.

173. Letter of A. B. Amri and editorial response, *Kwetu*, 26 December 1941.

174. In 1931, government employed 5,500 Africans; European and Asian households employed 3,500 Africans; and 3,000 were employed by private firms, petty trading, agriculture, or fishing. Baker, "Memorandum," 86–88, 59.

175. Shabani Gonga, interview by author, 5 October 1998.

176. Fryer to PC Eastern, 19 August 1931, TNA 61/167/A/f.25.

177. *Tanganyika Standard*, 1 June 1935.

178. Iddi Said Gure, interview by author, 2 January 1999.

179. Molohan, 1942 Labour Office Report, DSM TA, TNA 61/100/A/II/f.83&95; 1943 Uzaramo DAR, TNA 61/3/XVIII/A/f.11; Janet Bujra, *Serving Class: Masculinity and the Feminisation of Domestic Service in Tanzania* (Edinburgh: Edinburgh University Press, 2000), 192n9.

180. Baker to CS, 3 September 1941, TNA 30134/f.1.

181. Bujra, *Serving Class*, 57–59.

182. Revington, 1941 Dar es Salaam Annual Report, TNA 61/3/XVI/A/f.7. See minute of Molohan, 11 March 1943, TNA 28685/f.7; Baker to CS, 16 July 1942, TNA 28685/f.15; Pike, "Native Affairs Report," 5 June 1939, TNA 61/207/II/f.230.

183. Memorandum of meeting with Personal Servants Association, 23 January 1944, TNA 61/679/1/f.15.

184. Tsuruta, "Urban-Rural Relationships," 69n12.

185. Sayers, *The Handbook of Tanganyika*, 470; Jackson to Stanley, 29 November 1944, TNA 32744/f.17; Leslie, *A Survey*, 84–85.

186. Yunus Daud Mwinyikambi, interview by author, 29 December 1998.

187. Baker, "Memorandum," 98; Anthony, "Culture and Society," 147–49. See James R. Brennan, "Democratizing Cinema and Censorship in Tanzania, 1920–1980," *International Journal of African Historical Studies* 38 (2005): 481–511.

188. Mascarenhas, "Urban Development," 59.

189. Sayers, *The Handbook of Tanganyika*, 474; Bates, "Tanganyika under British Administration," 482; Alexander, *Tanganyika Memories*, 114–15.

190. Katharina Zöller, "Islamische Feste im kolonialen Dar es Salaam (1905–1938)" (MA thesis, Humboldt University, 2009), 69.

191. J. K. Chande, *A Knight in Africa: Journey from Bukene* (Manotick, Ontario: Penumbria Press, 2008), 44.

192. *Tanganyika Standard*, 17 October 1941 and 18 September 1942.

193. Chande, *A Knight in Africa*, 44; *Tanganyika Standard*, 12 July 1958.

194. Chiponde to CS, 23 August 1921, TNA 3246; Iliffe, *A Modern History*, 265–68.

195. Maxwell to CS, 10 December 1921, CO 691/54/f.477.

196. Charles Strachey, "Tanganyika: Education of Native Africans for Government Service," 9 February 1923, CO 691/58/f.447.

197. Hollis to Churchill, 1 March 1922, CO 691/54/f.517. Acting Governor Hollis supported recruiting Indians only days after Governor Byatt had endorsed the Maxwell Committee recommendations. Byatt to Churchill, 22 February 1922, CO 691/54/f.473; and Hollis to Churchill, 4 March 1922, CO 691/54/f.577.

198. Desai to CS, 14 February 1922, CO 691/54/f.582.

199. Tanganyika Railways Asiatic Employees to Railways Manager, 16 June 1924, CO 691/82/f.309. Indian railway workers were contracted labor and not included in the Asian Civil Service Association.

200. Quotation from note by Cameron on Mumford Memorandum, 24 December 1927, TNA 19390/II, cited in Andreas Eckert, *Herrschen und Verwalten: Afrikanische Bürokraten, Staatliche Ordnung und Politik in Tanzania, 1920–1970* (Munich: Oldenbourg, 2007), 66. On African education policy in this period, see ibid., 63–79.

201. Rivers-Smith to CS, 24 July 1925, TNA 7017, cited in Eckert, *Herrschen und Verwalten*, 71.

202. Chiponde to CS, 6 April 1925, TNA 3246; Scott to Amery, 10 September 1927, CO 691/93/f.9.

203. Madalito to Cameron, 11 September 1925, CO 691/93/f.22.

204. Madalito to Cameron, 11 January 1926, CO 691/93/f.31.

205. Viswanathan to Cunliffe-Lister, 13 February 1934, CO 691/135/f.5; TACSA to Cunliffe-Lister, 20 March 1934, CO 691/135/f.11.

206. *Tanganyika Opinion*, 16 February and 20 April 1934. See also Eckert, *Herrschen und Verwalten*, 80–87.

207. *Tanganyika Opinion*, 13 February 1934.

208. *1935 Annual Report of Police Administration*, 4, CO 736/15.

209. Donald Cameron, *My Tanganyika Service and some Nigeria* (London: Allen and Unwin, 1939), 128.

210. In 1935 Zone I had 34 night patrols; Zone II, 28; and Zone III, 17. Police Commissioner to CS, 8 November 1935, TNA 21963/I/f.24.

211. Martin Bystrom, *Letters from Africa* (Rock Island: Augustana Book Concern, 1951), 120.

212. *Dar es Salaam Times*, 7 October 1922.

213. Dar es Salaam DAR 1931, TNA library; *Tanganyika Herald*, 4 August 1931; *Dar es Salaam Times*, 19 March 1921; *1925 Police Administration Report*, 38, CO 736/5; ibid. (1926), 50, CO 736/6; *Tanganyika Standard*, 7 September 1935.

214. *Tanganyika Herald*, 4 February 1939.

215. Burton, *African Underclass*, 133.

216. *Tanganyika Herald*, 5 January 1932; ibid., 4 September and 20 November 1937.

217. *Tanganyika Herald*, 25 March 1939.

218. *Africa Sentinel*, 1 March 1942, in TNA 21963/II/f.5.

219. *Tanganyika Herald*, 4 June 1932.

220. *Tanganyika Herald*, 18 December 1929; Police Commissioner to CS, 24 December 1929, TNA 13986.

221. *Tanganyika Herald*, 8 November 1937; Police Commissioner to CS, 13 November 1937, TNA 21963/I/f.47. See especially Burton, *African Underclass*, 179–81.

222. *Tanganyika Herald*, 15 January 1937.

223. Letter of Idi Salim, *Kwetu*, 13 April 1938.

224. Masud bin Seleman to PC Eastern, 7 December 1934, TNA 61/146/f.351.

225. Richa Nagar, "Communal Discourses, Marriage, and the Politics of Gendered Social Boundaries among South Asian Immigrants in Tanzania," *Gender, Place and Culture* 5, no. 2 (1998): 127–30. Gender ratios in Dar es Salaam between Indian men and women shifted from 3,294 men and 1,682 women in 1931, or a 196:100 ratio; to 8,718 men and 6,881 women in 1948, or a 127:100 ratio. Baker, "Memorandum," 78; *Report on the Census of the Non-Native Population Taken on the Night of 25th February, 1948* (Dar es Salaam: Government Printer, 1948), 58. The 1948 figures include the surrounding Uzaramo District.

226. *Kwetu*, 8 June 1939.

227. The humorous yet bitter effect of the following words from an Indian cinema usher to an African customer is difficult to translate: "Ve kabila gani? . . . Senzi hapana ruksa, Zungu dio, Gova dio, Hindi dio, Bonyani dio

hata Arab katoona ile koti defu na jari zunguka singoni dio." Letter of Sulemani Bajuma, loc. cit.

228. Iliffe, *A Modern History*, 375.

229. Abbasi Athmani, "Ujinga wetu hawishi," *Kwetu*, 14 January 1938.

230. Letter of Mbucho Songoro, *Kwetu*, 13 April 1938; letter of W. C. Gondwe, *Kwetu*, 14 January 1939.

231. *Tanganyika Herald*, 20 October 1934.

232. Letter of Saidi Kholbon & Ahmed Hussein, *Kwetu*, 13 April 1938.

233. This is a summary of Brennan, "Nation, Race, and Urbanization," 139–45.

CHAPTER 3: POSING THE URBAN QUESTION

Epigraphs: A. H. Pike, "Report on Native Affairs in Dar es Salaam Township," 5 June 1939, TNA 61/207/II/f.231; and *Kwetu*, 14 January 1939.

1. These figures are based on: J. M. L. Kironde, "The Evolution of the Land Use Structure of Dar es Salaam" (PhD thesis, University of Nairobi, 1994), 81; R. H. Sabot, *Economic Development and Urban Migration: Tanzania, 1900–1971* (Oxford: Clarendon Press, 1979), 44–50; Deborah F. Bryceson, "A Century of Food Supply," in *Feeding African Cities: Studies in Regional Social History*, ed. Jane I. Guyer (Manchester: Manchester University Press, 1987), 194; Aili Mari Tripp, *Changing the Rules: the Politics of Liberalization and the Informal Economy in Tanzania* (Berkeley: University of California Press, 1997), 52–53; Richard Stren, *Urban Inequality and Housing Policy in Tanzania* (Berkeley: Institute for International Studies, 1975), 54–55; Karl Vorlaufer, *Dar es Salaam* (Hamburg: Deutches Institut für Afrika-Forschung, 1973), 21.

2. Nicholas J. Westcott, "The Impact of the Second World War in Tanganyika" (PhD diss., Cambridge University, 1982), 322.

3. Frederick Cooper, *Decolonization and African Society: The Labor Question in French and British Africa* (Cambridge: Cambridge University Press, 1996); Lisa Lindsay, *Working with Gender: Wage Labor and Social Change in Southwestern Nigeria* (Portsmouth, NH: Heinemann, 2003); Timothy Sander Oberst, "Cost of Living and Strikes in British Africa, c.1939–1948: Imperial Policy and the Impact of the Second World War" (PhD diss., Columbia University, 1991).

4. For examples from Libreville and Zanzibar, see Jeremy Rich, *A Workman Is Worthy of His Meat: Food and Colonialism in the Gabon Estuary* (Lincoln: University of Nebraska Press, 2007), 86–87, 102–4; Laura Fair, *Pastimes and Politics: Culture, Community, and Identity in Post-Abolition Urban Zanzibar, 1890–1945* (Athens: Ohio University Press, 2001), 46–51.

5. Literature on Europe stresses how expanding state responsibility over consumption has shaped political culture: Susan Pedersen, *Family, Dependence, and the Origins of the Welfare State* (Cambridge: Cambridge University Press, 1993), and Peter Gurney, *Co-operative Culture and the Politics of Consumption in England, 1870–1930* (Manchester: Manchester University Press, 1996).

6. Oberst, "Cost of Living," 202.

7. Robert Bates, *Markets and States in Tropical Africa: The Political Basis of Agricultural Policies* (Berkeley: University of California Press, 2005), chapter 2.

8. My definition is a descriptive one that focuses narrowly on colonial state regulation of exchange, rather than on a wider range of economic rights, which the analytical term "entitlement" evokes, most famously discussed in Amartya Sen, *Poverty and Famines: An Essay on Entitlement and Deprivation* (Oxford: Oxford University Press, 1983).

9. Cooper, *Decolonization*, 111.

10. Tanganyika [W. E. H. Scupham], *Report of Commission Appointed to Enquire into Tanga Disturbances* (Dar es Salaam: Government Printer, 1940), 20–21.

11. Frederick Cooper, *On the African Waterfront: Urban Disorder and the Transformation of Work in Colonial Mombasa* (New Haven, CT: Yale University Press, 1987), 60.

12. Ibid., 274–75.

13. Cooper, *Decolonization*, 238.

14. Monthly Intelligence Bulletin, 31 July 1934, KV 4/276; Westcott, "The Impact," 38.

15. Elmer Danielson, *Forty Years with Christ in Tanzania* (New York: Lutheran Church in America, 1977), 86.

16. *Kwetu*, 7 June 1942; Jackson to Stanley, 1 June 1943, CO 968/73/5/f.133.

17. "Notes on Mr. McCleery's Report," n.a., n.d. [*ca.* 1939], TNA 26177.

18. 1941 Temeke DAR, TNA 61/3/XVI/I/f.15.

19. Deborah F. Bryceson, *Liberalizing Tanzania's Food Trade: Public and Private Faces of Urban Marketing Policy, 1939–1988* (London: James Currey, 1993), 38–39; Bryceson, "Food Supply," 154–202.

20. Dawkins to PC Eastern, 10 January 1928, TNA 61/295/I/f.27; DO Dar es Salaam to PC Eastern, 18 December 1929, TNA 61/295/I/f.21; Baker, "Memorandum," 53–60; DO Dar es Salaam to PC Eastern, 31 October 1938, TNA 25912; Westcott, "The Impact," 40–41.

21. General Notices 217 and 268 of 1939 and 365 of 1940; Ordinance 4 of 1940; minute of H.S. to CS, 28 October 1939, TNA 27592/f.3.

22. Nicholas J. Westcott, "The Impact of the Second World War on Tanganyika, 1939-49," in *Africa and the Second World War*, ed. David Killingray and Richard Rathbone (New York: St. Martin's Press, 1986), 144. All other references to Westcott refer to his unpublished dissertation.

23. Werner Biermann, *The Tanzanian Economy, 1920–1985* (Münster: Lit Verlag, 1988), 70.

24. Westcott, "The Impact," 165–67.

25. Tanganyika, *Tanganyika Territory Trade Report for 1946* (Dar es Salaam: Government Printers, 1947), introduction.

26. Westcott, "The Impact," 49.

27. Stanton to Secretary of State, 11 July 1944, NARA RG 59 862S.5017/7-1144.

28. PC Tanga to CS, 11 April 1940, TNA 28594/f.1; Secretariat Circular, 27 July 1940, TNA 28594/f.19.

29. Minute of Railways General Manager to CS, 23 May 1940, TNA 28594.

30. Minute of Director of Public Works to CS, 12 June 1940, TNA 28594.

31. M. J. B. Molohan, "Unemployment and Wage Rates in Dar es Salaam," enclosed in Molohan to LC, 27 September 1941, TNA 61/443/1/f.7.

32. Report of Labour Board, 3 March 1942, TNA 30271/f.12.

33. Bryceson, "A Century of Food Supply," 174–75; Karim Janmohamed, "A History of Mombasa, c. 1895–1939" (PhD diss., Northwestern University, 1978), 446–47. Rent ran a distant second to food in terms of household expenditures in Dar es Salaam between 1938 and 1956, never accounting for more than 16 percent of household outlays, although such figures disguise advance fee "key money" and other real total costs. See John Campbell, "Race, Class and Community in Colonial Dar es Salaam," in *Gender, Family and Work in Tanzania*, ed. Colin Creighton and C. K. Omari (Aldershot: Ashgate, 2000), 33.

34. Labour Board minutes, 23–24 January 1942, TNA 30271/I/f.11; Clerk of Council to CS, 18 May 1942, TNA 30271/f.19; *Tanganyika Standard*, 25 June 1942.

35. M. J. B. Molohan, "Report of Enquiry into Wages and Cost of Living," 22 October 1942, TNA 30598.

36. Revington, 1941 Uzaramo DAR, TNA 61/3/XVI/A/f.7.

37. Westcott, "The Impact," 130–35.

38. Minute of Baker to A.S., 23 June 1943, TNA 30602/I/f.39.

39. Molohan, "Report of Enquiry," 22 October 1942, TNA 30598; Molohan, 1942 Labour Office Report, Dar es Salaam Township, TNA 61/100/A/II/f.95.

40. African Employees of Tanganyika Boating Company to CS, 22 May 1943, TNA 540/16/25.

41. LC to Labour Office, 12 September 1943, TNA 540/16/25. See also Oberst, "Cost of Living," 277–80.

42. 1943 Uzaramo DAR, TNA 61/3/XVIII/A/f.10.

43. ECB minutes, 12 April 1943, TNA 31555/0.

44. Ibid.; CS to Governor, 20 April 1943, TNA 31543/f.2; Uzaramo Report for May 1943, TNA 61/7/A/f.27; *Tanganyika Herald*, 15 April 1943; Westcott, "The Impact," 176; 1943 Uzaramo DAR, TNA 61/3/XVIII/A/f.13.

45. Uzaramo Report for June 1943, TNA 61/7/A/f.29; Food Distribution Committee minutes, 2 May 1944, TNA 540/27/13/4; Westcott, "The Impact," 288; ECB minutes, 4 January 1944, enclosed in Crawford to CS, 13 January 1944, TNA 61/443/1/f.42.

46. Molohan, 1943 Uzaramo DAR, TNA 61/3/XVIII/A/10; Political Kisarawe to Political Uzaramo Dar es Salaam, 12 July 1944, TNA 540/7/20/0/f.27.

47. *Tanganyika Standard*, 19 July 1945.

48. William E. Smith, *Nyerere of Tanzania* (Nairobi: Transafrica Publishers, 1974), 47–48.

49. Fair, *Pastimes and Politics*, 73; Jeremy Prestholdt, *Domesticating the World: African Consumerism and the Genealogies of Globalization* (Berkeley: University of California Press, 2008), 57.

50. *Kwetu*, February 1945.

51. Charlotte Leubuscher, *Tanganyika Territory* (London: Oxford University Press, 1944), 128; *Tanganyika Standard*, 29 April 1933; Leubuscher, *Tanganyika Territory*, 123. For an empire-level view, see Oberst, "Cost of Living," 81–92.

52. See comparative price list in TNA 30271/Annexure B; and Westcott, "The Impact," 330.

53. *Hansard*, 9 December 1942, 23; minute of Baker to CS, 30 September 1942, TNA 10849/863.

54. Molohan, "Unemployment and Wage Rates," 27 September 1941, TNA 61/443/1/f.8; Baker to CS, 19 December 1941, TNA 30271/I/f.1.

55. 1942 Uzaramo DAR, TNA 61/3/XVII/A/f.7.

56. Westcott, "The Impact," 167–69.

57. R. H. Mtandiko to PC Eastern, 2 June 1943, TNA 61/146A/f.133.

58. 1944 Uzaramo DAR, TNA 61/3/A/f.11; DSM TA minutes, 19 October 1944; Information Officer to Editor, *Kwetu*, 24 February 1948, TNA 23754/IV/f.204.

59. CS Tanganyika to Ministry of War Transport, Mombasa, 8 October 1944, TNA 591/16403/f.11.

60. Figures taken from *East Africa and Rhodesia*, 1 February 1947.

61. *Tanganyika Opinion*, 22 April 1937.

62. Kanji to CS, 20 June 1941, TNA 27313/I/f.6; minute of PC Eastern to CS, 5 July 1941, TNA 27313/I; Gulamhusein Brothers et al. to CS, 3 December 1941, TNA 27313/I/f.28. The 1941 rent restriction ordinance limited rental increases to 10 percent of the rent paid on 3 September 1939; enforcement depended on parties bringing disputes to rent control boards. The Property Owners Association successfully lobbied to replace the ordinance in 1950 with a law that allowed landlords to collect annual rents up to 50 percent of building value for prewar properties, and annual rents up to 12.5 percent of construction and ground rent costs for later properties. Ordinance 26 of 1941; *Tanganyika Standard*, 21 November 1941; Rent Restriction Board minutes for 1943–45 in TNA 61/750/f.2; Walji to Rent Bill Chairman, 2 October 1950, TNA 41222/f.20; *Tanganyika Standard*, 22 September 1950 and 12 June 1951; Philip Biron, "Dar es Salaam Rent Restriction Board," 4 April 1952, TNA 30595/II/f.607A.

63. DC Dar es Salaam to PC Eastern, 6 April 1945, TNA 61/750/f.1.

64. Sabot, *Economic Development*, 34.

65. Granville St. John Orde-Browne, *Report by Orde Browne, upon Labour in Tanganyika Territory* (London: H.M.S.O., 1926); Orde-Browne, *Labour Conditions in East Africa* (London: H.M.S.O., 1946); Cooper, *On the African Waterfront*, 116–18. Orde-Brown had been an early advocate of a pass system and repatriation of the urban unemployed, but for him this was a social problem of "detribalization" and adopting urban "evil ways," and not an economic problem. Orde-Browne, *Report*, 58–61. His influence among officials in African colonies had noticeably waned by 1945. Oberst, "Cost of Living," 263. By 1946, however, even Colonial Office skeptics like Sidney Caine were beginning to "define urban Africa as a distinct domain and to think about it in social terms." Cooper, *Decolonization*, 209.

66. See Luise White, *The Comforts of Home: Prostitution in Colonial Nairobi* (Chicago: University of Chicago Press, 1990); Timothy Scarnecchia, "Poor Women and Nationalist Politics: Alliances and Fissures in the Formation of a Nationalist Movement in Salisbury, Rhodesia, 1950–56," *Journal of African History* 37 (1996): 283–310; and T. Dunbar Moodie, *Going for Gold: Men, Mines, and Migration* (Berkeley: University of California Press, 1994).

67. A. H. Pike, "Report on Native Affairs in Dar es Salaam Township," 5 June 1939, TNA 61/207/II/f.242.

68. Minute of PC Eastern to CS, 12 July 1940, TNA 28594. Also Baker to CS, 21 May 1940, TNA 28685/f.6.

69. Burton, *African Underclass*, 101–2.

70. Andrew Burton, "'The Eye of Authority': 'Native' Taxation, Colonial Governance and Resistance in Inter-war Tanganyika," *Journal of Eastern African Studies* 2 (2008): 75, 85.

71. Westcott, "The Impact," 289; Westcott, *Daily News*, 21 December 1979; Burton, "The Eye of Authority," 86–87.

72. Extract of minute of Scupham to CS, 2 May 1940, TNA 28685/f.2. Government had previously thought costs of repatriation too high to justify executing them en masse. Under Township Rule 136, only eighty-two Africans were removed from Dar es Salaam from 1938 to 1940. Hutt to Twining, 24 June 1952, TNA 21616/III/f.403.

73. *Kwetu*, November 1941.

74. Burton, *African Underclass*, 105. For a full account, see ibid., 102–5.

75. Ag. Municipal Secretary to CS, 27 August 1941, TNA 30134/f.1A.

76. Secretary ECB to CS, 13 January 1944, TNA 28685/f.19.

77. Jackson to Stanley, 26 February 1944, CO 691/191/8/f.3.

78. Minute of Wild, 29 February 1944, CO 691/191/8.

79. J. P. Moffett, *Handbook of Tanganyika* (Dar es Salaam: Government Printer, 1958), 120–21.

80. Director of Man Power to CS, 11 December 1939, TNA 27427/f.46.

81. Burton, *African Underclass*, 105–11.

82. *Hansard*, 27 April 1944, 156–57. See especially Burton, *Underclass*, chapters 8-9.

83. Nickol, September 1948 Social Welfare Report, TNA 38616/1A.

84. "Native Policy: Detribalized Natives and Natives in Towns," February 1933, TNA 11601.

85. John Iliffe, *A Modern History of Tanganyika* (Cambridge: Cambridge University Press, 1979), 375.

86. CS to Presidents, Ismailia Council, Hindu Mandal, Sunni Jamat, Bohora Community, Ithnasheri Community, Anjuman Islamia, Goan Community, Sikh Temple, Sinhalese Association, and Arab Association, 15 April 1943, TNA 31555/f.7.

87. *Tanganyika Herald*, 8 and 12 May 1943, TNA 31555.

88. *Africa Sentinel*, 9 May 1943, TNA 31555/f.42.

89. Minute of R. L. to Y. H., 31 July 1945, TNA 31665/I.

90. ECB minutes, 12 April 1943, TNA 31555/o; PC Eastern to CS, 12 April 1943, TNA 31555/o/f.1.

91. *Tanganyika Gazette*, 7 May 1943; *Economic Control Board Bulletin*, 24 November 1944.

92. *Tanganyika Standard*, 12 February 1944.

93. Kanyama Chiume, *Autobiography of Kanyama Chiume* (London: Panaf, 1982), 28.

94. Donald C. Flatt, "Man of Four Worlds: A Story of Mission in Three Continents," 72, Pa 131, ELCA.

95. *Kwetu*, 29 February 1944.

96. Mbaramaki et al. to CS, 1 May 1944, TNA 10849/962/f.18.

97. Letter of "Blackest African," *Tanganyika Standard*, 10 September 1945.

98. 1943 Eastern PAR.

99. Saidi Pazi et al. to CS, 16 February 1944, TNA 10849/962/f.1.

100. Eastern PAR, 1946.

101. Ramadhani Mwaruka, *Masimulizi juu ya Uzaramo* (London: Macmillan, 1965), 143.

102. Westcott, "The Impact," 227; Bryceson, "A Century of Food Supply," 169; *Economic Control Board Bulletin*, 7 December 1945.

103. "Mabama African Association," *Askari*, 3 October 1946.

104. Battershill to Cohen, 10 April 1946, CO 691/192/15/f.38; *Tanganyika Standard*, 4 April, 2 and 28 May 1946.

105. Letter of Sembuyagy, *Tanganyika Standard*, 9 May 1946.

106. *Tanganyika Standard*, 28 June 1946.

107. *Tanganyika Standard*, 19 July, 10 and 13 August 1946.

108. Westcott, "The Impact," 310–11; *Tanganyika Standard*, 5, 7, and 10 September 1946.

109. Letter of "Starving African," *Tanganyika Standard*, 9 September 1946.

110. Letter of "Blackest African," *Tanganyika Standard*, 10 September 1946.

111. *Hansard*, 27 April 1944, 147–50; *Kwetu*, 15 July 1939.

112. Wilson to Municipal Secretary, 29 October 1945, TNA 29631/II/f.201A.

113. Letter of S. Asmani, *Kwetu*, 24 September 1942.

114. *Tanganyika Standard*, 10 September 1946.

115. Page-Jones to CS, 25 September 1947, TNA 591/16756. I thank John Iliffe for lending me his notes on this file.

116. Mohamed Said, *Life and Times of Abdulwahid Sykes (1924–1968): The Untold Story of the Muslim Struggle against British Colonialism in Tanganyika* (London: Minerva Press, 1998), 49.

117. 1947 Eastern PAR; DC Dar es Salaam to PC Eastern, 23 October 1948, TNA 540/7/20/o/f.72.

118. *Tanganyika Standard*, 14 February 1950.

119. *Tanganyika Standard*, 2 April 1949.

120. 1947 Uzaramo DAR, TNA 540/1/4/B; *Tanganyika Herald*, 29 September 1947; PC Eastern to DC Uzaramo et al., 3 August 1948, TNA 540/28/27/f.503; *Tanganyika Standard*, 23 September 1947.

121. Tanganyika, *Report of Committee on Rising Costs* (Dar es Salaam: Government Printers, 1951), 13.

122. Moffett, *Handbook of Tanganyika*, 122; *Tanganyika Opinion*, 26 September 1947; minute of Hoope to CS, 22 March 1945, TNA 32982.

123. Molohan and Pike memorandum, 22 July 1943, enclosed in Jackson to Stanley, 27 November 1943, TNA 24387/II/f.10. Medical officers later declared 68.9 percent of Zone III's 3,661 inspected rooms overcrowded. *Tanganyika Standard*, 22 May 1947.

124. In 1943, government drafted plans to create 2,000 residential plots for an African pilot housing scheme, but land was not acquired until 1947; only 1,762 of approximately 5,000 planned houses were constructed between 1946 and 1956. Ibid.; "African Housing, Dar es Salaam," n.a., n.d. [*ca.* 1948], DSM Extra-Provincial District Book, TNA; Twining to Gorell-Barnes, 7 November 1953, CO 822/589/f.5; A. J. Dixon, "The Evolution of Indirect Rule and the Development of Rural and Urban Local Government in Tanganyika During the British Administration, 1940–1961" (BA thesis, Oxford University, 1969), 137–38.

125. J. A. K. Leslie, *A Survey of Dar es Salaam* (London: Oxford University Press, 1963), 173, 176–77, 264–67, 275–80. Of Dar es Salaam's surveyed Indian residents in Kariakoo, 96 percent had cement floors, 57 percent piped water, and 77 percent electricity; for Africans overall, figures were 16 percent, 2 percent, and 2 percent, respectively. Leslie, appendix to unpublished "Survey of Dar es Salaam" (1957), 44, 54, 72, and 77.

126. John Logan and Harvey Molotch, *Urban Fortunes: The Political Economy of Place* (Berkeley: University of California Press, 2007), 29.

127. E. C. Baker memorandum on Dar es Salaam housing conditions, 5 September 1943, TNA 31751/f.2.

128. Leslie, *A Survey*, 153, 155, 168, 261.

129. Adolfo Mascarenhas, "Urban Development in Dar es Salaam" (MA thesis, UCLA, 1966), 90.

130. DSM TA minutes, 26 January 1940, 15 November 1940, & 14 November 1941; Director of Intelligence to PC Eastern, 14 November 1944, TNA 61/4/14/f.2.

131. DC Uzaramo to Municipal Secretary, Dar es Salaam, 22 August 1947, TNA 61/255/f.45.

132. Pike, "Development of African Areas of Dar es Salaam Township," n.d. [*ca.* June 1944], TNA 61/643/3/f.37.

133. Wilson to PC Eastern, 12 February 1945, TNA 61/4/15/f.1; Director of Intelligence to PC Eastern, 27 January 1945, TNA 61/4/14/f.8.

134. Minute of Nayar to CS, 21 November 1949, TNA 32697/I. Emphasis in original.

135. Said, *Life and Times*, 92–93.

136. Minute of Page-Downs to CS, 13 March 1947, TNA 35905; minute of LC to CS, 2 April 1947, ibid.

137. *Dunia*, 25 May 1944, TNA 61/750/2/f.52.

138. *Dunia*, 27 October 1944, in Director of Intelligence to PC Eastern, 30 October 1944, TNA 61/4/14/f.1.

139. *Dunia*, 20 February 1945, TNA 61/4/4/f.20.

140. Letter of "Savage," *Tanganyika Standard*, 15 February 1945.

141. *Dunia*, 16 and 20 February and 7 July 1945, TNA 61/4/14/f.18-26.

142. Minute to PC Eastern, December 1945, TNA 61/4/14.

143. TAGSA to CS, 5 February 1945, TNA 61/4/2/II/f.2.

144. *Dunia*, 14 April 1945, TNA 61/4/14/f.25.

145. Letter of A. W. Sykes, *Tanganyika Standard*, 8 May 1947.

146. Daisy Sykes Buruku, "The Townsman: Kleist Sykes," in *Modern Tanzanians*, ed. John Iliffe (Nairobi: EAHP, 1973), 109.

147. *Tanganyika Standard*, 26 April and 19 September 1947.

148. Notes of meeting between A. B. Cohen and members of the Committee of the Dar es Salaam African Association, 28 May 1951, enclosed in Hutt to Cohen, 23 June 1951, CO 822/644/f.1.

149. Hutchinson notes, 3 June 1946, in PC Conference Minutes, UDSM East Africana Collection; Municipal Secretary to Baluchi Association, 17 May 1946, TNA 540/11/12/f.17; PC Eastern to CS, 2 March 1945, TNA 61/4/4/f.21.

150. PC Eastern to DC Uzaramo, 19 November 1948, TNA 61/255/f.97; DC Dar es Salaam to Land Officer and PC Eastern, 8 November 1948, TNA 61/255/f.95. Exceptions to the ban were made in extraordinary circumstances.

151. Dar es Salaam DAR, 1950, TNA 540/1/4/B/f.4.

152. Dar es Salaam DAR, 1951, TNA 540/1/4/B/f.5.

153. The only areas with a greater Indian population percentage were the Central Commercial Center (11,589 people, or 85 percent); Chang'ombe Estate (414, or 79 percent); Upanga (876, or 29 percent); and Seaview (282, or 19 percent). Census figures for 1952 in Burton, *African Underclass*, 209. Kariakoo's Indian population had risen to 6,000 and its Arab population to 2,000 by 1956, but this marked a proportional decline, for Indians and Arabs totaled only 12 percent and 4 percent, respectively, of Kariakoo's overall population. Leslie, *A Survey*, 171.

154. EACFIN, 5 January 1951, CO 537/7218/f.1.

155. 1951 Dar es Salaam DAR, TNA 540/1/4/B/f.5.

156. Frederick Cooper, "Urban Space, Industrial Time, and Wage Labor in Africa," in *Struggle for the City: Migrant Labor, Capital, and the State in Urban Africa*, ed. Frederick Cooper (Beverly Hills: Sage, 1983), 7–50; Cooper, *On the African Waterfront*, 247–78.

157. Norman Pearson, "Trade Unionist on Safari," n.d. (*ca.* 1947), RH MSS Afr.s.394, 184.

158. Yunus Daud Mwinyikambi, interview by author, 29 December 1998.

159. Letter of "Mwenyeji," *Kwetu*, 7 June 1942.

160. Question of Chief Abdiel Shangali, *Hansard*, 7 March 1946, 130.

161. *Kwetu*, 1 August 1941.

162. Letter of "Africans," *Tanganyika Standard*, 15 January 1944. In Tanganyika's

Local Service, Asians were regularly hired at Grade II, and Africans at Grade III. Freeston to Moyne, 26 February 1942, CO 691/181/15/f.1.

163. Cooper, *Decolonization*, 445–46.

164. Iliffe, *A Modern History*, 396; TAGSA representatives meeting, 18 August 1952, CO 822/660/f.3; Ally Sykes, interview by Nestor Luanda, 29 February 1996. TAGSA succeeded the defunct TTACSA in the late 1940s and numbered three thousand members by 1952. Sykes was rusticated for confronting P. K. G. Nayar, an Asian civil servant unionist who recruited hundreds of civil servants from southern India after the war.

165. Overview of staff rates (*ca.* 1943), TNA 30271/f.35.

166. Hamidu Bisanga, "From War Books to Sandals," *Sunday News*, 4 July 1976.

167. DC Dar es Salaam to Chief Mechanical Engineer, 13 November 1943, TNA 540/16/1/f.49; Molohan, 1943 Uzaramo DAR, TNA 61/3/XVIII/A/f.10; Native Employees, Locomotive Department to Railways General Manager, 13 January 1940, TNA 10849/621/f.1.

168. Norman Pearson, "Trade Unionist on Safari," RH MSS Afr.s.394, 48–51.

169. Ibid.

170. Helps to CS, 29 November 1946, TNA 10849/1226/f.6. For an overview of petty commerce, see Leslie, *A Survey*, 133–37.

171. Msellem Abedi et al. to Member for Law and Order, 23 August 1952, TNA 10849/1848/f.1.

172. Burton, *African Underclass*, 158–61.

173. Helps to PC Eastern, 20 September 1944, TNA 61/390/I/f.92; Riddell, "Report of Native Sea Fishing Industry," 12 December 1948, enclosed in Maddocks to DC Dar es Salaam, 9 November 1951, TNA 540/6/7/f.1; Nickol, September 1948 Social Welfare Report, TNA 38616/1A.

174. There were between 300 and 400 *hamali* carts in Dar es Salaam by 1954, many belonging to Africans. *Tanganyika Standard*, 20 October 1954.

175. Said, *Life and Times*, 120; Mohamed Said, *Uamuzi wa busara wa Tabora* (Dar es Salaam: Abantu Publications, 2008), iv–viii; Mtoro Seif, interview by author, 4 January 1999; and Omari Ali Ndume, interview by author, 18 September 1998; Ally Kleist Sykes and Mohamed Said, "Under the Shadow of British Colonialism in Tanganyika," n.d., 76–77.

176. Susan Geiger, *TANU Women: Gender and Culture in the Making of Tanganyikan Nationalism* (Portsmouth, NH: Heinemann, 1997), 34–35.

177. Burton, *African Underclass*, 56, 282; Sabot, *Economic Development*, 90. Cf. 1930s Nairobi, with a female/male ratio ranging from 25:100 to 12:100, or 1950 Salisbury's 6:100 ratio. Burton, ibid., 56n42.

178. Cooper, *Decolonization*, 326–27, 356–57.

179. See Lindsay, *Working with Gender*, 4–8, 53–76.

180. Tim Harris, *Donkey's Gratitude: Twenty Two years in the Growth of a New African Nation—Tanzania* (Edinburgh: Pentland Press, 1992), 287.

181. Ahmed Seifu Salum Mponda, interview by author, 22 September 1998.

182. Westcott, "The Impact," 291; Justin Willis, "Unpretentious Bars: Munici-

pal Monopoly and Independent Drinking in Colonial Dar es Salaam," in *Dar es Salaam: Histories from an Emerging African Metropolis*, ed. James R. Brennan, Andrew Burton, and Yusuf Lawi (Dar es Salaam: Mkuki na Nyota, 2007), 168–70; Burton, *African Underclass*, 154–58.

183. *Kwetu*, 6 December 1942.

184. *Kwetu*, 9 January 1944; Westcott, "The Impact," 292; Leslie, *A Survey*, 232–37; Burton, *African Underclass*, 56; Baker, "Memorandum," 83–84. See also Geiger, *TANU Women*, 35–38. Female Haya migrants pioneered similar work patterns in Nairobi; see White, *The Comforts of Home*, 103–25.

185. "Sanitary Survey of Dar es Salaam, Tanganyika, 6 June 1942" by Colonel Leon Fox, 10. Unpublished typescript, National Library of Medicine, Bethesda, Maryland.

186. Scott to CS, 12 December 1944, TNA 20887/f.19.

187. *Kwetu*, 13 April 1938.

188. DC Dar es Salaam to PC Eastern, 18 June 1952, TNA 540/16/32/f.8.

189. John Iliffe, "A History of the Dockworkers of Dar es Salaam," *Tanzania Notes and Records* 71 (1970): 119–48.

190. All Cools Dar es Salaam to DO Dar es Salaam, 19 July 1939, TNA 61/679/f.6; Molohan to PC Eastern, 4 January 1940, TNA 25912; Cooper, *Decolonization*, 127–28.

191. Petition from African Wharfage Company workers, 1 January 1943, TNA 10849/879/f.1.

192. African Employees of Tanganyika Boating Company to CS, 22 May 1943, TNA 540/16/25; "Proceedings of Lighterage Dispute Tribunal," TNA 32594/f.1; Iliffe, "A History of the Dockworkers," 128–31; Westcott, "The Impact," 310.

193. Minute of Baker, 28 August 1943, TNA 61/679/f.32.

194. Ali Mohamed et al. to CS, 22 December 1943, TNA 61/679/1/f.8; PC Eastern to CS, 18 January 1944, TNA 61/679/1/f.9.

195. CS to LC, 9 March 1944, TNA 32594/f.3.

196. Iliffe, "A History of the Dockworkers," 131.

197. Pearson, "Trade Unionist," 221.

198. *Tanganyika Opinion*, 12 September 1947.

199. Abdulwahid Sykes first accepted decasualization despite considerable rank-and-file dissent; his successor, Salum Mohamed, threatened to break this pledge in 1949. Surridge to Creech Jones, 11 February 1950, CO 691/209/8/f.24; Iliffe, "A History of the Dockworkers," 134–38; Tanganyika Political Intelligence Summaries, July and August 1949, in CO 537/4717/f.3&5.

200. *Tanganyika Standard*, 9 February and 1–2 March 1948. Servant wages had increased from 40 percent to 70 percent over the period 1939–48.

201. Gerald F. Sayers, *The Handbook of Tanganyika* (London: Macmillan, 1930), 489; minute of Baker to CS, 18 January 1944, TNA 61/679/1; Director of Intelligence and Security to LC, 19 January 1945, TNA 61/679/1/f.28; Dar es Salaam Chamber of Commerce et al. to Member for Finance, 3 March 1948, TNA 32744/f.32.

202. *Tanganyika Standard*, 13 March 1948; letter of "Employer," *Tanganyika Standard*, 5 June 1948; Iliffe, *A Modern History*, 397–98; Janet Bujra, *Serving Class: Masculinity and the Feminisation of Domestic Service in Tanzania* (Edinburgh: Edinburgh University Press, 2000), 64; LC to CS, 1 September 1948, TNA 32744/f.55.

203. *Tanganyika Standard*, 14 April 1949.

204. Tanganyika Political Intelligence, September 1949, CO 537/4717/f.5.

205. This narrative is constructed from the following sources, many of which do not agree on vital details: "Industrial Dispute: Dar es Salaam Docks, February 1950," n.a., n.d., CO 691/209/42540; EACFIN, 1 February 1950, CO 537/5920/f.3; Deputy Governor to Creech Jones, 7 February 1950, CO 691/209/42540/f.15; Washhouse to Admiralty, 7 March 1950, ADM 1/21822; EACFIN, 1 April 1950, CO 537/5920/f.7; Bushwaller to DOS, 24 February 1950, NARA RG 84 File 560.3; *Hansard*, 7 June 1950, 132–35; Eastern PAR, 1950; Twining to Dowler, 6 February 1950, WO 276/133/f.22; EACFIN, 1 August 1950, CO 537/5920/f.16; LC memorandum, 21 May 1952, CO 892/11/4/f.7; *Tanganyika Standard*, 4 February 1950. Twenty-seven hundred workers were eventually registered. Molohan to Parry, 30 June 1950, CO 691/209/42540/f.30.

206. Tanganyika Police Special Branch Intelligence Summary, January 1950, WO 276/133.

207. EACFIN, 1 April 1950, CO 537/5920/f.7. Government later determined that the strike was led by Nyagatwa from Rufiji region, who made up more than one-quarter of the dock workforce and had "a notorious animosity to lawful authority." Dar es Salaam DAR, 1950, TNA 540/I/4/B.

208. John Iliffe, personal communication, 27 April 2004; Said, *Life and Times*, 70–77.

209. Stevedores and Dockworkers Union, which numbered fifteen hundred members until its dissolution, was officially deregistered by the High Court in June 1950 for embezzlement; the Motor Drivers and Commercial Transport Union financially collapsed that same year. Unsigned letter dated 22 February 1948, TNA 27306/f.22; EACFIN, 1 August 1950, CO 537/5920/f.16; Twining to Griffiths, 28 May 1951, CO 691/206/42065/f.115; EACFIN, 15 September 1950, CO 537/5920/f.19.

210. African Cooks to Tanganyika Government, 16 December 1952, TNA 38636/f.159.

211. Petition of Omali Asani et al., African Cooks to UN Visiting Mission, 16 September 1954, ARMS S-0720 Box 1 File 4, Acc. Dag 13/1.4.0.

212. Omari Hassani [Tanganyika Government Trade Union] to Queen Elizabeth, 10 September 1953, TNA 37681/5/25/f.11, in Ullrich Lohrmann, *Voices from Tanganyika: Great Britain, the United Nations and the Decolonization of a Trust Territory, 1946–1961* (Berlin: Lit Verlag, 2007), 523.

213. Tanganyika Intelligence Summary, May 1951, CO 537/7225/f.9; Barltrop to Twining, 28 September 1952, CO 822/660/f.1; Tanganyika Intelligence Summary, February 1951, CO 537/7225/f.3.

214. *East Africa Royal Commission, 1953–1955 Report* (London: HMSO, 1955), 158.

215. *1952 Town Planning Department Annual Report*, 7, CO 736/36.

CHAPTER 4: CONTINENTAL SHIFT

1. Jonathon Glassman, *War of Words, War of Stones: Racial Thought and Violence in Colonial Zanzibar* (Bloomington: Indiana University Press, 2011), 10.

2. John Iliffe, *A Modern History of Tanganyika* (Cambridge: Cambridge University Press, 1979), chapter 10.

3. See especially Alamin Mazrui and Ibrahim Noor Shariff, *The Swahili: Idiom and Identity of an African People* (Trenton: African World Press, 1994).

4. A survey carried out a decade later found that 41 percent of African men and 12 percent of African women were literate in Roman-script Swahili; 15 percent of men and 4 percent of women in Arabic-script Swahili, and 8 percent of men and 2 percent of women in English. J. A. K. Leslie, "Survey of Dar es Salaam" (1957), appendix A/1. For the newspaper culture of public reading and argument in Zanzibar, see Glassman, *War of Words*, 150–51.

5. Benedict Anderson, *Imagined Communities: Reflections on the Origin and Spread of Nationalism* (London: Verso, 1991), 44.

6. Heather Sharkey, *Living with Colonialism: Nationalism and Culture in the Anglo-Egyptian Sudan* (Berkeley: University of California Press, 2003), 3.

7. David Goldberg, *Racist Culture: Philosophy and the Politics of Meaning* (London: Blackwell, 1993); Goldberg, "The Semantics of Race," *Ethnic and Racial Studies* 15 (1992): 543–69.

8. Glassman, *War of Words*; Glassman, "Sorting out the Tribes: The Creation of Racial Identities in Colonial Zanzibar's Newspaper Wars," *Journal of African History* 41 (2000): 395–428; Glassman, "Slower Than a Massacre: The Multiple Sources of Racial Thought in Colonial Africa," *American Historical Review* 109 (2004): 720–54.

9. See, for example, the letter of R. M. R. MacRamson in *Kwetu*, 21 August 1938, which offers the aphorism, "kila makabila hukuza taifa lake na sisi *tusilegee*" or "each of the tribes glorifies its *taifa* [here, plainly, "race"] and *we should not grow faint*." Emphasis in original.

10. In one exception, African schoolboys at Dar es Salaam Central School were organized "according to tribes and groups of tribes" into four companies termed *mataifa*, each with subsections termed *makabila* for sports, drills, and general administration. *Annual Report of the Department of Education for 1925*, 28, CO 736/4.

11. J. Spencer Trimingham, *Islam in East Africa* (Oxford: Clarendon Press, 1964), 33.

12. The anthropologist A. H. J. Prins found in 1960s Lamu that *taifa* and *mji* (town) were used synonymously for "high-level, inclusive communities" in which the town of Lamu counted as one *taifa*, "the 'tribe' of the Wa-amu." The next level was *kabila*, which implied "more definite notions of descent"; both *taifa*

and *kabila* denoted shared descent and shared residence. A. H. J. Prins, *Didemic Lamu* (Groningen: Instituut voor Culturele Antropologie der Rijksuniversiteit, 1971), 6–7. See also Trimingham, *Islam in East Africa*, 144–45. In Mombasa, *taifa* described the twelve principal Swahili "tribes," as well as their two principal confederations, "three tribes" (*taifa thelatha*) and "nine tribes" (*taifa tisa*). John Middleton, *The World of the Swahili: An African Mercantile Civilization* (New Haven, CT: Yale University Press, 1992), 92. Lamu's "twelve tribes" were not *taifa* but *kabila*. The earliest *taifa* in Mombasa formed in the sixteenth and seventeenth centuries among urban refugees fleeing disorder along the northern Swahili coast; like *mji* (town), *taifa* "partakes of the nature of a political association ('a faction') with territorial overtones. . . . On the other hand it implies kinship ('a tribe')." The single constant was that *taifa* "was determined by patrilineal descent." F. J. Berg, "The Swahili Community of Mombasa, 1500–1900," *Journal of African History* 9 (1968): 35–56. *Kabila* lay curiously unused in Mombasa.

13. *Taifa* is a loanword from the Arabic طائفه meaning "group" or "faction." Contemporary Swahili lexiconists translate *taifa* first as "nation," and second alternatively as "race" and "tribe."

14. Philip Yale Nicholson, *Who Do We Think We Are? Race and Nation in the Modern World* (London: M. E. Sharpe, 1999).

15. Igor Kopytoff, "The Internal African Frontier: The Making of an African Political Culture," in *The African Frontier: The Reproduction of Traditional African Societies*, ed. Igor Kopytoff (Bloomington: Indiana University Press, 1987), 50, 57, cited in Glassman, *War of Words*, 11.

16. Jonathon Glassman, *Feasts and Riot: Revelry, Rebellion, and Popular Consciousness on the Swahili Coast, 1856–1888* (Portsmouth: Heinemann, 1995), 33–34, 61–62; Randall Pouwels, *Horn and Crescent: Cultural Change and Traditional Islam on the East African Coast, 800–1900* (Cambridge: Cambridge University Press, 1987), 128–30, 182; Mtoro bin Mwinyi Bakari, *The Customs of the Swahili People: The Desturi za Waswahili of Mtoro bin Mwinyi Bakari and Other Swahili Persons*, ed. J. W. T. Allen (Berkeley: University of California Press, 1981), 221–27; Jeremy Prestholdt, *Domesticating the World: African Consumerism and the Genealogies of Globalization* (Berkeley: University of California Press, 2008), 140–42.

17. Mazrui and Shariff, *The Swahili*, 27.

18. As Glassman argues, the term *asili* carried "the full force of an ethnic or racial paradigm, in which descent is imagined to determine not only one's social identity but also one's behavioral characteristics and most essential qualities." *War of Words*, 136.

19. A. H. J. Prins, *The Swahili-Speaking Peoples of Zanzibar and the East African Coast* (London: International African Institute, 1967), 108.

20. Katrin Bromber, "Ustaarabu: A Conceptual Change in Tanganyikan Newspaper Discourse in the 1920s," in *The Global Worlds of the Swahili: Interfaces of Islam, Identity, and Space in 19th and 20th Century East Africa*, ed. Roman Loimeier and Rüdiger Seesemann (Berlin: Lit Verlag, 2006), 67–81. The term was particularly important in Zanzibar—see Glassman, *War of Words*, 85–89.

21. Glassman, *War of Words*, 81; R. W. Hollingsworth, *Milango ya Historia* (London: Macmillan, 1965) [originally printed in 3 vols., 1925, 1929, and 1931, written with assistance of Ahmad Sayf al-Kharusi, A. M. al-Hadhrami, and Muhammad Salim Hilal al-Barwani], vol. 2, 49–53 and vol. 3, 101–2; Roman Loimeier, *Between Social Skills and Marketable Skills: The Politics of Islamic Education in Twentieth Century Zanzibar* (Leiden: Brill, 2009), 355–56.

22. Martin Lewis and Kären Wigen, *The Myth of Continents: A Critique of Metageography* (Berkeley: University of California Press, 1997), 120, quoted in Glassman, *War of Words*, 339.

23. Edwin Smith, *Aggrey of Africa* (London: Student Christian Movement Press, 1929), 212–14; Daisy Sykes Buruku, "The Townsman: Kleist Sykes," in *Modern Tanzanians*, ed. John Iliffe (Dar es Salaam: EAPH, 1973), 101; Mohamed Said, *The Life and Times of Abdulwahid Sykes (1924–1968): The Untold Story of the Muslim Struggle against British Colonialism in Tanganyika* (London: Minerva Press, 1998), 40–41.

24. Kenneth King, "James E. K. Aggrey: Collaborator, Nationalist, Pan-African," *Canadian Journal of African Studies* 3 (1969): 511–30; King, *Pan-Africanism and Education: A Study of Race Philanthropy and Education in the Southern States of America and East Africa* (Oxford: Clarendon Press, 1971), 97–126.

25. Chedieli Yohane Mgonja, *Johari ya Maisha Yangu* (Dar es Salaam: UDSM Press, 2003), 5.

26. Matola to Passfield, 25 July 1930, TNA 19325/f.2.

27. Buruku, "The Townsman," 105.

28. "Kanuni na Sheria za Chama [TAWCA]," n.d. [*ca.* August 1936], TNA 22444/f.102.

29. *Kwetu*, July 1938.

30. "Lugha ya Kiswahili," *Kwetu*, June 1938.

31. G. Hajivayanis, A. Mtowa, and John Iliffe, "The Politicians: Ali Ponda and Hassan Suleiman," in Iliffe, *Modern Tanzanians*, 238.

32. See *Kwetu*, 22 November 1938 and 21 February 1939.

33. Letter of Samuel Simon, *Kwetu*, 26 December 1941.

34. Joel Bakama, "Mtu Asiyejivuna kwa rangi," *Kwetu*, 16 January 1940.

35. Letter of James Aly, *Tanganyika Standard*, 16 April 1943.

36. "African or Native," *Tanganyika Opinion*, 23 June 1939.

37. Erica Fiah, "Native," *Kwetu*, 26 March 1942. Emphasis in original. Fiah was anticipating the emphasis on physical appearances that would later be central to the racial thought in Zanzibar's *Africa Kwetu* newspaper from the mid-1950s onward. See Glassman, *War of Words*, 132–37.

38. Letter of James Wapo, *Kwetu*, 23 August 1940; letter of R. M. R. Mac-Ramson, *Kwetu*, 21 August 1938.

39. "Ati Mazulu si Waafrika?" by Saleh bin Juma, *Kwetu*, June 1944.

40. Lorne Larson, "A History of the Mahenge (Ulanga) District, c. 1860–1957" (PhD diss., University of Dar es Salaam, 1976), 338.

41. George Stocking, *Victorian Anthropology* (New York: Free Press, 1987), 169–79.

42. Letter of "Native," *Tanganyika Standard*, 10 December 1932.

43. Letter of Simeon Mbaruku Muya, *Mambo Leo*, August 1936.

44. Letter of "Rojorojo," *Kwetu*, 31 March 1941.

45. "Tamaa na kuiga mambo ya upuzi," *Kwetu*, 31 July 1942; "Tamaa," *Kwetu*, 15 July 1939.

46. "Kukua kwa Taifa," *Kwetu*, 31 March 1944.

47. "Lugha ya Kiswahili," *Kwetu*, June 1938; *Kwetu*, 26 March 1942.

48. John Iliffe, "The Spokesman: Martin Kayamba," in Iliffe, *Modern Tanzanians*, 67; *Kwetu*, 10 December 1938 and 29 June 1940.

49. Martin Kayamba, *African Problems* (London: United Society for Christian Literature, 1948), 7. See also Iliffe, "The Spokesman," 86–91.

50. Kayamba, *African Problems*, 36.

51. Ibid., 76.

52. Ibid., 77–78.

53. Middleton, *The World of the Swahili*, 190.

54. Ann Biersteker, *Kujibizana: Questions of Language and Power in Nineteenth- and Twentieth-Century Poetry in Kiswahili* (East Lansing: Michigan State University Press, 1996), 28–66; Iliffe, *A Modern History*, 379–80.

55. Salum Kombo, *Ustaarabu na Maendeleo ya Mwafrika* (Nairobi: EALB, 1966, first published in 1950), 2.

56. Ibid., 18.

57. Brett Shadle, "Bridewealth and Female Consent: Marriage Disputes in African Courts, Gusiiland, Kenya," *Journal of African History* 44 (2003): 241–62.

58. James Giblin, *A History of the Excluded: Making Family a Refuge from State in Twentieth-Century Tanzania* (Oxford: James Currey, 2005), 63.

59. Jon Soske, "Navigating Difference: Gender, Miscegenation and Indian Domestic Space in Twentieth-Century Durban," in *Eyes Across the Water: Navigating the Indian Ocean*, ed. Pamila Gupta, Isabel Hofmeyr, and Michael Pearson, 197–219 (Pretoria: UNISA Press, 2010).

60. Letter of Samwil Kiama, *Mambo Leo*, April 1945.

61. Letter of K. S. J. Mbalaminwe, *Mambo Leo*, July 1945.

62. Letter of Ramsay Mwamanda, *Mambo Leo*, September 1945.

63. Letter of Olimpa Emanuel, *Mambo Leo*, November 1945. Lack of sexual reciprocity between races was a long-standing theme among African intellectuals—see Abbasi Athmani's *shairi* verse "Ujinga wetu hawaishi," *Kwetu*, 14 January 1938; and Fiah's excerpted story from *Uganda Voice* in *Kwetu*, 30 April 1944.

64. "Mwafrika na Mzungu" by Athumani bin Athumani, *Kwetu*, February 1945.

65. Cited in Bernard Lewis, *Race and Color in Islam* (New York: Harper and Row, 1971), 6.

66. Letter of Flowarose Salama binti Arubati, *Mambo Leo*, November 1945.

67. Letter of G. E. Naftal, *Mambo Leo*, December 1945.

68. Ibid.

69. Letter of Peter Joseph, *Mambo Leo*, March 1946.

70. Letter of Aaron Mzoo, *Mambo Leo*, January 1946.

71. Letter of Flowarose Salama binti Arubati, *Mambo Leo*, June 1946.

72. Ibid.

73. Letter of S. M. Mtengeti, *Mambo Leo*, August 1946. My emphasis.

74. Letter of Hatibu Yusufu Juma, *Mambo Leo*, May 1947.

75. Letter of Peter Joseph, *Mambo Leo*, March 1946. National interest in Flowarose grew so great that an African training officer sought her out in Tabora, and described her as "black, has an average body, neither tall nor short, pretty enough. Surprise, she has an African husband named Abdi Kandoro." He told readers to ignore Flowarose, for, he alleged, "bibi Flowerose knows how to read, but cannot write news in the paper, rather her husband writes for her." Letter of Mzee Ramadhani, *Mambo Leo*, January 1947. Authorship of Flowarose's letters remains unclear—Abdi Kandoro was undoubtedly Saadani Abdu Kandoro, a renowned *shairi* poet who was then treasurer of Uyumi Usagara Federation in Tabora, and later became a major political figure and author of the Tanzanian nationalist history *Mwito wa Uhuru* (Dar es Salaam: Thakers, 1961).

76. C. M. Binti Hassani, "Mwafrika kwa weupe ni tamaa ya dunia," *Mambo Leo*, September 1946.

77. "Kuoa mke suriama," *Kwetu*, 25 March 1938. Fiah uses the ambiguous term "mpagazi"—literally "carrier," but a term that also captures a wider range of nineteenth-century master-servant relationships from wage worker to slave.

78. Letter of Alimas, *Kwetu*, 19 May 1942.

79. Minute of Director of Education to CS, 17 September 1931, TNA 18675/I/f.33.

80. 1943 Eastern PAR, 17.

81. "Tupa," *Kwetu*, November 1945.

82. Downie to East African Governors Conference, 20 April 1931, TNA 18675/I/f.11.

83. Minute of Whitlamsmith to D. A. S., 23 May 1946, TNA 18675/III. In his survey of Dar es Salaam conducted in 1956, Leslie noted there were 300 members of the "Chotara" tribe in Dar es Salaam, the fortieth-largest "tribe" accounting for 0.3 percent of population. Ninety-four percent of "Chotara" lived in Kariakoo; 6 percent in Kinondoni/Msasani. Leslie, "Survey of Dar es Salaam" (1957), appendix A/13.

84. Letter of "Sympathizer," *Tanganyika Standard*, 18 November 1944. Leslie notes that "half-caste" prostitutes lived in eastern Kariakoo, nearest to customers from Zone II (Uhindini). J. A. K. Leslie, *A Survey of Dar es Salaam* (London: Oxford University Press, 1963), 234.

85. Letter of J. M. Mwigulila, *Kwetu*, 15 July 1939.

86. Letter of J. A. Zimba, *Tanganyika Standard*, 2 December 1944.

87. Letter of "African II," *Tanganyika Standard*, 2 December 1944.

88. David Anthony, "Culture and Society in a Town in Transition: A People's

History of Dar es Salaam, 1865–1939" (PhD diss., University of Wisconsin, 1983), 155–56.

89. Letter of M. M. Abushiri wa Mbwana, *Mambo Leo*, November 1946.

90. Minutes of African Association's East Africa Conference, Zanzibar, 4–5 April 1947, TNA 19325/II/f.67A, 13.

91. Ordinance to provide for Maintenance of Illegitimate Children, No. 42 of 1949.

92. *Hansard*, 6 July 1949, 226–28.

93. Letter of Ali bin Shamte, *Mambo Leo*, January 1947; letter of H. Salian Omar Bahawereth, *Mambo Leo*, June 1947. Frederick Johnson, *A Standard Swahili-English Dictionary* (Oxford: Oxford University Press, 1938), gives a tentative etymology for *chotara* as "half"; *suriama* means one born from a *suria* or "concubine slave"; the Gujarati term for mixed-race children and their subsequent offspring was *jotawa*, implying "bastard" or "mongrel." Agehananda Bharati, *The Asians in East Africa: Jayhind and Uhuru* (Chicago: Nelson-Hall, 1972), 160–61. Lodhi describes *chotara* as a person of mixed Africa-Asian, African-European, or Asian-European descent, originally a Kachchhi/Gujarati/Hindi/Punjabi vulgar expression for "offspring of the vagina" but now a nonderogative Swahili term. Abdulaziz Lodhi, *Oriental Influences in Swahili* (Göteborg: Acta Universitatis Gothoburgensis, 2000), 153–54.

94. Jan Knappert, *Swahili Proverbs* (Ndanda TZ: Ndanda Mission Press, 1997), 55.

95. For overviews of the KAR in Burma and South Asia, see Timothy Parsons, *The African Rank-and-File: Social Implications of Colonial Military Service in the King's African Rifles, 1902–1964* (Portsmouth, NH: Heinemann, 1999), 28–35; and David Killingray, *Fighting for Britain: African Soldiers in the Second World War* (Woodbridge: James Currey, 2010), chapter 5. The authoritative military history remains H. Moyse-Bartlett, *The King's African Rifles* (Aldershot: Gale and Polden, 1956), 610–82.

96. Iliffe, *A Modern History*, 376.

97. Larson, "A History of Mahenge," 329n15.

98. Waruhiu Itote, *"Mau Mau" General* (Nairobi: EAPH, 1967), 13–15, 33–34; quotation at 34.

99. "War Cabinet Morale and Welfare in the Far East," 7 November 1944, CO 968/98/f.1.

100. Kevin Brown, "The Military and Social Change in Colonial Tanganyika: 1919–1964" (PhD diss., Michigan State University, 2001), 305–6.

101. Letter of K. K. Kasumba, *Heshima*, 15 September 1943.

102. Letter of Rishiwani bin Kassim Msegeju, *Askari*, 11 October 1944; *Heshima*, 15 September 1943.

103. "Report on Welfare in 21st (EA) Infantry Brigade" by Griffith Quick, enclosed in Howes to Stanley, 25 June 1943, CO 820/55/3.

104. Ibid.

105. Killingray, *Fighting for Britain*, 170; Westcott, "The Impact," 295.

106. Brown, "The Military and Social Change," 268–70. On territorial football teams, see *Askari*, 5 April 1944.

107. Abdul Hamid el Zein, *The Sacred Meadows: A Structural Analysis of Religious Symbolism in an East African Town* (Evanston: Northwestern University Press, 1974), 62.

108. Middleton, *The World of the Swahili*, 194. See also Iliffe, *Honour in African History* (Cambridge: Cambridge University Press, 2005), 32–34.

109. T. C. McCaskie, *Asante Identities: History and Modernity in an African Village, 1850–1950* (Edinburgh: Edinburgh University Press, 2000), 170–71.

110. John Iliffe, *Honour*, 234.

111. For a thorough account of *Heshima* that focuses on discipline, see Katrin Bromber, "Do Not Destroy Our Honour: Wartime Propaganda Directed at East African Soldiers in Ceylon (1943–44)," in *Limits of British Colonial Control in South Asia*, ed. Ashwini Tambe and Harald Fischer-Tiné, 84–101 (London: Routledge, 2009). I thank Katrin Bromber for generously providing me with hard-to-find copies of *Heshima* and *Askari*.

112. Editorial, *Heshima*, 4 August 1943.

113. Clerk Stephens Raphael, "Tusiharibu Heshima, Wakatuita Wajinga," *Heshima*, 24 November 1943.

114. Killingray, *Fighting for Britain*, 113–14, 247–49.

115. Gerald Hanley, *Monsoon Victory* (London: Collins, 1946), 30, quoted in Bromber, "Do Not Destroy Our Honour," 88. Killingray estimates that 90 percent of all African soldiers recruited to serve in the war had been nonliterate. Killingray, *Fighting for Britain*, 75.

116. 1944 Eastern PAR, 25.

117. Letter of F. N. Ndirangu, *Heshima*, 8 December 1943.

118. Letter of Aiston Herrie, *Askari*, 3 May 1944.

119. Letter of Cpl. Abdullah Pombe, *Heshima*, 30 May 1945; letters of L/Cpl Simon Kiliba and J. M. Jacob, *Heshima*, 11 July 1945.

120. Letter of Cpl. Dixon, *Heshima*, 9 May 1945; letter of John Macumpason, *Heshima*, 4 July 1945.

121. Letter of Albert Isaac, *Heshima*, 9 May 1945; letter of Joseph Ganira, ibid., 27 June 1945; letter of Moshi Said, ibid., 4 July 1945.

122. Iliffe, *Honour*, 232.

123. See, inter alia, letter of Ali Saleh Ali, *Askari*, 20 October 1943; letter of Y. Sezzilwa, *Askari*, 11 October 1944; and letter of Tobia Paulo, *Askari*, 15 November 1944.

124. Darrell Bates, *A Fly-Switch from the Sultan* (London: Rupert Hart-Davis, 1961), 106.

125. Parsons, *The African Rank-and-File*, 158–66; Killingray, *Fighting for Britain*, 108–10.

126. John Nunneley, *Tales from the King's African Rifles* (Petersham: Askari Books, 1998), 111–13.

127. Dimoline to Rossiter, 8 January 1946, DIMONLINE 9/3-4, Liddell-Hart Centre for Military Archives, London.

128. C-in-C India, Adjutant Generals Branch, Medical Directorate, New Delhi to War Office London, 5 November 1945, DIMOLINE 9/3-4.

129. Brown, "The Military and Social Change," 274, 280, 294–300.

130. Letter of Mani Mwongela, *Heshima*, 15 December 1943.

131. Said, *The Life and Times*, 51.

132. The following is based on Ally Kleist Sykes and Mohamed Said, "Under the Shadow of British Colonialism in Tanganyika," n.d. (unpublished manuscript of Ally Sykes memoir); and Ally Sykes, interview by Nestor Luanda, 29 February 1996.

133. Said puts the meeting on Christmas Eve of 1945 (mistakenly) at Imphal; Listowel puts it in early 1946 in Bombay; Sykes puts it in Bombay in late 1945. Said, *The Life and Times*, 57–58; Judith Listowel, *The Making of Tanganyika* (London: Chatto and Windus, 1965), 121–22; Ally Sykes, interview by Nestor Luanda, 29 February 1996.

134. Brown, "The Military and Social Change," 419. For a thorough criticism of the myth that Asian nationalists honed African soldiers' political awareness, see Killingray, *Fighting for Britain*, 208–9.

135. Ally Sykes, interview by Nestor Luanda, 29 February 1996.

136. Ally Sykes, interview by author, 31 July 1999.

137. Randal Sadleir, *Tanzania: Journey to Republic* (London: Radcliffe Press), 37–38.

138. Morale Report, SEAC, February–April 1945, WO 203/2268/f.8A.

139. Brown, "The Military and Social Change," 343. See also Bates, *A Fly-Switch*, 107.

140. Morale Report, SEAC, May–July 1945, WO 203/2268/f.9.

141. Morale Report, SEAC, November 1945–January 1946, WO 203/2268/f.15.

142. For criticisms of this myth, see Brown, "The Military and Social Change," 417–18; Parsons, *The African Rank-and-File*, 255–56; Gregory Mann, *Native Sons: West African Veterans and France in the Twentieth Century* (Durham, NC: Duke University Press, 2006), 22–23; and especially Killingray, *Fighting for Britain*, chapter 7.

143. "Give Tanganyika to India," *Tanganyika Opinion*, 12 April 1946.

144. Letter from D. R. Dharani, *Tanganyika Standard*, 26 April 1946; letter from Shariff Anwari, *Tanganyika Standard*, 1 May 1946.

145. "Indians and Africans," *Tanganyika Herald*, 26 April 1946

146. Letter of B. A. Minga, *Tanganyika Standard*, 2 May 1945.

147. Letter of "Observers," *Tanganyika Standard*, 17 April 1946.

148. Letter of "African Observer," *Tanganyika Standard*, 30 April 1946. The language and detail of the letter indicate that its author was likely Abdulwahid Sykes.

149. Letter of Abdulwahid Sykes, *Tanganyika Standard*, 14 September 1946.

150. Letter of "Observers," *Tanganyika Standard*, 17 April 1946.

151. See Susan Geiger, *TANU Women: Gender and Culture in the Making of Tanganyikan Nationalism* (Portsmouth, NH: Heinemann, 1997); and Said, *The*

Life and Times. For a review see James R. Brennan, "Revisiting Nationalism in Tanganyika," *Afrika Spectrum* 37 (2002/3): 367–71.

152. Among the many accounts, the best by far remains Iliffe, *A Modern History*, 485–576.

153. PC Eastern to CS, 27 September 1945, TNA 28946/f.8; PC Eastern to CS, 9 January 1946, TNA 33136/f.12.

154. African Association conference minutes, enclosed in Korowe to Battershill, 1 October 1945, TNA 19325/II/f.18.

155. TAA memorandum to U.N. Visiting Mission, 20 September 1948, enclosed in Surridge to Creech Jones, 13 November 1948, CO 691/202/1; Tanganyika Intelligence Summaries for September and October 1949, CO 537/4717/f.5&18.

156. Iliffe, *A Modern History*, 406; East African Political Intelligence Report, July–September 1948, CO 537/3646/f.36, 18; EACFIN, 1 August 1950, CO 537/5920/f.16.

157. TAA constitutional memorandum, 21 May 1950, RH MSS Brit. Emp.365, Box 123/3/f.3.

158. *Hansard*, 15 and 16 April 1947, 32–52; Listowel, *The Making of Tanganyika*, 147–49.

159. Political Intelligence Summary Tanganyika, September 1949, CO 537/4717/5; EACFIN, 5 January 1951, CO 537/7218/1; Intelligence Summary, February, 1951, CO 537/7225/3.

160. Kenya Colony Political Intelligence, 31 October 1950, CO 537/5931/f.31.

161. Tanganyika Intelligence Summary, April–June 1949, CO 537/4717/f.2.

162. Westcott, "The Impact," 179–80; Leechman to David, 4 June 1954, CO 822/1092/f.1.

163. Hugh Tinker, *The Banyan Tree: Overseas Emigrants from India, Pakistan, and Bangladesh* (Oxford: Oxford University Press, 1977), 124; James R. Brennan, "South Asian Nationalism in an East African Context: The Case of Tanganyika, 1914–1954," *Comparative Studies of South Asia, Africa, and Middle East* 19 (1999): 32–34.

164. *Tanganyika Standard*, 31 January 1952; Margaret Bates, "Tanganyika under British Administration, 1920–1955" (DPhil diss., Oxford University, 1957), 274.

165. Darrell Bates, *A Gust of Plumes* (London: Hodder and Stoughton, 1972), 221–22, 251–52.

166. Gijsbert Oonk, "'After Shaking His Hand, Start Counting Your Fingers': Trust and Images in Indian Business Networks, East Africa, 1900–2000," *Itinerario* 27 (2004): 76–77, 80; Oonk, "The Changing Culture of the Hindu Lohana Community in East Africa," *Contemporary South Asia* 13 (2004): 12; Richa Nagar, "Communal Discourses, Marriage, and the Politics of Gendered Social Boundaries among South Asian Immigrants in Tanzania," *Gender, Place and Culture* 3 (1998): 131.

167. Tanganyika Intelligence Summary, March 1955, CO 822/859/f.13; Oscar Kambona to Secretary, Fabian Society, 18 October 1955, RH MSS Brit. Emp.365, Box 121/2/f.32; Twining to Lennox-Boyd, 31 October 1955, CO 822/859/f.33;

circulars and presidential addresses of D. K. Patel, 1 August 1955, 26 May 1956 and 28 February 1959, Indian Merchants Chamber microfilm, UDSM East Africana collection; Dinesh Vaishnav, interview by author, 15 September 1998; Lois Lobo, *They Came to Africa: 200 Years of the Asian Presence in Tanzania* (Dar es Salaam: Tanzania Printers, 2000), 86.

168. Nyerere to Thanki, 4 January 1959, CCM 5/336/f.137.

169. Letter of Julius Nyerere, *Tanganyika Standard*, 22 February 1956.

170. *Tanganyika Standard*, 18 February 1958.

171. Tanganyika Intelligence Summary, March 1960, CO 822/2061/f.4, 6.

172. TAA memorandum to Cohen, excerpted in Tanganyika Political Intelligence Summary, May 1951, CO 537/7225/f.9; see also Ulrich Lohrmann, *Voices from Tanganyika: Great Britain, the United Nations and the Decolonization of a Trust Territory, 1946–1961* (Berlin: Lit Verlag, 2007), 175–76.

173. Tanganyika Political Intelligence Summary April 1951, CO 537/7225/f.7; EACFIN, 28 May 1951, CO 537/7218/f.9.

174. Extract from Tanganyika Intelligence Summary for October 1955, CO 822/859/f.39.

175. Leslie, *A Survey*, 268,

176. "TANU ilipambana na misukosuko mingi," *Uhuru*, 3 July 1974; Said, *The Life and Times*, 181–82, 238–44, 255–56; extracts from Tanganyika Intelligence Summaries, July and August 1956, CO 822/859/f.72, 97. On the Youth League, see James R. Brennan, "Youth, the TANU Youth League, and Managed Vigilantism in Dar es Salaam, Tanzania, 1925–1973," *Africa* 76 (2006): 221–46.

177. See James R. Brennan, "Nation, Race and Urbanization in Dar es Salaam, Tanzania 1916–1976" (PhD diss., Northwestern University, 2002), chapter 4.

178. At the same time, colonial officials were discreetly enlisting witchcraft eradicators to help solve criminal cases. Tim Harris, *Donkey's Gratitude: Twenty Two years in the Growth of a New African Nation—Tanzania* (Edinburgh: Pentland Press, 1992), 452–54.

179. J. C. Cairns, *Bush and Boma* (London: John Murray, 1959), 145–47.

180. Lorne Larson, "Covens, Control and Coercion: An Examination of the Career of Nguvumali Mpangile, Witchcraft Eradicator," unpublished paper in author's possession; *Tanganyika Standard*, 10 March 1956.

181. Leslie, *A Survey*, 270.

182. Ulotu Abubaker Ulotu, *Historia ya TANU* (Dar es Salaam: East African Literature Bureau, 1971), 48.

183. Julius Nyerere to Editor, *Tanganyika Standard*, 27 December 1955, in CCM 5/149/f.54.

184. Iliffe, *Honour*, 309.

185. Iliffe, *A Modern History*, 554; Governor's Deputy to Lennox-Boyd, 19 February 1957, CO 822/1361/f.12.

186. Minute of Twining, 16 March 1957, CO 822/1361/f.29. See also Andrew Burton, *African Underclass: Urbanisation, Crime and Colonial Order in Dar es Salaam, Tanzania* (Oxford: James Currey, 2005), chapter 12.

187. Grattan-Bellew to Mathieson, 18 March 1957, CO 822/1361/f.29; Twining to Gorell-Barnes, 3 April 1957, CO 822/1361/f.37.

188. See, for example, 1957 party circulars in CCM 5/87 & CCM 5/115; and Dar es Salaam branch correspondence, 1958–1960, CCM 5/248.

189. Iliffe, *A Modern History*, 552. On Twining's "multiracial" policy blunder that brought Tanganyika, arguably the region's least developed colonial territory, to independence before any of its neighbors because of the decision to have common rather than communal electorates, see John Iliffe, "Breaking the Chain at Its Weakest Link: TANU and the Colonial Office," in *In Search of a Nation: Histories of Authority and Dissidence in Tanzania*, ed. Gregory Maddox and James Giblin, 168–97 (Oxford: James Currey, 2005).

190. "Oral Hearing at the Trusteeship Council, 1955," in Julius Nyerere, *Freedom and Unity* (Oxford: Oxford University Press, 1966), 36.

191. Letter of "Agricola," *Tanganyika Standard*, 27 December 1957.

192. *Tanganyika Standard*, 28 November 1962. Amir Jamal was the first non-African to join TANU, followed by Derek Bryceson.

193. Letter of Julius Nyerere, *Tanganyika Standard*, 25 November 1958.

194. Excerpted in *Tanganyika Standard*, 11 September 1958.

195. Sophia Mustafa, *The Tanganyika Way: A Personal Story of Tanganyika's Growth to Independence* (Nairobi: East African Literature Bureau, 1961), 78–80.

196. Minute of ALD to Gorell Barnes, 19 December 1958, CO 822/1210/f.78.

197. For example, Juma Mwindadi, a Dar es Salaam school teacher and ex-president of the African Association, explained that "our world today as it is we can divide into three major parts, or let's call it three races/nations (*mataifa*): 1. Race/nation of people of Europes (whites) 2. Race/nation of people of Asia ("red-skinned" people [sic]) 3. Race/nation of people of Africa (blacks). Juma Mwindadi, "Ubora wa lugha ya Kiswahili katika lugha za dunia," *Journal of East African Swahili Committee* 28 (1958): 17.

198. Letter of "A Tanganyikan," *Tanganyika Standard*, 27 January 1956.

199. Letter from Rodricks Simkoko, *Tanganyika Standard*, 1 February 1956.

200. Letter of E. B. M. Barongo, *Tanganyika Standard*, 22 March 1956.

201. Letter of John Ochieng, *Tanganyika Standard*, 28 January 1954.

202. Tanganyika Intelligence Summary, September 1955, CO 822/859/f.38.

203. Ware to DOS, 17 May 1958, NARA RG 59 778.00/5-1758.

204. Isa Moosa [District Secretary, Mwanza, Tanganyika Coloured People National Society] to Nyerere, 4 July 1960, CCM 5/316/f.343. It is unclear when this organization was founded.

205. "Mwafrika nani?" *Ngurumo*, 10 May 1961.

206. Brennan, "Youth," 227–33.

207. Leslie, *A Survey*, 115.

208. Burton, *African Underclass*, 282.

209. Burton, *African Underclass*, 234; William H. Friedland, *Vuta Kamba: The Development of Trade Unions in Tanganyika* (Stanford, CA: Hoover Institution Publications, 1969), 45–58.

210. R. H. Sabot, *Economic Development and Urban Migration: Tanzania, 1900–1971* (Oxford: Clarendon Press, 1979), 183–84, 207–8; Andrew Burton, "Raw Youth, School-Leavers and the Emergence of Structural Unemployment in Late-Colonial Urban Tanganyika," *Journal of African History* 47 (2006): 364. This localized labor stabilization policy later became national policy with enactment of a territorial minimum wage, implemented in 1963.

211. DC Dar es Salaam to Principal Immigration Officer, 22 July 1955, TNA 540/19/1/f.73.

212. *Zuhra*, 31 January 1958; Leslie, *A Survey*, 6–7, 278–79; Juma Manjenga, interview by author, 12 August 1999.

213. Colman Titus Msoka, "Informal Markets and Urban Development: A Study of Street Vending in Dar es Salaam Tanzania" (PhD diss., University of Minnesota, 2005), 39–40, 48–49, 80–82.

214. Letter of P. Mamodo, *Tanganyika Standard*, 29 March 1955. On the reconstruction of slavery "memories," see Glassman, *War of Words*, 138–44 passim.

215. For an elaborate analysis of "nonutilitarian" violence in far more violent Zanzibar, see Glassman, *War of Words*, chapter 7.

216. Superintendent of Police to DC Dar es Salaam, 13 May 1955, TNA 540/1/19/f.190; *Tanganyika Standard*, 14 September 1960.

217. For a full account, see James R. Brennan, "Destroying *Mumiani*: Cause, Context, and Violence in Late Colonial Dar es Salaam," *Journal of Eastern African Studies* 2 (2008): 95–111.

218. Moyez G. Vassanji, *The Gunny Sack* (Portsmouth, NH: Heinemann, 1989), 153.

219. Lobo, *They Came to Africa*, 80; Mohsin Virjee, interview by author, 30 September 1998; Hasnain Virjee, interview by author, 4 August 1999.

220. For a full account, see James R. Brennan, "The Short History of Political Opposition and Multi-Party Democracy in Tanganyika, 1958–1964," in Maddox and Giblin, *In Search of a Nation*, 250–76.

221. These statements are from ANC Press Release, n.d., *ca.* 30 January 1958, CO 822/1370/f.E2/3; and "What We Believe in—Our Political Philosophy," n.d. [*ca.* 30 January 1958], CO 822/1370/f.E3/3.

222. Tanganyika Intelligence Summary May 1959, CO 822/1363/f.267.

223. "Mtanganyika ni nani?," TANU circular by Roland Mwanjisi, n.d. [*ca.* July 1959], TNA 561/2/58.

224. Minute of Pearce to Rolfe, 25 November 1960, CO 822/2806; Fletcher-Cooke to Rolfe, 1 March 1961, CO 822/2806/f.9; Ross to Rolfe, 9 March 1961, CO 822/2806/f.10.

225. Memorandum on Tanganyika Citizenship, enclosed in Rolfe to Morgan, 22 March 1961, CO 822/2806/f.12.

226. Summary record of Tanganyika Pre-Independence Discussions, 28 June 1961, CO 822/2806/f.36.

227. Stanley to Chitty, 13 July 1961, DO 176/30/f.26.

228. Morgan to Turnbull, 7 September 1961, DO 176/30.

229. Carmen Voigt-Graf, *Asian Communities in Tanzania: A Journey Through Past and Present Times* (Hamburg: Institut für Afrika-Kunde, 1998), 88; minute of Last to Cleary, 8 August 1961, DO 176/30. Pakistan terminated dual citizenship in 1951, as did India in 1955. In 1957, roughly two-thirds of Asians in Tanganyika (50,330) were British Subjects, and the other third (22,621) were British Protected Persons, the distinction being that British Subjects were those born in either the UK or British colonies, while British Protected Persons were born in British-controlled Princely States or other Protectorates. This distinction created considerable legal confusion, as British Protected Persons were regarded as British subjects only while in foreign territories, and not while in British-controlled ones, bedeviling applications of Protected Persons for British citizenship or residency, particularly after 1960. See Voigt-Graf; and also Randall Hansen, *Citizenship and Immigration in Post-War Britain* (Oxford: Oxford University Press, 2000). The Aga Khan had encouraged Ismailis to naturalize as United Kingdom citizens in the early 1950s, in part to compensate for the general reluctance among Muslim Indians in East Africa to approach the India High Commission in Nairobi to acquire necessary certificates of origin. The High Commission meanwhile busily registered (mostly) Hindu applicants for British citizenship. Rogers to Hutson, 2 February 1952, CO 1026/15/f.2.

230. *Hansard*, 13 October 1960, col. 143.

231. *Hansard*, 14 December 1960, col. 186.

232. *Hansard*, 18 October 1961, col. 334. See Listowel, *The Making of Tanganyika*, xviii; *Tanganyika Standard*, 19 October 1961; and Stanley to Cleary, 20 October 1961, DO 176/30/f.57.

233. "It is considered that in a country like Tanganyika, which has several different races, there should be no division of loyalty and that Tanganyika citizens should owe loyalty only to Tanganyika. It is therefore proposed that dual citizenship should not be permitted to Tanganyika citizens." Tanganyika Citizenship Bill, section 4 subsection 2.

234. *Hansard*, 17 October 1961, cols. 313–14.

235. Ibid., col. 314.

236. *Hansard*, 18 October 1961, col. 353.

237. Ibid., col. 363.

238. Stanley to Cleary, 20 October 1961, CO 822/2806/f.E73.

239. For an example of the first strategy, see Nyerere's policy shift from "Africanization" to "localization" in January 1964, shortly before (and perhaps precipitating) the army mutiny; for the second strategy, see the April 1971 Acquisition of Buildings Act discussed in chapter 5; for the third strategy, see the "government" decision, which was fully Nyerere's decision, to refuse requests to allow Indians recently expelled by Idi Amin from Uganda to disembark at Dar es Salaam in 1972.

240. *Hansard*, 17 October 1961, col. 304.

241. Ibid., col. 306.

242. Ibid., col. 307.

CHAPTER 5: NATIONALIST THOUGHT

1. The best work on Tanganyikan nationalism remains John Iliffe, *A Modern History of Tanganyika* (Cambridge: Cambridge University Press, 1979). For Iliffe, TANU nationalist ideology owes much to trailblazing predecessors in India and Ghana. For works locating nationalist thought as product of local resistance to colonialism, see E. B. M. Barongo, *Mkiki Mkiki wa Siasa Tanganyika* (Dar es Salaam: East African Literature Bureau, 1966); Uloto Abubaker Uloto, *Historia ya TANU* (Dar es Salaam: East African Literature Bureau, 1971); and Susan Geiger, *TANU Women: Gender and Culture in the Making of Tanganyikan Nationalism* (Portsmouth, NH: Heinemann, 1997). Several works conflate Nyerere's thought with the nation's thought, particularly Cranford Pratt, *The Critical Phase in Tanzania, 1945–1968: Nyerere and the Emergence of a Socialist Strategy* (Cambridge: Cambridge University Press, 1976).

2. Geiger, *TANU Women*, 15.

3. Joan Vincent, "The Dar es Salaam Townsman: Social and Political Aspects of City Life," *Tanzania Notes and Records* 71 (1970): 155. See also Uloto, *Historia ya TANU*, 27–29.

4. King to DOS, 7 March 1961, NARA RG 59 778.00/3-761.

5. Barongo, *Mkiki Mkiki*, 212.

6. Tanganyika Intelligence Summary September 1961, CO 822/2062/f.27.

7. Administrative Secretary Tanga Region to DC Same, 25 July 1962, TNA 304/A6/28/f.218, cited in Steven Feierman, *Peasant Intellectuals: Anthropology and History in Tanzania* (Madison: University of Wisconsin Press, 1990), 230.

8. Feierman, *Peasant Intellectuals*, 228; Henry Bienen, *Tanzania: Party Transformation and Economic Development* (Princeton, NJ: Princeton University Press, 1970), 66–68.

9. Claire Mercer, Ben Page, and Martin Evans, *Development and the African Diaspora: Place and the Politics of Home* (London: Zed Books, 2008), 121; Kelly Askew, *Performing the Nation: Swahili Music and Cultural Politics in Tanzania* (Chicago: University of Chicago Press, 2002), 64.

10. This chapter uses the term "TANU government" only when it is clear that the government is pursuing official TANU policy. In a number of fields there was considerable difference between the demands and policies of TANU radicals and the subsequent actions of more-conservative government bureaucrats. This chapter does not explore this issue in any depth, but addresses its existence by taking care not to conflate party and state except when the differences do not exist or are inconsequential. For an important overview of party-state differences, see Jeannette Hartmann, "The Arusha Declaration revisited," *African Review* 12 (1985): 1–11.

11. Mathias Mnyampala, *The Gogo: History, Customs, and Traditions*, ed. Gregory Maddox (Armonk, NY: M. E. Sharpe, 1995), 3. See also Andreas Eckert, *Herrschen und Verwalten: Afrikanische Bürokraten, Staatliche Ordnung und Politik in Tanzania, 1920–1970* (Munich: Oldenbourg, 2007), 175–78.

12. Harvey Glickman, "Traditional Pluralism and Democratic Processes in

Tanganyika," paper delivered at American Political Science Association Meeting, 9–12 September 1964, 9.

13. Askew, *Performing the Nation*, 171.

14. This new sentiment was best captured by the journalist E. R. Munseri, who argued that Tanzania must follow Kemal Ataturk's example to form a national culture that encouraged modern development and expunged traditional elements that stood in its way. E. R. Munseri, "Kusitawisha na Kuhifadhi Utamaduni Wetu," n.d. [*ca.* 1966], reprinted from *Nchi Yetu* in TNA 540/CD/CR/46. See Askew, *Performing the Nation*, 171–91; and Andrew Ivaska, *Cultured States: Youth, Gender and Modern Style in 1960s Dar es Salaam* (Durham, NC: Duke University Press, 2010), 42–59.

15. "Taifa leo lawakumbuka mashujaa," *Uhuru*, 1 September 1971; "Ni nani shujaa?" and "Wimbo wa mashujaa," *Uhuru*, 1 September 1976.

16. Letter of K. K. Kondo, *Standard*, 13 September 1968.

17. "Kiswahili," in K. K. Kahigi and M. M. Mulokozi, *Malenga wa Bara* (Nairobi: East African Literature Bureau, 1976), 84.

18. *Sunday News*, 28 October 1973.

19. Julius Nyerere, *Ujamaa—The Basis of African Socialism* (Dar es Salaam: Government Printers, 1962).

20. Pratt, *The Critical Phase*, 120. These 1962 works include *Ujamaa*, *TANU na Raia*, and *Tujisahihishe*.

21. Most studies on the intellectual content of *ujamaa* are simply intellectual biographies of Nyerere. See J. L. Kanywanya, "Theoretical Problems of Ujamaa," in *Re-thinking the Arusha Declaration*, ed. Jeannette Hartmann, 45–53 (Copenhagen: Center for Development Research, 1991), 45–53; and Victoria Stöger-Eising, "Ujamaa Revisited: Indigenous and European Influences in Nyerere's Social and Political Thought," *Africa* 70 (2000): 118–43. An important exception that takes national political thought seriously is Denis-Constant Martin: *Tanzanie: l'invention d'une culture politique* (Paris: Karthala, 1988).

22. James R. Brennan, "Destroying *Mumiani*: Cause, Context, and Violence in Late Colonial Dar es Salaam," *Journal of Eastern African Studies* 2 (2008): 95–111; and Marja-Liisa Swantz, *Ritual and Symbol in Transitional Zaramo Society* (Uppsala: Almqvist and Wiksells, 1970), 320–26.

23. Territorially famous *waganga* predecessors of Hamedi Said Matoroka (or "Matoloka") who had also administered *dawa* in outer Dar es Salaam include Ngoja bin Kimweta (d. 1932), Amri Makwera Kasongo ("Songo," d. 1950), and Nguvumali (d. 1957).

24. "Mganga Buguruni," *Ngurumo*, 14 February 1961; "Wachawi wabuguruni waona cha mtema kuni," *Ngurumo*, 17 January 1969; Lloyd Swantz, *The Medicine Man among the Zaramo of Dar es Salaam* (Uppsala: Scandinavian Institute of African Studies, 1990), 47–51.

25. "African Political Affairs," enclosed in Grattan-Bellew to Webber, 16 February 1959, CO 822/1325/f.1B.

26. John Magotti, *Rashidi Mfaume Kawawa* (Dar es Salaam: Matai and Company Limited, 2007), 21.

27. J. C. Cairns, *Bush and Boma* (London: John Murray, 1959), 133–35; "Campaign to Explain What Uhuru Means," *Tanganyika Standard*, 10 October 1959; Msema Kweli, "Baada ya Uhuru ni Nini?" *Mwafrika*, 12 December 1959; Randal Sadleir, *Tanzania: Journey to Republic* (London: Radcliffe Press, 1999), 102, 227–30; Randal Sadleir, interview by author, 14 June 2000.

28. Shabani Gonga, interview by author, 5 October 1998.

29. *Uhuru*, 13 February 1965.

30. "Uchumi wa Tanganyika," *Uhuru*, 6 January 1962.

31. For word lists, see Carol Scotton, "Some Swahili Political Words," *Journal of Modern African Studies* 3 (1965): 527–41; V. Ostrosky and J. Tejani, "Second Tentative Word List," *Swahili* 37 (1967): 209–24; and ibid. 38 (1968): 54–99; Harold Goldklang, "Current Swahili Newspaper Terminology," *Swahili* 37 (1967): 194–208; ibid. 38 (1968): 42–53; C. W. Temu, "The Development of Political Vocabulary in Swahili," *Kiswahili* 41 (1971): 3–17; and Deo Ngonyani, "Ujamaa [Socialism] Metaphors: The Basis of President Nyerere's Political Terminology," in *Surviving Through Obliqueness: Language of Politics in Emerging Democracies*, ed. Samuel Obeng and Beverly Hartford, 31–43 (Hauppauge: Nova Science, 2002).

32. TANU, *Mafunzo ya Azimio la Arusha na Siasa ya TANU juu ya Ujamaa na Kujitegemea* (Dar es Salaam: Idara ya Elimu ya Siasa, 1967), appendix III, 36–37. TANU defined *unyonyaji* (exploitation) as "condition of life that enables a person or group of people or class of people to get necessities without working by using a person or another class of people"; and *mrija* ("straw") as "apparatus used for sucking sweat of another person or people."

33. *Ngurumo*, 6–13 and 24 February and 20 September 1967.

34. Letter of S. B. Kimbokota, *Standard*, 22 March 1967.

35. Joseph Namata, *Huduma Serikalini na Siasa ya Kujitegemea* (Dar es Salaam: Government Printers, 1967).

36. See letter of "Onlooker," *Standard*, 27 August 1968; and letters of K. M. Mpenda and "Oppressed," *Standard*, 30 September 1968.

37. M. A. Rupembecho, "Adhabu Gani Tuwape," *Uhuru*, 22 December 1971.

38. For a persuasive analysis of Tanzanian "urban bias" that also criticizes Bates's general argument, see Michael Lofchie, "The Politics of Agricultural Policy," in *Beyond Capitalism vs. Socialism in Kenya and Tanzania*, ed. Joel Barkan (Boulder, CO: Lynne Rienner, 1994), 129–73. See also R. H. Sabot, *Economic Development and Urban Migration: Tanzania, 1900–1971*, (Oxford: Clarendon Press, 1979), 52–59, 240–44.

39. Richard Stren, Mohamed Halfani, and Joyce Malombe, "Coping with Urbanization and Urban Policy," in Barkan, *Beyond Capitalism*, 175–200.

40. Julius Nyerere, "The Arusha Declaration," in *Ujamaa: Essays on Socialism* (New York: Oxford University Press, 1968), 28.

41. *Kusare*, 23 September 1967.

42. International Labour Office, *Report to the Government of the United Republic*

of *Tanzania on Wages, Incomes and Prices Policy* (Dar es Salaam: Government Printer, 1967), 5. See also Sabot, *Economic Development*, 237–39.

43. Tanzania, *Wages, Incomes, Rural Development, Investment and Price Policy* (Dar es Salaam: Government Printer, 1967), 24–25. See also Pratt, *The Critical Phase*, 215–16, 227.

44. Sabot, *Economic Development*, 235–40.

45. Larry Sawers, "Urban Primacy in Tanzania," *Economic Development and Cultural Change* 37 (1989): 841–59; and Rodger Yeager, *Tanzania: An African Experiment* (Boulder, CO: Westview Press, 1989), 74–76. Dar es Salaam was stripped of its municipal status in the nationwide abolition of local authorities brought about by "decentralization" policy; local authorities were reintroduced in 1978, when Dar es Salaam regained municipal status.

46. Richard Stren, "Urban Local Government in Africa," in *African Cities in Crisis*, ed. Richard Stren and Rodney White (Boulder, CO: Westview Press, 1989), 23.

47. Richard Stren, "Administration of Urban Services," in Stren and White, *African Cities*, 51–53; Saitiel Kulaba, "Local Government and the Management of Urban Services in Tanzania," in Stren and White, ibid., 219–25, 239–43.

48. Sabot, *Economic Development*, 248.

49. Andrew Burton, "The 'Haven of Peace' Purged: Tackling the Undesirable and Unproductive Poor in Dar es Salaam, ca. 1950s–1980s," *International Journal of African Historical Studies* 40 (2007): 119–51.

50. *Nationalist*, 21 October 1964; *Tanganyika Standard*, 21 October 1964; *Mwafrika*, 21 October 1964; *Ngurumo*, 9 March 1967. The Labor Commissioner announced his disappointment that only 109 of 1,279 workers registered in Kifagio Songambele agreed to work on sisal plantations, which had 885 jobs waiting. *Ngurumo*, 22 October 1964.

51. Letter of Peter Mrima, *Standard*, 20 March 1967.

52. *Standard*, 16 March 1967. For an unusually reflective account of the theory, practicalities, and internal debates of repatriations, see letter of Kitwana Kondo, *Standard*, 17 March 1967.

53. *Standard*, 16 December 1970.

54. Askew, *Performing the Nation*, 5–26, 157–95; Geiger, *TANU Women*, 156–62; and Thomas Burgess, "The Young Pioneers and the Rituals of Citizenship in Revolutionary Zanzibar," *Africa Today* 51 (2005): 3–29.

55. James R. Brennan, "Youth, the TANU Youth League and Managed Vigilantism in Dar es Salaam, Tanzania, 1925–73," *Africa* 76 (2006): 227–42.

56. "'Shenzi' Case," *Nationalist*, 4 June 1968.

57. Cartoons from *Ngurumo*, 15 February, 14 and 18 March 1967.

58. Transcript of Nyerere's Union Day speech at the National Stadium, enclosed in Richardson to Shepherd, 30 April 1966, DO 213/103/f.85.

59. See, inter alia, numerous *ujamaa* village articles in the Kivukoni College journal *Ujamaa*, 1968–74; and Tanganyika African National Union, *Maisha ya Ujamaa* (Dar es Salaam, National Printing Company, ca. 1972).

60. *Uhuru*, 6 March 1976; Rosaleen Smyth, "The Feature Film in Tanzania," *African Affairs* 88 (1989): 389–96. "Fimbo ya Mnyonge" had been an *ujamaa* village propaganda program on Radio Tanzania since the mid-1960s. "Taarifa ya Mwalimu wa Radio Kipindi cha 'Fimbo ya Mnyonge,'" *Ujamaa* 14, n.d. [*ca.* 1969], 4–10.

61. E. Mizambwa, "Wavivu ni Maadui," *Diwani Yetu*, ed. F. E. Mlingwa (Arusha: Longman Tanzania, 1970), 6–7.

62. Letter of "Mkazi mwingine wa Buguruni," *Uhuru*, 7 December 1967; *Standard*, 1 April 1967.

63. Circular of Tata Kabwera Foola Union, by Bakari Kondo et al., dated 25 March 1962, CCM 5/57/f.27.

64. Letter of "Embarrassed," *Standard*, 25 July 1969.

65. John Iliffe, *Honour in African History* (Cambridge: Cambridge University Press, 2005), 279; Alhaji Iddi Sungura, interview by author, 28 September 1998; Ivaska, *Cultured States*, 111–19.

66. Sabot, *Economic Development*, 91, 94.

67. "Vijana watoa maoni," *Uhuru*, 6 June 1970.

68. Ostrosky and Tejani, "Second Tentative Word List"; letter of Joel Kitubika, *Ngurumo*, 28 September 1967.

69. Aili Mari Tripp, *Changing the Rules: The Politics of Liberalization and the Informal Economy in Tanzania* (Berkeley: University of California Press, 1997), 118.

70. Nyerere, "Ujamaa," 169.

71. The best starting point is Issa Shivji, *The Silent Class Struggle* (Dar es Salaam: Tanzania Publishing House, 1973); and Shivji, *Class Struggles in Tanzania* (London: Heinemann, 1976).

72. On its origins, see the following newspaper letters: R. A. Chambuso, *Ngurumo*, 3 July 1965; S. Mbonde, *Ngurumo*, 26 May 1967; Mahamad Jume, *Uhuru*, 2 December 1967; Mohamed Juma, *Ngurumo*, 29 November 1967; Nyanza Omari, *Ngurumo*, 8 August 1968.

73. *Nationalist*, 15 July 1967 and 27 April 1971. The best Marxist analysis of the elusive *naizi* class is Susanne Mueller, "The Historical Origins of Tanzania's Ruling Class," African Studies Center Working Paper 35, Boston University, 1980.

74. Letters of Ali Rusonzo and G. B. Kaputula, *Ngurumo*, 23 July 1964; *Uhuru*, 12 May 1966.

75. "Mzegamzega naizi-siye kabwela," *Ngurumo*, 17 April 1969.

76. Alex Banzi, *Zika Mwenyewe* (Dar es Salaam: Tanzania Publishing House, 1977), quoted in (and translated by) Rajmund Ohly, *The Zanzibarian Challenge* (Windhoek: Academy, 1990), 90–92. For a superlative survey, see Elena Zubkova Bertoncini, *Outline of Swahili Literature* (Leiden: E. J. Brill, 1989).

77. "Naize na Visa Vyao" by S. S. Nyanzugu, *Civil Service Magazine*, November/December 1965; various *mashairi* in ibid., January/February 1966.

78. Scotton, "Some Swahili Political Words," 532.

79. Letter of Abdulla Salum, *Ngurumo*, 22 February 1967; Ostrosky and Tejani, "Second Tentative Word List."

80. "Neno 'Kabwela' halifai katika Jamhuri lisitumike," *Ngurumo*, 19 June 1965.

81. TANU, *Mafunzo ya Azimio la Arusha na Siasa ya TANU juu ya Ujamaa na Kujitegemea* (Dar es Salaam: Idara ya Elimu ya Siasa), 36–37. This Arusha Declaration primer defines *kabwela* as "person of low standing," and *naizi* as "person of high standing or person of a certain rank."

82. Letter of Peter Shizya, *Ngurumo*, 22 February 1964; letter of E. P. Isakwisa, *Ngurumo*, 11 February 1966; letter of Mohamed Mziwanda, *Ngurumo*, 18 February 1966.

83. For rare glimpses of this in socialist Dar es Salaam, see "Watumishi majumbani wana matatizo!" *Uhuru*, 28 March 1973; for socialist Tanga, see Janet Bujra, *Serving Class: Masculinity and the Feminisation of Domestic Service in Tanzania* (Edinburgh: Edinburgh University Press, 2000), 112–33.

84. "Socialism Is Not Racialism" by Julius Nyerere, *Nationalist*, 14 February 1967.

85. *Zuhra*, 22 November 1957.

86. Alhaji Iddi Sungura, interview by author, 28 September 1998.

87. "Uhusiano Mwema na Dharau," *Mwafrika*, 17 September 1960.

88. Scotton, "Some Swahili Political Words," 532–33; "Wahindi," *Uhuru*, 1 February 1967; letter of Raia Asili, *Standard*, 21 April 1971.

89. Letter of R. J. Rukombe, *Daily News*, 5 May 1972.

90. "Huu ni 'Udugu' wa Kabila Gani?" *Mwafrika*, 6 August 1960.

91. Letter from Justin Mungia, *Uhuru*, 30 January 1965.

92. Letter of Nietzsche Dixon Mubeya, *Standard*, 17 November 1967.

93. Letter of Salam Mtimbwa, *Zuhra*, 10 February 1961.

94. Alhaji Iddi Sungura, interview by author, 28 September 1998.

95. *Uhuru*, 21 July 1966; letter of Iddi Selemani, *Uhuru*, 23 December 1965.

96. *Nationalist*, 17 November 1964.

97. Letter of "Asian," *Tanganyika Standard*, 29 June 1964; "Wahindi hawajasikia," *Uhuru*, 11 July 1964.

98. See especially Shija Msafiri, "Tanzanian Control of the Economy," *Nationalist*, 21 February 1969, and response by Eliab Mrema, ibid., 31 March 1969.

99. *Standard*, 26 October 1965.

100. Letter of Kalimile Malagila, *Sunday News*, 10 December 1967.

101. *Nationalist*, 2 May 1970.

102. *Standard*, 18 September 1970. For an overview of the forced marriage crisis, see George Triplett, "Zanzibar: The Politics of Revolutionary Inequality," *Journal of Modern African Studies* 9 (1971): 612–17.

103. See letters in *Standard*, 25 and 28 September; and 2 October 1970; and *Nationalist*, 26 September 1970.

104. *Standard*, 30 September 1970.

105. Letter of John Bundala, *Nationalist*, 6 May 1970; letter of E. C. Ambali, *Nationalist*, 7 May 1970; letter of Francis Mihayo, *Nationalist*, 6 May 1970.

106. Letter of Linda Wabuliba, *Nationalist*, 6 May 1970.

107. Ibid.

108. *Nationalist*, 16 May 1970. Cf. *Uhuru*, 9 May 1970.

109. A. M. Khamis, "Swahili as a National Language," in *Towards Ujamaa*, ed. Gabriel Ruhumbika (Dar es Salaam: East African Literature Bureau, 1974), 291. Characterized by lack of affixes, excessive pronouns, and substitution of "j" for "z," *Kiswahili cha Kihindi* reflects its origins as a commercial bridge between Indians and Africans, and symbolized the failure of many Indians (though certainly not all) to fully master the language's complexities.

110. Letter of G. E. Mwanasasu, *Mwafrika*, 21 March 1964.

111. See especially the incendiary editorials by Roland Mwanjisi on Indian duplicity, racism, and exploitation shortly after independence. *Uhuru*, 6 January and 10 February 1962.

112. For Miye's conversations with Mamujee, see *Uhuru*, 7 February 1972, 18 April 1973, 2 May 1973, 11 July 1973, 4 November 1973, 3 February 1974, 2 November 1975.

113. "Miye," *Uhuru*, 11 October 1972.

114. Ibid.

115. *Uhuru*, 25 July 1973.

116. "Miye," *Uhuru*, 8 May 1971. Original reads *Sisi hapana wananchi. Kadi TANU weja?*

117. Hugh Tinker, *The Banyan Tree: Overseas Emigrants from India, Pakistan, and Bangladesh* (Oxford: Oxford University Press, 1977), 133.

118. Letter of "Mwananchi," *Nationalist*, 30 March 1968.

119. Sayyeda Salam, "The Politics of Nationalization and Denationalization of Asian Properties and Businesses in Dar es Salaam, 1971–2005" (MA thesis, University of London [SOAS], 2005), 17.

120. Letter of M. J. D. Kwanoga, *Ngurumo*, 2 October 1964.

121. *Nationalist*, 26 November 1966.

122. Agehananda Bharati, "Political Pressures and Reactions in the Asian Minority in East Africa," Program of East African Studies, Syracuse University, Occasional Paper 12 (1965), 1.

123. Letter of Jack Muruguranza, *Nationalist*, 3 February 1967.

124. Julius Nyerere, interview by Derek Taylor, *Times of Zambia*, n.d. [*ca.* February 1967], FCO 47/46/f.1.

125. *Standard*, 25 January 1967; *Nationalist*, 13 August 1969; "Kwa Heri Patel!" *Uhuru*, 13 August 1969; *Standard*, 27 November 1969; "17 Asians Expelled," *Nationalist*, 22 April 1970; Carmen Voigt-Graf, *Asian Communities in Tanzania: A Journey Through Past and Present Times* (Hamburg: Institut für Afrika-Kunde, 1998), 160.

126. *Mwafrika*, 25 June 1964.

127. Editorial, *Uhuru*, 5 April 1965.

128. Letter of Justini Mungia, *Uhuru*, 14 April 1965. The actual word Mungia uses is *wanatupepeta*; the verb *pepeta* has the double meaning of sifting or separating (as in the wheat from the chaff), but also of pulverizing.

129. *Standard*, 11 May 1966; letter of "Annoyed Citizen," *Nationalist*, 14 June 1966.

130. Letter of "Tanzanian," *Nationalist*, 1 July 1967.

131. *Standard*, 15 August 1968; Voigt-Graf, *Asian Communities*, 65.

132. *Nationalist*, 18 August, 28 August, and 18 September 1969.

133. *Nationalist*, 27 November 1969.

134. See *Nationalist*, 20 January 1966, 7 December 1968, 20 September 1969, and 22 April 1973; *Daily News*, 9 May 1973.

135. Ross to DOS, 17 April 1972, NARA RG 59 Pol 13-3 Tanzan.

136. Richa Nagar, "The Making of Hindu Communal Organizations, Places, and Identities in Postcolonial Dar es Salaam," *Environment and Planning D: Society and Space* 15 (1997): 717.

137. 1962 Annual Report for Dar es Salaam City, TNA Library, 12.

138. Voigt-Graf, *Asian Communities*, 105, 112.

139. Letter of K. R. Majura, *Uhuru*, 20 January 1962.

140. *Tanganyika Standard*, 8 January 1964.

141. Brennan, "Youth," 233–34.

142. Pratt, *The Critical Phase*, 124–34; Sabot, *Economic Development*, 209–10; Eckert, *Herrschen und Verwalten*, 231–36.

143. Voigt-Graf, *Asian Communities*, 111.

144. *Tanganyika Standard*, 17 and 24 July 1963. This Economist Intelligence Unit report was later published as H. G. C. Hawkins, *Wholesale and Retail Trade in Tanganyika* (New York: Praeger, 1965), quotation from 141.

145. Minutes of DSM Merchants Chamber, 24 August 1963 and circular of M. M. Devani, DSM Merchant's Chamber, 12 September 1963, Honey notes.

146. Special general meeting on Africanization, 16 August 1964, Dar es Salaam Merchants Chamber, Honey notes; *Tanganyika Standard*, *Mwafrika*, and *Nationalist* on 17 August 1964.

147. *Mwafrika*, 18 August 1964.

148. *Standard*, 11 March 1972; Hawkins, *Wholesale and Retail Trade*, 148–50.

149. *Nationalist*, 27 January 1967.

150. *Tanganyika Standard*, 14 April 1958.

151. Tom Torrance, *Dar es Salaam 1963: A New Graduate Encounters an Emerging African Nation* (Renfrew, ON: General Store Publishing House, 2010), 51; *Tanganyika Standard*, 31 July 1963.

152. *Nationalist*, 19 March 1965; "Focus on Credit Unions," *Nationalist*, 11 December 1967.

153. Letter of Simon Mwamasso, *Uhuru*, 23 March 1965.

154. Shop credit accounted for 8.18 shillings (24.5 percent) of average gross borrowing in Dar es Salaam per individual, compared to the 2.63 shillings (7.9 percent) from pawnshops. Household Budget Survey 1956/1957, J. A. K. Leslie, Kisarawe District Book, TNA. Of the total 33.38 shilling average received credit, wage advances accounted for 2.25 shillings (6.7 percent), and "Loans" accounted for the remaining 20.22 (60.6 percent). Leslie explains that these loans "were from relatives and friends and, although every effort to distinguish between loans and gifts was made, some of the items shown here may in fact be concealed gifts."

155. Thipa Msowoya, "Why African Traders Fail in Business," *Nationalist*, 16 March 1965. See Hawkins, *Wholesale and Retail Trade*, 119–20, 134–35; and J. A. K. Leslie, *A Survey of Dar es Salaam* (London: Oxford University Press, 1963), 279.

156. For rich case-study evidence from 1960s Bunju, just north of Dar es Salaam, see Marja-Liisa Swantz, *Ritual and Symbol*, 121–26.

157. *Nationalist*, 30 October 1970 and 17 March 1971; "Wahindi washika jembe," *Ngurumo*, 21 January 1967.

158. May Joseph, *Nomadic Identities: the Performance of Citizenship* (Minneapolis: University of Minnesota Press, 1999), 58.

159. Hasnain Virjee, interview by author, 30 September 1998.

160. Yash Ghai, "The Future Prospects," in *Portrait of a Minority*, ed. Dharam Ghai and Yash Ghai (Nairobi: Oxford University Press, 1970), 217.

161. *Standard*, 26 March 1966.

162. For an illuminating example, see J. K. Chande, *A Knight in Africa: Journey from Bukene* (Manotick: Penumbra Press, 2008), 91–105.

163. Kitwana Kondo, MP for Dar es Salaam, argued that many Asians "make known their citizenship only in times of hardship or when they want to obtain something." Amid cheers and applause from the House, Kondo added, "Asians are forming a community of their own. They show no willingness to co-operate and integrate with other people," and appealed to immigration authorities to be "very cautious when granting citizenship to such people." *Nationalist*, 17 July 1968.

164. Nyerere, *Ujamaa*; *Tanganyika Standard*, 16 April 1962. See generally Paul Bjerk, "Julius Nyerere and the Establishment of Sovereignty in Tanganyika" (PhD diss., University of Wisconsin, 2008), 237–45.

165. J. M. L. Kironde, "The Evolution of Land Use Structure in Dar es Salaam: A Study in the Effects of Land Policy" (PhD thesis, University of Nairobi, 1994), 315–17; R. W. James, *Land Tenure and Policy in Tanzania* (Dar es Salaam: East African Literature Bureau, 1971), 138–66; Great Britain, *East Africa Royal Commission, 1953–1955 Report* (London: H.M.S.O., 1955), 214–22, 346–66; *Tanganyika Standard*, 3 October 1959.

166. *Hansard*, 14 February 1961, cols. 80–82. Cf. James, *Land Tenure and Policy*, 192–93; Mzee Mbwana to DC Dar es Salaam, 3 February 1958, TNA 540/3/39/II/f.371.

167. *Standard*, 18 June 1966.

168. Richard Stren, *Urban Inequality and Housing Policy in Tanzania: The Problem of Squatting* (Berkeley, CA: Institute of International Studies, 1975), 37–43; Kironde, "The Evolution," 326–46, 380–85. On NHC's history, see *Uhuru*, 16 October 1972.

169. *Tanganyika Standard*, 15 February, 13 April, and 3 July 1962; 1962 Annual Report for Dar es Salaam City, TNA Library, 1; *Nationalist*, 17 December 1966.

170. Stren, *Urban Inequality*, 59–61; Kironde, "The Evolution," 83; Kulaba, "Local Government," 226–28.

171. Sabot, *Economic Development*, 47.

172. Kironde, "The Evolution," 459, 53.

173. "The House That Jack (Tried to) Build," *Sunday News*, 6 August 1972. See also Kironde, "The Evolution," 364.

174. Stren, *Urban Inequality*, 66. In 1972, the Lands Division issued 6,331 rights of occupancy plots in Dar es Salaam; at the end of the year, the waiting list for such plots stood at 15,000. Ibid., 47.

175. In 1980, 64 percent of all housing was financed entirely out of individual savings. The African Urban Housing Loan Scheme (est. 1953), which had targeted Magomeni, expired after independence. The main private lenders were Savings and Loan Society and First Rhodesian Building Society, which began lending in the early 1950s but stopped in the early 1960s following a regional panic among depositors. Tanzania Housing Bank formed in 1972 upon nationalization of Permanent Housing Finance Company, but had largely ceased lending by 1985. *1954 Town Planning Department Annual Report*, 21, CO 736/41; *Zuhra*, 14 January 1955; Tanzania and UN-HABITAT, *Re-Establishing Effective Housing Finance Mechanisms in Tanzania* (Nairobi: U.N. Human Settlements Programme, 2003), 43–49.

176. *Tanganyika Standard*, 25 May 1963; Stren, *Urban Inequality*, 56, 73–75.

177. Geoffrey Owens, "On the Edge of a City: An Historical Ethnography [sic] of Urban Identity in the Northwestern Suburbs of Dar es Salaam, Tanzania" (PhD diss., University of Wisconsin-Madison, 2004), 255.

178. *Nationalist*, 26 January 1967; *Standard*, 7 September 1968; *Daily News*, 2 September 1974; Kironde, "The Evolution," 367. For an overview of slum clearances, see G. M. Fimbo, "Law and Urban Housing: A Study in State Intervention in Urban Housing in Tanzania" (PhD diss., University of Dar es Salaam, 1988), chapter 7.

179. *Standard*, 17 May 1971; Stren, *Urban Inequality*, 69–70, 83. Compare these Dar es Salaam figures to a national owner-occupier rate of 36 percent among urban households in 1969. D. M. Mwita, "Urban Landlordism and the Acquisition of Buildings Act" (LLM diss., University of Dar es Salaam, 1978), 237.

180. Letter of M. Salim (Ilala), *Uhuru*, 5 December 1967; letter of Peter Shizya, *Ngurumo*, 22 February 1964; *Uhuru*, 21 July 1962.

181. Letter of Ali Said, *Standard*, 9 February 1970.

182. See accounts in *Standard* and *Nationalist*, 13 February 1965.

183. "Kodi za nyumba mjini," *Uhuru*, 17 December 1966.

184. *Nationalist*, 2 April 1965; East Africa Business Group Meeting, 3 November 1965, DO 214/100/f.97; Brennan, "Destroying *Mumiani*," 106.

185. See efforts of Kitwana Kondo in *Majadiliano ya Bunge (Hansard)*, 18 December 1965, cols. 376–80.

186. Geiger, *TANU Women*, 3. In her interviews with Susan Geiger, Bibi Titi exhibited a remarkably precise memory for dates, names, and prices relating to her two Dar es Salaam properties. Ibid., 172–79.

187. Pratt, *The Critical Phase*, 235–36.

188. *Standard*, 16 January 1971.

189. 1971 Tanzania Annual Review, enclosed in Ewans to Douglas-Home, 1 January 1972, FCO 31/1286/f.1.

190. Phillips to Le Tocq, 7 April 1971, FCO 31/968/f.7.

191. *Nationalist*, 6 April 1971.

192. Memorandum of conversation with Stephen Mhando, 14 July 1971, NARA RG 59 Pol 7 Tanzan.

193. *Nationalist*, 23 April 1971. See also *Ngurumo*, 23 April 1971; and Phillips to Le Tocq, 5 May 1971, FCO 31/968/f.9.

194. Nyerere Speech on Building Expropriation, 23 April 1971, in BBC Summary of World Broadcast Pt IV, 26 April 1971, FCO 31/997/f.7.

195. *Uhuru*, 14 May 1971.

196. *Ngurumo*, 3 May 1971.

197. Ahmed Seifu Salum Mponda, interviews by author, 22 September 1998.

198. "Uzawa: Ruffling Feathers in Tanzania," *Awaaz* (Nairobi), July 2005, cited in Salam, "The Politics of Nationalization," 10.

199. *Nationalist*, 24 April 1971.

200. *Nationalist*, 6 May 1971; *Ngurumo*, 18 May 1971.

201. Fimbo, "Law and Urban Housing," 81. 2,994 buildings were initially acquired nationwide, but 512 were returned to their owners.

202. Ally Kleist Sykes and Mohamed Said, "Under the Shadow of British Colonialism in Tanganyika" (unpublished memoir of Ally Sykes), 74.

203. Kreisberg to DOS, 27 April 1971, NARA RG 59 Soc 6-3 Tanzan.

204. *Daily News*, 23 August 1974.

205. Philip Ochieng, *I Accuse the Press: An Insider's View of the Media and Politics in Africa* (Nairobi: Initiatives Publishers, 1992), 130.

206. *Nationalist*, 24 April 1971; *Daily News*, 10 and 18 August 1972; *Uhuru*, 19 August 1972.

207. *Daily News*, 9 November 1973.

208. *Daily News*, 30 June 1972.

209. Aryes to Holmes, 1 December 1971, FCO 31/968/f.16.

210. Hashim Ismail, interview by author, 22 September 1998.

211. In 1962, Tanganyika had an Asian population of 92,000, and Zanzibar roughly 20,000—or 112,000 residing in not-yet-created "Tanzania." Robert Gregory, *South Asians in East Africa: An Economic and Social History, 1890–1980* (Boulder, CO: Westview Press, 1993), 13. During the two-year grace period after independence, 21,557 Tanganyika Indians registered for citizenship, overwhelmingly Ismaili acting at behest of the Aga Khan, although these official figures vary considerably. Tinker, *The Banyan Tree*, 128. Voigt-Graf puts the population at 115,000 in 1962 (Tanganyika and Zanzibar); 88,000 by 1967; and 78,000 by 1972. Voigt-Graf, *Asian Communities*, 43. Total South Asian population had declined to roughly 60,000 by 1973, with 30,000 holding British passports, 20,000 holding Tanzanian passports, 6,000–7,000 holding Indian passports, and the remainder mostly stateless. A. T. Lal, First Secretary, High Commission of India in Tanzania, interview by Martha Honey, 7 September 1973. Nagar states that 40,000 Asians left within six months of building nation-

alization. Richa Nagar, "The South Asian Diaspora in Tanzania: A History Retold," *Comparative Studies of South Asia, Africa, and the Middle East* 16 (1996): 70.

212. Paul Kaiser, *Culture, Transnationalism, and Civil Society: Aga Khan Social Service Initiatives in Tanzania* (Westport: Praeger, 1996), 46; Salam, "The Politics of Nationalization," 22.

213. Ross to DOS, 3 June 1971, NARA RG 59 Soc 14 Tanzan.

214. *Nationalist*, 24 November 1971.

215. Moyez G. Vassanji, *The Gunny Sack* (Portsmouth, NH: Heinemann, 1989), 247.

216. A. A. J. Thawer, interview by Martha Honey, 24 October 1973.

217. Carter to DOS, 31 July 1973, NARA RG 59 Pol 2 Tanzan.

218. Nagar, "The South Asian Diaspora."

219. *Daily News*, 22 March 1973; *Sunday News*, 11 February & 8 April 1973; Gregory, *South Asians*, 334–39; Salam, "The Politics of Nationalization," 11–12; Kironde, "The Evolution," 314.

220. Fundi Wakati, interview by author, 20 September 1998.

221. Ibrahim Chande, interview by author, 20 September 1998.

222. Mwinyimaji Musa wa Pazi, interview by author, 12 December 1998.

AFTERWORD

1. Issa Shivji, *Not Yet Democracy: Reforming Land Tenure in Tanzania* (Dar es Salaam: IIED, 1998), 26–39. The near-absolute discretionary powers of the president, who, like the colonial governor, is constitutionally invested with ultimate control of all land, is the most startling postcolonial continuity of Tanzania's land practice.

2. Allen Armstrong, "Colonial Planning and Neocolonial Urban Planning: Three Generations of Master Plans for Dar es Salaam, Tanzania," *Utafiti* 8 (1986): 44–53.

3. J. M. L. Kironde, "The Evolution of the Land Use Structure of Dar es Salaam 1890–1990: A Study in the Effects of Land Policy" (PhD diss., University of Nairobi, 1994), 448; Bashir Punja and Badru Velji, interviews by author, 1 August 1999, Dar es Salaam. Around three hundred properties were returned to their original owner because of mistakes or successful appeals to a tribunal. Richard Stren, *Urban Inequality and Housing Policy in Tanzania: The Problem of Squatting* (Berkeley: University of California Press, 1975), 42–43n58.

4. Carmen Voigt-Graf, *Asian Communities in Tanzania: A Journey Through Past and Present Times* (Hamburg: Institut für Afrika-Kunde, 1998), 135; Sayyeda Salam, "The Politics of Nationalization and Denationalization of Asian Properties and Businesses in Dar es Salaam, 1971–2005" (MA thesis, University of London [SOAS]), 2005.

5. T. C. McCaskie, *Asante Identities: History and Modernity in an African Village, 1850–1950* (Edinburgh: Edinburgh University Press, 2000), 15.

6. Stren, *Urban Inequality*, 59–76; Kironde, "The Evolution," 36, 53, 83, 301, 372–74.

7. Michael Mpuya, "Urban Poverty and Squatting in Marginal Lands: A Case

Study of Hananasif-Bondeni, Yombo-Kilakala, and Vingunguti-Msimbazi Valley in Dar es Salaam" (MA thesis, University of Dar es Salaam, 2000), 14–15, cited in Garth Andrew Myers, *Disposable Cities* (Aldershot: Ashgate, 2005), 55.

8. Saitiel Kulaba, "Local Government and the Management of Urban Services in Tanzania," in *African Cities in Crisis*, ed. Richard Stren and Rodney White (Boulder, CO: Westview Press, 1989), 213; Tanzania and UN-HABITAT, *Re-establishing Effective Housing Finance Mechanisms in Tanzania: The Potentials and Bottlenecks* (Nairobi: U.N. Human Settlements Programme, 2003), 12, 26–32.

9. J. M. Lusugga Kironde, "Rapid Urbanisation in Tanzania: The Government's Coping Strategies," in *Urbanising Tanzania: Issues, Initiatives and Priorities*, ed. Suleiman Ngware and J. M. Lusugga Kironde (Dar es Salaam: DUP, 2000), 27, 31–36, 40–41; Tanzania and UN-HABITAT, *Re-establishing Effective Housing*, 60–73.

10. *Tanzanian Affairs*, September–December 1997, 16.

11. Richa Nagar, "The South Asian Diaspora in Tanzania: A History Retold," *Comparative Studies of South Asia, Africa, and the Middle East* 16 (1996): 72; T. L. Maliyamkono and M. S. D. Bagachwa, *The Second Economy in Tanzania* (London: James Currey, 1990), ix–xix.

12. Voigt-Graf, *Asian Communities*, 120.

13. Nagar, "The South Asian Diaspora," 72–76.

Glossary

Terms are Swahili unless otherwise noted; plurals are noted if different or conventionally used in plural form.

aibu	shame, dishonor
akida (pl. *maadika*)	subaltern in German and early British direct rule structures
asili	ancestry, origins; essence
askari	African soldier
baraza	public meeting with didactic purpose
chama (pl. *vyama*)	association, party
chotara (pl. *machotara*)	mixed-race person
daftari	account book, ledger
fujo (pl. *mafujo*)	disorder; disturbance or riot
golo [Gujarati]	slave; black person
hartal [Gujarati]	closure of shops in political protest; commercial strike
heshima	honor, respect
kabila (pl. *makabila*)	tribe, nation, group
kabwela	poor man, usually in reference to urban poor
liwali (pl. *maliwali*)	governor; top "native authority" in colonial Dar es Salaam
maendeleo (pl.)	development
makuti (pl.)	thatched palm, used as roofing material
mbegu	seed; race or stock
mgeni (pl. *wageni*)	guest; foreigner
mhindi (pl. *wahindi*)	Indian
mhuni (pl. *wahuni*)	hooligan, criminal; unemployed male youth
mshenzi (pl. *washenzi*)	barbarian or savage; uncivilized
mwafrika (pl. *waafrika*)	African
mwananchi (pl. *wananchi*)	citizen (colloquial); "child of the land"
mwenyeji (pl. *wenyeji*)	native
mzungu (pl. *wazungu*)	European; white person

naizi	successful African civil servant or businessman in 1960s
nchi	country, land
ndugu	brother, sibling; in socialist years, "comrade"
ngoma	dance, drum, public performance
ote dugu moja	poorly spoken, "Indianized" version of "wote undugu mmoja" or "we are all one family," a nationalist phrase
pazi (pl. *mapazi*)	chief; term used by Zaramo people
raia	citizen (formal)
shairi (pl. *mashairi*)	genre of Swahili poetic verse
taifa (pl. *mataifa*)	nation, race
tamaa	desire; lust
Uhindini	Indian area; in colonial Dar es Salaam, colloquial term for the zoned "commercial" area or Zone II
uhuru	freedom; independence
ujamaa	"familyhood"; African socialism
unyonyaji	exploitation; literally "sucking"
ustaarabu	civilization; state of being civilized
Uswahilini	African area; in colonial Dar es Salaam, colloquial term for the zoned "native" area or Zone III
Uzunguni	European area; in colonial Dar es Salaam, colloquial term for the zoned "residential" area or Zone I
watu wa kuja (pl.)	immigrants; literally "people who came [later]"
wenye mji (pl.)	original inhabitants; literally "owners of the town"

Select Bibliography

ARCHIVES

Tanzania National Archives, Dar es Salaam (TNA)

Secretariat Minute Papers, Tanganyika Territory. There are two sets of Secretariat files—the early set (TNA 1522–8173) has four digits and covers the period 1920–1927; the latter set (10063–43664) has five digits and covers the period 1927–*ca.* 1953. I have dispensed with the cumbersome SMP (Secretariat Minute Papers) citation in my footnotes, allowing a four- or five-digit number citation to indicate an early or later secretariat file, respectively.

Citations from accessioned files (i.e., all other files not from German or Secretariat holdings) are indicated by accession number, followed by file numbers. For example, file number 7/A (Monthly Reports, Uzaramo, 1942–1944) from Accession 61, the provincial files of Eastern Province, is cited as: TNA 61/7/A. For TNA and other archival referencing in this book, folio numbers of documents within a file (for example, f.1 for "folio 1") are indicated after the file citation where applicable. Below are the most important accessions used in this book:

TNA Accession 57: District Files, Uzaramo/Kisarawe District
TNA Accession 61: Provincial Files, Eastern Province
TNA Accession 540: District Files, Ilala Boma
TNA Accession 561: District Files, Ilala Boma

I also consulted district books held at TNA, and district annual reports held at the TNA library.

Chama Cha Mapinduzi Party Archives, Dodoma (CCM)

With the gracious assistance of the late Said Ngwanga, I was able to consult Accession 5 of the TANU/CCM party archives, which include correspondence, circulars, and reports for the period 1953–1967.

East Africana Collection,
University of Dar es Salaam Library (UDSM)

Among the holdings of the East Africana Collection I consulted are: the Hans Cory Papers; J. A. K. Leslie's original report on Dar es Salaam; several newspapers; a volume of papers on constitutional development in the 1950s; minutes of provincial commissioners' meetings; BA, master's, and PhD theses by University of Dar es Salaam students; and a microfilm copy of minutes of the Dar es Salaam Indian Merchants Chamber, 1947–1960.

National Archives of the United Kingdom, Kew

Formerly the Public Records Office (PRO), all National Archives of the United Kingdom files are cited simply by their department code and number. I use this abbreviated system not only for the great frequency with which these citations are used, but also because PRO has now become obsolete, and its apparent replacement, "TNA" for "The National Archives," not only conflicts with this book's citations for the Tanzania National Archives, but rather absurdly distinguishes this national archive from all others by use of the article "The." Thus, Colonial Office record class 691, Tanganyika Original Correspondence, is simply cited here as CO 691, followed by the specific file and folio numbers. Below are the record class abbreviations used in this book:

ADM	Admiralty
CO	Colonial Office
DO	Dominions Office
FCO	Foreign and Commonwealth Office
KV	Security Service (MI-5)
WO	War Office

India Office Records, British National Library (IOR)

The main files consulted were from the accessions IOR L/P&J, L/E, and V, which cover Intelligence and Security Summaries for Eastern Africa, reports on Indian nationalist figures in East Africa, and legal reports on immigration and legal status of Indians.

Rhodes House Library, Oxford University (RH)

Rhodes House contains valuable collections pertaining to British colonial Tanganyika, in particular the Fabian Colonial Bureau Papers and the personal papers of former Tanganyikan colonial officials.

Special Collections, School of Oriental and African Studies, University of London (SOAS)

Wilfred Whiteley's papers are deposited here, which include valuable articles, newspapers, and circulars unavailable elsewhere. This collection also includes a copy of J. A. K. Leslie's original report on Dar es Salaam (1957), a photocopy of E. C. Baker's report on Dar es Salaam (1931), and valuable Tanzanian newspapers from the 1960s.

Liddell-Hart Centre for Military Archives, Kings College, University of London (LHCMA)

The Liddell-Hart Centre holds the papers of William Alfred Dimoline, commander of East Africa brigades in the Asian Theater during the Second World War.

Imperial War Museum, London (IWM)

The Imperial War Museum holds the papers of several KAR officers and the newspaper *Heshima*.

National Archives and Records Administration, College Park, MD, USA (NARA)

Twentieth-century records of the United States Department of State are located at the College Park (Archives II) branch of the National Archives and Records Administration. Citations are indicated first by the acronym NARA, followed by the RG (Record Group) from which the document originates, and finally by either the decimal or the alphanumeric reference on the original document.

RG 59   State Department Central Decimal Files, Central Foreign Policy Files, Subject Numeric Files, and Lot Files

United Nations Archives and Records Management Section, New York (ARMS)

The United Nations Archives contain a number of official petitions, sent to the United Nations from Tanganyika during the period ca. 1946–1961, concerning disputes between residents and the British government over the latter's policies and administration within the mandated territory.

Archives of the Evangelical Lutheran Church in America, Elk Grove Village (ELCA), Illinois

Donald Flatt's unpublished manuscript cited below and Elmer Danielson's papers were read at this archive.

INTERVIEWS

For several of these interviews, I benefited from the assistance of Hamisi
Msumi (HM) and Mohamed Kibanda (MK), who both located many of the
people interviewed, and assisted in translation when my spoken Swahili was
improving from poor to functional. I indicate with their initials the interviews
where they helped in any way.

Brennan Taped Interviews
Abdala, Ahmed Salum, in Gerezani, 14 August 1999 (HM)
Abdala, Mkegani, in Kariakoo, 12 August 1999 (HM)
Chande, Ibrahim, in Kariakoo, 20 September 1998 (HM)
Chibende, Haruna Mpazi, in Gerezani, 1 January 1999 (HM)
Devani, M. M., CBD, 2 August 1999
Gonga, Shabani, in Kariakoo, 5 October 1998 (HM)
Gude, Iddi Said, in Kariakoo, 2 January 1999 (HM)
Jhaveri, K. L., in Seaview, 4 August 1999
Kassum, Al Noor, at Sheraton Hotel, 9 August 1999
Kibanda, Rashidi Mohamed, in Kariakoo, 14 December 1998 (HM)
Kiswagala, Mohamed Hassan, in Kariakoo, 13 January 1999 (HM)
Majaliwa, Saidi, in Kariakoo, 8 January 1999 (HM)
Manjenga, Juma M., in Temeke, 12 August 1999 (HM)
Mawji, P. J., CBD, 4 August 1999
Mfaume, Abdala Mohamed, in Gerezani, 23 December 1998 (HM)
Mmanyema, Mshandani, in Kariakoo, 11 January 1999
Mponda, Ahmed Seifu Salum, in Kariakoo, 22 September 1998 (HM)
Musa, Habib Omari, in Kariakoo, 16 August 1999 (HM)
Mwaruka, Yahya, in Kariakoo, 10 August 1999 (HM)
Mwinyi, Fatuma, in Kariakoo, 23 September 1998 (HM)
Mwinyikambi, Yunus Daud, in Gerezani, 23 December and 29 December 1998
    (HM)
Ndume, Omari Ali, in Kariakoo, 18 September 1998 (HM)
Pazi, Mwinyimaji Musa wa, in Kariakoo, 12 December 1998 (HM)
Sadleir, Randall, in London, 14 June 2000
Seif, Mtoro, at Kariakoo, 4 January 1999 (HM)
Sheriff, Ahmed H. (Amdu), CBD, 2 August 1999
Sungura, Alhaji Iddi, in Kariakoo, 28 September 1998 (HM)
Wakati, Fundi, in Kariakoo, 20 September 1998 (HM)

Brennan Untaped Interviews
Abbas, Ali, in Mwananyamala, 31 May 2010
Bakar, Saidi, in Buguruni, 11 October 1998 (MK)
Bassaleh, Sheikh Ali, in Kariakoo, 27 and 28 May 2010
Buhecha, Manju, CBD, 1 August 1999

Chalamanda, Salehe, in Buguruni, 8 December 1998 (MK)
Chande, Andy, in London, 15 August 2009; and in Chang'ombe, 31 May 2010
Digega, Hassani Suleiman, in Buguruni, 11 December 1998 and 5 August 1999
   (MK)
Fazal, Nizar, CBD, 3 December 1998
Fazal, Roshanali, in Upanga, 4 August 1999
Haji, Mzee, in Buguruni, 10 October 1998 (MK)
Hemani, Abdalla, in Upanga, 3 August 1999
Ismail, Hashim, in Kariakoo, 22 September 1998
Jumbe, Ally Yusufu, in Buguruni, 8 December 1998 and 4 August 1999 (MK)
Khalfan, Mohammad, in Upanga, 4 August 1999
Khimji, Haidal, CBD, 4 December 1998
Mkasi, Mohamedi Ramadhani, in Buguruni, 6 December 1998 and 5 August 1999
   (MK)
Mzena, Charles, CBD, 23 September 1998
Nasser, Mohammad, CBD, 4 December 1998
Njechele, Mzee, in Buguruni, 10 October 1998 (MK)
Nyamato, Mzee, in Buguruni, 29 September 1998 (MK)
Punja, Bashir, CBD, 16 September 1998; 1 December 1998; and 1 August 1999
Rashad, Ahmed, in Upanga, 9 August 1999
Sachedina, Salim, Toronto, 7 July 1999
Said, Fatima, in Buguruni, 29 September 1998 (MK)
Said, Mohamed, in Tanga, 5 August 1999
Sykes, Ally, CBD, 31 July 1999
Tanna, B. K., CBD, 30 November 1998
Vaishnav, Dinesh, CBD, 15 September 1998
Velji, Badru, CBD, 31 July 1999
Velji, Noorali, in Masaki, 1 August 1999
Virji, Hasnain, CBD, 5 August 1999
Virji, Hassanali, in Upanga, 30 September 1998
Virji, Mohsin, in Upanga, 30 September 1998
Visram, Nizar, in Kariakoo, 29 November 1998

Martha Honey interviews, 1973–1974. I thank Martha Honey and Robert Gregory for allowing me access to these interviews, and for permitting their usage in this book. Copies of these interviews are in the author's possession.

Bhatia, Alibhai, in Dar es Salaam, 19 September 1973
Lal, A. T., in Dar es Salaam, 7 September 1973
Tejpar, Abdulla, in Dar es Salaam, 2 November 1973.
Thawer, A. A. J., in Dar es Salaam, 24 October 1973

Other interviews. I thank Robert Gregory, Nestor Luanda, and Andreas Eckert for providing me access to these interviews.

Robert Gregory interview with V. R. Boal, in Bombay, 2 July 1973
Nestor Luanda interview with Ally Sykes, in Dar es Salaam, 29 February 1996

UNPUBLISHED SOURCES

Aiyar, Sana. "Nation, Race, and Politics amongst the South Asian Diaspora: From Colonial Kenya to Multicultural Britain." PhD diss., Harvard University, 2009.

Anthony, David Henry, III. "Culture and Society in a Town in Transition: A People's History of Dar es Salaam, 1865–1939." PhD diss., University of Wisconsin-Madison, 1983.

Baker, E. C. Amendments to "Memorandum on the Social Conditions of Dar es Salaam, 4 June 1931," 1939. Enclosed in Deputy Information Officer to Chief Secretary, 10 January 1940, TNA 18950/II/1A/34.

———. "Memorandum on the Social Conditions of Dar es Salaam, 4 June 1931." Copy of report microfilmed by Nicholas J. Westcott and no longer available, apparently, at Tanzania National Archives or National Library. Printed copies from Westcott's microfilm are located at SOAS library special collections (MS 380738), University of London; and African Studies Centre, University of Cambridge.

Bates, Margaret L. "Tanganyika under British administration 1920–1955." DPhil thesis, Oxford University, 1957.

Bertz, Ned. "Race, Urban Space, and Nationalism in Indian Ocean World History: Schools, Cinemas, and the Indian Diaspora in Tanzania, 1920–2000." PhD diss., University of Iowa, 2008.

Bjerk, Paul. "Julius Nyerere and the Establishment of Sovereignty in Tanganyika." PhD diss., University of Wisconsin, 2008.

Brennan, James R. "Nation, Race and Urbanization in Dar es Salaam, Tanzania, 1916–1976." PhD diss., Northwestern University, 2002.

Brown, Kevin K. "The Military and Social Change in Colonial Tanganyika: 1919–1964." PhD diss., Michigan State University, 2001.

Burton, Andrew. "Wahuni (The Undesirables): African urbanization, Crime, and Colonial Order in Dar es Salaam, 1919–1961." PhD thesis, University of London, 2000.

Fimbo, Gamaliel M. "Law and Urban Housing: A Study of State Intervention in Urban Housing in Tanzania." PhD diss., University of Dar es Salaam, 1988.

Flatt, Donald C. "Man of Four Worlds: A Story of Mission in Three Continents." Pa 131, Archives of the Evangelical Lutheran Church in America (Elk Grove Village, Illinois), n.d. (ca. 1976).

Gibb, Sir Alexander, and Partners. "A Plan for Dar es Salaam." Unpublished town plan, located in University of Dar es Salaam East Africana Library, 1949.

Glickman, Harvey. "Traditional Pluralism and Democratic Processes in Tanganyika." Unpublished conference paper delivered at annual meeting of the American Political Science Association, Chicago, Illinois, 9–12 September 1964.

Honey, Martha. "A History of Indian Merchant Capital and Class Formation in Tanganyika c. 1840–1940." PhD dissertation, University of Dar es Salaam, 1982.

———. Notes from 1973–1974 interviews, Dar es Salaam Township records, Indian Merchants Chamber, Tanzania National Archives, Zanzibar National Archives, Dar es Salaam Indian Association, Asian Association, and G. M. Daya Files. I am deeply indebted to Martha Honey and Robert Gregory for allowing me access to these invaluable notes, many from documentary sources now lost or inaccessible, and also to Robert Gregory for graciously hosting me during my visit to Syracuse University in July 1999.

Janmohammed, Karim K. "A History of Mombasa, c. 1895–1939: Some Aspects of Economic and Social Life in an East African Port Town during Colonial Rule." PhD diss., Northwestern University, 1978.

Jones, Laird. "The District Town and the Articulation of Colonial Rule: The Case of Mwanza, Tanzania, 1890–1945." PhD diss., Michigan State University, 1991.

Kironde, J. M. L. "The Evolution of the Land Use Structure of Dar es Salaam 1890–1990: A Study in the Effects of Land Policy." PhD diss., University of Nairobi, 1994.

Larson, Lorne E. "Covens, Control and Coercion: An Examination of the Career of Nguvumali Mpangile, Witchcraft Eradicator." Unpublished seminar paper in author's possession, 1974.

———. "A History of the Mahenge (Ulanga) district, c. 1860–1957." PhD diss., University of Dar es Salaam, 1976.

Leslie, J. A. K. "Survey of Dar es Salaam." 1957. Copy at UDSM East Africana collection and SOAS special collection.

Lyall, A. B. "Land Law and Policy in Tanganyika: 1919–1932." LLM diss., University of Dar es Salaam, 1973.

Mascarenhas, Adolfo C. "Urban Development in Dar es Salaam." MA thesis, University of California Los Angeles, 1966.

McCleery, H. H. "Report of an Enquiry into Landownership in Dar es Salaam." Typescript, Rhodes House MSS Afr. s. 870, 1939.

Mwita, Donasian Marwa. "Urban Landlordism and the Acquisition of Buildings Act." LLD diss., University of Dar es Salaam, 1978.

Msoka, Colman Titus. "Informal Markets and Urban Development: A Study of Street Vending in Dar es Salaam Tanzania." PhD diss., University of Minnesota, 2005.

Nagar, Richa. "Making and Breaking Boundaries: Identity Politics among South Asians in Postcolonial Dar es Salaam (Tanzania)." PhD diss., University of Minnesota, 1995.

Oberst, Timothy Sander. "Cost of Living and Strikes in British Africa, c. 1939–1948: Imperial Policy and the Impact of the Second World War." PhD thesis, Columbia University, 1991.

Owens, Geoffrey Ross. "On the Edge of a City: An Historical Ethnography of Urban Identity in the Northwestern Suburbs of Dar es Salaam, Tanzania." PhD diss., University of Wisconsin-Madison, 2004.

Raimbault, Franck. "Dar-es-Salaam, Histoire d'une Societe Urbaine Coloniale en Afrique Orientale Allemande (1891–1914)." 3 vols. PhD diss., Universite Paris I—Pantheon Sorbonne, 2007.

Salam, Sayyeda. "The Politics of Nationalization and Denationalization of Asian

Properties and Businesses in Dar es Salaam, 1971–2005." MA history diss., University of London (SOAS), 2005.

Scotton, James F. "The Growth of the Vernacular Press in Colonial East Africa: Patterns of Government Control." PhD diss., University of Wisconsin, 1971.

Swantz, Lloyd W. "The Role of the Medicine Man among the Zaramo of Dar es Salaam." PhD thesis, University of Dar es Salaam, 1972.

Sykes, Ally Kleist, and Mohamed Said. "Under the Shadow of British Colonialism in Tanganyika." Unpublished memoir, no date (ca. 1998), in author's possession.

Walji, Shirin R. "A History of the Ismaili Community in Tanzania." PhD thesis, University of Wisconsin, 1974.

Westcott, Nicholas J. "The Impact of the Second World War on Tanganyika, 1939–1949." PhD diss., University of Cambridge, 1982.

Zöller, Katharina. "Islamische Feste im Kolonialen Dar es Salaam (1905–1938)." MA thesis, Humboldt-Universität zu Berlin, 2009.

PUBLISHED SOURCES

Newspapers

Askari (Nairobi)
Baragumu
Civil Service Magazine
Daily News
Dar es Salaam Times
Dunia
Economic Control Board Bulletin
Heshima
Kwetu
Mambo Leo
Mwafrika
Mwangaza
Mzalendo
Nationalist
Nchi Yetu
Ngurumo
Samachar
Sauti ya TANU
Standard
Sunday News
Tanganyika Gazette
Tanganyika Herald
Tanganyika Opinion
Tanganyika Standard
Tanganyika Times
Uhuru
Zuhra

Books and Articles

Aminzade, Ronald R. "From Race to Citizenship: The Indigenization Debate in Post-Socialist Tanzania." *Studies in Comparative International Development* 38, no.1 (2003): 43–63.

———. "The Politics of Race and Nation: Citizenship and Africanization in Tanganyika." *Political Power and Social Theory* 14 (2000): 53–90.

Anderson, Benedict. *Imagined Communities: Reflections on the Origin and Spread of Nationalism.* New York: Verso, 1991.

Armstrong, Allen. "Colonial Planning and Neocolonial Urban Planning: Three Generations of Master Plans for Dar es Salaam, Tanzania." *Utafiti* 8 (1986): 44–53.

Askew, Kelly M. *Performing the Nation: Swahili Music and Cultural Politics in Tanzania.* Chicago: University of Chicago Press, 2002.

Baker, E. C. "Mumiani." *Tanganyika Notes and Records* 21 (1946): 108–9.

———. "A Note on the Washomvi of Dar es Salaam." *Tanganyika Notes and Records* 23 (1947): 47–48.

Barongo, Edward B. M. *Mkiki Mkiki wa Siasa Tanganyika.* Nairobi: East African Literature Bureau, 1966.

Bates, Darrell. *A Gust of Plumes: A Biography of Lord Twining of Godalming and Tanganyika.* London: Hodder and Stoughton, 1972.

Bates, Robert H. *Markets and States in Tropical Africa: The Political Basis of Agricultural Policies.* 2nd ed. Berkeley: University of California Press, 2005.

Beidelman, T. O. *The Matrilineal Peoples of Eastern Tanzania.* London: International African Institute, 1967.

Berg, F. J. "The Swahili of Mombasa, 1500–1900." *Journal of African History* 9, no. 1 (1968): 35–56.

Berry, Sara. *No Condition is Permanent: The Social Dynamics of Agrarian Change in Sub-Saharan Africa.* Madison: University of Wisconsin Press, 1993.

Bertoncini, Elena Zubkova. *Outline of Swahili Literature: Prose Fiction and Drama.* Leiden: Brill, 1989.

Bhacker, Mohamed Reda. *Trade and Empire in Muscat and Zanzibar: The Roots of British Domination.* London: Routledge, 1992.

Bharati, Agehananda. *The Asians in East Africa: Jayhind and Uhuru.* Chicago: Nelson-Hall, 1972.

Bienen, Henry. *Tanzania: Party Transformation and Economic Development.* Princeton, NJ: Princeton University Press, 1970.

Bissell, William C. *Urban Design, Chaos, and Colonial Power in Zanzibar.* Bloomington: Indiana University Press, 2011.

Blij, Harm de. *Dar es Salaam: A Study in Urban Geography.* Evanston, IL: Northwestern University Press, 1963.

Bose, Sugata. *A Hundred Horizons: The Indian Ocean in the Age of Global Empire.* Cambridge, MA: Harvard University Press, 2006.

Brennan, James R. "Between Segregation and Gentrification: Africans, Indians, and the Struggle for Housing in Dar es Salaam, 1920–1950." In *Dar es Salaam:*

Histories from an Emerging African Metropolis, edited by James R. Brennan, Andrew Burton, and Yusuf Lawi, 118–35. Dar es Salaam/Nairobi: Mkuki na Nyota/BIEA, 2007.

———. "Blood Enemies: Exploitation and Urban Citizenship in the Nationalist Political Thought of Tanzania, 1958–1975." *Journal of African History* 47, no. 3 (2006): 387–411.

———. "Democratizing Cinema and Censorship in Tanzania, 1920–1980." *International Journal of African Historical Studies* 38, no. 3 (2005): 481–511.

———. "Destroying *Mumiani*: Cause, Context, and Violence in Late Colonial Dar es Salaam." *Journal of Eastern African Studies* 2, no. 1 (2008): 95–111.

———. "Lowering the Sultan's Flag: Sovereignty and Decolonization in Coastal Kenya." *Comparative Studies in Society and History* 50, no. 4 (2008): 831–61.

———. "Realizing Civilization through Patrilineal Descent: African Intellectuals and the Making of an African Racial Nationalism in Tanzania, 1920–50." *Social Identities* 12, no. 4 (2006): 405–23.

———. "Revisiting Nationalism in Tanganyika." *Afrika Spectrum* 37 no. 3 (2002/3): 367–71.

———. "The Short History of Political Opposition and Multi-Party Democracy in Tanganyika, 1958–64." In *In Search of a Nation: Histories of Authority and Dissidence in Tanzania*, edited by Gregory H. Maddox and James L. Giblin, 250–76. Oxford: James Currey, 2005.

———. "South Asian Nationalism in an East African Context: The Case of Tanganyika, 1914–1956." *Comparative Studies of South Asia, Africa and the Middle East* 19, no. 2 (1999): 24–39.

———. "Youth, the TANU Youth League, and Managed Vigilantism in Dar es Salaam, Tanzania, 1925–1973." *Africa: Journal of the International Africa Institute* 76, no. 2 (2006): 221–46.

Brennan, James R., and Andrew Burton. "The Emerging Metropolis: A History of Dar es Salaam, *circa* 1862–2000." In *Dar es Salaam: Histories from an Emerging African Metropolis*, edited by James R. Brennan, Andrew Burton, and Yusuf Lawi, 13–75. Dar es Salaam/Nairobi: Mkuki na Nyota/BIEA, 2007.

Bromber, Katrin. "*Ustaarabu*: A Conceptual Change in Tanganyikan Newspaper Discourse in the 1920s." In *The Global Worlds of the Swahili: Interfaces of Islam, Identity, and Space in 19th and 20th Century East Africa*, edited by Roman Loimeier and Rüdiger Seesemann, 67–81. Berlin: Lit Verlag, 2006.

Bromber, Katrin. "Do Not Destroy Our Honour: Wartime Propaganda Directed at East African Soldiers in Ceylon (1943–44)." In *The Limits of British Colonial Control in South Asia: Spaces of Disorder in the Indian Ocean Region*, edited by Ashwini Tambe and Harald Fischer-Tiné, 84–101. London: Routledge, 2009.

Brubaker, Rogers, and Frederick Cooper. "Beyond 'Identity.'" *Theory and Society* 29 (2000): 1–47.

Bryceson, Deborah F. "A Century of Food Supply in Dar es Salaam." In *Feeding African Cities: Studies in Regional Social History*, edited by Jane I. Guyer, 154–202. Manchester: Manchester University Press, 1987.

———. *Liberalizing Tanzania's Food Trade: Public and Private Faces of Urban Marketing Policy, 1939–1988*. Portsmouth, NH: Heinemann, 1993.

Bujra, Janet. *Serving Class: Masculinity and the Feminisation of Domestic Service in Tanzania*. Edinburgh: Edinburgh University Press, 2000.

Buruku, Daisy Sykes. "The Townsman: Kleist Sykes." In *Modern Tanzanians: A Volume of Biographies*, edited by John Iliffe, 95–114. Dar es Salaam: East African Publishing House, 1973.

Burton, Andrew. *African Underclass: Urbanisation, Crime and Colonial Order in Dar es Salaam, Tanzania*. Oxford: James Currey, 2005.

———. "'The Eye of Authority': 'Native' Taxation, Colonial Governance and Resistance in Inter-war Tanganyika." *Journal of Eastern African Studies* 2, no. 1 (2008): 74–94.

———. "The 'Haven of Peace' Purged: Tackling the Undesirable and Unproductive Poor in Dar es Salaam *ca.* 1950s–1980s." *International Journal of African Historical Studies* 40, no.1 (2007): 119–51.

———. "Raw Youth, School-Leavers and the Emergence of Structural Unemployment in Late-Colonial Urban Tanganyika." *Journal of African History* 47, no. 3 (2006): 363–87.

———. "Urchins, Loafers and the Cult of the Cowboy: Urbanisation and Delinquency in Dar es Salaam, 1919–1961." *Journal of African History* 42 (2001): 199–216.

Burton, Andrew, and Michael Jennings. "The Emperor's New Clothes?" *International Journal of African Historical Studies* 40, no.1 (2007): 1–25.

Cairns, J. C. *Bush and Boma*. London: John Murray, 1959.

Calhoun, Craig, ed. *Social Theory and the Politics of Identity*. Oxford: Blackwell, 1994.

Callahan, Michael D. *Mandates and Empire: The League of Nations and Africa, 1914–1931*. Brighton: Sussex Academic Press, 1999.

Cameron, Donald C. *My Tanganyika Service, and Some Nigeria*. Washington: University Press of America, 1939.

Campbell, John. "Race, Class and Community in Colonial Dar es Salaam: Tentative Steps Towards an Understanding of Urban Society." In *Gender, Family and Work in Tanzania*, Colin Creighton and C. K. Omari, 17–43. Aldershot: Ashgate Publishing, 2000.

Chande, J. K. *A Knight in Africa: Journey from Bukene*. Manotick, Ontario: Penumbra Press, 2008.

Chuo cha CCM, Kivukoni. *Historia ya Chama cha TANU 1954 hadi 1977*. Dar es Salaam: Government Printer, 1981.

Cohen, Ronald. "Ethnicity: Problem and Focus in Anthropology." *Annual Review of Anthropology* 7 (1978): 379–403.

Cooper, Frederick. *Decolonization and African Society: the Labor Question in French and British Africa*. Cambridge: Cambridge University Press, 1996.

———. *From Slaves to Squatters: Plantation Labour and Agriculture in Zanzibar and Coastal Kenya, 1890–1925*. New Haven, CT: Yale University Press, 1980.

———. *On the African Waterfront: Urban Disorder and the Transformation of Work in Colonial Mombasa.* New Haven, CT: Yale University Press, 1987.

———. "Urban Space, Industrial Time, and Wage Labor in Africa." In *Struggle for the City: Migrant Labor, Capital, and the State in Urban Africa,* edited by Frederick Cooper, 7–50. Beverly Hills: Sage Publications, 1983.

Coquery-Vidrovitch, Catherine. "The Process of Urbanization in Africa." *African Studies Review* 34 (1991): 1–98.

Cornell, Stephen, and Douglas Hartmann. *Ethnicity and Race: Making Identities in a Changing World.* Thousand Oaks, CA: Pine Forge Press, 1998.

Coulson, Andrew. *Tanzania: A Political Economy.* Oxford: Oxford University Press, 1982.

Curtin, Philip D. "Medical Knowledge and Urban Planning in Tropical Africa." *American Historical Review* 90 (1985): 594–613.

Dar es Salaam Merchants Chamber. *Silver Jubilee Souvenir (1941–1966).* Dar es Salaam: self-published, 1966.

Delf, George. *Asians in East Africa.* London: Oxford University Press, 1963.

Deutsch, Jan-Georg. *Emancipation without Abolition in German East Africa, c.1884–1914.* Oxford: James Currey, 2006.

Eastman, Carol. "Who Are the Waswahili?" *Africa* 41 (1971): 228–36.

Eckert, Andreas. *Herrschen und Verwalten: Afrikanische Bürokraten, Staatliche Ordnung und Politik in Tanzania, 1920–1970.* München: R. Oldenbourg Verlag, 2007.

Fair, Laura. *Pastimes and Politics: Culture, Community, and Identity in Post-Abolition Urban Zanzibar, 1890–1945.* Athens: Ohio University Press, 2001.

Feierman, Steven. *Peasant Intellectuals: Anthropology and History in Tanzania.* Madison: University of Wisconsin Press, 1990.

Fimbo, G. M. *Essays in Land Law, Tanzania.* Dar es Salaam: Dar es Salaam University Press, 1992.

Fox, Robin. *Kinship and Marriage: An Anthropological Perspective.* Hammersworth: Penguin, 1967.

Friedland, William H. *Vuta Kamba: The Development of Trade Unions in Tanganyika.* Stanford, CA: Hoover Institution Publications, 1969.

Freund, Bill. *Insiders and Outsiders: The Indian Working Class of Durban, 1910–1990.* Portsmouth, NH: Heinemann, 1995.

Furnivall, J. S. *Colonial Policy and Practice: A Comparative Study of Burma and Netherlands India.* Cambridge: Cambridge University Press, 1948.

Geiger, Susan. *TANU Women: Gender and Culture in the Making of Tanganyikan Nationalism.* Portsmouth, NH: Heinemann, 1997.

Ghai, Yash. *Racial and Communal Tensions in East Africa.* Nairobi: East African Institute of Social and Cultural Affairs, 1966.

Giblin, James. *A History of the Excluded: Making Family a Refuge from State in Twentieth-Century Tanzania.* Oxford: James Currey, 2005.

Gilman, Clement. "Dar es Salaam, 1860 to 1940: A Story of Growth and Change." *Tanganyika Notes and Records* 20 (1945): 1–23.

Glassman, Jonathon. *Feasts and Riot: Revelry, Rebellion and Popular Conscious-ness on the Swahili Coast, 1856–1888.* Portsmouth, NH: Heinemann, 1995.

———. "Slower Than a Massacre: The Multiple Sources of Racial Thought in Colonial Africa." *American Historical Review* 109 (2004): 720–54.

———. "Sorting Out the Tribes: The Creation of Racial Identities in Colonial Zanzibar's Newspaper Wars." *Journal of African History* 41 (2000): 395–29.

———. *War of Words, War of Stones: Racial Thought and Violence in Colonial Zanzibar.* Bloomington: Indiana University Press, 2011.

Goldberg, David Theo. *Racist Culture: Philosophy and the Politics of Meaning.* London: Blackwell, 1993.

———. "The Semantics of Race." *Ethnic and Racial Studies* 15 (1992): 543–69.

Goldklang, Harold A. "Current Swahili Newspaper Terminology." *Swahili* 37 (1967): 194–208; and *Swahili* 38 (1968): 42–53.

Great Britain. *East Africa Royal Commission, 1953–1955 Report.* London: H.M.S.O. (Cmd 9475), 1955.

Gregory, Robert G. *India and East Africa: A History of Race Relations within the British Empire 1890–1939.* Oxford: Oxford University Press, 1971.

———. *Quest for Equality: Asian Politics in East Africa, 1900–1967.* Hyderabad: Orient Longman, 1993.

———. *South Asians in East Africa: An Economic and Social History, 1890–1980.* Boulder, CO: Westview Press, 1993.

Hajivayanis, G. G., A. C. Mtowa, and John Iliffe. "The Politicians: Ali Ponda and Hassan Suleiman." In *Modern Tanzanians*, edited by John Iliffe, 227–53. Nairobi: East African Literature Bureau.

Harris, Tim. *Donkey's Gratitude: Twenty Two years in the Growth of a New African Nation—Tanzania.* Edinburgh: Pentland Press, 1992.

Hartmann, Jeannette, ed. *Re-thinking the Arusha Declaration.* Copenhagen: Center for Development Research, 1991.

Hawkins, H. C. G. *Wholesale and Retail Trade in Tanganyika: A Study of Distri-bution in East Africa.* New York: Frederick A. Praeger, 1965.

Hayuma, A. M. *Economic and Financial Constraints in the Implementation of the 1968 Dar es Salaam City Master Plan from 1969 to 1979.* Dar es Salaam: Ardhi Institute, 1984.

Hindu Mandal. *Hindu Mandal Golden Jubilee Souvenir, 1919–1969.* Dar es Sa-laam: Africa Printers, 1969. Photocopy in author's possession; thanks to B. K. Tanna for making this available.

Hollingsworth, Lawrence W. *The Asians of East Africa.* London: Macmillan, 1960.

———. *Milango ya Historia.* 3 vols. London: MacMillan, 1965.

Iliffe, John. "The Age of Improvement and Differentiation (1907–45)." In *A His-tory of Tanganyika*, edited by I. N. Kimambo and A. J. Temu, 123–60. Nairobi: East African Publishing, 1969.

———. "Breaking the Chain at Its Weakest Link: TANU and the Colonial Office." In *In Search of a Nation: Histories of Authority and Dissidence in Tanzania*, edited by Gregory H. Maddox and James L. Giblin, 168–97. Oxford: James Currey, 2005.

———. "A History of the Dockworkers of Dar es Salaam." *Tanzania Notes and Records* 71 (1970): 119–48.

———. *Honour in African History.* Cambridge: Cambridge University Press, 2005.

———. *A Modern History of Tanganyika.* Cambridge: Cambridge University Press, 1979.

———. "The Spokesman: Martin Kayamba." In *Modern Tanzanians*, edited by John Iliffe, 66–94. Nairobi: East African Literature Bureau, 1973.

———. "Wage Labour and Urbanisation." In *Tanzania under Colonial Rule*, edited by M. H. Y. Kaniki, 276–306. London: Longman, 1979.

Ivaska, Andrew. *Cultured States: Youth, Gender and Modern Style in 1960s Dar es Salaam.* Durham, NC: Duke University Press, 2010.

James, R. W. *Land Tenure and Policy in Tanzania.* Nairobi: East African Literature Bureau, 1971.

Joelson, F. S. *The Tanganyika Territory: Characteristics and Potentialities.* New York: D. Appleton, 1921.

Johnson, Frederick. *A Standard Swahili-English Dictionary.* Oxford: Oxford University Press, 1995.

Kandoro, Saadani Abdu. *Mwito wa Uhuru.* Dar es Salaam: National Printing, 1961.

Khamis, A. M. "Swahili as a National Language." In *Towards Ujamaa: Twenty Years of TANU Leadership*, edited by Gabriel Ruhumbika, 288–308. Dar es Salaam: East African Literature Bureau, 1974.

Killingray, David. *Fighting for Britain: African Soldiers in the Second World War.* Woodbridge: James Currey, 2010.

King, Kenneth. "James E. K. Aggrey: Collaborator, Nationalist, Pan-African." *Canadian Journal of African Studies* 3 (1969): 511–30.

———. *Pan-Africanism and Education: A Study of Race Philanthropy and Education in the Southern States of America and East Africa.* Oxford: Clarendon Press, 1971.

Kombo, Salum M. *Ustaarabu na Maendeleo ya Mwafrika.* Nairobi: East African Literature Bureau, 1966.

Kopytoff, Igor. "The Internal African Frontier: The Making of African Political Culture." In *The African Frontier: The Reproduction of Traditional African Societies*, edited by Igor Kopytoff, 3–84. Bloomington: Indiana University Press, 1987.

Lee, Christopher Joon-Hai. "The 'Native' Undefined: Colonial Categories, Anglo-African Status and the Politics of Kinship in British Central Africa, 1929–38." *Journal of African History* 46 no. 3 (2005): 455–78.

Leslie, J. A. K. *A Survey of Dar es Salaam.* London: Oxford University Press, 1963.

Leubuscher, Charlotte. *Tanganyika Territory: A Study of Economic Policy under Mandate.* London: Oxford University Press, 1944.

Lindsay, Lisa. *Working with Gender: Wage Labor and Social Change in Southwestern Nigeria.* Portsmouth, NH: Heinemann, 2003.

Listowel, Judith. *The Making of Tanganyika.* London: Chatto and Windus, 1965.

Lobo, Lois. *They Came to Africa: 200 Years of the Asian Presence in Tanzania.* Dar es Salaam: Tanzania Printers, 2000.

Lodhi, Abdulaziz. *Oriental Influences in Swahili: A Study in Language and Culture Contacts*. Göteborg: Acta Universitatis Gothoburgensis, 2000.

Lofchie, Michael. "The Politics of Agricultural Policy." In *Beyond Capitalism vs. Socialism in Kenya and Tanzania*, edited by Joel D. Barkan, 129–73. Boulder, CO: Lynne Rienner, 1994.

Lohrmann, Ullrich. *Voices from Tanganyika: Great Britain, the United Nations and the Decolonization of a Trust Territory, 1946–1961*. Berlin: Lit Verlag, 2007.

Lugalla, Joseph. *Crisis, Urbanization, and Urban Poverty in Tanzania*. Lanham: University Press of America, 1995.

Mamdani, Mahmood. *Citizen and Subject: Contemporary Africa and the Legacy of Late Colonialism*. Princeton, NJ: Princeton University Press, 1996.

———. *When Victims Become Killers: Colonialism, Nativism, and the Genocide in Rwanda*. Princeton, NJ: Princeton University Press, 2001.

Mangat, J. S. *A History of the Asians in East African, c. 1886 to 1945*. Oxford: Clarendon Press, 1969.

Mapunda, H. *Historia ya Mapambano ya Mtanzania*. Dar es Salaam: Tanzania Publishing, 1980.

Martin, Denis-Constant. *Tanzanie: l'invention d'une culture politique*. Paris: Presses de la Fondation nationale des sciences politiques and Karthala. 1988.

Mazrui, Alamin, and Ibrahim Noor Shariff. *The Swahili: Idiom and Identity of an African People*. Trenton, NJ: Africa World Press, 1994.

Mbilinyi, Marjorie. "'City' and 'Countryside' in Colonial Tanganyika." *Economic and Political Weekly* 20, no. 43 (1985): 88–96.

McCarthy, D. M. P. *Colonial Bureaucracy and Creating Underdevelopment: Tanganyika, 1919–1940*. Ames: Iowa State University Press, 1982.

McCaskie, T. C. *Asante Identities: History and Modernity in an African Village, 1850–1950*. Edinburgh: Edinburgh University Press, 2000.

Metcalf, Thomas R. *Imperial Connections: India in the Indian Ocean Arena, 1860–1920*. Berkeley: University of California Press, 2007.

Middleton, John. *The World of the Swahili: An African Mercantile Civilization*. New Haven, CT: Yale University Press, 1992.

Milingwa, F. E., ed. *Diwani Yetu*. Arusha: Longman Tanzania, 1970.

Moffett, J. P., ed. *Handbook of Tanganyika*. Dar es Salaam: 2nd ed. Government Printer, 1958.

Mtoro bin Mwinyi Bakari. *The Customs of the Swahili People: The Desturi za Waswahili of Mtoro bin Mwinyi Bakari and Other Swahili Persons*. Translated and edited by J. W. T. Allen. Berkeley: University of California Press, 1981.

Mustafa, Sophia. *The Tanganyika Way: A Personal Story of Tanganyika's Growth to Independence*. Nairobi: East African Literature Bureau, 1961.

Mwaruka, Ramadhani. *Masimulizi juu ya Uzaramo*. London: MacMillan, 1965.

Myers, Garth Andrew. *Disposable Cities: Garbage, Governance and Sustainable Development in Urban Africa*. Aldershot: Ashgate, 2005.

Nagar, Richa. "Communal Discourses, Marriage, and the Politics of Gendered

Social Boundaries among South Asian Immigrants in Tanzania." *Gender, Place and Culture* 5 (1998): 117–39.

——. "The Making of Hindu Communal Organizations, Places, and Identities in Postcolonial Dar es Salaam." *Environment and Planning D: Society and Space* 15 (1997): 707–30.

——. "The South Asian Diaspora in Tanzania: A History Retold." *Comparative Studies of South Asia, Africa and the Middle East* 16 (1996): 62–80.

Nagar, Richa, and Helga Leitner. "Contesting Social Relations in Communal Places: Identity Politics among Asian Communities in Dar es Salaam." In *Cities of Difference*, edited by Jane M. Jacobs and Ruth Fincher, 226–51. New York: Guilford Press, 1998.

Nyerere, Julius K. *Freedom and Development, Uhuru na Maendeleo: A Selection from Writings and Speeches, 1968–1973.* Dar es Salaam: Oxford University Press, 1973.

——. *Freedom and Socialism, Uhuru na Ujamaa: A Selection from Writings and Speeches, 1965–1967.* Dar es Salaam: Oxford University Press, 1968.

——. *Freedom and Unity, Uhuru na Umoja: A Selection from Writings and Speeches, 1952–65.* Dar es Salaam: Oxford University Press, 1966.

Oonk, Gijsbert. "'After Shaking His Hand, Start Counting Your Fingers': Trust and Images in Indian Business Networks, East Africa, 1900–2000." *Itinerario* 28, no. 3 (2004): 70–88.

——. "The Changing Culture of the Hindu Lohana Community in East Africa." *Contemporary South Asia* 13, no. 1 (2004): 7–23.

——. "'We Lost our gift of Expression': Loss of the Mother Tongue among Indians in East Africa, 1880–2000." In *Global Indian Diasporas: Exploring Trajectories of Migration and Theory*, edited by Gijsbert Oonk, 67–87. Amsterdam: Amsterdam University Press, 2007.

Ostrosky, V., and J. Tejani. "Second Tentative Word List." *Swahili* 37 (1968): 209–24; and *Swahili* 38 (1969): 54–99.

Owens, Geoffrey Ross. "The Secret History of TANU: Rumor, Historiography and Muslim Unrest in Contemporary Dar es Salaam." *History and Anthropology* 16, no. 4 (2005): 441–63.

——. "The Shomvi: a precursor to global ethnoscapes and indigenization in precolonial East Africa." *Ethnohistory* 53, no. 4 (2006): 715–51.

Parsons, Timothy. *The African Rank-and-File: Social Implications of Colonial Military Service in the King's African Rifles, 1902–1964.* Portsmouth, NH: Heinemann, 1999.

Pouwels, Randall. *Horn and Crescent: Cultural Change and Traditional Islam on the East African Coast, 800–1900.* Cambridge: Cambridge University Press, 1987.

Pratt, R. Cranford. *The Critical Phase in Tanzania, 1945–1968: Nyerere and the Emergence of a Socialist Strategy.* Cambridge: Cambridge University Press, 1976.

Prestholdt, Jeremy. *Domesticating the World: African Consumerism and the Genealogies of Globalization.* Berkeley: University of California Press, 2008.

Prins, A. H. J. *The Swahili Speaking Peoples of Zanzibar and the East African Coast: Arabs, Shirazi and Swahili*. London: International African Institute, 1961.

Raimbault, Franck. "Les stratégies de reclassement des élites arabes et indiennes à Dar-es-Salaam durant la colonization allemande (1891–1914)." *Hypothèses* 5 (2001): 109–18.

———. "L'évolution de l'espace péri-urbain à Dar-es-Salaam durant la colonisation allemande (1890–1914)." In *De Dar es Salaam à Bongoland*, edited by Bernard Calas, 35–105. Nairobi/Paris: IFRA, 2006.

Ranger, T. O. *Dance and Society in Eastern Africa, 1890–1970: The Beni "Ngoma."* London: Heinemann, 1975.

Sabot, R. H. *Economic Development and Urban Migration in Tanzania, 1900–1971*. Oxford: Clarendon Press, 1979.

Sadleir, Randal. *Tanzania: Journey to Republic*. London: Radcliffe Press, 1999.

Sahlins, Marshall. *Stone Age Economics*. New York: Aldine, 1974.

Said, Mohamed. *The Life and Times of Abdulwahid Sykes (1924–1968): The Untold Story of the Muslim Struggle against British Colonialism in Tanganyika*. London: Minerva, 1998.

Salim, Ahmed I. "'Native or Non-Native?': The Problem of Identity and the Social Stratification of the Arab-Swahili of Kenya." *Hadith* 6 (1976): 65–85.

Sayers, Gerald F., ed. *The Handbook of Tanganyika*. London: Macmillan, 1930.

Scott, R. R. "The Growth of a Public Health Service in a Tropical Town." *East African Medical Journal* 10 (1933): 130–44.

———. "Public Health Services in Dar es Salaam in the 'Twenties." *East African Medical Journal* 40 (1963): 339–53.

Scotton, Carol M. M. "Some Swahili Political Words." *Journal of Modern African Studies* 3 (1965): 527–41.

Shadle, Brett. "Bridewealth and Female Consent: Marriage Disputes in African Courts, Gusiiland, Kenya." *Journal of African History* 44 (2003): 241–62.

Sharkey, Heather J. *Living with Colonialism: Nationalism and Culture in the Anglo-Egyptian Sudan*. Berkeley: University of California Press, 2003.

Shivji, Issa G. *Not Yet Democracy: Reforming Land Tenure in Tanzania*. London: IIED, 1998.

Sidbury, James. *Becoming African in America: Race and Nation in the Early Black Atlantic*. Oxford: Oxford University Press, 2007.

Smith, Edwin William. *Aggrey of Africa: A Study in Black and White*. New York: Richard R. Smith, 1930.

Smith, William E. *Nyerere of Tanzania*. London: Gollancz, 1973.

Soske, Jon. "Navigating Difference: Gender, Miscegenation and Indian Domestic Space in Twentieth-Century Durban." In *Eyes Across the Water: Navigating the Indian Ocean*, edited by Pamila Gupta, Isabel Hofmeyr, and Michael Pearson, 197–219. Pretoria: UNISA Press, 2010.

Stocking, George W., Jr. *Victorian Anthropology*. New York: Free Press, 1987.

Stoler, Ann Laura. *Carnal Knowledge and Imperial Power: Race and the Intimate in Colonial Rule*. Berkeley: University of California Press, 2002.

Stren, Richard. *Urban Inequality and Housing Policy in Tanzania: The Problem of Squatting.* Berkeley: Institute of International Studies, 1975.

Strobel, Margaret. *Muslim Women in Mombasa, 1890–1975.* New Haven: Yale University Press, 1979.

Sturmer, Martin. *The Media History of Tanzania.* Ndanda: Ndanda Mission Press, 1998.

Sutton, J. E. G. "Dar es Salaam: A Sketch of a Hundred Years." *Tanzania Notes and Records* 71 (1970): 1–19.

Swantz, Lloyd W. *The Medicine Man among the Zaramo of Dar es Salaam.* Uppsala: Scandinavian Institute of African Studies, 1990.

Swantz, Marja-Liisa. *Ritual and Symbol in Transitional Zaramo Society with Special Reference to Women.* Lund: Gleerup, 1970.

Tanganyika. *Hansard.* Dar es Salaam: Government Printer, 1926–1964.

———. *Provincial Annual Reports.* Dar es Salaam: Government Printer, 1921–1961.

———. *Report of the Committee on Rising Costs.* Dar es Salaam: Government Printers, 1951.

———. *Tanganyika Territory Trade Reports.* Dar es Salaam: Government Printer. Annual reports, 1934–1948.

———. *A Report by Mr. E. C. Baker on the Social and Economic Conditions in the Tanga Province.* Dar es Salaam: Government Printer, 1934.

Tanganyika African National Union. *Mafunzo ya Azimio la Arusha na Siasa ya TANU juu ya Ujamaa na Kujitegemea.* Dar es Salaam: Idara ya Elimu ya Siasa, 1967.

———. *Maisha ya Ujamaa.* Dar es Salaam: National Printing Company, 1972.

Tanner, R. E. S. "Land Rights on the Tanganyika Coast." *African Studies* 19 (1960): 14–25.

Tanzania. *Majadiliano ya Bunge (Hansard).* Dar es Salaam: Government Printer, 1964–1976.

———. *Wages, Incomes, Rural Development, Investment and Price Policy.* Dar es Salaam: Government Printer, 1967.

Tanzania, and UN-HABITAT. *Re-establishing Effective Housing Finance Mechanisms in Tanzania: The Potentials and Bottlenecks.* Nairobi: U.N. Human Settlements Programme, 2003.

Temu, A. J. "The Rise and Triumph of Nationalism." In *A History of Tanganyika,* edited by I. N. Kimambo and A. J. Temu, 189–213. Nairobi: East African Publishing, 1969.

Temu, C. W. "The Development of Political Vocabulary in Swahili." *Kiswahili* 41 (1971): 3–17.

Tinker, Hugh. *The Banyan Tree: Overseas Emigrants from India, Pakistan, and Bangladesh.* Oxford: Oxford University Press, 1977.

Trimingham, J. Spencer. *Islam in East Africa.* Oxford: Clarendon Press, 1964.

Tripp, Aili Mari. *Changing the Rules: The Politics of Liberalization and the Informal Economy in Tanzania.* Berkeley: University of California Press, 1997.

Tsuruta, Tadasu. "Popular Music, Sports, and Politics: A Development of Urban

Cultural Movements in Dar es Salaam, 1930s–1960s." *African Study Mono-graphs* 24, no. 3 (2003): 195–222.

———. "Simba or Yanga?: Football and Urbanization in Dar es Salaam." In *Dar es Salaam: Histories from an Emerging African Metropolis*, edited by James R. Brennan, Andrew Burton, and Yusuf Lawi, 198–212. Dar es Salaam/Nairobi: Mkuki na Nyota/BIEA, 2007.

———. "Urban-Rural Relationships in Colonial Dar es Salaam: Some Notes on Ethnic Associations and Recreations, 1930s–1950s." *Memoirs of the Faculty of Agriculture of Kinki University* 36 (2003): 63–69.

Ulotu, Ulotu Abubaker. *Historia ya TANU*. Dar es Salaam: East African Literature Bureau, 1971.

Van den Berghe, Pierre L. *The Ethnic Phenomenon*. New York: Elsevier, 1981.

Vassanji, Moyez G. *The Gunny Sack*. Portsmouth, NH: Heinemann, 1989.

Vincent, Joan. "The Dar es Salaam Townsman: Social and Political Aspects of City Life." *Tanzania Notes and Records* 71 (1970): 149–56.

Voigt-Graf, Carmen. *Asian Communities in Tanzania: A Journey Through Past and Present Times*. Hamburg: Institut für Afrika-Kunde, 1998.

Vorlaufer, Karl. *Koloniale und Nachkoloniale Stadtplanung in Dar es Salaam*. Frankfurt am Main: Johann Wolfgang Goethe-Universität, 1970.

Waugh, Evelyn. *Remote People*. London: Duckworth, 1931.

Weber, Max. *Economy and Society: An Outline of Interpretive Sociology*. Edited by Guenther Roth and Claus Wittich. 2 vols. Berkeley: University of California Press, 1978.

Westcott, Nicholas J. "An East African Radical: The Life of Erica Fiah." *Journal of African History* 22 (1981): 85–101.

———. "The Impact of the Second World War on Tanganyika, 1939–49." In *Africa and the Second World War*, edited by David Killingray and Richard Rathbone, 143–59. New York: St. Martin's, 1986.

White, Luise. *The Comforts of Home: Prostitution in Colonial Nairobi*. Chicago: University of Chicago Press, 1990.

———. *Speaking with Vampires: Rumor and History in Colonial Africa*. Berkeley: University of California Press, 2000.

Willis, Justin. *Mombasa, the Swahili, and the Making of the Mijikenda*. Oxford: Clarendon Press, 1993.

Yaeger, Rodger. *Tanzania: An African Experiment*. 2nd ed. Boulder, CO: Westview Press, 1989.

Young, M. Crawford. "Nationalism, Ethnicity and Class in Africa: A Retrospective." *Cahiers d'Etudes Africaines* 26 (1986): 421–95.

Index

Abbasi, M. O., 56, 83
Abushiri wa Mbwana, M. M., 135–36
acquisition of buildings. *See* Building
    Acquisition Act of 1971
adverse possession, 31, 43–45
African (as term), 124–25
African Association, 19, 68–69, 105, 219nn135–
    36; civilization discourses of, 123–24;
    extraterritorial ambitions of, 144; on
    food and commodity shortages, 99–102;
    on housing shortages, 106–7; on inter-
    marriage, 135; labor activism of, 110, 113–15;
    racial recruitment of, 143–45, 158, 245n197
African Charcoal Dealers Union, 185
African community: civil service jobs in, 78–79,
    104, 108–9; commercial relationships of,
    70–76, 110–12, 152; as domestic servants,
    75–76, 82, 114; education in, 83, 183–84,
    186; ethnic map of, 59f; food rations in,
    99–102; Indian housing in, 36, 38, 104–7,
    230n125, 231n153; labor unions in, 78–79,
    113–16, 232n164, 233n199, 234n209; origins
    of, 60–62, 216n85; population density in,
    104, 197; population numbers of, 24, 48,
    211n5, 216n85; restricted labor migration
    of, 95–98, 151, 169–70, 227n65. *See also*
    nationalism; segregated urban zones
African identity, 2, 13, 18, 48, 58–70;
    associational life in, 66–69, 77,
    219nn135–36; coastal hierarchies in, 63–
    64, 84, 122–23, 125–26; firstcomer status
    in, 15, 18, 31, 47, 58–62, 83–84, 87, 124,
    216n92; insider-outsider rivalry in, 60,
    64–69, 84; interracial liaisons in, 128–36,
    151, 238n63; language use in, 82–83; of
    mercenaries, 65–66; in native/non-native
    categorization, 26, 125; resentment of
    Indians in, 80–83, 159, 176–81, 223n227,
    254n111; slave origins in, 65
African Muslims, 67, 83. *See also* Muslim
    population

African National Congress (ANC), 153–54
African nationalism. *See* nationalism; Pan-
    Africanism
African Problems (Kayamba), 126–27
African socialism. *See ujamaa*
African Tailors Union, 116
African Urban Housing Loan Scheme, 257n175
Afro-Shirazi Party, 152, 190
Aga Khan III, 4, 51, 54, 57–58, 77; on
    citizenship, 193, 247n229, 258n211;
    Diamond Jubilee of, 101–2; on nationalist
    movements, 150
Aga Khan IV, 150
Aggrey, James, 120, 123–24, 132
aibu, 17, 139–40
Aiyar, Sana, 6
Ali, Ramadhani, 69, 219n136
All-Muslim National Union of Tanganyika
    (AMNUT), 161
Amin, Idi, 2, 3, 190, 192, 247n239
Amri Abedi, Sheikh Kaluta, 127, 156
Anderson, Benedict, 13, 119
Andrews, Charles, 51–52, 212n23
Anjuman Islamiyya, 83
anticolonial discourses, 6–7, 48–49, 160. *See
    also* nationalism
Arab community, 63, 66–67; African domestic
    servants in, 76; commercial role of, 152;
    food rationing in, 99; immigration of,
    152; as *liwali*, 67–68, 144; in native/non-
    native categorization, 25; native quarter
    housing of, 231n153; population numbers
    of, 25, 204n12; social status in, 122
Arusha Declaration of 1967, 166, 168–69, 172,
    183, 186–87, 190, 253n81
Asian Association, 145, 146, 150
Asian Commercial Employees Association, 116
Asian community. *See* Indian community
askari, 59, 65–66, 131; discourses on *heshima* of,
    136–43, 157–58, 241n115; sexual liaisons
    of, 139–40

Association of Masuriama and Machotara, 135
Ataturk, Kemal, 249n14
Austin, Gareth, 202n23

Bakari, Mtoro bin Mwinyi, 61
Baker, E. C., 34, 38, 40–41, 64, 68, 96, 104
Banda, Hastings Kamuzu, 166, 171
Bantu Group, 147
Banzi, Alex, 175
Barber, Karin, 16–17
Barghash, Sultan of Zanzibar, 61
Barongo, E. B. M., 151
Barriers to Democracy (Nyerere), 149–50
Bates, Darrell, 139
Batetera Union, 65
beer brewing, 111–12
Berlin, Isaiah, 160
Berman, Bruce, 11, 34
Bharati, Agehananda, 182
Bissell, William C., 27
black markets, 35, 93–94, 100, 102–3, 110–11, 193
Boal, V. R., 54, 55, 56
Bohora community, 49, 83, 183
Bone, Dick, 95
Bose, Sugata, 7
British Nationality Act, 145
British Protected Persons, 155, 247n229
British Railways, 108–9
Brown, Kevin, 141–42
Brubaker, Rogers, 14, 211n1
Bryceson, Derek, 154
Buguruni neighborhood, 15, 153, 164, 172, 189–90, 192
Building Acquisition Act of 1971, 3–6, 10, 159, 187–94, 197, 199, 201n7, 247n239, 259n3
building codes, 29, 31–32, 38–39, 107, 206n38, 206n45
building ownership: nationalization of, 3–6, 10, 159, 187–94, 197, 199, 201n7, 247n239, 259n3; status achieved through, 64–65; by women, 65, 111–12
Burahim, Binti, 82
Bushiri Rebellion of 1888, 61
Byatt, Horace, 23, 29, 51–52, 55, 222n197

Cameron, Donald, 44, 78
caricature, 10–11, 16, 52–53, 70, 82, 159, 176–81, 254n111
Carrier Corps Building, 38
categories of identity, 1–3, 20, 47–48, 119–21, 197; in colonial urban spaces, 11–18, 69–70, 203n32; as native or non-native, 17–18, 21–46, 125; print media debates on, 16–17; processual nature of, 3, 16; role of the state in, 16. *See also* ethnicity/tribe;

nation; race
census of 1929, 24, 25, 204n12
Chagga Democratic Party, 161
chama, 66–67
Chama cha Mapinduzi (Revolutionary Party) (CCM), 199–200
Chande, Andy, 77
Chopra, I. C., 144–45
chotara, 129, 133–36, 151
citizenship, 153–57, 177, 200, 247n229; Indian community options in, 145, 155, 177, 247n229, 258n211; urban bias in, 167–72
civilization/barbarism discourses, 118, 119–28, 157, 236n18; female racial purity in, 128–36; self-improvement guides in, 126–28; terminology of nationalism and race in, 118, 119–26
civil service, 77–80, 104, 108–9, 221n174, 222n197; Africanization of, 184; in citizenship debates, 155–56; as *naizi*, 174, 175
class, 16; formation of, 9; in native half-caste designations, 25–26; in native/non-native categorization, 25; postcolonial language of, 172–76, 195; in workplace settings, 107–16
clothing distribution, 94–95
Colonial Development and Welfare Act of 1940, 88
colonial rule, 1–17; categories of identity under, 1–3, 11–15, 17–18, 21, 47, 69–70, 84, 119–20, 203n32; civil service in, 77–80, 104, 108–9, 221n174, 222n197; contradictions of accumulation and control under, 11–15, 18–19, 34–35; direct rule in, 61–62, 84; independence from, 4, 16, 143; indirect rule in, 61–64, 78, 84; legal-administrative system of, 22–26, 27, 28; literacy rates under, 17, 138–39, 241n115, 246n4; paternalist protectionism of, 23, 24, 26, 34–35, 38–39, 196–97; pluralistic society of, 7–8. *See also* postcolonial era; World War II
Colony for India, A (Morison), 51
Colson, Elizabeth, 44
commerce, 34–37; African work in, 110–11; Arab work in, 152; black markets in, 35, 102–3, 110–11; credit strategies in, 10–11, 35–37, 53, 57, 70, 72–75, 185–86, 214n63, 220n160; *dukas* in, 10, 34–35, 70–71, 152–53; Indian community in, 52–53, 57–58, 70–76, 102, 153, 184–85, 194; official city markets in, 37–38; pawnshops in, 36–37, 72–73, 220n156
communal lands, 32, 42–45
Communist Party, 115–16

Conveyancing Act of 1923, 187
Cooper, Frederick, 9, 14, 40; on commerce and
    credit, 70; on identity, 211n1; on labor
    policies, 86, 87–89, 108
Cost of Living Committee, 103
credit strategies, 10–11, 35–37, 53, 70, 72–75,
    214n63; *amana* system of, 220n160;
    of Indian community *hundi*, 57; of
    pawnshops, 36–37, 72–73, 220n156; in
    the postcolonial era, 185–86, 255n154;
    reciprocity in, 71, 73–74; of women's
    revolving credit societies, 172
Credit to Natives Act of 1923, 36–37, 187
customary tenure, 44–45

dance clubs, 67, 77
Dar es Salaam, 7–8, 15–19, 201n1; Buguruni
    neighborhood of, 15, 153, 164, 172, 189–
    90, 192; firstcomer status in, 15, 18, 31, 47,
    58–62, 83–84, 87, 124; founding of, 17, 61;
    Gerezani neighborhood of, 15; Kariakoo
    neighborhood of, 15; maps of, 30f, 168f;
    Mnazi Mmoja (neutral zone) of, 31,
    83, 115; native quarter of, 33–34; official
    market of, 37–38; original settlement
    of, 43; population of, 24, 25, 28, 48, 54,
    85–87, 198, 204n12, 211n5; postcolonial
    division of, 169; public health in,
    28–31, 35–36, 102, 206n29; Uhindini
    neighborhood of, 5, 32–34, 104–7, 197;
    Upanga neighborhood of, 31, 101, 197,
    231n153. *See also* African community;
    Arab community; European community;
    Indian community; segregated urban
    zones; urban spaces
Dar es Salaam Chamber of Commerce, 52, 55
Dar es Salaam Club, 77
Dar es Salaam Cultural Society, 77
Dar es Salaam Merchants Chamber, 185
Dar es Salaam Tenants Committee, 56
Daya, Suleiman, 153
descent, 13–15, 16, 19, 47, 48; in *askari*
    discourses, 136–43; interracial liaisons
    in, 128–36, 151, 238n63; in nationalism
    discourses, 118, 120–21, 123–24, 127–28; in
    native/non-native categorization, 25–26;
    as patrilineal, 14–15, 19, 118, 120–22,
    128–36, 157
descriptive sociology, 7–8
Diwan, H. P., 69
dockworkers, 92, 112–15, 234n207
Dodoma, 169
Domestic and Hotel Workers Union, 151–52
domestic service, 75–76, 82, 114, 176
duka (store) circuits, 10–11, 70–71; Indian

owners of, 34–35; as sites of racial
    tension, 152–53

East Africa Indian National Congress, 54
East African Indian community. *See* Indian
    community
East African Salary Commission, 108
East Africa Royal Commission, 197
Economic Control Board, 93, 94, 97; food
    politics of, 99; textile policies of, 103
economic rent, 9–10, 189
El Hatimi, Muhamed bin Shale, 60
English language, 1, 16–17
ethnicity/tribe, 1–2, 14–15, 47–48, 60–66,
    211nn3–4; *kabila* as term for, 120–21,
    160–62; map of, 59f
European community, 48–49; African
    domestic servants in, 76, 114; antipathy
    toward Indian merchants in, 52–53; civil
    service jobs of, 108–9; clubs of, 77; food
    rationing in, 99–100; non-native status
    of, 23–24; political power and privilege
    of, 22, 34; population numbers of, 48,
    204n12, 211n5; segregated urban spaces
    of, 28–31; tax policies for, 55–56. *See also*
    colonial rule
European Women's Service League, 114
exploitation, 147, 158, 160, 163–67, 172, 175–76,
    195

Fair, Laura, 12, 94
famine of 1946, 100–101
Fiah, Erica, 69, 73, 75, 221n170; on racial
    mixing, 132; on the term "native," 125,
    133, 237n37
film ratings, 77
Fimbo ya Mnyonge (*The Poor Man's Stick*), 171
firstcomer status, 15, 18, 31, 47, 58–62, 83–84,
    87, 124, 216n92
First Rhodesian Building Society, 257n175
Flowarose Salama binti Arubati, 130–34,
    239n75
Flurbuch field survey, 43–44
food rationing, 89–94, 113, 226n33; black
    markets in, 102–3; contaminated foods
    and, 102–3; racialized politics of, 98–107
football clubs, 66–67, 77
Fox, Robin, 13
freeholds, 23, 31, 42–44
Freehold Titles Act of 1963, 187
Freund, Bill, 8
Furnivall, J. S., 7–8

Gandhi, Mohandas, 51–52, 54, 55, 143
Garvey, Marcus, 124

Geiger, Susan, 160
gender contexts: of building ownership, 65,
    111–12; of literacy rates, 17, 235n4; of
    male/female ratios, 111, 172, 232n177;
    of matrilineal relationships, 129; of
    patrilineal descent traditions, 14–15, 19,
    118, 120–22, 128–36, 157; of postcolonial
    urban life, 172, 173; of racial purity, 128–
    36; of wage labor, 111. See also women
gentrification, 33–34, 37–39, 41, 107
Gerezani neighborhood, 15, 33–34, 208n73
German East Africa, 1, 17–18, 23–24, 201n1;
    Bushiri Rebellion in, 61; demise of,
    27–28; direct rule in, 61–62; as Indian
    colony, 51–52; Indian immigration to, 49;
    kiwanja plot tax in, 32, 207n59; land sales
    in, 43–44; mercenary soldiers in, 59, 65–
    66; rentier behavior in, 40; segregationist
    policies of, 29, 31–32, 206n38. See also
    colonial rule
Gillman, Clement, 77
Giri, Varahagiri Venkata, 180
Glassman, Jonathan: on identity
    categorization, 3, 12, 203n32; on racial
    thought, 118–20, 236n18
Goans, 49, 50, 55
Goldberg, David, 119
Great Britain, 2
Great Depression, 41, 56–57
Greater India discourses, 6–8, 51–58, 71;
    anticolonialism of, 6–7, 48–49;
    nationalist discourses in, 54–56, 58,
    142–46; Vande Mataram in, 57–58
Gregory, Robert, 213nn34–35
Gujarati language, 51, 54–55, 71, 82, 212n14
Gujarat region, 49–51, 211n7
The Gunny Sack (Vassanji), 4, 153
Gymkhana Club, 77

Hamilton, G. G., 115–16
Hanley, Gerald, 138–39
hartal strike of 1923, 54–55, 71
Hehe Democratic Party, 161
Helps, E. H., 41
heshima, 17, 81–82, 124, 157–58; askari
    discourses on, 136–43; definition of, 138;
    literacy in, 138–39, 235n4, 241n115
Hindu Mandal, 50, 56, 146, 184, 212n13
Hindus/Hinduism, 83; caste organization of,
    49–50; food rations for, 99; in India's
    communal divisions, 7, 18, 49–51, 56–58;
    religious practices of, 139. See also Indian
    community
honor. See heshima
housing, 197; financing of, 257n175; home

ownership in, 64–65; postcolonial
    shortages of, 187–88; rents and renters
    in, 9, 34, 41, 95, 187–88, 227n62; squatters
    and illegal buildings in, 188–89, 198,
    257n175; Swahili-style of, 104, 198; World
    War II shortages of, 95, 104–5, 227n62,
    230n124. See also rentiers; segregated
    urban zones
Hundred Horizons, A (Bose), 7

identity formation, 1–3, 17–18, 47–84, 211n1;
    conflation of categories with, 14; core
    elements of, 11; for East African Indians,
    49–58; firstcomer status in, 15, 18, 31, 47,
    58–62, 83–84, 87, 124, 216n92; idioms of
    descent in, 14–15, 16, 19, 47, 48. See also
    categories of identity
Ilala neighborhood, 32, 39
Iliffe, John: on African populations in Dar es
    Salaam, 58–60, 69; on askari life, 139;
    on creation of tribes, 84; on honor, 17;
    on labor organization, 112–15; on Martin
    Kayamba, 126; on nationalism, 160,
    248n1; on rationing, 98; on the strike of
    1950, 115; on TANU, 148, 160
Imagined Communities (Anderson), 13
India: African askari in, 138–43; citizenship in,
    155, 247n229; communalism of the 1930s
    in, 7, 18, 49–51, 56–58; Greater India
    discourses in, 6–8, 51–58, 71, 142–46;
    nationalist movement in, 54–56, 58, 144
Indian Association, 33, 51, 145; communal
    antagonism in, 56; strike leadership of,
    54–56, 71
Indian community, 2–3, 8, 20, 181–87;
    accumulation of wealth in, 10–11, 17–18,
    52–53, 71–72, 75, 159, 181–84, 194, 213n26,
    213nn34–35; African domestic servants
    of, 75–76, 82, 114; citizenship options of,
    145, 155, 177, 193, 247n229, 258n211; in
    civil service, 78–80, 108–9, 184, 221n174,
    222n197; colonial classification of,
    17–18, 21–24, 51; commercial activities
    of, 34–37, 52–53, 57–58, 70–76, 102,
    110–11, 152–53, 184–85, 194, 219n144;
    communal stratification of, 49–51, 56–58,
    83; Diamond Jubilee celebrations in,
    101–2; education in, 55, 183–84, 186;
    engagement with TANU of, 145–50, 186;
    European antipathy toward, 52–53; fear
    of crime and violence in, 80–81, 145,
    153; financial crime in, 182–84, 192–93,
    199–200; food rationing in, 99–100;
    gentrification in, 33–34, 37–39, 41, 107;
    Greater India discourses in, 6–8, 18,

48–49, 54, 71, 142–46; hoarding in, 103, 182, 185; identity formation in, 49–58; language use in, 54–55, 71, 82, 212n14; nationalization of buildings of, 3–6, 10, 159, 187–95, 197, 199, 201n7, 259n3; native quarter housing of, 34, 36, 39, 41, 46, 104–7, 230n125; pawnshops of, 36–37, 72–73, 185–86, 220n156; peri-urban land of, 42–46, 153, 189–90; political protests and strikes of, 54–56, 57, 71; population numbers of, 24, 25, 54, 193, 200, 204n12; postcolonial exodus of, 5, 19, 181, 186–87, 192–93, 258n211; postcolonial experiences of, 159, 176–87, 254n111; promotion to non-native status of, 21–24; rentier behavior in, 39–41, 56, 95, 104, 153, 159; residential quarter of, 5, 29, 31–34, 54, 194, 197, 231n153; rights of occupancy tenancies in, 32–33; self-segregation of, 76–83, 181–87; social institutions of, 56–58; tax policies for, 55–56; trade unions in, 56, 116; World War II restrictions on, 95. *See also* Uhindini neighborhood
Indian Merchants Chamber, 56, 146, 185
Indian National Congress, 54–55, 58
Indian Ocean region, 6–8
Indians Overseas Association, 54
indigeneity. *See* native/non-native categories
intermarriage, 178–79
International Labor Organization (ILO), 168–69
interracial liaisons, 81–82, 128–36, 151, 238n63
Investment Promotion Services (IPS) skyscraper, 4
Isherwood, A. A. M., 77
Ismailia Council, 50, 58, 212n13
Ismaili Khojas. *See* Khoja Ismaili community
Ithnasheri Khoja community, 49, 83, 193
Itote, Waruhiu, 136–37

Jamal, Amir, 146, 154, 186, 245n192
Jamiatul Islamiyya, 67, 83
Joelson, F. S., 52–53
Joseph, May, 186
Jubilee Insurance Company, 57

kabila, 120–21, 160–62
kabwela, 16, 172–76, 195, 253n81
Kachchhi language, 82
Kachchh region, 49–51
Kahama, George, 157, 185
Kalidas, Sheth Mathuradas, 57
Kamaliza, Michael, 156
Kambona, Oscar, 154, 190
Kandoro, Saadani Abdu, 127, 239n75

Kaplan, Martha, 13
Kariakoo neighborhood, 15, 33–34; diversity of, 197; gentrification in, 38–39, 41, 107; housing nationalization in, 195; Indian residents in, 36, 38, 104–7, 230n125, 231n153; Manyema landlords in, 65, 217n103; official market in, 37–38; rent-paying in, 40–41; street vendors in, 110, 152
Karimjee, A. Y. A., 163
Karume, Abeid, 178–79, 186–87, 190
Kawawa, Rashidi, 161, 184, 191–92
Kayamba, Martin, 126–27
Kelly, John D., 13
Kenya, 24, 49, 120, 144
Khoja Ismaili community, 49, 51, 83, 116; citizenship of, 247n229, 258n211; communalism of, 57–58; Diamond Jubilee celebrations of, 101–2; emigration of, 193; pawnshops of, 36–37, 72–73
Kibanda, Mohamed, 15
Kilama, Pazi (chief), 61, 215n78
King's African Rifles (KAR), Sixth, 136–43
Kirumbi, Yusuf, 67
Kisutu neighborhood, 31, 33–34, 37, 189, 208n73
Klamroth, Martin, 62
Kombo, Salum, 127–28
Kombo, Thaabit, 175
Kondo, Kitwana, 256n163
Kondo, K. K., 162
Kopytoff, Igor, 60
Kundya, M. R., 155
Kunzru, Hradayanath, 142
Kwetu newspaper, 69

labor, 8–9, 75, 221n174; in civil service, 77–80, 104, 108–9, 174, 175, 184; creation of a stable urban working class and, 88–89, 95–96, 108, 116–17, 246n210; in dockwork, 112–15, 234n207, 234n209; in domestic service, 75–76, 82, 114; in informal economies in, 74, 110–12, 221n164; living-wage policies for, 37, 89–93, 111, 226n33, 246n210; mass conscription of, 97; migration of the 1940s of, 85–87, 95–98; postcolonial reforms of, 186–87, 246n210; as street vendors, 110–11, 152; strikes and unrest of, 88, 90, 91, 92, 101, 102, 107–16, 151–52, 234n207; trade unions of, 56, 78–79, 113–16, 151–52, 232n164, 233n199, 234n209; women's roles in, 74, 110–12, 172, 221n164; World War II regulation of, 85–89, 95–98. *See also* urban entitlement
Land Act of 1999, 198

landlords. *See* rentiers

Land Ordinance, 187

land policies, 197; administration of, 42–43; of adverse possession, 31, 43–45; on communal lands, 32, 42–45; on freeholds, 23, 31, 42–44, 187; *kiwanja* plot taxes in, 32–33, 207n59; native protections in, 23, 35, 69, 144, 187, 196–97; in peri-urban areas, 41–46, 69, 104; in post-colonial Dar es Salaam, 198; of rights of occupancy tenancies, 32–33; segregationist goals of, 22, 27–34, 46; in title by prescription, 43

language of identity. *See* categories of identity

language use: in discourses on nationalism and race, 4–5, 19–20, 118–28, 159–67; English language use, 1, 16–17; in the Indian community, 54–55, 71, 82, 212n14; word borrowing in, 71–73, 120–23. *See also* Swahili language

Larson, Lorne, 136

League of Nations mandate, 11, 23, 54

Leslie, J. A. K., 65, 147, 239nn83–84, 255n154

literacy rates, 17, 138–39, 235n4, 241n115

liwali, 67–68, 144

Lonsdale, John, 11, 34

Lugard, Frederick, 44

machotara. *See* mixed-race individuals

Madalito, Cecil, 79

maendeleo, 146–48, 157–58, 164

Maintenance of Illegitimate Children Act, 135

Majid, Sultan of Zanzibar, 61, 65

Makaranga, H. M., 5

Makwaia, Kidaha, 144–45

malaria, 28, 31, 206n29

Mamdani, Mahmood, 21–22

Manyema people, 59, 64–65, 216n92; as landlords, 65, 217n103; as street vendors, 111

maps: of African ethnic groups, 59f; of Dar es Salaam in 1925, 30f; of Dar es Salaam in 1976, 168f; of the Western Indian Ocean and Gujarat, 50f

marriage practices, 129, 137, 172, 178–79

Martin, Denis-Constant, 249n21

Masasi African Democratic Union, 161

Mascarenhas, Adolfo, 62

Maswanya, Saidi, 187

Matoroka, Hamedi Said, 164, 249n23

Maxwell, G. A. P., 78

Maxwell Committee, 78–79, 222n197

Mazrui, Alamin, 122

Mbwana, Makisi, 69

McCaskie, Tom, 138, 198

McCleery, Hugh, 45

Metcalf, Thomas R., 7

Mgonja, Chedieli, 123

Mhando, Stephen, 147, 191

Mhaville, John, 190–91

middlemen, 8

Middleton, John, 138

Milango ya Historia, 123

Ministry of National Culture, 161–62

Mission Quarter neighborhood, 33–34

Mitchell, Philip, 26, 39, 205n20, 241n163

mixed-race individuals: education of, 134; legal status of, 134–36, 240n93; in native/non-native categorization, 25–26, 205n14; social status of, 179; in *taifa* debates, 129–36, 151, 238n63, 239nn83–84

"Miye" column, 180–81

Mkande, James, 140

Mnazi Mmoja (neutral) zone, 31–32, 101, 115

Mnyampala, Mathias, 127

Moffett, J. P., 77

Mohamed, Bibi Titi, 154, 164, 190, 257n186

Mohammed, Salum, 233n199

Molohan, M. J. B., 91–92

Monsoon Victory (Hanley), 138–39

Morison, Theodore, 51

Motor Drivers and Commercial Transport Union, 234n209

Msumi, Hamisi, 15

mswahili, 162–63

Mtemvu, Zuberi, 153–54

Mtikila, Christopher, 199–200

multiracialism, 77, 121, 145; Twining's policies of, 148–49; vs. Nyerere's nonracial policies, 148–50, 153–57, 245n192

Munduli, Mrs. B., 179

Munseri, E. R., 249n14

Muslim League, 57–58

Muslim population, 49–50, 67, 83; citizenship of, 247n229; in Indian communal divisions, 7, 18, 49–51, 56–58; in Kariakoo neighborhood, 33–34; of Manyema, 59; self-segregation of, 83

Muslim School Association, 146

Mwakangale, John, 164

Mwanjisi, Roland, 254n111

Mwaruka, Ramadhani, 63

Mwindadi, Juma, 245n197

naizi, 16, 173–76, 195

Namfua, J. D., 191

nation, 1–3, 13–15, 19, 47–48. *See also* taifa

National Heroes Day, 162

National Housing Corporation, 187–88, 191

nationalism, 13–14, 18, 118–58, 198–200; African

writings on, 121; *askari* discourses on, 136–43; in citizenship debates, 153–57, 247n229; concept of *taifa* in, 119–21; conflation with race of, 14, 19; Indian community participation in, 145–46, 186; intellectual content of, 159–67; interracial liaisons in, 128–36, 238n63; language/terminology of, 118–28; multiracial discourses in, 121, 145; in postcolonial urban contexts, 159–95; role of descent in, 118, 123–24, 127–36; TANU's racial recruitment in, 143–53, 158, 160; *ujamaa* discourses in, 4–5, 19–20, 127, 159–76, 198–200, 249n21
Nationals of India Association, 146
native (as term), 124–25
native half-caste status, 25–26
native/non-native categories, 17–18, 20–46, 125, 196–97; ambiguity and improvisation in, 24–26; in commercial relationships, 34–37, 70–76; legal-administrative contexts of, 22–26, 45–46; of mixed-race individuals, 25–26, 205n14; in peri-urban land rights, 41–46; population numbers of, 24, 25, 204n12; racial basis of, 24–26, 39, 48–49; of rentiers and renters, 39–41; segregated urban spaces of, 22, 27–34, 46; in tax policies, 24, 32–33, 55–56, 207n59; as terms, 20
native quarter of Dar es Salaam, 29, 33–41; gentrification in, 38–39, 41, 107; Ilala neighbrhood of, 32, 39; Indian residents in, 34, 36, 38, 41, 46, 230n125, 231n153; trade and markets in, 37–38, 39. See *also* Kariakoo neighborhood; segregated urban zones
Nazerali, V. M., 144–45
Ndengereko people, 65, 66, 76, 216n92
Nehru, Jawaharlal, 145
Ngoni people, 60
Nguvumali Mpangile, 147, 249n23
Nyamwezi people, 60, 62, 64, 66, 161, 216n85
Nyasaland identity case, 25–26
Nyerere, Julius, 14, 93, 127, 160, 200; on agriculture and rural development, 167–68, 171, 186; on citizenship, 155–56, 247n239; on cultural assimilation, 176–77, 182, 249n14; elimination of tribal offices by, 161; housing policies of, 189–91, 194–95; localization policies of, 184; mutiny of 1964 against, 184; nationalization policies of, 4–6, 147–48, 199; nonracial politics of, 19, 148–50, 154, 157–58, 159; *ujamaa* discourses of, 163, 165, 166, 172–73, 249n21; UN visit of, 146, 173

Oberst, Timothy, 86
Orde-Brown, Granville St. John, 37, 96, 227n65
"Others," 2–3

Pakistan, 155, 247n229
Pan-Africanism, 2, 69, 118–20, 123–24, 136, 158, 200. See *also* nationalism
Pan-Islamic *khilafat* movement, 7
parasitism, 160, 163, 165
Pawnbrokers Ordinance of 1930, 220n156
pawnshops, 36–37, 72–73, 185–86, 220n156, 255n154
Pearson, Norman, 108–9, 113–14
peri-urban areas, 41–46, 69, 104; Arab street vendors in, 152; farming in, 74, 111, 221n164; native land alienation in, 42–46, 144, 153; squatters and illegal building in, 188–89, 198; witchcraft in, 164–65
Permanent Housing Finance Company, 257n175
Pinda, Mizengo, 200
Plantan, Effendi, 66
Plantan, Kleist Sykes. See Sykes, Kleist
Plantan, R. M., 105–6
plural societies, 7–8
political economy. See urban entitlement
Ponda, Ali, 124
postcolonial era, 2, 4, 15–17, 159–95, 248n10; Africanized urban life of, 181–87; Arusha Declaration of 1967 of, 166, 168–69, 172, 183, 186–87, 190; Building Acquisition Act of 1971, 3–6, 10, 159, 187–94, 197, 199, 201n7, 259n3; categories of identity in, 15; citizenship debates in, 153–57, 167–72, 247n229; credit strategies in, 185–86, 255n154; decentralization policy in, 169, 184, 251n45; equitable incomes policy in, 169; Indian exodus of, 5, 19, 181, 186–87, 192–93, 258n211; Indian racial distance in, 156, 176–87, 254n111; labor reforms of, 186–87; language of class and poverty in, 172–76, 195; minimum wage policies in, 246n210; mutiny of 1964 in, 184; presidential power in, 259n1; removal of evil in, 165; segregated urban zones in, 170–72, 189–91, 197; tribal culture in, 161–62; *ujamaa* of, 4–5, 19–20, 159–67; union with Zanzibar in, 200; urban planning and development of, 197–98. See *also* nationalism
postcolonial studies, 5–6
precedence, 60. See *also* firstcomer status
Prestholdt, Jeremy, 10, 94
Prins, A. H. J., 235n12
Property Owners Association, 95, 227n62

prostitution, 65, 111–12, 172, 239n84
public health policies, 28–31, 35–36, 102–3, 112, 206n29
Punja, Habib, 4
Punjabi language, 51, 82, 212n14
Punjab region, 49

race, 1–3, 14–15, 19, 47–48, 83–84, 199–200; caricatures of, 10–11, 16, 156, 176–81, 254n111; conflations with nation of, 14, 19; creation of categories of, 3, 11–15, 17–18, 47, 69–70, 84, 119–20, 197, 203n32; in domestic-service settings, 76, 82, 114; in intermarriage, 178–79; in interracial liaisons, 81–82, 128–36, 151, 238n63; language/terminology of, 119–21; in native/non-native categories, 24–26, 39, 48–49, 196–97. *See also* African identity; Indian community; segregated urban zones; *taifa*
racialization: of the civil service, 77–80, 108–9; of colonial protectionist policies, 38–39, 196–97; of crime and violence, 80–81, 145; of intergroup relationships, 48–49; of social structures, 14–15, 18–19; of TANU's nationalist activism, 143–53; of World War II urban entitlements, 85–87, 98–117
racial recruitment, 143–53, 158, 160
racial thought, 118–21. *See also* nationalism
Railways African Association, 113
Rattansey, Mohamed, 150
reciprocity practices, 71, 73–74
relational modes of identification. *See* descent
rentiers, 39–41, 159, 165, 196; African landlords as, 40–41, 65, 104–7, 159, 217n103; commodification of urban spaces by, 9–10, 39–40, 202nn22–23; female landlords as, 65, 111–12, 172, 257n186; Indian landlords as, 40, 56, 95, 104–5, 153, 159; numbers of, 40; Nyerere's views on, 163, 189–91; race-based policies of, 40–41; of squatter housing, 188–89; of Swahili-style housing, 104; World War II controls on, 95
rents/renters, 9, 34; legal protections for, 41, 95, 187–88, 227n62; in Swahili-style houses, 104. *See also* housing
repatriation of labor migrants, 95–98, 151, 169–70, 227n65
research methods, 15–17
respect. *See* heshima
Ricardo, David, 10
rights of occupancy tenancies, 32–33, 41, 107, 187, 257n174
Rivers-Smith, Stanley, 78

Road Workers Union, 114
Robert, Shaaban, 127
Rupia, John, 192, 195
rural development, 167–73, 186, 251n50

Sadleir, Randal, 15, 141
Sahlins, Marshall, 73
Said, Mohamed, 65
Saleh, Ali, 67
Saleh bin Fundi, 114
Salim bin Omar, Sharif, 68
sanitation, 28–31
Saurashtra region, 49–51
Savings and Loan Society, 257n175
Scott, R. R., 28
segregated urban zones, 22, 27–34, 46, 83–84, 145; building codes of, 29–31, 38–39, 206n38, 206n45; commerce and markets in, 34–39; contradictory implementation of, 37–39; health and sanitation in, 28–31, 36, 102, 206n29; neutral zone (Mnazi Mmoja) in, 31–32, 83, 115; postcolonial discourses on, 170–72, 189–91, 197; postwar resegregation of, 105–7; self-segregated spaces in, 76–83; tax policies in, 32–33, 207n59
self-improvement guides, 126–28
self-segregation practices, 76–83
Shagaan *askari*, 65–66
Shah, Sultan Muhammad, 51
Shangali, Abdiel, 144–45
Shariff, Ibrahim Noor, 122
Sharkey, Heather, 119
Shia Muslims, 49–50, 51, 83
Shirazi identity, 12, 60–61, 63
Shomvi people, 15, 31, 59–64
Sidbury, James, 13
Sikhs, 49, 50
socialism. *See* ujamaa
"Socialism Is Not Racialism" (Nyerere), 176
Somji, Mohamed Baker, 186
Songambele, Mustafa, 169, 183
Soske, Jon, 7
South Asian community. *See* Indian community
spatial belonging. *See* urban entitlement
squatters, 42, 153, 188–89, 198
Stevedore and Dock Workers Union, 114–15, 234n209
Stocking, George W., Jr., 126
Stoler, Ann Laura, 12
subaltern studies, 6
Sudanese mercenaries, 65
Sukuma people, 66
Sultani, Juma, 66

Sunni Muslims, 49–50, 83
Swahili houses, 40, 104, 189, 198
Swahili identity, 63, 216n85; assimilatory
capacity in, 122; coastal hierarchies in,
63–64, 84, 122–23, 125–26; patrilineal
descent in, 14–15, 19, 118, 120–22, 128–36;
wenye mji in, 18, 60, 64–69, 83–84
Swahili language, 1–2, 16–17, 82; Arabic words
in, 120–23; Indianized usage of, 179–80,
254n109; Indian words in, 71, 219n144;
literacy in, 138–39, 235n4, 241n115; native
and foreigner in, 48; racial-national
discourses in, 118–28. See also taifa
Sykes, Abdulwahid: military service of, 136, 140,
143; political work of, 106, 110, 143, 145,
233n199, 242n148
Sykes, Ally, 108, 136, 140–41, 192, 232n164
Sykes, Kleist, 66, 67, 83, 102, 123–24, 140

taifa, 1, 13, 16, 19, 68, 119–21, 157–58, 196;
fluidity as term of, 120–21, 160–61, 235–
36nn12–13; Kenya's use of, 120; Kombo's
definition of, 128; moral considerations
in, 128–36, 151, 238n63; in postcolonial
discourses, 159–95; in racial-national
discourses, 124–28; TANU's uses of,
143–53, 158, 199; Zanzibar's use of, 200
Tambaza, Mtumwa Msakara bin Jumbe, 63,
217n103
Tanganyika, 2, 201n1
Tanganyika African Association (TAA), 143–44,
147
Tanganyika African Government Servants
Association (TAGSA), 106, 108, 232n164
Tanganyika African National Union (TANU),
113, 136, 199, 248n10; African National
Congress opposition to, 153–54; Arusha
Declaration of, 166, 168–69, 183, 186–87,
190; citizenship debates of, 153–57;
Indian engagement with, 145–50, 186;
membership in, 186; nationalist rhetoric
of, 160; origins of, 136; racial politics
of, 19, 121, 147–54, 161, 245n192; racial
recruitment by, 143–53, 158; Youth
League of, 147, 151, 170–72. See also
ujamaa
Tanganyika African Welfare and Commercial
Association (TAWCA), 69, 124
Tanganyika Asian Civil Service Association
(TACSA), 78–79
Tanganyika Citizenship Bill, 154–57, 247n233
Tanganyika Coloured People National Society,
151, 245n204
Tanganyika Ismailia Co-operative Society, 57
Tanganyika Railways Asiatic Union, 78

Tanganyika Territory African Civil Service
Association (TTACSA), 78–79, 232n164
Tanzania Housing Bank, 257n175
"Tata Kabwera Foola Union," 172
tax policies, 24; on kiwanja plots, 32–33,
207n59; local enforcement of, 96–98; for
non-natives, 55; on prostitution, 112
textiles, 94–95, 100, 103, 152
title by prescription, 43
transport workers, 86, 88, 107–9, 112–16
Trimingham, J. Spencer, 120
Tumbo, Christopher, 156
Turnbull, Richard, 148
Twining, Edward, 115, 145, 147–49, 245n189

Uhindini neighborhood, 5, 194, 231n153;
crime and violence in, 80–81, 145,
153; gentrification of, 33–34; housing
shortages in, 104–7; rights of occupancy
tenancies in, 32–33; segregation in, 189,
197
uhuru, 100, 164–65, 195
ujamaa, 4–5, 19–20, 127, 159–67, 198–99,
249n21; agriculture and rural
development in, 167–72, 186, 251n250;
labor reforms in, 186–87; language of
class and poverty in, 172–76; removal
of evil and enemies in, 165–66; uhuru
discourses in, 164–65; unyonyaji
discourses in, 163–67, 176, 250n32
Ujamaa—The Basis of African Socialism
(Nyerere), 163, 172–73
Union of African Cooks, Washermen, and
House Servants, 113, 114
United Nations, 14, 146, 173
United Republic of Tanzania, 2, 201n1
United Tanganyika Party (UTP), 149–50
unyonyaji, 147, 158, 159, 163–67, 176, 250n32
Upanga neighborhood, 31, 101, 197, 231n153
urban citizenship, 170–72
urban entitlement, 18–19, 85–117, 196, 225n8;
clothing and textiles in, 94–95, 103; food
rations in, 89–94, 98–107, 113, 226n33;
housing distribution in, 95, 104, 227n62,
230n124; illegal economies in, 102–3;
in labor issues, 107–16; labor migration
restrictions in, 95–98, 151, 169–70,
227n65; minimum guarantees of, 89–95;
in the postcolonial era, 159, 167–72;
racialized hierarchies of, 98–107, 117;
regulatory control of, 87–89
urban question, 86, 88–89, 95
urban social history, 5–6
urban socialist ideology, 19–20. See also urban
entitlement

urban spaces, 5, 8–15, 17–18; categories of identity in, 11–15, 17–18, 47, 203n32; class formation in, 9; commodification by rentiers of, 9–10, 39–40, 202nn22–23; contradictions of accumulation and control in, 11, 18–19, 34–35; creating a stable working class in, 88–89, 96, 108, 116–17; *duka* (store) circuits in, 10–11, 70–71, 152–53; gentrification of, 33–34, 37–39, 41, 107; multiracial public venues in, 77; native/non-native status in, 17–18, 21–46; official planning of, 27, 197–98; regulation of commerce in, 34–37, 70–76; self-segregation practices in, 76–83. *See also* peri-urban areas; segregated urban zones

ustaarabu, 122–23, 125–29, 138–39, 146, 148, 157–58

Ustaarabu na Maendeleo ya Mwafrika (Kombo), 127–28

Uzaramo Native Authority, 44–45

uzawa, 199–200

Uzunguni. *See* European community

Vande Mataram, 57–58

Van den Berghe, Pierre L., 8

Vassanji, Moyez G., 4, 153, 193

Wabuliba, Linda, 179

wahuni, 80, 97–98, 110, 148, 169, 171–76, 194

Wamburga, R. S., 155

Wanubi people, 65

Washington, Booker T., 124

watu wa kuja, 18, 60, 64–69, 83–84, 99, 120–21

Waugh, Evelyn, 33, 53

Wazaramo Union, 68, 69, 144, 147

Weber, Max, 48, 211n4

wenye mji, 18, 60, 64–69, 83–84, 87, 100, 144, 217n103. *See also* firstcomer status

Westcott, Nicholas J., 85–86, 90

White, Luise, 40

Willis, Justin, 12

witchcraft, 106, 147, 160, 164–65, 244n178

women, 14–15; accumulation of wealth and property by, 65, 111–12, 217n107;

economic autonomy of, 112, 172; informal economies of, 74, 110–12, 221n164; interracial liaisons of, 121, 128–36, 151, 238n63; as landlords, 65, 111–12, 172; misogyny toward, 15, 65; purity and virtue discourses on, 121, 172; revolving credit societies of, 172. *See also* prostitution

World War II, 16, 18–19, 85–117; African *askari* in, 19, 97, 136–43, 235n14; Burma campaign of, 136–38; international commodity boom of, 90; population growth during, 85, 86, 95, 117, 197; security concerns during, 89; segregated soldiers in, 137–38; urban immigration restrictions during, 95–98; war charities of, 89. *See also* urban entitlement

Yao people, 60, 216n92

Youth League of TANU, 147, 151, 170–72

Zanzibar: categories of identity in, 12, 24–25, 63, 118–20, 237n37; Indian settlers in, 49, 54; land policies of, 43; nationalist discourses in, 152–53, 175; Omani culture in, 122–23; Revolution of 1964 in, 184; separation from Tanganyika African Association of, 144; *taifa* of, 200; union with Tanganyika of, 200; urban planning in, 27

Zaramo people, 44–45, 76; colonial Native Administrations of, 62; as firstcomers, 15, 59–60, 216n92; on food shortages, 100; informal commercial work of, 111–12; origins of, 60–63, 216n85; political engagement of, 219n136. *See also* Wazaramo Union

Zika Mwenyewe (Banzi), 175

Zimba, J. A., 134–35

Zone I. *See* native quarter of Dar es Salaam

Zone II. *See* Uhindini neighborhood

Zone III. *See* European community

Zulu *askari*, 65–66. *See also askari*

www.ingramcontent.com/pod-product-compliance
Lightning Source LLC
Chambersburg PA
CBHW021852020426
42334CB00013B/295